SUBMARINES
OF THE WORLD

SUBMARINES
OF THE WORLD

DAVID MILLER

ORION BOOKS

New York

A SALAMANDER BOOK

Copyright ©1991 by Salamander Books
Ltd.

Published in the United States in 1991
by Orion Books, a division of Crown
Publishers, Inc., 201 East 50th Street,
New York, New York 10022.
Member of the Crown Publishing Group.

Originally published in 1991 in Great
Britain by Salamander Books Ltd.

ORION and colophon are trademarks of
Crown Publishers, Inc.

Manufactured in Hong Kong

Library of Congress Cataloging-in-
    Publication Data available

ISBN 0-517-58666-5

10 9 8 7 6 5 4 3 2 1

First American Edition

CREDITS

Editor:
Philip de Ste. Croix

Designer:
Richard Hawke

Color and black and white artwork:
Tony Gibbons, Terry Hadler, Janos
Marffy, Maltings Partnership, Stephen
Seymour, TIGA ©Salamander Books Ltd
and
©John Batchelor

Index:
Stuart Craik

Filmset:
The Old Mill, England

**Color and monochrome
reproduction:**
P&W Graphics PTE Ltd, Singapore

Printed in Hong Kong

THE AUTHOR

Until May 1991 David Miller was a
serving officer in the British Army, a
career which took him to Singapore,
Malaysia, Germany, the Falkland
Islands and Holland, and which has
included service in the Royal Corps of
Signals, several staff jobs at Army
headquarters and the command of a
regiment in the UK. On leaving the
Army, he became a full-time author
specializing in military and technical
subjects. He has contributed numerous
articles to defense journals on subjects
ranging from guerrilla warfare to
missile strategy, and is the author of
several books, including *Modern
Submarine Warfare (*with John
Jordan), *Modern Naval Combat* (with
Chris Miller), *An Illustrated Guide to
Modern Submarines, An Illustrated
Guide to Modern Subhunters,* and the
Combat Arms Guide *Modern
Submarines.*

CONTENTS

INTRODUCTION

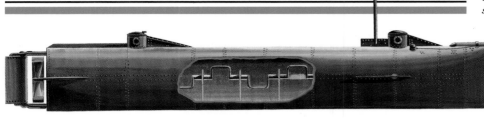

The submarine is one of the most important strategic and tactical weapons systems of the 20th Century, and this importance will increase yet further in the 21st Century. The tiny, creaking, leaking and unsafe 'submarine-boats' of the 1890s, displacing under two hundred tons and carrying a handful of men and a few torpedoes have grown into massive, sophisticated and deadly weapons sytems, displacing as much as 26,000 tons, carrying a crew of over a hundred and armed with missiles which can destroy vast areas of the Earth.

Every day hundreds of submarines are patrolling the oceans of the world. Many of them are on routine training, but some of them are armed with strategic missiles and for them every patrol is as fully operational as if they were at war. The surface of the ocean is hostile enough on occasion, but the depths are *always* hostile to man. Yet, for many centuries man has dreamed of penetrating the depths of the oceans and now this dream has become possible. This book describes some of the milestones on that journey.

Early Days

The early history of the submarine bears remarkable similarities to that of the aeroplane. The concept of a device to take man underwater was mooted as early as the 16th Century, first of all in theoretical works such as *De Motu Animalium* by the Abbé Borelli, which was published in 1680, and secondly in the shape of actual submersible devices. Quite who conducted the first ever submarine descent is a matter of some dispute. A Dutchman, Cornelius van Drebbel, is alleged to have carried out a dive in 1620 in London's River Thames before a large crowd. Some reports suggest that King James I watched, others that he personally was on board during the dive; the former seems possible, the latter fanciful.

Man knew virtually nothing about the nature of the ocean, nor about the physical properties of the depths and thus the testing of submarine devices was as fraught with peril as testing the first flying machines. An English wagon-maker named

John Day converted an old sailing vessel into a form of submarine by constructing a watertight compartment and adding heavy ballast, part of which could be jettisoned whilst submerged, whereupon the device would return to the surface, assisted by the buoyancy of seventy-five empty hogsheads. In June 1774 Day demonstrated his device off the port of Plymouth, but he failed to return to the surface, becoming the first known person to be killed in a submarine disaster.

Men such as Day wanted simply to be able to submerge, travel underwater and, of course, then to return to the surface. All of this was a difficult enough feat. It was an American, David Bushnell, who was the originator of the ideas of the submarine as a weapon of war. He supervised attacks on two British warships, one in 1776 in his submersible called *Turtle* and the other in 1812. Both missions were to no avail, although the submarines and their single-man crews survived on both occasions.

The first successful demonstration of the effect of the threat posed by a submarine came in 1850. A Bavarian carpenter, Wilhelm Bauer, was serving as a corporal in the Prussian artillery at Kiel during a blockade by the Danish fleet brought about by one of the succession of crises over the Schleswig-Holstein dispute. He built a submarine with a wooden frame covered with iron sheets, weighing about 38 tons (38,610kg) and with ballast tanks to control the boat's buoyancy. Propulsion was by a propeller turned by a handwheel; the water-pump was also hand-driven. Two sets of leather gloves in the bows could be used by the crew to place explosive charges on an enemy vessel. The device certainly floated and was driven towards

the enemy fleet by its crew. The Danes, thoroughly daunted by the threat from this mysterious craft, withdrew, making this the first example of the effectiveness of the *threat* of submarine action.

A year later Bauer, accompanied by a crew of two, submerged the boat, but he lost control and plunged to the bottom at a depth of some 60ft (18.5m), ending up in a vertical position with the bows stuck in mud. There appeared to be no means of escape, as the crew could not open the hatch against the pressure of water outside. But the redoubtable Bauer reasoned that if they waited until the air pressure inside the hull equalled that of the water outside then they would be able to open the hatch with ease and float to the surface. Persuading the two simple seamen of the merits of this plan was not an easy task, but eventually they were convinced and all waited for the time when they would be able to test the theory. When the time came Bauer was proved correct and the three men shot to the surface in an air bubble, becoming the first men in history to escape from a sunken submarine.

During the American Civil War the Confederacy was blockaded by the Union Navy. One of the means of trying to combat this was the submarine. Various designs were tested, and the *HL Hunley*, despite having proved exceptionally dangerous in trials, drowning numerous volunteers in the process, managed to sink the USS *Housatonic*, being lost with all hands herself in the process.

Thereafter an increasing number of submarines appeared. The three principal lines of development evolved in France, the United States and Italy. Finally, after all the years of experimenting, workable

submarines started to appear more or less simultaneously in numerous countries. In France Maxime Laubeuf produced the *Narval* in 1898, while in the United States J.P. Holland at last persuaded the Navy to buy one of his submarines, and in Italy the *Pullino* was launched. Thereafter progress was rapid, and once the major navies had started to buy submarines, many of the smaller powers were quick to follow their lead.

World War I

By the outbreak of World War I there were many submarines in service. It was generally expected that their principal tactical use would be against surface warships, a view which seemed to be endorsed when the German submarine *U-9* sank three British cruisers in just 60 minutes on 22 September 1914. However, although submarines went on to sink numerous warships, their greatest single contribution to the war was in their attack on merchant fleets, which had been foreseen by only a very few. One of that few was the British Admiral of the Fleet Lord Fisher who in 1912, ie, two years before war started, said:

> 'Again the question arises as to what a submarine can do against a merchant ship when she has found her? She cannot capture the merchant ship; she has no spare hands to put a prize crew on board; little or nothing would be gained by disabling her engines or propeller; she cannot convoy her into harbour . . . there is nothing else the submarine can do except sink her capture . . . this submarine menace is a truly terrible one for British commerce and Great Britain alike.' (*Records*, 1919, pp 183-184.)

The High Seas Fleet of the Imperial German Navy (IGN) as a 'fleet-in-being' certainly tied down the British Grand Fleet throughout the war, but it did little, if anything, to bring Great Britain anywhere nearer defeat. The submarines of the IGN, however, very nearly did just that, exactly as Admiral Fisher had predicted, sinking a vast amount of shipping. The British merchant ship losses in the twelve months following the opening of the unrestricted campaign in February 1917 illustrate the point only too clearly:

Above: *Japanese* Submarine No 1 *was a standard Holland design, strengthened to suit the IJN's needs.*

The table shows what fearful losses the U-boats wrought — no less than 2,684 British merchant-ships lost and many more damaged — in the course of a year. It also shows how the one really effective countermeasure, the convoy system, finally began to counterbalance the efforts of the U-boat crews.

By the end of the war the submarine had emerged as a mature system, with a strategic influence beyond anything which could have been imagined five years previously. The submarines of the other combatant navies had, of course, been active, but their roles had been fundamentally different. British and French (and from 1917, American) submarines, for example, were not faced with a vast enemy merchant fleet to attack and they had to seek out every target.

Three new types of submarine appeared during the war: minelayers, cruisers and ASW submarines. The sole example of the latter, the British R class, was quite exceptional, being the first since the original Hollands to be optimsed for submerged rather than surfaced performance, having an underwater speed of some 15kt. They suffered from two fundamental problems: first, they developed instability at high underwater speeds, a phenomenon that was not understood for another thirty years and, secondly, the sensors with a performance adequate enough to allow them to achieve their role just did not exist.

Above: *The Imperial Austro-Hungarian Navy's submarine U-6 was a Holland design, built by the firm of Whitehead.*

Below: *A photograph of the German submarine U-9, taken by a British merchant captain before it sank his ship.*

British Merchant Ship Losses 1917-1918			
Month	Average number of U-boats at sea	British Losses Number of ships	British Losses Gross Registered Tonnage (grt)
February 1917	38	254	500,573
March	40	310	556,775
April	47	413	873,754
May	47	285	589,603
June	55	286	674,458
July	41	224	545,021
August	46	186	509,142
September	55	158	338,242
October	56	159	448,923
November	39	126	289,085
December	48	160	382,060
January 1918	46	123	302,088
Totals	46.5	2,684	6,009,724

The Inter-War Years

As the nations began to recover from the effects of the war, a Naval Conference was convened in Washington, DC to hold what were, in effect, the first-ever arms limitation talks. There the British proposed the total abolition of the submarine as a weapon of war, which, in view of their recent experiences, was partly understandable. However, they received little support from other participant nations, and although limits were placed on submarine tonnages, calibres of guns and so on, there was no question of banning of the submarine itself.

The navies proceeded to rebuild their fleets in the 1920s, in line with the treaty limits, but incorporating the lessons of the war. Most navies built a number of small classes of what were generally known as 'patrol submarines', but it was also a time of experimentation. Submarines were armed with exceptionally large guns, a number of minelayers were constructed and a few navies tried to produce a submarine aircraft-carrier. Few of these ideas proved to be a success, however.

One will-o'-the-wisp pursued by several navies was the 'fleet submarine'. It was argued that there should be a type of submarine which could act as a distant scout for the main battle fleet, signalling sightings and, if possible, sinking a few major units before the main engagement took place. To achieve this the submarines needed the same range and speed as the battle fleet and much effort was directed to attaining this end. One of the main problems was that every time the designers coaxed greater surface speed out of their submarines it transpired that the fleet's speed had increased also, so that the discrepancy remained the same! Eventually it was realised that the basic tactical concept was flawed, although even as late as the early 1950s the nuclear radar picket *Triton* (SSRN-586) was built in order to keep up with carrier task groups.

Overall, however, submarine design and development proceeded smoothly in most countries, while even Germany, which was supposedly banned from building any submarines until 1935, managed to keep abreast of developments.

World War II

The outbreak of World War II found most navies with submarines which were technically similar to those with which they had ended the previous conflict, although obviously there had been some improvements. The navies operating submarines had, however, grown in number as had the numbers of submarines:

The World's Submarine Fleets: September 1939			
Europe		**Europe**	
Denmark	11	UK	69
Estonia	2	USSR	(approx) 150
Finland	5	Yugoslavia	4
France	77		
Germany	65	**North America**	
Greece	6	United States	100
Italy	107		
Latvia	2	**South America**	
Netherlands	24	Argentina	3
Norway	9	Brazil	4
Poland	5	Chile	9
Portugal	4	Peru	4
Romania	1		
Spain	9	**Asia**	
Sweden	24	Japan	65
Turkey	9	Siam	4

Submarines operated in every theatre throughout the war, but there were three principal battlegrounds. First, as in World War I, was the Atlantic where again the German U-boats sought to break the lines-of-communication between North America and the United Kingdom. Once more they came very near to succeeding. There was also a major submarine conflict in the Mediterranean, where for several years Allied maritime traffic flowed in a West-East direction supplying Malta and Egypt, while Axis traffic flowed North-South supplying troops in North Africa, both lines of supply providing ideal pickings for submarines. Finally, there was the submarine war in the vast expanses of the Pacific, where the United States' and Japanese submarines fought quite different battles from those in the Atlantic.

At a lower level submarines provided the only means by which the two European Axis partners were able to co-operate with their Far Eastern ally. Several visits were paid by Japanese submarines to German-

Below: U-124, *a Type IXB, here under the guns of a German warship, was sunk on 2 April 1943 by a British sloop.*

controlled ports in France, whilst German involvement in the Far East grew to such a level that they opened a submarine base in Penang in the Federated Malay States (today's West Malaysia).

For the German submariners a major difference in World War II was that they suddenly found themselves in control of most of France's Atlantic seaboard and they were thus able to avoid the long haul to the north of the British Isles to reach the Atlantic. Also, very strong central command was exercised by Admiral Karl Dönitz, who commanded the submarine force from the outbreak of war until 30 January 1943 when he became the Commander-in-Chief of the Navy.

The German submarine war was, to a large extent, fought with just two types of boat — the Type VII and the Type IX — both of which had been developed in the 1930s. They were not outstanding in any respect, but they were sound and capable designs, which were produced in large numbers. Up to May 1945 705 Type VIIs of various sub-types were constructed of which 437 were lost in action, while of 194 Type IXs 150 were lost.

Although the U-boats sank large amounts of Allied shipping they were eventually defeated. Allied naval ASW became very effective, and was substantially aided by the increasing range and capabilities of ASW aircraft and by the very significant contribution of the electronic warfare organisation, which had broken *Enigma* and other German naval codes. Crucially, the U-boats, despite the quantity of the shipping they sank, never succeeded in outstripping the Allied capability to replace these losses.

The vast U-boat losses spurred the Germans to seek revolutionary types of submarine, which would swing the balance in their favour. This led, amongst others, to the Types XXI and XXIII, which, had they entered service in effective numbers, would have caused the Allies a severe problem. The Allies did not develop such submarines themselves, because they simply had no need of them. German ASW capability was insignificant in comparison to that of the Allies.

The second great campaign was that in the Pacific. The Japanese possessed a big submarine fleet, which included some of the largest boats then in service. However, their overall performance during the war was not as good as had been anticipated. Their big submarines were slow to dive, difficult to manoeuvre underwater, and, despite their size, remarkably uncomfortable for their crews. They were also very easy for Allied ASW forces to find, returning excellent sonar echoes.

The primary mission of the IJN's submarine force was to attack warships and they sank many, including two aircraft carriers, two cruisers, ten destroyers and numerous smaller vessels, together with a meagre 184 merchant ships (907,000grt). Such results came nowhere near causing replacement problems to the United States. Some 126 boats entered service during the war and total losses came to 129. Like the Germans, the Japanese developed two

types of revolutionary fast submarines. However, again as in Germany, they did not reach service in time to affect the outcome of the war.

The United States' submarine fleet was based on the excellent 'fleet' boats, which were large, capable, comfortable and available in considerable numbers. They proved ideally suited to the Pacific campaign and, following the order to wage 'unrestricted submarine warfare against Japan', they sank large numbers of merchant ships. They lost 53 submarines during the war, 45 of them in action. One interesting aspect of the American campaign is that they fought the whole war with essentially one design of submarine. There were, of course, some older boats in service, but these did not play a significant role. From the P class of 1935 onwards the difference between each succeeding class was not great and, although it appears at first glance that three classes were constructed during the war (Gato, Balao and Tench), these were to all intents minor variations of a single design. Thus, the military benefits of standardization were well proven.

British submarines also fought a hard war, but of a quite different type. They sank only 84 Axis merchant ships (270,000grt) in the North Sea and Atlantic, compared to 361 ships (1,157,000grt) in the Mediterranean and 48 ships (97,000grt) in the Far East. They also sank or damaged a large number of warships, including six cruisers, sixteen destroyers and 35 submarines, together with many smaller vessels. Against this they lost 68 submarines in action and twelve to other causes.

The Cold War

Immediately the war had ended large proportions of the Allied submarine fleets were placed into reserve, while the active fleet was updated in the light of the German and (to a lesser extent) Japanese advances in fast submarine technology. Thus, many US and British submarines were streamlined and given new sensors. The US Guppys (Greater Underwater

Above: *A control position in USS* Ohio *illustrates the complexity and sophistication of today's submarines.*

Propulsive Power) proved particularly successful and when they were replaced by nuclear submarines they were passed on to many Allied navies to give them experience with the new technology.

The new potential enemy was the Soviet Union which had also gained access to German technology and was rumoured to be building vast submarine fleets. This confrontation has spurred the developments of the past 45 years.

There have been three great advances in submarine technology since World War II. The first is the advent of nuclear propulsion, which at last freed the submarine from the necessity of having to approach the surface regularly to obtain supplies of air with which to run its diesels to recharge the batteries. This still left those who could not afford (or were politically opposed to) nuclear propulsion with the old problem, albeit alleviated to a certain extent by the perfection of the schnorkel. However, it now appears that a viable, non-nuclear, air-independent propulsion (AIP) system may soon be widely available.

The second major advance has been in hull design. The previous long, narrow hull could not be driven faster than about 18-20kt before control began to be lost. This problem was experienced by a variety of types starting with the British R class of 1918. It was not until the US Navy researched the phenomenon properly in the late 1940s and early 1950s that the solution was found: a shorter, fatter hull, as epitomized by the research submarine USS *Albacore* (AGSS-569).

The third great advance has been in the development of ballistic and cruise missiles which give the submarine a truly global strategic capability. Thus, the US Ohio and the Soviet Typhoon class SSBNs are probably the most potent single weapons systems ever constructed.

Perhaps less obvious has been the advance in sensors, as submarines have been equipped with ever more sophisticated devices to enable them to find surface ships and other submarines, and to reduce the chances of themselves being found. Another major influence on the nature of submarine warfare is the advent of computerised command-and-control systems, which enable the submarine to become a far more effective fighting unit.

Below: *This cutaway shows the interior of the British submarine HMS* Upholder, *one of the most sophisticated of modern diesel-electric designs. The cylindrical pressure-hull is capped forward and aft by domed bulkheads, and is constructed of high-tensile steel to permit diving to*

depths in excess of 656ft (200m). Two watertight bulkheads sub-divide the space into three main compartments, while the after compartment has an additional acoustic bulkhead to isolate the propulsion motor room. Forward of the engine-room there are two levels.

Attack periscope | ESM antenna

Snort induction mast | Radar antenna

Exhaust mast

Main propulsion motor | Engine room

Search periscope

Five-man lock-out chamber | Intercept sonar array

Passive ranging sonar

Torpedo tubes

Passive bow sonar

Auxiliary machinery room | Control room | Accommodation

Submarine Weapons

The weapon that made the submarine an effective weapon of war was the torpedo, which is, itself, a miniature, self-contained submarine. The earliest device was a spar-torpedo, which consisted of an explosive charge mounted on a long, wooden spar, which was detonated on contact with an enemy warship, an inherently dangerous device. This defect was solved when Whitehead invented the automotive torpedo. Early torpedoes had a diameter of 14in (356mm), but this was quickly increased to 17.7in (450mm) in some navies (eg, the French) and 18in (457mm) in others. The 21in (533mm) torpedo was introduced just before World War I, and it became the virtual international standard for the next eighty years. The French chose the marginally different diameter of 21.7in (550mm), although even they changed to 21in (533mm) in the 1960s.

Any torpedo consists of three elements: a warhead, a propulsion system and a guidance/control system. The original explosive used was wet guncotton, but this was replaced in most cases by TNT just before World War I. In World War II normal TNT was replaced by Torpex, which was essentially TNT with an additive to increase its explosive power. Further additives in the post-war years have either increased explosive power yet further or have made the explosive more stable over a longer period.

Torpedo propulsion systems originally used compressed-air, while later steam was favoured. Both systems entailed a stream of exhaust bubbles which could be spotted in daylight by an alert watchkeeper on the target ship. The Germans developed an electrically-driven torpedo in the 1930s, which was copied by both the British and Americans during the war. Attempts have also been made in various countries to use hydrogen-peroxide as a propellant, but this substance is notoriously difficult to handle and it caused explosions on at least one submarine in the 1950s. Nevertheless, it is now in use in the Swedish TP 617 torpedo.

Control, for torpedoes, originally meant running on a set course and at a set depth. Indeed, the famous 'secret' of the Whitehead torpedo was the device which maintained it at a precise depth. The achievement of consistently reliable control has always been difficult and one of the problems with the US Navy's Mark XIV torpedo in the early years of World War II was that it frequently ran deeper than had been set, thereby passing well under the targets.

Above: *A scene familiar to all submariners as a Soviet sailor aligns the depth setting on a torpedo with that on the tube gear, prior to it being loaded.*

During the war both active and passive homing heads were developed for torpedoes. An active head transmitted sonar pulses, which, when reflected by a target, were detected and used to home the torpedo onto the target. Being active, these were, of course, detectable by the target. Passive heads homed on the acoustic signals transmitted by a target.

Since the war there have been numerous very expensive programmes to develop new torpedoes. Current models have maximum speeds which are being equalled or even exceeded by those of their quarry; the US Mark 46, for example, has a speed of 46kt, which is exactly that of the Soviet Alfa class SSN, so a stern chase is out of the question. The problem is partly solved by the use of weapons such as SUBROC, but there is still a need for a faster torpedo. The US Navy's Advanced Capability programme (ADCAP) for the Mark 48 torpedo has raised its speed to 55kt, while the British Mark 24 Tigerfish is reported

Below: *The Swedish FFV TP 617 torpedo weighs 4,078lb (1,850kg) and is 23ft 0in (7m) in length. The thermal propulsion system uses hydrogen peroxide (H_2O_2), alcohol and water as propellants.*

to be capable of even higher speeds.

Most modern torpedoes have complicated guidance systems including an active/passive sonar transducer which works initially in the passive mode and then changes automatically to the active mode once the target indicates that it has become aware of the attack. Sonar information from the torpedo's sensors is transmitted back to the submarine by wires and guidance commands to the torpedo are passed forward by the same means.

Warhead design is also becoming more important as submarine hulls become ever stronger, perhaps the most difficult target being the immense double-hulls of the Soviet Typhoon class SSBN and Oscar class SSGN. Some form of directed-energy (shaped) charge is necessary to meet such challenges. Further, since the effectiveness of such a charge is directly proportional to its diameter, various navies are now examining the feasibility of larger diameter torpedoes. The US Navy will soon start sea trials of a 30in (762mm) torpedo, while the Soviet Navy is believed to be starting to deploy a 26in (660mm) torpedo. In general terms, however, the capabilities of modern torpedoes lag behind those of the sonars that support them. They are slow, lack range and are noisy.

Torpedoes have proved to be unreliable and sometimes wayward weapons over the years. Submariners of all nations have experienced problems with them. A particularly tragic example is that of USS *Tang* (SS-306), one of the most successful of all US submarines in World War II. During an attack on a Japanese convoy on 24 October 1944 she fired her last torpedo, which veered in a half circle and hit the *Tang* herself, causing immediate and fatal damage. The bridge party of ten were thrown into the water, while the boat sank with the rest of the crew. Thirteen escaped from the submarine, which was lying at a depth of 180ft (55m), of whom five were still alive next morning. The Japanese picked up a total of fifteen men, of whom six succumbed to the rigours of Japanese prisoner-of-war camps. Thus, one rogue torpedo accounted directly for the lives of 81 men and indirectly for another six.

Lest it be thought that this is a problem which has been overcome by modern technology it is worth noting that the Norwegian submarine *Ula* was hit by one of her own practice torpedoes on 11 November 1989, whilst undergoing pre-delivery trials. Fortunately the damage was slight.

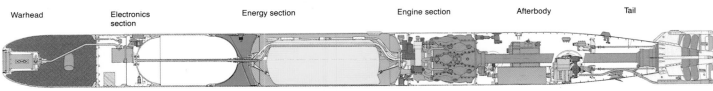

Warhead	Electronics section	Energy section	Engine section	Afterbody	Tail
Homing head	Computer unit	Tanks for compressed air,	Catalyst	Course and depth control	Gearbox	Power supply
Charge	Control	alcohol, fresh water and	Steam generator	Wire dispenser	Propellers	connection
Safety device	Signal processing	hydrogen peroxide	Engine	Alternator	Rudders	Wire outlet
Impact fuze	Proximity fuze		Speed and oxidiser	Servo control electronics		
			switching unit	Tube safety lock		

Launching Torpedoes

The most common method of launching torpedoes is by use of fixed tubes, mounted within the pressure-hull. The earliest submarines had all such tubes in the bows, but in 1907 the Russian submarine *Kaiman* was launched with two torpedo tubes in the stern, complementing the bow tubes. From then on most submarines had stern tubes, whose main tactical purpose was to fire torpedoes at pursuing ASW surface warships. Such an installation became impossible when the use of single propellers was introduced in the 1960s and today very few submarines have such an installation.

There was a brief British fashion in World War I for beam tubes, which actually launched their torpedoes at 90° to the hull, but this idea was soon dropped and no other navy took it up. Many US Navy SSNs and the latest Japanese SSKs have allocated all available space in the bows to very large sonar arrays, which has entailed moving the torpedo tubes back in the hull almost to a beam position. However, the tubes are angled to fire forward at about 20° from the hull.

The French tried to obtain the best of both worlds by using rotating mountings. These devices contained two, three or four tubes and their direction of launch was controlled from within the submarine. However, they conferred little advantage, for they could not be reloaded at sea, and they upset the trim of the boats. They were first installed before World War I and French submarines continued to be built with such devices until the late 1930s.

The French also showed a penchant for the Russian-designed Drzewiecki drop-collars, which were installed on the upper casing and which fell sideways before releasing the torpedo. The devices were somewhat vulnerable to damage, were inherently inaccurate and could not, of course, be reloaded whilst at sea. First used on the Russian *Delfin* in 1903 and later on French submarines, they had fallen out of fashion by the 1920s.

Above: *Modern torpedo warheads have a devastating effect on surface targets, as this strike on an old destroyer shows.*

Below: *Special devices, such as this Strachan & Henshaw system, are needed to embark, stow and load torpedoes.*

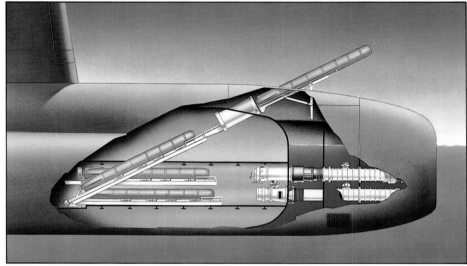

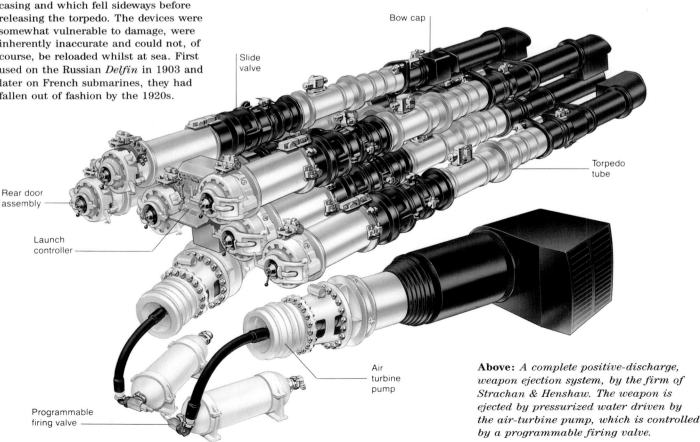

Bow cap

Slide valve

Torpedo tube

Rear door assembly

Launch controller

Programmable firing valve

Air turbine pump

Above: *A complete positive-discharge, weapon ejection system, by the firm of Strachan & Henshaw. The weapon is ejected by pressurized water driven by the air-turbine pump, which is controlled by a programmable firing valve.*

Guns

The first gun to be installed on a submarine was the 'dynamite gun' mounted in the early US Navy Holland class, but this was soon deleted, both because the weapon was practically useless and because no use could be seen for it. For some years submarines were armed only with torpedoes, but in 1911 the Royal Navy launched *D-4*, which, after lengthy discussions at the highest level, was armed with one 12pdr. The gun was on a complicated disappearing mount, as was the case with other classes which followed (eg, the US Navy's L class), but it was soon realised that a fixed mounting was cheaper, lighter and easier to maintain.

Once World War I had started, and the value of the gun in saving the use of valuable torpedoes against merchant ships had been demonstrated, virtually all submarines were so fitted. An idea then developed for a big-gun armed submarine, which started with the German U-151 class, armed with two 5.9in (150mm) guns and the British K class with two (later three) 4in (102mm). Then came the British M class, very large submarines for their time with a displacement of 1,946 tons and armed with one 12in (305mm) gun. After the war the British developed the *X-1* with four 5.2in (132mm) guns, which, it was assessed, was sufficient for her to take on a destroyer. Finally, in 1927

Above: The largest gun ever installed in a submarine was the 12in/23cal (305mm), installed in the British M class of 1918.

came the French *Surcouf*, which had two 8in (203mm) guns, the largest calibre permitted under the recently agreed Washington Naval Treaty.

It turned out, however, that the tactical concept behind such designs was flawed. If the target was a merchant ship, then the submarine was better off getting closer and engaging with smaller guns, while if such a submarine was to attempt to take on a destroyer in a surface engagement its chances of survival were slim. Thus, this concept had been discarded by 1930 and only *Surcouf* served on until she was sunk in 1942.

Until near the end of World War II all submarines had one, sometimes two deck guns, usually accompanied by one or two AA guns. Such gun armament changed quickly throughout the war and in virtually all combatant navies there seems to have been little standardisation, even within classes, the weapon fit even depending upon the captain's beliefs and what he could persuade the dockyards to fit!

Below: A typical World War II gun installation, in this case a 3in/45cal on a British S class submarine.

However, the Germans realised that the gun and its mount created a great deal of hydrodynamic resistance and that, in any case, radar and the threat of aircraft virtually precluded the use of the submarine on the surface. So, their Type XXI and XXIII *Elektroboote* did away with guns altogether; after the war other navies quickly followed suit. By the late 1950s there were virtually no deck guns left, although the Royal Navy fitted some of their submarines with guns during the 'Confrontation' campaign against Indonesia in the 1960s. Curiously, the Peruvian Navy still retains a gun on its Dos de Mayo class submarine in the 1990s.

Air Defence

Since World War I aircraft have posed a particular threat to submarines. Initially, the response was to mount anti-aircraft cannon or machine-guns to provide defence while on the surface. However, time spent on the surface became increasingly hazardous, and the entry into service of the schnorkel meant that submarines stayed below, even when running their diesels. So, the need for air defence weapons reduced, although there was a brief rekindling of interest when the British firm of Vickers developed a device called SLAM (Submarine-Launched Air-Defence Missile) in the 1960s, which consisted of a quadruple Blowpipe missile launcher mounted on an extending mast. However, this weapon presupposed that the submarine was travelling at periscope depth, which still made it vulnerable; in the event SLAM never entered service.

However, the aircraft threat persists, especially as a submerged submarine often has no idea that an aircraft is even in the area, let alone tracking it, until an ASW weapon is launched. The Euromissile consortium is now developing the *Polyphem* missile, which can be launched through the torpedo tube of a deeply submerged submarine and which ascends to the surface in a capsule before launching itself at the attacking aircraft.

Cruise Missiles

The original naval missile was the US Navy's Loon, which was a straight copy of the German V-1 missile adapted for firing from a surface submarine; the first launching took place on 12 February 1947 from the USS *Cusk* (SSG-348). Having proved its potential the navy developed a new missile which was essentially a small, unmanned, swept-wing aircraft, powered by a turbojet, with rocket-assisted take-off (RATO). Designated Regulus 1, this was the first Submarine-Launched Cruise Missile (SLCM) to enter service, being deployed from 1950s to 1964. Two fleet submarines were converted to take two Regulus 1 each in a large, cylindrical hangar on the after-deck: *Tunny* (SSG-282) and *Barbero* (SSG-317).

Two further submarines were modified during construction to carry four Regulus 1s and these were followed by the nuclear-propelled *Halibut* (SSGN-587), which could carry five of the missiles. Regulus 1, which could only be launched from the

surface, was only capable of attacking large area targets and required mid-course guidance from radar picket submarines (SSRs). The next US Navy SLCM was the Regulus 2, which, despite the similarity of name, was a totally different and much more capable SLCM. However, the entry into service of Polaris meant its development ended without any deployment.

The Soviet Navy also had an SLCM development programme which led to the testing of the first missiles at sea during 1947, although the first service missile, the SS-N-3A, did not actually enter service until the mid-1960s aboard the converted Whiskey Single-Cylinder, Whiskey Twin-Cylinder, and, later, the Whiskey Long-Bin conversions. From that time, however, there has been constant development of the Soviet Navy's SLCMs and the associated submarine launchers.

The first purpose-built SLCM carriers were the nuclear-powered Echo I (six SS-N-3A missiles). However, these Soviet missiles were not, as was the US Navy's Regulus, intended for anti-city operations, but instead for anti-ship missions against US aircraft-carrier task groups. The SS-N-3A had a number of serious limitations: it could only be launched from the surface and it needed an airborne platform for over-the-horizon targetting (usually, a Bear-D or Hormone-B).

Above: *An early US cruise missile was the Regulus 1, here being launched from USS* Halibut *in the early 1960s.*

Next came the shorter range SS-N-7 sea-skimming missile for which the Charlie class SSGN was built. Unlike the SS-N-3, the SS-N-7 is launched from a submerged submarine. In 1979 the Oscar I class SSGN appeared, a huge (15,400 tons submerged displacement) submarine, armed with twenty-four SS-N-19 anti-ship missiles, with a range of some 250nm (463km).

Following the US development of the Tomahawk missile system the USSR has developed a strategic SLCM of its own, designated SS-NX-24. A Yankee class SSBN, disarmed of its SLBMs to comply with the SALT-II Treaty, has been converted to carry at least four of this new missile. Designated by NATO the 'Yankee Notch' this submarine is almost certainly a trials vessel and a purpose-built SS-NX-24 carrier will doubtless soon appear.

After the Regulus 2 missile the US Navy abandoned SLCMs altogether for many years, only returning to the field in the late 1970s to develop the Tomahawk missile. However, there was no attempt to

Below: *The ultimate submarine weapons — Trident missiles — here being loaded into an Ohio class SSBN, have a range well in excess of 4,000nm.*

develop a specialised SSG/SSGN submarine, instead of which the missile was designed to fit a standard 21in (533mm) torpedo tube. Initial deployment was on Los Angeles class SSNs, where Tomahawks were included as part of the torpedo load, but from *Providence* (SSN-719) onwards the Tomahawks will be housed in 12 separate vertical tubes, thus restoring the original complement of torpedoes. These weapons saw their first combat use in January 1991, being used in the attack on Iraqi installations.

Ballistic Missiles

The first nation to consider firing ballistic missiles from underwater was Germany, who in 1944 had a design on the drawing-boards for a submerged towing-body which would have transported and launched V-2 rockets, possibly for use against New York. At the end of World War II, both the USA and the USSR worked on the V-2s they had captured, helped, in both cases, by German scientists.

The first ballistic missile submarines (SSB) to enter service were the four boats of the Zulu V class, which had been converted to take two SLBMs mounted vertically in the fin. The missile was designated SS-N-4 by NATO and was probably a version of the Soviet R-10, which was itself a development of the German V-2. These were closely followed by the first SSB to be designed specifically for the purpose of launching ballistic missiles, the Golf class, 23 being built.

The US Navy meanwhile briefly considered an 8,500 ton submarine armed with six liquid-fuel Jupiter-S missiles, but then settled on the more ambitious, solid-fuelled Polaris project. Few weapons in history have combined more dramatic technological innovations than this SLBM, which was designed by Admiral WF Raborn, USN, and a team from Lockheed. When Polaris entered service in 1960 it changed the nature of strategic confrontation. Since then US SLBMs have been steadily developed from Polaris through Poseidon to Trident, with increases in range and reliability in each model. Warheads, too, developed from a single large Re-entry Vehicle (RV) through Multiple Re-entry Vehicles (MRVs) and Multiple Independently-targetted Re-entry Vehicles (MIRV) to today's Manoeuvrable Re-entry Vehicles (MaRV).

The Soviet Navy meanwhile persisted with liquid-fuelled missiles, but nevertheless developed some very effective missiles, whose great range enabled them to withdraw their SSBNs into the two sanctuaries of the Sea of Okhotsk and the Arctic Ocean. Soviet SSBNs progressed through the Yankee to the Delta (now in its Delta-IV form) and thence to the largest submarine ever built, the Typhoon class, armed with 20 SS-N-20 missiles.

Having seen the strategic power available in the SLBM/SSBN combination, first the UK, then France and China developed their own fleets. The only other nation which looks as though it might soon join this elite club is India.

Submarine Propulsion

The earliest inventors had no alternative to manpower with which to propel their submarines. Initially, this involved oars, then came propellers turned by hand, either by a single person, as in David Bushnell's *Turtle*, or by several people turning a crank, as in the Confederate *Hunley* and the German *Brandtaucher* in the mid-19th Century. Later in the 19th Century compressed-air was used, as were electrical accumulators, but both were of very limited endurance and required the submarine to return to port to recharge, which was tactically unacceptable. There were also a number of attempts to harness steam, not only for surface propulsion, but also to provide power when submerged, using stored-energy devices, but none worked satisfactorily.

Eventually it was realised that the ideal solution was to combine the efficiency of batteries for underwater propulsion with some form of power which could be used on the surface both to propel the submarine and to recharge the batteries. For some years steam was used for the latter purpose by many navies as the technology was well understood and relatively efficient, but it had numerous disadvantages. The steam plant made the interior of the submarine very hot and humid, while the furnace had to be both cooled and damped down prior to submerging. Further, the system required funnels to expel the smoke, which needed vents to the outside, which, in turn, had to be closed by watertight valves, and these were always a source of vulnerability.

The French produced a number of steam-driven classes of submarine, which were reasonably successful. The British produced rather fewer classes powered by such means, and these tended to be troublesome, especially the notorious K class. These were steam-driven because that was the only way to obtain the power required for the 'fleet speed' (24kt) in the Admiralty's specification. The boats were unpopular in the navy and suffered more than their fair share of accidents, although analysis indicates that, despite popular legend, very few were acutally due to the steam-propulsion system.

Above: *The French* Narval, *launched in 1899, was one of many early submarines to have a steam propulsion plant.*

The petrol engine was the obvious replacement for steam, and it was introduced in some submarines at the turn of the century. This may have solved the steam engine's problems with the vents, but equally it introduced the hazards of fire and explosion, which led to a number of losses and deaths. Indeed, the Imperial German Navy was so concerned with the dangers of petrol engines that they insisted on the use of Körting paraffin (kerosene) engines in their early submarines. This fuel was certainly safer to use, but when the submarine was running on the surface it left a cloud of dense white exhaust fumes behind it, which was a serious tactical shortcoming.

The answer to all these problems was the diesel engine, which was first introduced in the French submarine

Below: *The first submarine fitted with a schnorkel enabling diesels to be run at periscope depth was the Dutch O-19.*

Aigrette, launched in 1904. Its use spread rapidly, although it was some years before it proved thoroughly reliable. However, the limited technology of the day meant that the diesel engines of the 1910s and 1920s were long, heavy and with low r.p.m., which generated considerable acoustic signature, while there were certain critical speeds at which the vibration became so bad as to make the engine inoperable. The answer was high-speed diesels, but these required much development work. In the USA a fortunate coincidence of events meant that the navy was seeking such engines for its submarines just as the railroads were seeking suitable diesels for their locomotives. A fortuitous combination of naval money to fund the research and commercial pressure to produce the equipment led to the appearance of some potentially excellent engines in the mid-1930s. Although some very serious problems were encountered in the first two or three years of service, these were rapidly sorted out.

The diesel engine had effectively been perfected by the time of World War II, but the advent of long-range ASW aircraft, coupled with the increasing use of radar meant that submarines on the surface became extremely vulnerable. This weakness affected German U-boats far more than Allied submarines during the war years, and as a consequence the Germans developed a Dutch invention to produce the *schnorkel*. This enabled the submarine to travel at periscope depth to evade detection.

This device, too, was not without its problems at first. The early schnorkel tubes proved to be vulnerable to physical damage and for a time there were problems if a wave or a sudden change in depth caused the automatic valve to close suddenly. If they were not quickly closed-down, the diesels then sucked up the air within the submarine, to the acute discomfort of the crew.

After the war the US Navy again pressed for even more powerful diesels, the result being a small, radial engine, known colloquially as a 'pancake'. These were installed in Tang class submarines and proved so troublesome that they were replaced, the hulls having to be lengthened by 16ft (4.87m) to accommodate the more conventional propulsion units.

The vulnerability of a submarine running just below the surface has long been recognised and thus the need for an air-independent propulsion (AIP) system has remained a goal for many navies. There have been numerous attempts to perfect such a device, but the first serious system was that developed by the German engineer, Helmuth Walter, in the 1930s. His closed-cycle system included the use of hydrogen peroxide as an oxidant and was potentially very efficient. However, it also needed a new type of hull to take advantage of the speed being offered, and the effort needed to develop the two simultaneously proved too much, even for German industry. Fortunately for the U-boat service, the hull design was capable

of a rapid adaptation to take conventional diesel engines and a large number of batteries, the result being the excellent Type XXI.

After the war the Royal Navy became very interested in Walter's work and the professor himself worked at the Vickers Yard at Barrow in England from 1946 to 1949. The outcome was two trials submarines, *Explorer* and *Excalibur*, whose propulsion system proved to be very hazardous in service. The research was discontinued. The apparent cheap alternative to nuclear propulsion had proved to be too dangerous.

The matter rested there for some years, with some talk of using fuel-cells and other exotic systems, but with little serious action. However, there was a resurgence of

Above: *HMS* Excalibur *was built to test a hydrogen-peroxide propulsion system based on Professor Walter's design.*

interest in the 1980s as new technology appeared to offer workable systems. Most major navies, with the exception of the US navy, now claimed to be working on AIP technology and at least three submarines have carried out tests of working systems.

The Swedish submarine *Näcken* was taken in hand in late 1987 and had a 26ft 3in (8m) section added to enable Kockums to install two Stirling engines, together with associated liquid oxygen tanks and auxiliary machinery. Following trials she was recommissioned in late 1989. During her trials she demonstrated the ability to remain submerged for two weeks and has

since returned to full service as the first operational submarine with an AIP system.

In Germany *U-1* has been converted to accommodate six oxygen/hydrogen fuel cells, which are used to recharge the batteries. She returned to sea with the new system in 1987. RDM in the Netherlands is also working on a closed-cycle system.

Previous AIP systems, such as the Walter system, aimed to produce enough power to propel a submarine at all speed ranges while submerged. However, the latest systems now under trial are designed to power the boats at only slow speeds — high submerged speed will still be produced by the batteries. This considerably eases the technical problems involved in an AIP system.

Below: *The Stirling Air-Independent Propulsion system on board the modified Swedish submarine* Näcken.

Below: *The Swedish submarine* Näcken *after modification to house a Stirling AIP installation. It is now clear that*

non-nuclear submarines must have an affordable AIP system if they are to survive in a modern ASW environment.

Nuclear Propulsion

The great majority of modern nuclear-propelled submarines used pressurized-water reactors (PWR), in which water acts as both coolant and moderator, a tried and tested technique which has proved very reliable in the West, although a little less so in the Soviet Navy. In such a system water travels around a primary circuit, passing several times through the nuclear reactor and thence to a steam generator (heat exchanger). The water in the primary circuit has to be kept at a high pressure to prevent it from boiling and turning to steam. This is achieved by a pressurizer. Steam at the top of the pressurizer is used to compensate for changes in coolant volume as the reactor inlet and outlet temperatures vary.

The heat energy is transferred in the steam generator from the pressurized water in the primary circuit to unpressurized water in the secondary circuit, which then becomes steam and drives the turbine. Having driven the turbine it passes into a series of condensers, becoming water once again and returning in liquid form to the steam generator to continue the cycle. PWR condensers use sea water as a heat sink and require a constant throughput, provided either by the forward motion of the submarine, or, at slow speeds, by the use of pumps.

The operation of a PWR installation requires considerable auxiliary power, mainly to operate the circulation pumps in the primary circuit and the electrical heater elements in the pressurizer. The system can be designed to use natural circulation resulting from the thermal gradients set up by the nuclear reaction, but at higher power levels pumps still have to be switched in. Some systems, in an effort to minimize noise and vibration, use several pumps which can be selectively activated according to the power level. Whatever the system, however, all these pumps create low-level noise, which can be detected by suitable sensors.

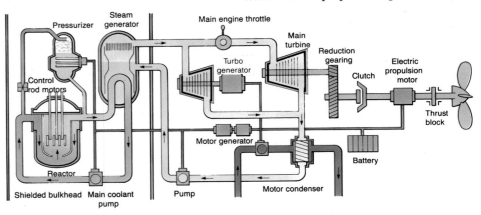

Below: *This is the layout of a pressurized-water nuclear propulsion system.*

Various alternative coolants have been tried. USS *Seawolf* (SSN-575), launched in 1955, was fitted with an S2G liquid sodium-cooled reactor, which effected a much more efficient heat transfer, but was very troublesome in service. There were two particular problems, the more intractable being that the sodium had to be kept liquid at all times, otherwise it solidified and ruined the primary circuit pipes. The second was that the plant was plagued by high-pressure steam leaks. After two years the S2G was changed for an S2Wa PWR, virtually identical to that installed in the *Nautilus*. The Soviet Alfa and Mike class SSNs are both agreed to have liquid metal-cooled reactors, but it should be noted that the Mike suffered an explosion and sank in 1989. The French Rubis class were thought for some years to have liquid metal cooled reactors but it has recently been confirmed that they have a new type of smaller PWR.

Right: *The nuclear reactor vessel is lowered with care into a French SSBN.*

Below: *USS* Miami *(SSN-755), one of the US Navy's outstanding Los Angeles class nuclear-propelled attack submarines.*

Submarine Types

The basic role of the submarine since its inception has been to attack surface vessels, both warships and merchant ships, and, more recently, also to attack other submarines. Although the name has changed from time to time (for example, cruiser, patrol submarine, hunter/killer are just a few), the basic role has not. However, not surprisingly, various types of specialisation have come about. This concluding section of the Introduction examines the special roles that submarines have undertaken in their history.

Minelayers

The idea of a specialised submarine minelayer originated with the Russian *Krab*, which was laid down in 1908 (although she was not completed until 1915). She was followed by the Germans with their UC-1 class in 1915. Thereafter small numbers of minelayers were built for most navies, following one of two basic concepts. In one the mines were placed on a horizontal conveyor, located under the upper casing, which moved the mines towards the stern where they dropped through two holes clear of the propellers. This was the system pioneered in *Krab* and similar systems were used by the Americans and British. The various systems worked quite well, but the complicated mechanical devices, plus the mines, placed a lot of weight high on the submarine, which interfered with their stability.

The second concept, which was pioneered by the Germans, was quite different and consisted of vertical tubes holding one, two or three mines and from which the mines were dropped. In some installations the tubes were mounted in the hull and in others (for example, the French Normand-Fenaux system) they were in the ballast tanks.

The loss rate among specialised minelayers was quite high. Eventually the requirement for such a type faded out

Above: *The French submarine* Surcouf *standing out to sea. She was intended to be a commerce raider and the circular hangar below the bridge houses a specially-designed reconnaissance aircraft to find her potential victims.*

during World War II because mines were developed which could be launched from standard torpedo tubes. However, two types of 'strap-on' mine-laying 'girdles', have appeared in the late 1980s, with which a submarine can be given an additional minelaying capability without interfering with the number of torpedoes being carried. One system is being produced in Germany, the other in Sweden.

Aircraft-Carrying Submarines

During World War I it became apparent that visibility from a submarine running on the surface was very limited. One possible way of extending this was by carrying an aircraft, which could both observe and perhaps also attack distant targets. Initially, such combinations simply involved a floatplane sitting on the deck of a submarine, which submerged to enable the aircraft to taxi away and then take-off,

with the procedure being reversed on landing.

The first time this was tried was by the Germans in January 1915, when the technique was proved feasible, using a Friedrichshafen FF-29a floatplane and the submarine *U-12*. The same system was tested by the British, also in 1915, with two Sopwith Schneider aircraft mounted on twin rails on the after deck of the submarine HMS *E-22*; the aim was to extend the fighters' range to enable them to attack raiding Zeppelins before they reached the British coast. In both cases the fundamental problem was that the aircraft simply sat on the submarine's deck, thus preventing the boat from submerging and making the whole combination highly vulnerable.

The solution to this occured to the Germans first. They realised that the answer was to have a small aircraft which could be dismantled and carried in a watertight tube, and thus submerge with the submarine. To fly off, the submarine surfaced and the aircraft was quickly assembled. The first aircraft of this type was the Hansa Brandenburg W20, designed by Dr Ernst Heinkel, which was intended for use on board the new U-139 class cruiser submarines. It first flew in 1917, required a container 20ft x 6ft (6m x 1.83m) and took three minutes to assemble. It was never tested at sea.

The US Navy also became interested in the idea and towards the end of World War I they flight-tested several aircraft intended for use aboard submarines, but no submarines were converted. There was renewed interest in 1923 when the Glenn Martin MS-1, which could be stowed in a cylinder, was tested aboard the submarine *S-1* (SS-105). As with the earlier German and British systems, the MS-1 was floated off from the submarine after assembly, but this process took no less than four hours, which was completely unacceptable. After a lot of redesign over a period of three years, assembly time was reduced to just twelve minutes. However, the US Navy still saw little point in the idea and it was again dropped. There was yet another resurgence of interest in the early 1930s when trials were conducted with the Loening XSL-1, but the news of the loss of the British *M-2* provided the excuse to stop once again.

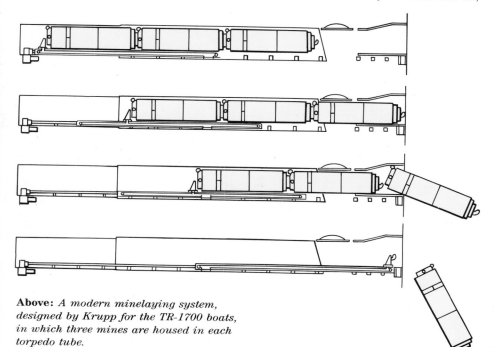

Above: *A modern minelaying system, designed by Krupp for the TR-1700 boats, in which three mines are housed in each torpedo tube.*

The Germans and the Americans had used small cylindrical hangars inside which the aircraft was completely disassembled. The British took a slightly different approach, using a large hangar aboard HMS *M-2*. The aircraft, a Parnall Peto floatplane, was stowed in the hangar completely assembled except that its wings were folded. On surfacing the aircraft was moved out of the hangar onto a short catapult, the wings extended and then launched, all in under five minutes. To be recovered it taxied alongside the submarine where it was picked out of the water by a crane and lowered onto its launching trolley, which, the wings having been folded, was then pushed back into the hangar. The overall concept was successful but the submarine was lost on 26 January 1932 and the idea was dropped.

Meanwhile the French had constructed the first purpose-built aircraft-carrying submarine, the *Surcouf*. Completed in 1933 she displaced 4,304 tons and carried a Marcel-Besson MB-411 aircraft in a large hangar. She also mounted two 8in (203mm) guns and was intended as a commerce raider. *Surcouf* escaped to Britain in 1940 and then went to the USA for a refit. She was sunk en route to the Pacific on 18 February 1942.

The Italian Navy designed one cruiser submarine to take an aircraft, the *Ettore Fieramosca* (1,965 tons). However, the plans were changed before she was completed and the hangar door was plated over.

It was the Japanese who developed the aircraft-carrying submarine to a fully operational system. First trials took place in 1927, using a small floatplane mounted on the after casing of the submarine *I-21*. These were successful and the *I-51* was fitted with a hangar and a catapult on her after casing. Again the trials were successful, but after three years the submarine was returned to normal duties. However, this led to the purpose-built aircraft-carrying submarine of the J2 type, which had two small hangars abaft the conning-tower, one of which housed the fuselage and the other the wings and floats of a small aircraft. Next came the J3 type, two submarines, which were fitted with a catapult facing aft. It was then realised that it was more logical to launch the aircraft into wind and the next series, the B1 type, and all subsequent aircraft-carrying submarines had the catapult on the foredeck.

Altogether the IJN built some 38 aircraft-carrying submarines, all of which served during World War II. Aircraft used were the Yokosuka E14Y1 (known to the Allies as 'Glen') and, at the end of the war, the Aichi M6A1 *Seiran*, both designed specifically for submarine operations. They carried out numerous missions, including reconnaissances of Pearl Harbor in Hawaii, Sydney Harbour in Australia and Wellington in New Zealand. One E14Y1 aircraft operating from *I-25* was the only Axis aircraft to penetrate United States' airspace when, on two successive days in September 1942, it

Above: *The Japanese aircraft-carrying submarine* I-8; *note the catapault aft.*

dropped bombs on Oregon forests.

The Germans also briefly flirted with the idea during World War II. They first considered using a tiny monoplane, the Arado Ar 231, but this was dropped in favour of a unique, collapsible, rotary-wing kite, the Focke-Achgelis Fa 330. These autogyro kites were tethered by a wire to a winch aboard the submarine and considerably extended the spotting range of the submarine. However, it took some time to wind the kite down, which boded ill for the intrepid pilot if any enemy ship was spotted! The Fa 330s were allocated to the Type IX submarines which served in the Far East, but there are no records of how successful they were.

Seaplane Tenders

In a variation on the aircraft theme, various navies have toyed with the idea of using the submarine as a seaplane tender. The British tested the submarine *L-8* in

Below: *Three Japanese aircraft-carrying submarines lie alongside the US submarine base in Pearl Harbor in 1946.*

such a role in the 1920s, but did not pursue the idea. The Japanese tested the concept in the 1930s, with at least one submarine, *I-22*, modified for the role. Then, in February 1942 they modified three more submarines to refuel seaplanes, which were used later in the month to enable two seaplanes to carry out a bombing raid on Pearl Harbor. The aircraft completed a round trip of some 4,000 miles (6,440km) in 24 hours, being refuelled by the submarines once on the outward leg and again on the homebound leg. A special class of seaplane tenders was designed, the SH class, although only one boat was completed. These carried 365 tons of aviation fuel, together with bombs and torpedoes.

The US Navy also tested the concept in the late 1930s, converting some fuel tanks in a few submarines to carry aviation fuel. Tests were successful, but as far as is known, the idea was not pursued during the war. The concept reappeared in the early 1950s when the Gato class submarine *Guavina* (AGSS-362) was converted to carry 159,864 gallons (605,149 litres) of aviation fuel. However, despite successful tests the idea was not carried forward.

Transports

Submarines have been used as transports on numerous occasions and, at its most basic, men or stores are simply fitted in where feasible without any modification to the submarine. Numerous missions have been accomplished in such a way. The Germans used submarines as extempore transports during the invasion of Norway in 1940, *U-101*, for example, carrying one 88mm anti-aircraft gun, with its accessories, 774 rounds of 88mm ammunition, eight 250kg bombs, 60m³ of aircraft fuel and 1,200kg of lubricating oil. A number of Japanese combat submarines visited Europe during the war and all carried what supplies they could in both directions. The British also used submarines to run supplies to Malta in 1942 and to the Aegean islands in 1943.

During World War I the Allied blockade of Germany began to bite very quickly and one proposed method of breaking it was by the construction of purpose-built transport submarines of the Deutschland class (1,875 tons). *Deutschland* herself made one return trip to the USA in 1916, but after the USA entered the war there was no further use for the class in a commercial role and the survivors were converted into cruisers as the U-151 class.

In World War II Germany suffered similar problems, but this time the only possible source of supplies was her distant ally in the Far East. Operational U-boats returning home from the Far East were used to transport whatever could be fitted in, while nine Italian submarines were taken over and rapidly converted before being sent to the Far East as transports. Not one of these returned to Europe, for a variety of reasons, and the idea was abandoned. Six German U-boats were then converted to the transport role: two Type IXD₁, two Type XB and two Type VIIF. Several specialised transport designs were considered, including the Kohrs' 4,000 ton 'U-ship', the Type XX and a conversion of the Type XXI, but none was built.

In Japan the transport problem was different. The most urgent requirement was to resupply outlying garrisons scattered across the Pacific. As usual combat submarines were first used, no less than sixteen large I-series submarines being placed on this duty in late 1942 when the situation on Guadalcanal became critical. These large submarines could carry some 50 tons of supplies, their aircraft hangar proving particularly useful, but the task was highly unpopular with the crews.

One unusual device was the *unkato*, a

Above: *The German U-151 was initially built as the cargo vessel* Deutschland.

streamlined cylindrical canister capable of carrying 337 tons of cargo. The *unkato* was towed behind a submerged submarine to its destination, where both submarine and cylinder surfaced and the latter was towed ashore by local boats. Only a small number of *unkato* missions were successful. The Germans also tested a similar device.

The IJN also built a number of specialised transport submarines. The D1 class (2,215 tons) could carry 22 tons of stores and 110 soldiers, but of the twelve built eight were lost. An improved type, the D2 (2,240 tons), was designed of which only one was completed and that, too, was sunk. A much smaller boat was then designed, the SS Type (493 tons) of which ten were completed in 1944/45; six made successful resupply runs. Astonishingly, the Japanese Army also built a number of its own transport submarines. Twenty-six were built of two

Below: *US Navy special forces on board a Swimmer Delivery Vehicle (SDV); many navies use such clandestine methods.*

types, the Yu1 and Yu1001 classes, the great majority of which were sunk by US forces.

During the war the US Navy also used a number of combat submarines on transport missions, particularly to resupply isolated island garrisons and on clandestine missions in support of guerrillas in the Philippines. One submarine, *Argonaut* (SS-166) was converted as a troop transport and was given the first 'transport' designation, becoming APS-1. After the war three fleet submarines were converted to the transport role, to fit them to carry 111 troops, 85 tons of supplies, a tracked amphibious vehicle (LVT), a jeep and eight 10-man rubber dinghies in support of amphibious landings on hostile beaches. This involved considerable internal modifications and a large watertight cylindrical hangar was installed on the after casing. These submarines were given the classification APSS.

When the Regulus cruise-missile programme ended, two boats were converted to become transport submarines for US Navy special forces. *Tunny* (SS-282), built originally as a Gato class fleet submarine, was converted into a troop transport (as APSS-282, later changed to LPSS-282) in 1966, but was stricken in 1969. Her place was taken by a former purpose-built Regulus submarine, *Grayback* (SSG-574), whose large hangars were ideal for her new transport role. Redesignated LPSS-574, *Grayback* was stricken in 1984. Two Ethan Allen class former SSBNs were then converted to this role in the mid-1980s: *John Marshall* (SSN-611) and *Sam Houston* (SSN-609). They can carry up to 67 SEAL swimmers and a swimmer delivery vehicle (SDV), which is housed in a large Dry Dock Shelter (DDS) on the upper casing.

The Soviet Navy has built two India class submarines, very large (4,800 tons submerged displacement) diesel-electric submarines, whose role is said to be 'salvage' and 'rescue'. For this role they carry two tracked submersibles on the after casing. It is believed that, in addition to their announced role, they are also used to transport Soviet special forces such as *Spetsnaz* troops.

Although other navies can carry small numbers of special forces in their operational attack submarines, none is known to have converted any to carry such large numbers.

Oilers

The German *Kriegsmarine* seems to have been the first to hit upon the idea of using one submarine to refuel another at sea. Occasionally during the early years of World War II a U-boat returning to base with excess fuel was directed to rendezvous with another U-boat short on fuel and resupply her, but it proved to be an exceptionally difficult undertaking. Also in those early years, surface resupply ships were at sea to replenish the surface commerce raiders and these occasionally supplied U-boats, as well.

This led to a requirement being stated for specialised supply boats, which resulted

in the Type XIV U-boat, of which six were built. Each Type XIV, known in the U-boat service as *'milch-kuhe'* (milk cows) could replenish twelve Type VIICs with four week's or five Type IXC with eight week's supply of fuel oil. The Type XIV could also supply fresh bread, a variety of spares and torpedoes (of which only four were carried). Transfer at sea proved difficult and very time-consuming and could not take place in sea states worse than Force 4. Also, of course, both boats were exposed to enemy aircraft and surface ships. Experiments took place in which, having transferred the hoses on the surface, both boats then submerged for the resupply operation, spending some 3-4 hours at periscope depth while the fuel was transferred. As far as is known, this technique was not used operationally.

The Allies made special efforts to dispose of the Type XIVs. Aided by interception of enemy radio traffic, the last of the six boats was sunk on its maiden voyage in mid-1944.

In 1950 the US Navy converted one submarine to the oiler role, *Guavina* (SS-362). However, unlike the German Type XIV she was designed not to resupply other submarines at sea, but to carry fuel to beachheads during amphibious landings. She could carry 42,268 gal (160,000 l) of fuel. She was redesignated SSO-362, but after some trials the idea was dropped and the submarine was reroled.

Radar Pickets

In the latter days of the Pacific campaign surface warships were used as radar pickets to help guide bombers towards their targets in Japan, but their losses were heavy, especially to Japanese *kamikaze* aircraft. Consequently, after the war the US Navy developed the idea of submarine radar pickets, designated SSR. Radar sets were installed inside the submarines, where the equipment and operators took up a great deal of space. The antennas were mounted on the upper casing or on the fin.

Two boats were given quick and simple modifications in 1946, which proved rather unsatisfactory. As a result a proper conversion was designed, codenamed 'Migraine', of which there were three versions totalling ten boats. In addition, three new, purpose-built submarines were constructed as radar pickets: two were diesel-electric and one nuclear-powered, *Triton* (SSRN-586). These pickets were also all designed to control friendly aircraft and some of them were also able to provide mid-course guidance to submarine-

Above: *German World War II Type XIV supply submarine at an Atlantic RV.*

launched Regulus 1 cruise-missiles.

This project suffered from two fundamental weaknesses. First, in order to operate their antennas the submarines had to remain awash, if not fully surfaced, which made them almost as vulnerable as the surface ships they were replacing. Secondly, except for the nuclear-propelled *Triton,* they did not have the speed to operate with a carrier task force. When carrier-based airborne early warning aircraft (eg, the Grumman E-2 Hawkeye) entered service in the late 1950s the project was dropped and the boats were either converted to other duties or scrapped.

Target Submarines

Elderly submarines ready for scrapping have from time to time been disposed of by several navies by serving as targets. Also, submarines are frequently used as targets for ASW exercises in which sensors are used, but which stop short of actually firing a weapon.

However, following World War II there was a brief interest in the use of

Below: *The Combat Information Centre (CIC) in a Dutch Walrus class submarine.*

submarines as targets for homing torpedoes with dummy warheads, in order to carry out trials and to practise operational crews. In the US Navy *Manta* (SS-299) was converted in 1949, being given considerable extra protection for the role, which only lasted until 1953. In the Royal Navy one submarine HMS *Scotsman* was given a similar conversion and used as a target for some years.

The Soviet Navy actually built a specialised class of target submarines in the late 1960s, which are still in service. The Bravo class (3,000 tons) is fitted with considerable protection. Four were built.

Command and Control

Only two navies have ever used 'command-and-control' (C^2) submarines. The Imperial Japanese Navy (IJN) actually envisaged submarines being fought as 'fleets' under the command of an admiral afloat with his forces. As a result, the admirals needed flagships in order to command their forces and these were provided in the A1 Type (4,149 tons), which had additional accommodation for the admiral and his staff, together with special radio equipment. Three were completed, of which two were sunk by US forces and the third sank as an operational loss in 1944. The STo Type aircraft-carrying submarines (6,560 tons) also included C^2 facilities for an admiral and his staff.

The Soviet Navy fitted three elderly Golf-1 class submarines with extra communications in the 1970s. These may have been intended for a special C^2 task, but as the submarines have now been deleted the role has presumably been dropped.

The German U-boat commander in World War II, Admiral Dönitz, often organised his submarines into 'wolf packs' and he considered the idea that these should be

commanded by special flagship U-boats. However, not only would this have meant the pack commander transmitting a lot of radio signals (which would have been intercepted and DFed by Allied warships) but it would also have meant that the flagship would have had to remain separate from the immediate battle in order to exercise command properly. In such a case it was deemed better to exercise command from ashore and the idea of a flagship was dropped, although the senior captain of the 'pack' was often given certain local responsibilities.

One submarine was briefly considered for what might be termed the ultimate C^2 role. When the US Navy's nuclear-propelled radar picket *Triton* (SSRN-586) became redundant in its radar picket role, plans were prepared to convert it into a submerged Alternative National Command Post (ANCP) for the President and his staff to use during a nuclear war. The project never came to fruition.

Submarine Accidents

Despite the sophistication of today's submarines, accidents continue to happen; indeed, it is no exaggeration to say that submarines are inherently dangerous. Perhaps surprisingly, submarines are at their most vulnerable when on or near the surface, and remarkably few accidents occur to submarines when running deep.

Surface ships are a special hazard for submarines and in such a collision the submarine, no matter how strong, stands very little chance of surviving. Since 1900 there have been at least thirty such collisions in peacetime in which the submarine was lost, and many more in which the submarine received serious damage but without actually sinking. Human error, too, takes its toll, although today's sophisticated checking devices have diminished this likelihood. Leaving a hatch

Above: *Submarines are vulnerable, even in peacetime: USS* Stickleback *was rammed by USS* Silverstein *in 1958.*

Below: *Even today, the potential of the submarine has barely begun to be realised. This is one of the very capable* Västergötland *class boats.*

open or incorrect drills with a schnorkel can happen, even in the best navies. Mechanical failure can happen occasionally, too, and it seems reasonably certain that USS *Scorpion* suffered from some sort of catastrophic failure when she disappeared in the Atlantic on 21 May 1968.

This Book

In this book are the details of some sixty-nine submarines, which have all been carefully selected to represent a cross-section of the history of submarines. Most, but not all, of the countries which operate submarines are represented. The national entries have been arranged by grouping the major navies (USA, Soviet Union, Germany, Great Britain, Japan, France, Italy and the PRC) at the front of the book, and then following these with entries for the smaller navies, organised alphabetically by country name. Each country entry starts with an overview of submarine development in that particular navy and summarises the reasons why that navy needs submarines. This is followed by entries giving details of the more important classes to have served in that navy.

It should be noted that throughout the book, where a submarine's displacement is given to indicate its size (for example, 'Type VIIA (745 tons)') this figure is always the submerged displacement, unless it is specifically stated otherwise.

Finally, in all my researches into the history of submarines one factor stands out above all others, which is the courage of all submariners, regardless of nationality. They spend their working lives in an essentially hostile environment which, while it may give them shelter from view, is also utterly merciless if the slightest error is made. It is to all these men that this book, with respect, is dedicated.

USA

The first submerged attack on an enemy warship was carried out on 6 September 1776 by the American submarine *Turtle* against the British frigate HMS *Eagle*. Designed by David Bushnell and piloted by Sergeant Ezra Lee the tiny, one-man craft was made of wood and driven by a hand-cranked propeller. Although the attack was unsuccessful, thwarted by *Eagle*'s copper sheathing, *Turtle* seems to have been a sound design for her time. Nevertheless, no further progress was made until the War of 1812 when Bushnell produced a new submersible which carried out an attack against HMS *Ramillies*. A hole was drilled in the ship's side, but the screw broke as the explosive was being attached and the attack again failed, although, as before, the submarine escaped unscathed.

Next on the American scene was Robert Fulton, who, after failing to interest various European powers in his submarine designs, persuaded Congress to fund a new submarine, the first to be powered by a steam engine. However, he died during the trials and the project was abandoned.

During the American Civil War the Union maritime blockade of the Confederacy inspired Horace L. Hunley to finance the construction of several submarines. The first two were not particularly successful but the third, named *HL Hunley*, became the first submarine to sink an enemy warship. During training the *Hunley* was swamped while running on the surface and sank on no less than three occasions, twenty-three men dying in the process. Each time she was recovered and recommissioned. Finally, with yet another crew attracted by huge financial rewards, she attacked the Federal sloop *Housatonic* on 17 February 1864 off Charleston harbour with a spar torpedo. The attack was successful, *Housatonic* sinking with the loss of five men, but the *Hunley* also succumbed to the force of the explosion and was lost, again with all hands, and this time for good.

Above: *A Confederate Navy 'David' submersible at Charleston in 1865. Note the 'spar torpedo' in the bows.*

The Federal Navy funded the construction of two submarines, the *Alligator* and the *Intelligent Whale*. Despite official support both were failures.

Some twenty years later the US Navy became aware of growing foreign interest in submarines, so in 1888, following one of the fashions of the time, it sponsored an open competition for a design. There were five contenders, of whom the principle were the Swedish inventor Thorsten Nordenfelt and a puckish Irishman who had come to America in 1872, John P. Holland. Holland won both this and a second competition, but the government then withdrew its support. Yet another competition was set up on 3 March 1893, which Holland again won. His design was built as *Plunger*; it displaced 168 tons submerged and was driven by a steam engine. It was not a success and did not complete its trials. Holland then turned his energies to a new design, which he designated *Holland VI*. This boat was funded by Holland and was launched in 1897. Its success was clear from the start and it was purchased by the US Navy in 1900, being commissioned as *Holland* and later being given the historic hull number 'SS-1'.

Below: *J.P. Holland's steam-propelled* Plunger *of 1896 was not a success, and did not even complete her trials.*

Holland's only real rival during this period was another American, Simon Lake, who built a series of submarines, originally for commercial use in the exploration of the sea-bed. He later became involved in designing and building submarines for naval use, but although they were built in some numbers, few were successful.

World War I

With the success of the *Holland* the place of the submarine in the US Navy's order of battle was assured and new classes appeared at regular intervals. The early submarines, with their limited capabilities, were employed in the harbour defence role and were deployed to defend naval ports on the mainland United States, at the entrances to the Panama Canal and in the Philippines. By the time it entered the war in April 1917 the US possessed 53 submarines, of which the most modern were the L class, then building.

Much of the US surface fleet deployed to the European war zone to aid the other Allied navies, but only two classes of submarine were despatched. Four boats of the K class were sent to the Azores and seven L class to Bantry Bay in Ireland. Although many patrols were conducted, there were few contacts as there were very few ships of the Central Powers left at sea, apart from U-boats. Nevertheless the crews gained invaluable practical experience.

The lessons learned early in the war were incorporated into the R and S classes. The R class, 27 of which were built between 1917 and 1919 consisted of two groups, one designed by the Electric Boat Company, the other by Lake. The latter's seven boats were all stricken in 1930, but the remainder served through World War II. No less than 47 of the S class were built between 1918 and 1924, the same specifications being used to produce three designs, one by the Electric Boat company (31 built), the second by Lake (five built) and the third by the Navy's Bureau of Construction (11 built). Careful attention to streamlining gave some of these boats the high underwater speed (for the time) of 13.3kt. The S boats provided the bulk of the US Navy's submarine fleet in the 1920s and 1930s and, despite their obsolescence, many fought in World War II.

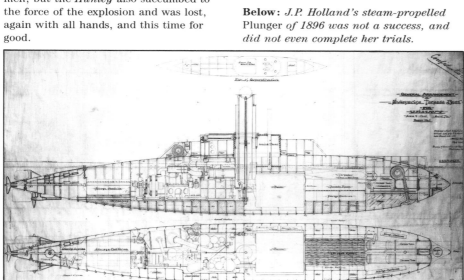

The Inter-War Years

After the war the navy reassessed the strategic situation. It was clear that the principal potential enemy was Japan and naval planners concluded that the strategy must be to carry the offensive to the enemy. This led to a requirement for submarines with long range, heavy armament with plenty of reloads, and good habitability. The result was the classic US Navy 'fleet submarine', which was developed through a process of gradual evolution over a period of some twenty years.

The first 'fleet submarines' were the four boats of the Schley class, also known as the T and AA class, which were constructed between 1918 and 1919. Displacing 1,482 tons (submerged) these were the largest submarines built in the USA up to that time. Also, with a surface range of 3,000nm (5,560km) at 14kt and an armament of six 18in (457mm) torpedo tubes (two of which were later removed) and two 3in (76mm) guns, they were, at least on paper, the most powerful submarines of their day.

Although they were not a success in service, the Schley class pointed the way and the next to appear was the three-boat Barracuda class in 1924/25, displacing 2,506 tons (submerged) and with a surface range of 11,000nm (20,378km). Large as they were, the next class, the Narwhal class, was larger still, displacing 3,960 tons (submerged). They remain the largest diesel-electric submarines ever to be built for the US Navy.

These were considered too large and had a poor underwater performance, and so an attempt was made to incorporate the best features of the Narwhal class into a much smaller hull. The result was the single-boat Dolphin class (2,215 tons) launched in 1932, which had much better manoeuvrability when submerged and carried the same armament. However, it only had half the range. The Cachalot class of two boats, commissioned in 1933, were smaller than the *Dolphin*, but they were the first US submarines to make widespread use of electric welding, which gave much stronger hulls and avoided the problem of fuel leakage, which plagued submarines with rivetted tanks, and was a certain give-away to surface warships. The Cachalots were also the first to be fitted

Above: *S-48 (SS-159), one of five S class boats constructed by Simon Lake. The deck gun is a 4in (102mm)/50 calibre.*

with Torpedo Data Computers (TDC), a mechanical analogue device which led to much more accurate torpedo firings.

Although it may not have been obvious at the time, the US Navy was now well on course. The P class of 1935 was the first of the World War II 'fleet boats'. Displacing 1,960 tons, they had a surface range of 11,000nm (20,370km) at 10kt and a maximum surface speed of 19kt, with an armament of six 21in (533mm) torpedo tubes (4 forward, 2 aft). The P class (ten boats) was followed by the Salmon/Sargo class (sixteen boats) and the Tambor class (twelve boats), each of which represented

Below: *USS* Pickerel *(SS-524), a Tench class boat surfaces from a depth of 150ft (45m) off Oahu, during a 1952 test.*

an incremental improvement, culminating in the outstanding Gato class, the first of which entered service just as the Japanese attacked Pearl Harbor. The next class, the Balao class, differed principally in having a high-tensile steel hull which gave an additional 100ft (30m) in diving depth, while the Tench class had minor internal differences. Total strength of each class was: Gato, 73; Balao, 122; Tench 30 (of which 11 were completed before the end of the war).

There were two diversions from this steady line of development during the inter-war years. First was *Argonaut*, the only purpose-built submarine minelayer ever to serve in the US Navy. A huge boat displacing 4,164 tons (submerged) she was derived from the *Barracuda* design, but incorporated lessons learned from examining German World War I minelayer plans. She had an exceptional range of 18,000nm (33,330km), but her engines were a constant source of trouble. During World War II she was converted into a troop transport.

The other divergence was the Mackerel class. In the late 1930s the powers-that-be in the surface navy had been watching the increasing size and sophistication (computers *and* air-conditioning!), and the growing cost of the fleet submarines with some alarm. So, in 1939 the chairman of the General Board compelled the submarine force to accept two smaller Mackerel class vessels if they also wanted to receive the six new, large Tambor class that they were asking for. Displacing 1,190 tons, with a poor range and insufficient armament the Mackerel class were highly unpopular in service and spent most of their service careers in training units.

World War II

US submarine activity in the Atlantic was limited and by far the greater proportion of the force was deployed, as it had always been intended it should, in the Pacific against the Japanese. At the time of Pearl Harbor the force comprised a number of elderly R and S class submarines, which had been constructed at the end of the previous war, together with all the inter-war boats; a total of 112 submarines.

From the start, US submarines conducted an aggressive campaign, penetrating into Japanese-controlled waters at every opportunity. The policy throughout the war against Japan was officially declared to be 'unrestricted submarine warfare' and thus both warships and merchant ships were attacked. During the war Japan lost 2,117 merchant ships (over 8 million grt) of which some 60 per cent was sunk by submarines, 30 per cent by aircraft and ten per cent by surface warships or mines. These losses reduced the merchant fleet to a shadow and few worthwhile targets were left as the war drew to a close. US submarines also accounted for 201 warships of the Japanese surface fleet, including one battlecruiser, three aircraft carriers, two cruisers and many smaller ships.

In general, the Japanese anti-submarine capability was low, with surface warships accounting for nineteen US boats, air and combined air/surface eleven boats, and mines six. Only one US submarine was sunk by a Japanese submarine. The remainder of the losses were: unknown, 7; accident, 1; and operational losses, 8, which included one sunk in error by a US Navy warship and one sunk by a rogue torpedo it had just launched.

One of the saddest chapters in the submarine war concerned the Mark XIV torpedo, which had been insufficiently tested during peacetime, due mainly to a misguided wish to maintain 'secrecy'. As a consequence its guidance and depth-setting features were extremely unreliable, the detonator was inefficient, the warhead was the smallest in a torpedo in any navy, and, to cap it all, it was available in inadequate quantities.

Despite repeated failures in combat the authorities strenuously resisted the notion that there was a problem and therefore did not seek a solution, the failures being blamed on the inexperience of the captains and crews. Then, in mid-1942, it was shown that one of the problems was that the torpedoes were running too deep; this was quickly corrected but other problems persisted. They were finally traced in mid-1943 to the Mark VI detonator, which proved to be faulty in both its primary magnetic mode and in its secondary contact mode. Thus, the Mark XIV torpedo was finally debugged, but only after a shocking number of duds had been fired on operational missions by courageous crews.

One example among many is the case of the *Tunny* (SS-282), which in April 1943 managed to reach the centre of a formation of three Japanese aircraft-carriers (a submarine skipper's dream!)

Above: *The US submarine campaign in the Pacific was an outstanding success. Here* Tinosa *(SS-283) returns to Pearl Harbor in August 1945, each Japanese flag signifying an enemy vessel sunk.*

and fired a spread of ten torpedoes. Of these, six exploded prematurely, three missed and just one scored a hit, damaging one of the carriers.

At the end of the war the submarine force had every reason to be proud of its achievements. It had sunk large numbers of Japanese ships and had been among the first to take the war to Japan. Further, it had not only sunk ships but had also laid mines, transported troops on amphibious raids, carried supplies, rescued downed fliers (including the future President Bush) and acted as radar pickets. To achieve all this the US Navy lost 53 submarines out of a total of 336 that served during the war, costing the lives of 3,509 men.

The Cold War

After World War II the United States found itself in a totally new strategic situation. It was by far the strongest and richest of the victorious powers, it was expected to take up global responsibilities and it had a new potential enemy — the Soviet Union. The threat from the USSR made itself felt almost immediately and it posed itself in a variety of ways and in various directions. At sea the problem was that the Soviet Fleet was a relatively unknown quantity, but there was reason to believe that large-scale building programmes for cruisers, destroyers and submarines had been initiated. These submarines were thought to be coming off the ways in large numbers and to incorporate technological lessons derived from the German Types XXI and XXIII in their design. With hindsight the threat may have been overestimated, but to those involved at the time it seemed very real.

For the longer term the US Navy pinned its hopes on nuclear-propulsion and long-range missiles, but in the short term what was needed was large numbers of reasonably fast and capable submarines. Fortunately, many of the World War II fleet submarines were on hand and these provided a good basis for modernisation in a variety of undertakings, such as the Fleet Schnorkel and the Greater Underwater Propulsive Power (Guppy, for short) programmes.

The first priority was to streamline the hulls and to build in greater battery power. Next the German-perfected schnorkel was fitted. Then more and more equipment (for example, new sonars, radars and

US Submarine Losses 1941-1945										
Class	Surface Attack	Air Attack	Air/Surface Attack	Submarine	Mine	Accident	Unknown	Operational Losses[1]	Total War Losses	Killed
R						1			1	46
S	1						1	4	6	151
Barracuda									0	
Argonaut	1								1	105[2]
Narwhal									0	
Dolphin									0	
Cachalot									0	
P	3				1				4	217
Salmon	2	1						1[3]	4	256
Tambor	4	1	2				1		8	464
Mackerel									0	
Gato	4	1	3	1	4		4	2	19	1,450
Balao	4	2	1		1		1	1	10	820
Tench									0	
Totals	19	5	6	1	6	1	7	8	53	3,509

Notes:
[1] Operational loss covers losses at sea during the war, but not caused by the enemy.
[2] The largest single loss of life in the loss of any US submarine.
[3] Sunk by a US surface warship in error.

computers) was packed into existing hulls, so that some of the hulls had to be lengthened to create more space. Surprisingly, the results were outstanding and 'fleet submarines' proved themselves again excellent in service, bridging the gap until the new generation of nuclear submarines joined the fleet. Even after that they gave further sterling service on transfer to foreign navies.

There were also a variety of smaller programmes undertaken, which enjoyed differing degrees of success. There were apparently requirements for submersible radar pickets, seaplane resupply submarines, specialised anti-submarine submarines (SSK) and submarines capable of firing cruise missiles. All these and more were tried. There were also two post-war classes of diesel-electric submarines, the Tang class and the Barbel class. After relatively short service with the US Navy the Tangs were sold abroad, but the three Barbels served on for some years as ASW training targets. This ended when *Blueback* (SS-581) was stricken in 1990, not only the last of her class, but also the last operational diesel-electric submarine in the US Navy, descended in a direct and unbroken line from the *Holland* (SS-1).

By the 1950s it was clear that the US Navy's submarine requirements had effectively reduced to two: she needed a ballistic-missile submarine, and a very high performance attack and ASW submarine, both nuclear-powered. To support these plans there appeared a number of experimental submarines, of which two stand out as turning-points in submarine development. First was *Nautilus* (SSN-571), the world's first-ever nuclear-propelled submarine; the second was *Albacore* (AGSS-569), whose revolutionary hull-shape enabled submarine designers to take full advantage of the power available from nuclear propulsion.

The US Navy's strategic deterrent submarine force in 1991 comprises 36 SSBNs. The oldest in service is the Lafayette class, which was built between 1961 and 1967. Of the 31 built, 24 remain

Above: Sabalo *(SS-302), was launched in 1944, converted to a Fleet Schnorkel (as seen here) in 1952, stricken in July 1971.*

in service. Twelve of these are armed with Poseidon SLBMs and another twelve have been modernised to take the Trident I C-4 missile, while the others have already been stricken to comply with SALT-II treaty limits.

There are currently twelve of the latest Ohio class SSBNs in service with another eight due to join the fleet at a rate of one per year until 1998. The ninth and subsequent submarines have the Trident II D-5 missile, while the first eight, which were built to take the Trident I C-4, are being backfitted to take the newer missile at a rate of one every other year.

Below: *The Ohio class SSBNs are among the mightiest weapons of war ever built.*

There are 90 SSNs, of which 42 are of the highly successful Los Angeles class, with a further 20 on order. There are 37 Sturgeon class, built between 1963 and 1975, and one of the closely related Narwhal class, which used a lengthened Sturgeon hull to test the natural-circulation S5G reactor. There are also eight remaining Permit class, although these will all be stricken in the early 1990s, as will the first few units of the Sturgeon class. Finally, there are two former SSBNs of the Ethan Allen class, which are now used as troop transports and swimmer delivery submarines. The first of the new SSN-21 (or Seawolf) class, is currently under construction, but the programme costs are bound to be extremely high and its is questionable that many will be authorized in the new strategic environment following the end of the Cold War.

Holland Class

(Coastal patrol submarine)

Displacement:
64 tons surfaced; 74 tons submerged
Performance:
Max speed 8kt surfaced; 5kt submerged
Range 500nm/7kt surfaced
Maximum Operational Diving Depth:
75ft (23m)
Dimensions:
53ft 10in (16.4m) x 10ft 3in (3.1m) x 8ft 6in (2.6m)
Machinery:
One Otto gasoline engine, 45bhp; one Electro
Dynamic Co electric motor, 50shp; one shaft
Complement:
1 officer; 6 ratings
Construction:
Crescent Shipyard, Elizabethport. *Holland*
(SS-1). One boat. Launched 17 May 1897

Above: *USS* Holland I *alongside, clearly showing the muzzle of the 8in (203mm) dynamite gun, a useless weapon which was not installed on other submarines.*

Design: Not the first submarine, but certainly the first effective underwater weapons system and the first commissioned submarine in the US Navy, John P. Holland's craft included many design features which are still in use today. The *Holland* was optimised for underwater performance, with a streamlined, 'teardrop' hull and single propeller, and, unlike many contemporary designs, she dived with her ballast tanks full, relying for control on her aft-mounted hydroplanes.

She combined an air-breathing, gasoline-powered, drive system for surface propulsion and charging the batteries with an air-independent, battery-powered, electrical drive system for underwater propulsion. Other features, too, have stood the test of time, such as the controls and the clutches, which could enable the petrol engine to drive either the propeller direct or could be used to recharge the batteries, using the motor as a generator, with or without turning the propeller; ie, the batteries could be charged either while moving at sea or while at rest alongside.

Having returned the money he had received from the Government for the abortive *Plunger*, Holland designed the *Holland VI* (the inventor's designation) and had it built at his own expense at the

Crescent Shipyard, Elizabethport, New Jersey, where she was launched on 17 May 1897. Trials went well despite a major hitch in October of that year when a shipyard workman left a valve open while the boat was on the slip. This resulted in her being flooded when the tide came in, but potential damage to the entire electrical cabling system was prevented and the boat passed all her tests.

Armament: Main armament was a single, bow-mounted 17.7in (450mm) torpedo tube, covered by a watertight bow-cap, which was raised for firing by a worm-gear. Compensation to maintain the trim when a torpedo was fired was extremely effective. Three torpedoes were carried. She also carried two 8in (203mm) 'dynamite guns', one in the bow above the torpedo tube, the second aft. These were fixed mounts intended to be fired with the muzzle just clear of the water, but as far as is known they were never fired; indeed, the after gun was soon removed.

Service History: She was bought by the US Government on 11 April 1900 and named USS *Holland*, subsequently also being allocated the number SS-1. She was commissioned on 12 October 1900, the first commanding officer being Lieutenant Harry H. Caldwell, USN.

In service the *Holland* carried out trials and was used as a training boat at the US Naval Academy, Annapolis until 17 July 1905. She was finally stricken on 21 November 1910 and sold to a breakers yard in June 1930. Unfortunately, no trace of this truly historic submarine remains, although a close sister, the British *Holland No 1* is on display at the Royal Navy Submarine Museum at Gosport, England.

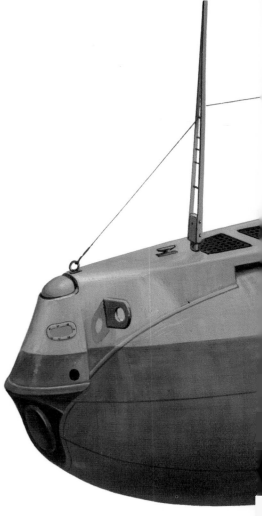

Left: *Following the lead of the US Navy, the Royal Navy constructed a number of identical boats. This is submarine No 1 running on the surface.*

Above: *J.P. Holland's design had a 'teardrop' hull, a single propeller and minimal protuberances, all of which were intended to optimise underwater performance. These concepts were to be lost between 1900 and the 1950s, being rediscovered in USS* Albacore (AGSS-569).

Above: *USS* Holland, *the US Navy's first submarine. She was armed with one 17.7in (450mm) torpedo tube, for which three torpedoes were carried.*

Right: *USS* Holland *spent most of her operational life as a training boat, serving at the US Navy Academy at Annapolis from 1901 to 1905. The relaxed attitude and casual rig of her crew contrasts strongly with the very correct Royal Navy 'types' opposite.*

L Class

(Patrol submarines)

Displacement:
Electric Boat Co design 450 tons surfaced; 548 tons submerged
Lake design 456 tons surfaced; 524 tons submerged

Performance:
Max speed 14kt surfaced; 10.5kt submerged
Range 3,300nm/10.5kt surfaced; 150nm/5kt submerged

Maximum Operational Diving Depth:
200ft (61m)

Dimensions:
Electric Boat Co design 167ft 5in (51.0m) x 17ft 5in (5.3m) x 13ft 7in (4.1m)
Lake design 165ft 0in (50.3m) x 14ft 9in (4.5m) x 13ft 3in (4.0m)

Machinery:
Electric Boat Co design Two NELSECO diesels, 900bhp; two Electro Dynamic Co electric motors, 680shp; two shafts
Lake design Two Busch-Sulzer diesels, 1,200bhp; two Diehl electric motors, 800shp; two shafts

Complement:
2 officers; 26 ratings

Construction:
Electric Boat Co design Fore River Yard. L-1 to L-4; L-9 to L-11. Seven boats. Completed 1916
Lake design Lake TB Co, Bridgeport. L-5. One boat. Completed 1918. California Shipbuilding Co. L-6, L-7. Two boats. Completed 1917. Portsmouth Naval Shipyard. L-8. One boat. Completed 1917.

Design: This was the class entering service as the United States became a belligerent in World War I. They were built, as was normal US Navy practice at the time, to the same general specifications, but to two slightly different designs: one group (L-1 to L-4 and L-9 to L-11) from the Electric Boat Company, the other (L-5 to L-8) from Simon Lake.

As usually happened the Lake boats took considerably longer to build than those constructed by the Electric Boat Company, but the latter's did suffer some teething problems. The first four boats (L-1 to L-4) failed their acceptance tests on surface-running and two of them failed on submerged runs, as well! However, following some frantic work at the yards, they all subsequently passed. The Electric Boat Company boats were powered by NELSECO diesels, which, at that stage, had a reputation for unreliability, whereas the Lake boats had the rather more trustworthy and more powerful Busch-Sulzer engines.

Armament: The L class was armed with four bow 18in (457mm) torpedo tubes, for which a total of eight torpedoes were carried. They were the first American submarines to mount a deck gun, a result of observing the progress of the submarine war across the Atlantic. The gun was the 3in (76mm)/23 Mark 9, which was adapted from a boat gun, firing a 13lb (5.9kg) shell to a maximum range of 8,800yd (8,047m).

The gun was mounted just forward of the conning-tower, but in order to reduce underwater resistance to a minimum, the gun retracted through 90° into a recess in the casing when not in use. The complete barrel could not fit into the housing and some 5ft (1.52m) protruded vertically. This installation was, however, a complication which was not to be repeated in other classes, particularly as it added to the time required to get the gun into use when surfacing to attack an enemy vessel with direct fire.

Service History: Once the USA joined the Allied Powers the US Navy hastened to join the fray and a large proportion of the available fleet was sent across the Atlantic. The L boats, the latest in the fleet, were no exception, and L-1, L-2, L-4, L-9, L-10 and L-11 (plus the older *Skipjack* (SS-24)) were formed into Submarine Division 5 and sent to Bantry Bay in South-west Ireland. They arrived in two groups in January/February 1918 and stayed to the end of the war. Later, L-5, L-6, L-7 and L-8 (all Lake boats) formed Submarine Division 6 which was sent to the Azores, but they arrived on 7 November 1918, just four days before the war's end.

All US Navy submarines operating in European waters wore large markings on their conning towers, the letter 'A' for 'American' followed by their class and class number (eg, 'AL-10') to avoid confusion with British submarines.

Division 5 carried out numerous patrols, making some 21 contacts with enemy submarines. They did not sink any, although L-2 (SS-41) carried out an attack on a U-boat, which apparently exploded before any weapon was fired at it.

The class did not last long after the war, all being decommissioned in 1922-23.

Below: *The first operational deployment of US submarines was to Ireland in 1918. A crewman of USS L-3 (SS-42) signals by flag to another US Navy submarine at sea off Bearhaven.*

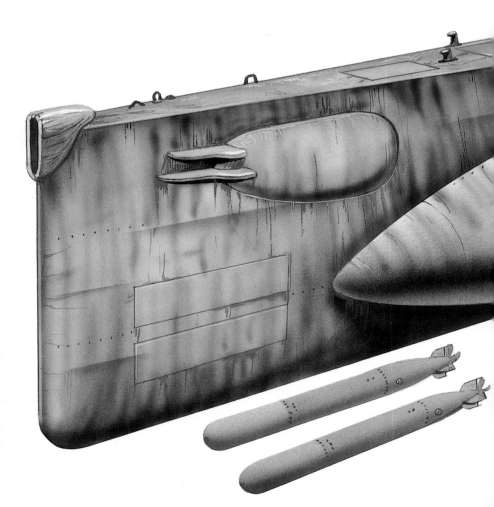

Above: *Like all US submarines deployed to the British Isles in 1918, these US Navy L class submarines wear the letter 'A' before their class numbers to distinguish them from British submarines with the same class name. Seen here are (from left to right) L-6 (SS-45), L-9 (SS-49), L-11 (SS-51) and L-2 (SS-41).*

Below: *USS L-1 (SS-30) putting to sea, with a large number of people on the upper deck, including some who are about to go ashore in the motor-boat.*

Above: *USS L-11 (SS-51). The artwork clearly shows the unusual gun mount, in which the 3in/23 Mark 9 retracted through 90° into a recess in the casing, leaving part of the barrel exposed.*

Argonaut Class

(Minelaying submarine)

Displacement:
2,710 tons surfaced; 4,164 tons submerged
Performance:
Max speed 15kt surfaced; 8kt submerged
Range 18,000nm/8kt surfaced; 10nm/8kt submerged
Maximum Operational Diving Depth:
300ft (91m)
Dimensions:
381ft 0in (116.1m) x 33ft 10in (10.3m) x 15ft 4in (4.67m)
Machinery:
Two M.A.N diesel engines, 3,175bhp; two Ridgeway electric motors, 2,400hp; two shafts (see design notes)
Complement:
8 officers; 80 ratings
Construction:
Portsmouth Naval Shipyard. *Argonaut* (SS-166). One boat. Completed 1928.

Design: Submarine minelayers had proved fairly successful in World War I. The Russians had pioneered the idea with the *Krab*, but it was the Imperial German Navy which had the greatest influence, with a series of small coastal minelayers (UC-1, UC-16 and UC-80 classes), which were built in large numbers, and the larger ocean-going types (U-71 class). The idea was then taken up by a number of other navies, the British, for example, building small numbers of E and L class minelayers, as well as converting the large M-3 in the late 1920s.

Thus, the US Navy was following an international fashion when it decided to construct a large minelaying submarine in the mid-1920s. Only one example was built, *Argonaut* (SS-166), whose design was derived from that of the *Barracuda* (SS-163), but incorporating lessons learned from examination of German World War I submarines and plans. One example of this was that the unique American bulbous bow which had appeared on the Barracuda class was discontinued in favour of the German sloping bow, which possessed far superior sea-keeping qualities. In the event, she turned out to be the only

purpose-built minelaying submarine ever constructed for the US Navy.

Designed for operations in the Pacific, she had an exceptional range. However, there were constant problems with her original diesel engines, which seldom delivered better than half their rated power and this, combined with poor manoeuvrability led to her not being judged a success.

She underwent a major modernisation in the USA in 1942. Her two troublesome M.A.N engines were replaced by four General Motors diesels with reduction gears and hydraulic couplings, raising power from 2,800bhp to 4,800bhp. Her electrical and electronic systems were also updated.

Armament: *Argonaut* was armed with four 21in (533mm) torpedo tubes, for which 16 torpedoes were carried. During her 1942 refit she was fitted with two additional torpedo tubes, mounted externally on the afterdeck. The gun armament was heavy, with two 6in/53cal (152mm) guns and two 0.3in machine-guns.

Her minelaying arrangements were unique, but highly complicated and

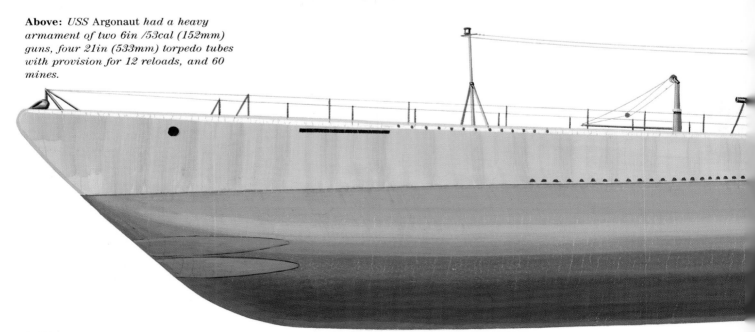

Above: *USS* Argonaut *had a heavy armament of two 6in /53cal (152mm) guns, four 21in (533mm) torpedo tubes with provision for 12 reloads, and 60 mines.*

difficult to operate. The mines were moved by a hydraulic system and loaded, four at a time, into two 40in (101.6cm) diameter tubes, from which they were discharged through two holes just under the stern. There was a complicated compensation system to maintain the submarine's trim during the laying process, which, at least in theory, was capable of discharging the load of 60 mines at a rate of eight mines every ten minutes.

Service History: *Argonaut* was scheduled for a major overhaul in 1941, but this was postponed because of the threatening

international situation and she was actually on patrol when the Japanese attacked Pearl Harbor. She was then sent back to the United States for the long-promised refit, but on return was hurriedly converted to a troop transport to carry US Marines for the raid on Makin Island on 17-19 August 1942. After this, she was sent to Australia, where she was lost on a special mission (intended to be her final

Below: *USS* Argonaut *(SS-166) remains the only purpose-built minelaying submarine to have served in the US Navy.*

operational task). She was sunk by Japanese destroyers off Rabual on 10 January 1943 with the loss of 105 men, the largest number in any US submarine in World War II.

Argonaut's designations illustrate the changing fashions in the inter-war US Navy. She was originally designated *V-4*, but in 1931 this was changed to the name, *Argonaut*. Her hull number was SS-166, but this was later changed to SM-1 to indicate her minelaying role and changed yet again to APS-1 when she became a transport boat in 1942.

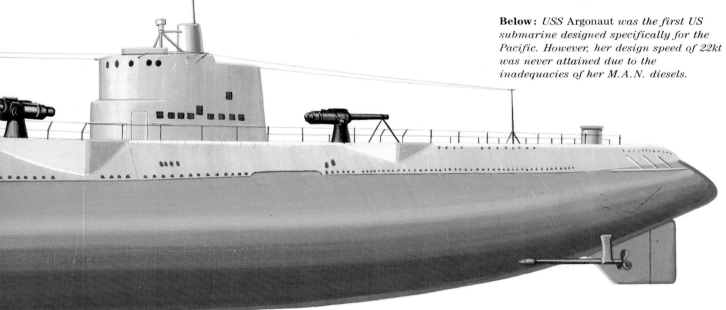

Below: *USS* Argonaut *was the first US submarine designed specifically for the Pacific. However, her design speed of 22kt was never attained due to the inadequacies of her M.A.N. diesels.*

Gato Class

(Fleet submarines)

Displacement:
1,825 tons surfaced; 2,391 tons submerged
Performance:
Max speed 20.25kt surfaced; 8.75kt submerged
Range 10,000 to 13,000nm/14kt surfaced;
95nm/5kt submerged
Maximum Operational Diving Depth:
300ft (91m)
Dimensions:
311ft 9in (95.02m) x 27ft 3in (8.3m) x 15ft 3in
(4.65m)
Machinery:
Four Fairbanks, Morse or General Motors or
Hooven, Owens, Rentschler (H.O.R) diesel
engines, 5,240shp; two General Electric or
Elliott or Allis-Chalmers electric motors,
2,740shp; two shafts
Complement:
6 officers; 54 ratings
Construction:
Electric Boat Company. SS-212 to SS-227.
Sixteen boats. SS-240 to SS-264. Twenty-five
boats. Completed 1942-44.
Portsmouth Naval Yard. SS-228 to SS-235,
SS-275 to SS-280. Fourteen boats. Completed
1941-42.
Mare Island Naval Yard. SS-236 to SS-239,
SS-281 to SS-284. Eight boats. Completed
1941-42.
Manitowoc Shipbuilding Company. SS-265 to
SS-274. Ten boats. Completed 1942-43.

Above: Perch, *one of many post-war conversions, became a transport boat, under the designation APSS-313.*

Design: The 73 submarines of the Gato class were the 'fleet boats' which, together with the essentially similar Balao and Tench classes, bore the brunt of the US submarine war in the Pacific. As such, they have come to epitomise the US Navy's long-range attack submarine, a concept which started with the Schley class in 1918. All these boats operated with great success and distinction, playing a significant part in bringing Imperial Japan to the verge of surrender.

The first of the Gato class — *Drum* (SS-228) — was commissioned on 1 November 1941, the only one to be in service at the time of the attack on Pearl Harbor. Developed from the six-boat Tambor class, the Gatos were 4ft (1.22m) longer, with 350 tons greater displacement, most of which was used to provide better diesels and batteries to give improved range and performance, as well as increased water bunkerage. These 'fleet boats' had a high surface speed (just over 20kt), but despite their name they were never used as part of a surface fleet, their speed and range being used instead to enable them to reach their distant patrol areas rapidly. They were, however, slow underwater, with a maximum submerged speed of only 8.75kt. However, even this could not be sustained for any great period as it caused too great a drain on the batteries.

The all-welded construction facilitated production, which was confined to four yards: Electric Boat, Groton; Portsmouth

Naval Yard; Mare Island Naval Yard; and Manitowoc, Wisconsin. The last-named was the most unusual, being on the banks of a narrow, winding river some 1,000 miles (1,610km) inland. The boats had to be launched sideways into the river (itself no mean feat) and were then tested to their operational depths in Lake Michigan, following which they travelled down the Mississippi on barges to reach the sea.

Gatos were the first US boats to be fitted with a comprehensive electronics fit, eventually having a full range of radar, sonar, communications and electronic warfare equipment. During the war the actual fit was in a constant state of change as new equipment became available. Masts and antennas proliferated, with little effort at reducing underwater drag, until by the war's end there was a veritable forest atop every submarine's conning-tower.

The Gato class was followed by the Balao class, which was virtually identical in layout and armament, but was constructed of stronger steel, giving a maximum operating diving depth of 400ft (122m). 132 Balao class were ordered, of which ten

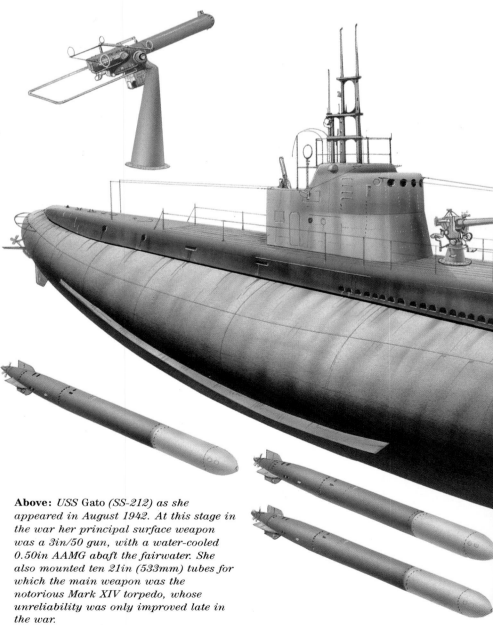

Above: *USS* Gato *(SS-212) as she appeared in August 1942. At this stage in the war her principal surface weapon was a 3in/50 gun, with a water-cooled 0.50in AAMG abaft the fairwater. She also mounted ten 21in (533mm) tubes for which the main weapon was the notorious Mark XIV torpedo, whose unreliability was only improved late in the war.*

were cancelled, 101 saw war service and 21 arrived after the end of hostilities; there were ten war losses.

The Tench class was virtually identical. 134 were ordered, but 104 were cancelled and of the 30 completed only 11 joined the fleet before VJ-day. There were no war losses.

Armament: As built, the Gatos were armed with one 3in (76mm)/50, in line with the US Navy's somewhat unusual pre-War policy of ensuring that a submarine captain would not be given a gun which might encourage him to 'fight it out' on the surface. However, as combat experience was gained, weapons were progressively added and by 1945 armament normally comprised one 5in (127mm)/25 gun, two 40mm Bofors and two 2x20mm cannon.

There were ten 21in (533mm) torpedo tubes — six forward and four aft — with 24 reloads. The Gato, Balao and Tench classes themselves were very reliable, but as has so often been the case in the history of the submarine, the torpedoes in the first years of the war were far less so.

Above: *July 1945: five famous boats running on the surface, flying their* warflags. *Nearest is USS* Flying Fish *(SS-229); beyond is* Spadefish *(SS-411).*

Service History: A small number of the Gatos operated in the Atlantic and Mediterreanean for a short period in 1943. *Herring* (SS-233) sank *U-136* in the Bay of Biscay, while another, *Dorado* (SS-248) was lost in the Atlantic. Those apart, the Gato class was employed in the Pacific, where it bore the lion's share of the US Navy's submarine campaign against the Japanese. They were capable of very long patrols and their main task was to carry out offensive action in enemy sea lanes, although they were also used to lay mines, run supplies to Philippine guerrillas, reconnoitre landing beaches, pick up downed US aircrew and even carry out shore bombardments.

Their primary targets were Japanese warships and merchant vessels, and these boats were supremely successful in attacking both. Highest tonnage of Japanese merchant ships sunk by a single boat was *Flasher* (SS-249) with 100,231grt, but *Barb* (SS-220), *Rasher* (SS-269) and *Silversides* (SS-236) were close behind with more than 90,000grt each. Several Congressional Medals of Honor were won by captains of these boats, including Commander Eugene Fluckey, *Barb*'s commanding officer.

In summary, the Gato class consisted of 73 boats launched between 1941 and 1943. There were 16 war losses: 11 due to enemy action; one was sunk by friendly forces in error; three were lost as a result of accidents and one due to unknown causes.

After the war the Gatos continued to give sterling service for many years, although their reduced diving depth compared to the later Balaos and Tenches, plus their greater length of war service made them marginally less preferred for conversions. Of the 57 boats still serving at the war's end some were sold abroad, some were converted in the various post-war programmes, but most served out their years as Naval Reserve Trainers (NRT) or as auxiliaries (AGSS) before being scrapped in the 1960s.

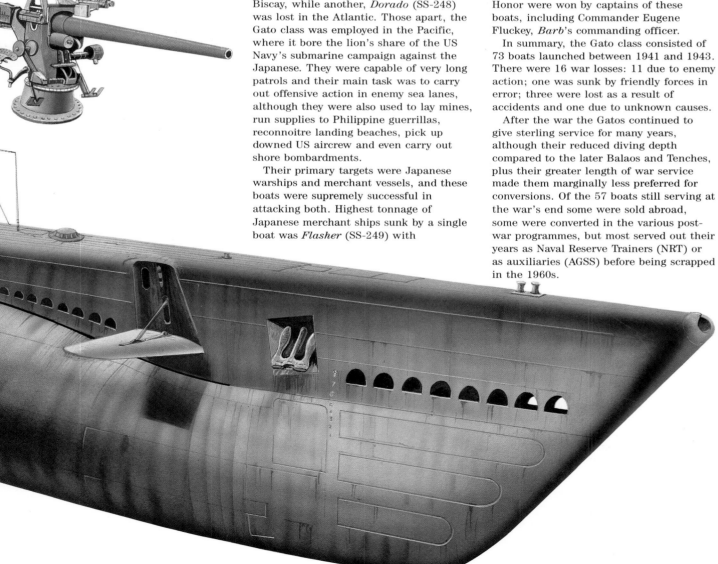

Albacore Class

(Experimental submarine)

Displacement:
1,500 tons surfaced: 1,850 tons submerged
Performance:
Max speed 25kt surfaced; 33kt submerged
Range
Not known

Maximum Operational Diving Depth:
Not published
Dimensions:
203ft 8in (62.1m) x 27ft 6in (8.4m) x 18ft 6in
(5.64m). Length was later increased to 210ft 6in
(64.2m)
Machinery:
Two General Motors radial diesels; one
Westinghouse electric motor; 15,000shp; one
shaft
Complement:
52
Construction:
Portsmouth Naval Shipyard. Albacore
(AGSS-569). One boat. Completed 1953.

Design: There have been four truly
revolutionary submarine designs. First was
the *Holland*, the world's first practicable
submersible. Second was the German Type
XXI, the first true submarine, able to
carry out underwater operations, rather
than to submerge for brief periods. Third
was *Nautilus* (SSN-571), whose nuclear
power released her from the requirement
for regular returns to the surface to
replenish the air supply. The fourth in this
elite group was the *Albacore* (AGSS-569),
which demonstrated the totally new hull
design without which the new nuclear-
propelled submarines could not achieve
manoeuvrability and control at high
speeds.

Although John P. Holland had, quite
correctly, advocated a tear-drop hull shape,
other designers had quickly adopted a
long, narrow type of hull and this hull
shape prevailed from about 1905 well into

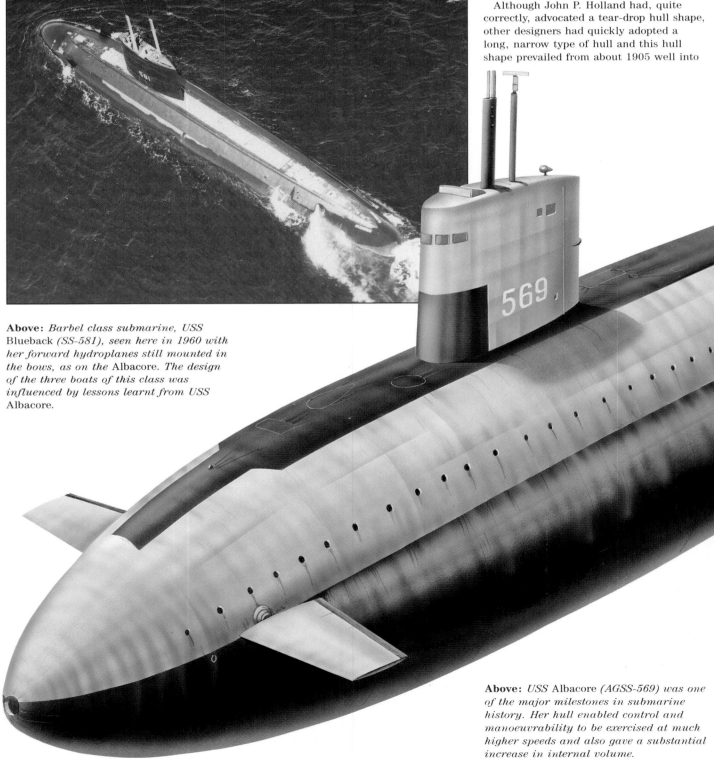

Above: *Barbel class submarine, USS*
Blueback *(SS-581), seen here in 1960 with
her forward hydroplanes still mounted in
the bows, as on the* Albacore. *The design
of the three boats of this class was
influenced by lessons learnt from USS*
Albacore.

Above: *USS* Albacore *(AGSS-569) was one
of the major milestones in submarine
history. Her hull enabled control and
manoeuvrability to be exercised at much
higher speeds and also gave a substantial
increase in internal volume.*

the 1960s. Even the German Type XXI and the first few classes of American nuclear-powered submarines followed this pattern. However, many years ago (in 1916) the British had built the R class, one of the first to be optimised for underwater performance, which achieved the then remarkable underwater speed of 16kt. It was observed at the time that at such speeds control became very difficult. Similar characteristics were noted with the Japanese *Number 71* in the late 1930s, but in neither case was research into these observations pursued.

In the late 1940s, however, the US Navy discovered that the new, fast Guppys started to pitch at high underwater speeds. Indeed, under certain conditions control could be lost, and so it was decided to undertake a proper investigation of the phenomenon.

This programme resulted in the development of a new hull-form to overcome these problems, based on that of an airship. An experimental submarine was built to test this new shape: USS *Albacore* (AGSS-569). The Albacore hull-form was a body-of-revolution, ie, symmetrical around its long axis. Results showed that the new shorter, fatter hull was much more manoeuvrable, being capable of turning at some 3.2 degrees per second compared with 2.5 degrees per second or less for the more traditional hull. Indded, the Albacore proved that a submarine could be 'flown' in three dimensions like an aircraft. There were internal benefits, too, since the fatter hull could accommodate a multi-deck layout, leading to greater storage space and habitability.

Armament: *Albacore* carried no weapons.

Service History: *Albacore* was used to test a variety of features. In her original state she could travel at 26kt submerged, but with silver-zinc batteries and contra-rotating propellers — both fitted in Phase IV of the programme — she achieved an amazing 33kt. Another feature was an aircraft type dive brake abaft the fin, used to control an inadvertent dive. Because German World War II research had shown that at underwater speeds above 12kt bow planes tended to destabilise the submarine in a vertical plane, *Albacore* was built without bow hydroplanes; this was apparently very successful, although such hydroplanes were later mounted and the idea was not adopted for subsequent production classes.

She originally had cross-shaped (+) after control surfaces but was later modified (Phase III) to test an X-configured stern empennage. Although this configuration has certain advantages, and has since found favour with some other navies (eg, Sweden and the Netherlands), it has not been pursued further by the US Navy.

As a result of the dramatic demonstrations by the *Albacore* the hull-forms of the next class of US Navy SSN (the Skipjack class) and of the last class of US diesel-electric submarines (the Barbel class) were altered, with great benefits to their performance. The details were also made available to the United States' allies, as a result of which a number of designs, among them the Japanese Uzushio/Yuushio and the Dutch Walrus/Zwaardvis classes, made use of what has now become known as the 'Albacore hull'.

Albacore tested various sonar and other sensor fits, such as a bow-mounted BQR-2 with DIMUS (digital multi-beam steering), which enabled a submarine to listen in all directions and to detect weak signals which might otherwise have been lost in the background noise. DIMUS increased detection range by a quiet submarine against a schnorkelling submarine from 50 to 70nm and also enhanced multi-target tracking capability.

Albacore was decommissioned in 1972 and stricken on 1 May 1980.

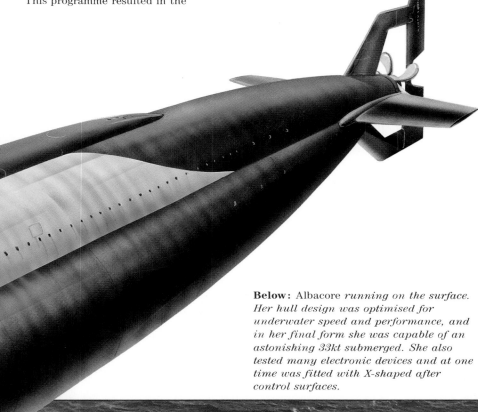

Below: Albacore *running on the surface. Her hull design was optimised for underwater speed and performance, and in her final form she was capable of an astonishing 33kt submerged. She also tested many electronic devices and at one time was fitted with X-shaped after control surfaces.*

Nautilus

(Nuclear-powered patrol submarine) (SSN)

Displacement:
3,674 tons surfaced; 4,092 tons submerged
Performance:
Max speed 18kt surfaced; 23kt submerged
Maximum Operational Diving Depth:
In excess of 400ft (122m)
Dimensions:
323ft 0in (98.45m) x 27ft 0in (8.23m) x 22ft 0in (6.7m)
Machinery:
One S2W nuclear reactor, 15,000shp; two shafts
Complement:
11 officers; 100 ratings
Construction:
Electric Boat Company, Groton. *Nautilus* (SSN 571). One boat. Completed 1954.

Design: From the earliest days in the US nuclear programme it had been realised that, apart from its use for the most powerful explosions known to man, a nuclear reaction could be controlled and thus used as a source of power. One particularly advantageous application would be in submarines, where, since air would no longer be needed to run the motors, the boat would become virtually independent of the surface. So, as soon as the war ended, a naval research and development team assembled at the Oak Ridge nuclear research centre, led by a Captain Hyman G. Rickover, USN, an outspoken, but hitherto little-known electrical engineer.

Rickover forced the pace and eventually contracts were placed with the Electric Boat Company for the first SSN and with Westinghouse for the power plant. This led to the first operational reactor, the Submarine Thermal Reactor Mark II, which, under the designation S2W, was installed in the hull of *Nautilus* during her 27-month construction period.

The first funds for the construction of a nuclear-powered submarine were authorized by Congress in the FY52 Budget and the keel was laid by President Harry S. Truman on 14 June 1952. USS *Nautilus* (SSN-571) was launched on 21 January 1954 and on 17 January 1955 was able to send her historic signal 'Underway on nuclear power'.

Nautilus was designed with a conventional, long, streamlined hull, with twin propellers, not dissimilar in most respects from the German Type XXI hull. Her great power gave her a submerged speed of about 23kt, but she then began to experience the control problems inherent in such a design.

Armament: *Nautilus* was armed with six 21in (533mm) torpedo tubes.

Service History: Considering her revolutionary propulsion system *Nautilus* was a remarkably successful boat. Within three months of her first run on nuclear power she made a 1,381nm (2,558km) underwater voyage from New London to San Juan, Puerto Rico in 90 hours at an average speed of some 16kt.

By August 1958 there was sufficient confidence in her nuclear plant for her to make the first-ever Polar transit, starting from Pearl Harbor, Hawaii and finishing at Portland, England. She steamed 62,562nm (115,865km) on her first nuclear core, 91,324nm (169,132km) on her second and some 150,000nm (277,800km) on the third.

After a very successful career she was withdrawn from active service in 1980 and is now a museum at Groton, Connecticut.

Right: *USS* Nautilus *(SSN-571), the world's first nuclear-propelled submarine, first moved under nuclear power on 17 January 1955. After a very active operational career she was withdrawn from service in 1980 and is now a permament memorial at the US Navy Submarine Museum at Groton, Connecticut.*

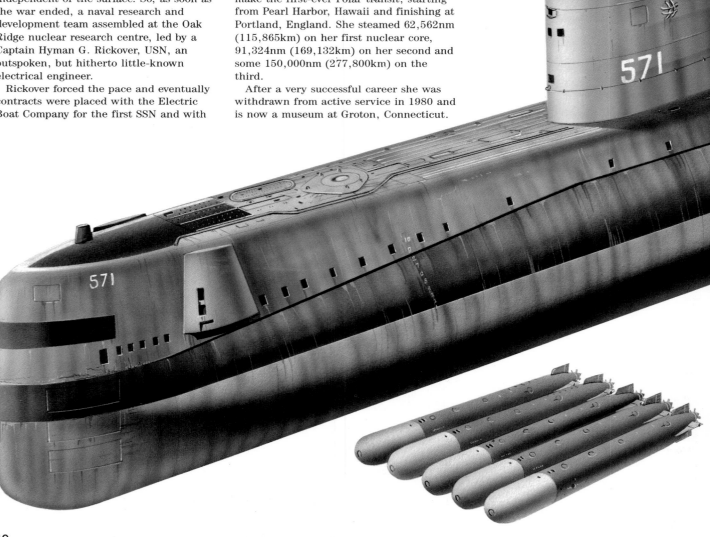

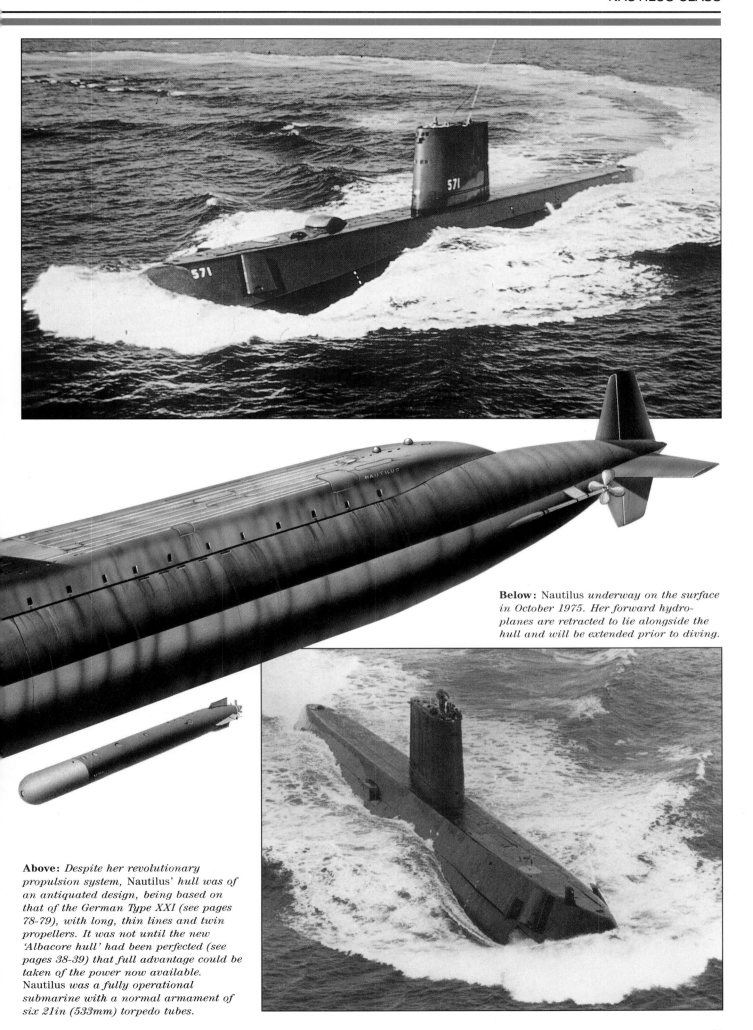

Below: Nautilus *underway on the surface in October 1975. Her forward hydroplanes are retracted to lie alongside the hull and will be extended prior to diving.*

Above: *Despite her revolutionary propulsion system, Nautilus' hull was of an antiquated design, being based on that of the German Type XXI (see pages 78-79), with long, thin lines and twin propellers. It was not until the new 'Albacore hull' had been perfected (see pages 38-39) that full advantage could be taken of the power now available. Nautilus was a fully operational submarine with a normal armament of six 21in (533mm) torpedo tubes.*

Los Angeles Class

(Nuclear-powered attack submarines) (SSN)

Displacement:
6,080 tons surfaced; 6,900 tons submerged
Performance:
Max speed 30+kt submerged
Maximum Operational Diving Depth:
1,476ft (450m)
Dimensions:
360ft 0in (109.7m) x 33ft 0in (10.1m) x 32ft 4in (9.9m)
Machinery:
One pressurized-water cooled S6G nuclear reactor; two geared turbines; 35,000shp; one shaft
Complement:
12 officers; 127 ratings (berths for 95)
Construction:
Newport News Shipbuilding & Drydock Company. SSN-688, SSN-689, SSN-691, SSN-693, SSN-695, SSN-711, SSN-712, SSN-713, SSN-714, SSN-715, SSN-716, SSN-717, SSN-718, SSN-721, SSN-722, SSN-723, SSN-750, SSN-753, SSN-756, SSN-758, SSN-759, SSN-764, SSN-765, SSN-766, SSN-767, SSN-769, SSN-770, SSN-772, SSN-773. Twenty-nine boats. Completed 1976 to 1995(?).
General Dynamics, Electric Boat Division. SSN-690, SSN-692, SSN-694, SSN-696, SSN-697, SSN-698, SSN-699, SSN-700, SSN-701, SSN-702, SSN-703, SSN-704, SSN-705, SSN-706, SSN-707, SSN-708, SSN-709, SSN-710, SSN-719, SSN-720, SSN-724, SSN-725, SSN-751, SSN-752, SSN-754, SSN-755, SSN-757, SSN-760, SSN-761, SSN-762, SSN-763, SSN-768, SSN-771. Thirty-three boats. Completed 1977 to 1994(?).

Above: *USS* Miami *(SSN-755). Built by General Dynamics, she is one of the latest Los Angeles class SSNs to join the fleet. From SSN-751 onwards the forward hydroplanes have been moved from the fin to the bows to aid breaking through ice.*

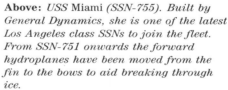

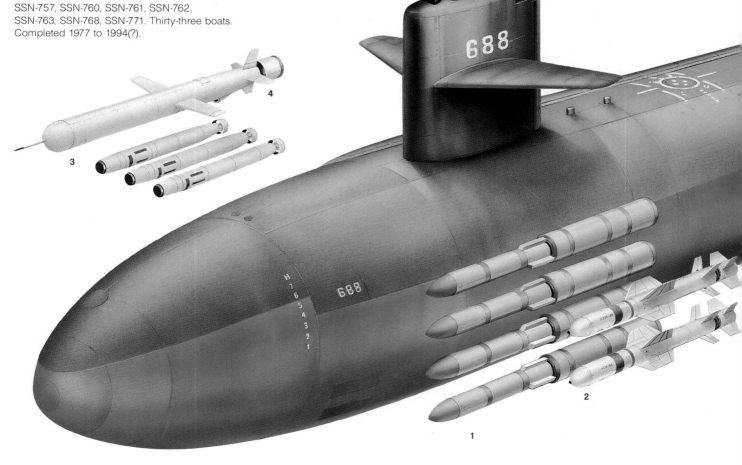

Design: The Los Angeles (SSN-688) class will eventually number 66 boats, making it one of the most sophisticated, expensive, effective and important weapons systems ever to have reached operational status. Its origins go back to the late 1960s when the US Navy considered two classes of future SSNs: one was to be a high-speed attack and ASW submarine, and the second a very quiet type intended for 'barrier' operations.

The latter requirement led to the *Glenard P Lipscomb* (SSN-685) and the former to the *Los Angeles* (SSN-688). However, it was subsequently decided that, rather than incur the considerable extra expense of two separate classes, the Los Angeles class could perform both roles and only one Lipscomb class boat was built.

The Los Angeles boats are 67ft 10in (20.7m) longer than the Sturgeon class and the hull is optimised for high submerged speed with a very small sail. One unfortunate outcome was that, because the sail-mounted planes cannot be rotated to the vertical, the early Los Angeles boats could not break through ice. This problem is being overcome from *San Juan* (SSN-751) onwards, which have their diving-planes moved forward to the more

traditional bow position. Together with some new electronic equipment this enables them to be declared 'Arctic-capable'.

The sensor fit is comprehensive and includes the BQQ-5 sonar system in the bows and a passive tactical towed sonar array. The cable and winch are mounted in the ballast tanks, but there is no room for the array itself, which is, therefore, housed in a prominent fairing which runs along almost the entire length of the hull.

There has been much criticism of the complexity and cost of the Los Angeles, and it is alleged that too many sacrifices were made to achieve the very high speed. A design for a cheaper and smaller SSN, under consideration in 1980 as a result of Congressional pressure, was later shelved, but may well reappear, especially if the proposed new Seawolf (SSN-21) class should turn out to be even more expensive than the Los Angeles, which is highly possible. Meanwhile there are plans to improve the Los Angeles boats, especially their sensors, weapons systems and control equipment. Such improvements will include moving the torpedo tubes back to the bow, and increasing their number to eight. Further, the later Los Angeles boats

are being given anechoic coatings, the first to be applied to a US submarine.

The Los Angeles class is very sophisticated and each boat is an extremely potent fighting machine. With a production run of at least sixty-six it must be considered an outstandingly successful design. However, these boats are becoming very expensive: the first cost $221.25 million, while the boat bought in 1979 cost $325.6 million, the two in 1981 $495.8 million each, and the four in 1987 $656.25 million each.

Armament: The most remarkable feature of the Los Angeles class is its armament. These powerful submarines are armed with Subroc and Sub-Harpoon, as well as conventional and wire-guided torpedoes. All boats from SSN-688 to SSN-718 carry up to eight Tomahawk as part of their torpedo loads. All these are fired from the four 21in (533mm) torpedo tubes located amidships and angled outwards. From SSN-721 onwards, however, twelve Mark 36 vertical launch tubes for Tomahawk are fitted in the space in the bow between the inner and outer hulls, thus restoring the torpedo capacity. So, although their primary mission is still to hunt other submarines and to protect SSBNs, the Los Angeles class can be used without modification to sink surface ships at long-range with Sub-Harpoon, while Tomahawk enables them to operate against strategic targets well inland, as well. Also the later boats have a mine-laying capability.

Service History: USS *Los Angeles* (SSN-688) entered service on 18 November 1976 and since then these highly effective boats have joined the fleet at a somewhat fluctuating rate: 1976, 1; 1977, 3; 1978, 4; 1979, 1; 1980, 1; 1981, 6; 1982, 4; 1983, 5; 1984, 2; 1985, 4; 1986, 2; 1987, 2; 1988, 4; 1989, 4; 1990, 5; 1991, 6. The Reagan Administration ordered a speeding-up of the Los Angeles building programme; two were completed in 1986, two in 1987, four in 1988, five in 1990 and six in 1991.

The Tomahawk missile programme was also accelerated, with these missiles being fitted in USS *Providence* (SSN-719) onwards.

USS *Groton* (SSN-694) travelled around the world submerged between 4 April and 8 October 1980.

Below: USS Los Angeles *(SSN-688), and the full range of weapons of her class, including Subroc ASW missiles (1), Sub-Harpoon anti-ship missiles (2), Mark 48 torpedoes (3) and a Tomahawk missile (4). From SSN-721 onwards 12 Tomahawks are mounted in vertical tubes.*

Below: Practising emergency surfacing drills, USS Birmingham *(SSN-695) gives an excellent view of her bow sonar dome.*

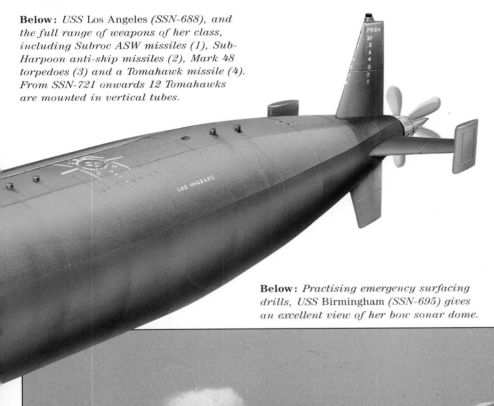

Ohio Class

(Nuclear-powered ballistic missile submarines) (SSBN)

Displacement:
16,600 tons surfaced; 18,700 tons submerged
Performance:
Max speed 20+kt submerged
Maximum Operational Diving Depth:
984ft (300m)

Dimensions:
560ft 0in (170.7m) x 42ft 0in (12.8m) x 35ft 6in (10.8m)
Machinery:
One pressurized-water-cooled General Electric S8G nuclear reactor; two geared turbines; 60,000shp; one shaft
Complement:
15 officers; 142 ratings
Construction:
General Dynamics, Electric Boat Division. SSBN-726 to SSBN-743. Eighteen boats. Completed 1981 to 1996(?).

Design: While the upgrading of Lafayette class SSBNs to carry Poseidon was under way in the early 1970s, development of the entirely new Trident I C-4 missile was started. With a range of 3,830nm (7,100km), this missile is now in service aboard 12 converted Lafayette class and eight Ohio class ballistic missile submarines (SSBN-726 to SSBN-733, inclusive).

In order to take full advantage of these missiles (and to accept the already-planned and slightly larger successor — Trident II D-5), a new class of larger SSBNs was ordered. At first it was intended that these would be improved and enlarge Lafayettes, using the same Westinghouse S5W pressurized-water reactor. There was, however, an urgent need to reduce noise levels as much as possible and it was decided to install an S8G natural-circulation reactor, based on the S5G which had been successfully tested in *Narwhal* (SSN-671). The S8G drives two sets of turbines: one for high-speed and the other for low-speed, and all machinery is mounted on noise-insulating rafts. It was also decided that it would be more cost-effective to design the new ships to take twenty-four missiles rather than sixteen, a payload increase of 50 per cent.

Congress baulked at the enormous costs, but when the Soviet Navy introduced its own new long-range SLBM, the 3,650nm (6,760km) SS-N-8 in the Delta class, US reaction was to authorize and speed up the Trident programme. The first of the Ohio class boats was laid down on 10 April 1976. The eventual number of Trident-carrying submarines depends upon two

Above: *The launch ceremony of USS West Virginia (SSBN-736) on 14 October 1989. The turtleback covers twenty-four launch tubes for Trident II D-5 missiles.*

Above: *USS* Ohio *(SSBN-726) is shown here armed with Trident I C-4 missiles, and four Mk 48 torpedoes. As with the others of the class up to SSBN-733, she will eventually be backfitted with the more advanced Trident II D-5 missile. SSBN-734 and subsequent boats were fitted for the D-5 missile during construction.*

Left: *A Trident missile launch canister is lowered into an Ohio class SSBN.*

Left: *USS* Tennessee *(SSBN-734), ninth in the class. The long, narrow bulge on the port side abaft the turtleback houses a towed passive sonar array for detecting hostile submarines.*

principal factors: first, the outcome of the Strategic Arms Reduction Talks (START) between the USA and USSR, and, second, expense.

Armament: The first eight Ohio class SSBNs (SSBN-726 to SSBN-733) are armed with twenty-four Trident I C-4 missiles, mounted vertically abaft the sail. The Trident II D-5 missile is being deployed on new Ohio class SSBNs starting from the ninth (*Tennessee*, SSBN-734) and will be retrofitted into the first eight. (The D-5 cannot, however, be backfitted to the converted Lafayettes, now armed with Trident I C-4) Trident II D-5 carries larger payloads and is more accurate than Trident I, thus providing the SSBN force with the potential to put 'hard' targets at risk, a significant expansion of the SSBN/SLBM role, which up to now has been regarded as a survivable, second-strike, counter-value, deterrent system.

Ohio class SSBNs have four torpedo tubes firing conventional torpedoes. There are also eight launchers mounted below the sail to fire 'countermeasure' devices to decoy incoming torpedoes.

Service History: The great advantage of the current generation of long-range US and Soviet SLBMs is that they can be launched from their respective home waters. This makes detection of the launch platform and destruction of the submarine or the missiles very difficult, if not virtually impossible, which enhances their deterrent role. This great increase in missile range has also enabled the US Navy to operate the Ohio Class SSBNs from home ports in the contiguous USA. The first eight operate out of Bangor, Washington and the remainder out of King's Bay, Georgia.

Current US Navy plans are for a force of eighteen Ohios, nine each in the Pacific and Atlantic Fleets respectively, and all with two crews. With an anticipated availability of 66 per cent, these boats carry out 70-day patrols, followed by a 25-day short refit, each boat having a full 12-month refit every nine years.

USSR

It is essential to an understanding of Russian naval development to appreciate that she faces a unique naval dilemma in that she must plan to fight campaigns in four geographically separated areas: the Arctic Ocean, the Baltic Sea, the Black Sea and the Pacific Ocean. The fleets in each of these areas are unable to provide support to any of the others, whilst exits from the Baltic and Black Seas are completely dominated by hostile powers. Further, even in the Far East the majority of the Russian bases lie on the mainland coast with their exits from the Sea of Japan and the Sea of Okhotsk also dominated by foreign powers, the sole exception being the base at Petropavlovsk on the Kamchatka Peninsula.

Early Days
Despite the generally-accepted picture of an indolent aristocracy ruling a horde of ignorant serfs, pre-Revolutionary Russia actually kept up with global technological developments and in some cases led the field. Thus, the first submarine to be built in Imperial Russia was the *Diable Marin* (Sea Devil), constructed by the Bavarian pioneer Wilhelm Bauer at St Petersburg in 1855. After over one hundred successful trials she sank, without loss of life; she was recovered but later sank a second time and was lost for good. A Russian, Ivan Aleksandrovski designed the next submarine, which was built between 1863 and 1866. Displacing 355 tons she operated successfully for some years, but was lost in 1877 when the hull collapsed at depth.

In that year Stepan Dzhevetsky (1843-1938) produced his first submarine, a one-man 13ft (4m) long device. He followed this in 1879 with a four-man submarine, which included in its equipment the first periscope, with prisms and a magnifying lens, enabling the helmsman to see the surface while submerged.

Russia ordered one of Nordenfelt's steam submarines in 1886, but she ran aground in the Kattegat and was not accepted into the fleet. A further pause followed until the outbreak of the Russo-Japanese War in 1904 led to an urgent requirement for a number of different types. Orders were placed for indigenous designs from Dzhevetsky, Bubnov, another famous Russian submarine engineer, and a Lieutenant Botkin (for a wooden submarine!). Other orders were placed overseas with Germany and the United States.

Russian submarines failed to play a significant role in the Russo-Japanese War and attention focussed once again on the Baltic and Black Sea fleets. An ambitious five year plan in 1907 postulated a force of 40 submarines in the Baltic and a further 26 in the Black Sea. However, the reality

Above: *Russia's first submarines,* Karp, Karass *and* Kambala, *arriving with their surface escort on delivery from Germany.*

was more prosaic, with a number of designs being produced in small numbers, including the first-ever submarine minelayer. However, more ambitious schemes were in train and by 1914 the Navy was working on a plan to assemble the largest submarine fleet in the world by 1920. In 1916 two 3,000 tons displacement 'submarine cruisers' were laid down, with a proposed range of 12,000nm (22,255km) and an armament of 19 torpedo tubes, four 100mm guns and two 57mm AA guns. They were never finished, but are early evidence of the Russian fascination with sheer size.

World War I
World War I involved the Baltic and Black Sea Fleets only. In the Baltic extensive mining operations were carried out by the Russians, supported by submarines, but the latter's tasks were mainly concerned with reconnaissance. It was not until September 1915 that the Russian boats began to undertake offensive operations against German shipping, although these efforts were hampered by a lack of aggressiveness, due (at least in part) to a desire not to aggravate the relationship with neutral Sweden. Fifteen German merchantmen were sunk in 1915, mostly by gunfire or demolition charges.

Little of note occurred in the Baltic in 1916 although the submarine fleet began to receive major reinforcements, including the first of the Amerikanski Golland (American Holland) boats, which were identical in all respects to the H class boats then being supplied to the British, and Italian navies. Some operations were undertaken in both 1916 and 1917, but with little result and by the time the ceasefire with the Germans came into force on 15 December 1917 the somewhat ineffective Baltic submarine war had already petered out.

In the Black Sea the naval war began with a dramatic German/Turkish bombardment of Sevastopol and Odessa, but thereafter took the form of a series of inconclusive operations by both sides. Russian submarines carried out patrols of up to twelve days' duration, but were hampered by shortage of numbers, over-strict patrol orders and poor mechanical reliability.

The Inter-War Period
In the period of the Revolution, the Intervention War and the Civil War the former Imperial submarine force ceased to exist. Some boats were scuttled by their Russian crews, others were captured first by the Germans then by the British and *then* scuttled, whilst yet another group was operated by the forces under Wrangel before being taken to Bizerta, where they were interned.

As the new government imposed its rule the navy found itself in a parlous state, especially in the North. There, not only had they lost the naval bases now in independent Finland, Estonia, Latvia and Lithuania, but they also faced what appeared to be a serious threat from Great Britain. Some 20 submarines of various classes survived, all of them in a state of disrepair, and these became the nucleus of the new Soviet Navy. These were repaired and a few unfinished AG class boats completed. It was not until 1926 that the first new boats were authorised, the 12-strong Dekabrist (or Series I) class, which joined the fleet between 1928 and 1931. Not particularly successful, they were followed by the Leninetz class (Series II) minelayers. Feeling themselves cut off from modern technology in 1928 the Soviet Navy raised the hulk of the British submarine *L-55*, which had been sunk off Kronstadt in 1919 and its construction was carefully analysed.

Building continued with the Shchuka class of medium-sized patrol submarines and the Malodki (an abbreviation of *Maliye lodki*, or 'small submarine') class. As seems invariably to happen with small submarines, the initial Malodkis (Series VI) proved to be too small and there was a steady escalation in size through several 'series' until the final Series XV had a displacement of 351 tons. At the other end of the scale thoughts turned to large 'cruiser-submarines', of which the first, the Pravda class (Series IV), proved to be outright failures.

In the early 1930s the Soviet Navy, like a number of others, turned to the most experienced submarine navy — Germany — for assistance. The exports office at The Hague (I.v.S) designed the Series IX Stalinetz class (1,070 tons displacement), very similar in size and design to the German Navy's Type IA, which led, by coincidence, to the German Type IX. Finally, came the K class (Series XIV), another excellent design. These were large

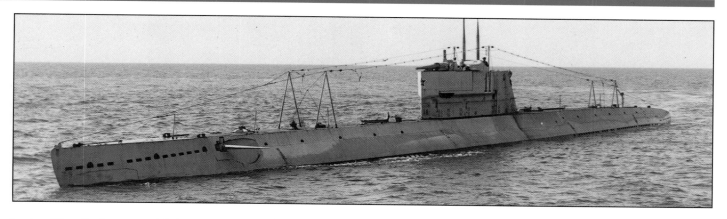

boats with a displacement of 2,600 tons and armed with no less than ten torpedo tubes, two 100mm guns, two 45mm AA guns and 20 mines.

World War II

So intense were the efforts put into submarine construction that when war broke out on 21 June 1941 the Soviet Navy possessed no fewer than 213 operational submarines, greater in numbers than the next two strongest submarine fleets (the USA and Italy) *combined*. However, these were split, as always, between the various fleets: Baltic, 69; Black Sea, 44; Northern, 15; Pacific, 85.

Despite its size the submarine force did not perform as well as was expected. In the North the boats operated out of Murmansk and Polyarny, attacking German supply routes along the Norwegian coastline, with the large, well-armed K class boats being particularly effective. The submarines were also used to establish screens between the coast and Anglo-US convoys heading for Murmansk.

In the Baltic, Soviet submarines suffered a number of strategic problems. First, the Gulf of Finland freezes over for about half of every year, permitting the submarines a 'campaigning season' of only some seven months. Secondly, the sea is neither large nor deep and no German merchant ship was ever very far from friendly aircraft or ships. Thirdly, the unfettered voyages permitted to neutral Swedish vessels required Soviet submarine captains to be extra vigilant before carrying out an attack.

Twenty-nine Soviet submarines were destroyed in port as German armies advanced along the Baltic coast. The Germans and Finns then constructed a mine barrier across the Gulf of Finland to bottle up the remaining Soviet naval forces, particularly their submarines. Thirteen thousand mines were laid, but the effectiveness of the barrier was reduced by the Soviet retention of several small islands in this stretch of sea. In 1943 the Germans placed even more mines and also laid a double anti-submarine net, some 30 miles (48km) long and 180ft (55m) deep. This latter prevented any Soviet submarine from leaving the Gulf of Finland throughout 1943 and until September 1944 when Finland capitulated and Soviet forces were able to take control of both ends of the barrier. Between then and the end of the

Above: *Submarine* Yakobinec *(D-6), a Series I submarine, was completed in 1929 and lost by bombing in 1941. Note the 100mm gun in the high mounting.*

war the Baltic submarines undertook a number of patrols and a number of German ships were sunk, the principal victims being several large liners transporting German refugees fleeing from East Prussia.

In the Black Sea the war opened with spectacular Axis advances; the great naval base and construction yards at Nikolayev fell on 17 August. During the siege of Sebastopol submarines were pressed into service as supply vessels, moving men and freight into the beleaguered garrison. Thereafter the submarines concentrated on attacking Axis shipping, but with very disappointing results. Over the war as a

whole they claim to have sunk 72 ships (105,000grt) and their own losses are estimated to have been 28 submarines.

In the Pacific, Soviet submarines saw virtually no action. Indeed, the opportunity was taken to transfer a number of boats from the Pacific to the Northern Fleet, a journey which involved a voyage across the Pacific, through the Panama Canal and across the Atlantic into the Arctic Ocean.

Despite their strategic and tactical problems, and some successes, there is no doubt that the performance of the Soviet submarine force in World War II was disappointing. A reasonable estimate of their successes is 160 merchantmen (402,000grt) sunk in all theatres for a loss of approximately 110 submarines, some of them admittedly sunk in harbour as a result of land action.

Above: *The Malodki types of small submarines were simple in construction and appeared in several versions; this is a Series XII-bis.*

Below: *Shchuka type* Shch-203, *a Series V-bis, coming alongside a jetty in a Black Sea port. She was lost with all hands in the Black Sea in October 1943.*

The Cold War

Following the cessation of hostilities in Europe the Soviet Navy obtained German submarines and technology to catch up with the latest advances. They were allocated four complete Type XXI submarines from the Allied war booty, together with several Type XXIII coastal submarines, a number of older Type VII and Type IX boats, and two ex-Italian submarines. They also obtained a number of incomplete hulls when the Schichau Yard at Danzig was overrun. In addition, several thousand German technicians were transported to the USSR, together with technical documents and machine tools, to assist in making good the damage inflicted on the submarine yards during the war.

As the relationship between the former Allies cooled rapidly in the late 1940s the old Western problem of estimating Soviet military strength began anew, a process hindered by the Soviet love of secrecy. As always, Western intelligence staffs over-estimated and as early as 1946 were predicting a force of 500 boats by 1950, of which 300 would have been new construction, based on the Type XXI. In fact, by 1950 the Soviet Navy possessed some 288 submarines, of which 92 were ocean-going types, 80 medium-range and 116 coastal.

Once the Soviet Navy had recovered from the aftermath of the war its submarine force evolved along four major lines of development: diesel-electric patrol submarines (SS), nuclear-powered attack submarines (SSN), ballistic missile submarines (SSB/SSBN) and guided-missile submarines (SSG/SSGN).

Diesel-electric patrol submarines were the first development line and the USSR

Soviet Submarine Construction: 1945-1990	
Diesel-electric:	
Patrol/Attack (SS)	472
Guided-missile (SSG)	16
Ballistic missile (SSB)	29
Miscellaneous	8
	525
Nuclear-propelled	
Attack	82
Guided-missile	59
Ballistic missile	90
Research	2
	233

Above: *Juliett class SSG, armed with four SS-N-3A cruise missiles. Sixteen were commissioned 1961-63, of which twelve remain in service, one of which has been modified to launch SS-N-12.*

has long possessed the largest single force of this type in the world, especially since the USA opted out of this particular field. The first post-war design was the Whiskey, which appeared in 1951 and was immediately (and incorrectly) declared by Western experts to be based upon the German Type XXI; it was, in fact, based upon the pre-war Stalinetz. Indeed, the early Whiskeys did not even have schnorkels and were armed with guns for surface actions. The first class to incorporate lessons from the German Type XXI was the Zulu class, 26 of which were produced between 1952 and 1957.

The third type produced in the 1950s was the Quebec, which, in the event, proved to be the last in the series of small, coastal submarines. They were designed to use a closed-cycle engine and since the Germans had worked at length on the Walter system it was assumed that it was this that was being used. It is now evident that the Soviets were using another German system called *Kreislauf*, but this device also proved dangerous and all 30 Quebecs were subsequently fitted with diesel-electric propulsion.

In 1958 two more designs emerged, the first being the Foxtrot, which became the standard 'workhorse' of the submarine arm, carrying out missions in all the oceans of the world. Sixty-two were constructed for the Soviet Navy and many more for export. The second was the Romeo, which was generally similar to the Foxtrot, although somewhat larger, more heavily armed (ten torpedo tubes as opposed to six on the Foxtrot) and with much better sensors. Twenty Romeos were constructed for the Soviet Navy and well over one hundred have been constructed in China.

There was then a pause before the first Tango class submarine was launched in 1971. By far the largest conventional submarine produced by any navy since the war, the Tango has a displacement of 3,900 tons and, like many Western conventional types, is quieter than

nuclear-propelled submarines. The Tango, however, still had a Type XXI hull and it was not until the Kilo class that the Soviet Navy produced a disel-electric submarine with a beamier hull more closely resembling the Albacore hull developed by the US Navy in the 1950s.

SSNs

The Soviet Navy has produced some outstanding and important SSN designs. The first SSN was commissioned on 8 April 1958, a November class boat of 5,300 tons displacement, but with a long narrow hull, which would almost certainly have prevented her obtaining maximum advantage from the 22,000shp nuclear reactor. Like USS *Nautilus*, the design featured two propellers, which did little for silent operations, but did enable four 16in (406mm) stern torpedo tubes to be fitted. Fifteen Novembers were constructed between 1956 and 1964.

The November class was succeeded by the Victor class. Sixteen Victor Is were built (1965-74), followed by seven of the longer Victor II (1972-78) carrying SS-N-16 missiles, as well as the original SS-N-15 and torpedoes. Latest in this line are 26 Victor IIIs, which are longer again. They also introduced a large streamlined pod atop the vertical rudder, whose purpose caused intense arguments in Western circles.

In the early 1980s two new SSNs appeared: the Sierra class (7,550 tons) and the Akula class (10,000 tons). The development of two apparently competing designs is a not infrequent occurrence in areas the Soviet military consider very important. This is apparently intended both to ensure the survival of more than one design bureau in each major area and also to guard against failures of any one project. In this particular case, it now appears that the Akula has been selected for future production.

There has, however, been a third strand of development. The Alfa class was first detected in 1967, causing great alarm in Western military circles. Of a totally new hull design, it was powered by a liquid-metal cooled nuclear reactor and showed an underwater speed during a NATO exercise in excess of 40kt. The first Alfa was scrapped, but six more have since

Above: *This Yankee class SSBN suffered an explosion in a missile tube while on patrol off the United States' Atlantic seaboard and eventually sank on 6 October 1986. Three died and others were injured.*

been produced. The apparent successor to the Alfa, the single vessel of the Mike class appeared in 1983, but sank in 1989 and is unlikely to be replaced.

SSGs

For many years a major concern of the Soviet Navy has been the threat from US Navy carrier task forces. One obvious defensive tactic was the use of lines of patrol submarines in the North Atlantic, a method used during both World Wars I and II in the Baltic and Black Seas, and one suited to the Russian doctrine of issuing firm, detailed and very limiting orders to subordinate commanders.

The first cruise-missile installations were on converted Whiskey class submarines in the mid-1950s, producing clumsy, ugly and reportedly top-heavy boats. They served their purpose, however, of getting missiles to sea and identifying some of the technological problems which purpose-built boats could overcome. These then appeared in the early 1960s, using the usual Soviet twin-track approach, with one nuclear-powered design — Echo I — and one conventionally-powered design as a back-up — Juliett. Both were initially armed with the SS-N-3b land-attack cruise-missile, presumably to insure against failure of the SLBMs then going to sea for the first time. Once these had proved themselves, both types converted to the anti-ship role with the SS-N-3A missile.

Both Echo and Juliett classes were very noisy when submerged and had to surface to launch their missiles. They were followed by much better designed Charlie class SSGNs carrying eight SS-N-7 missiles, which, although having a shorter range than the earlier SS-N-3, could be launched while the submarine was submerged.

Latest of the Soviet SSGNs is the huge Oscar class with a displacement of 14,500 tons. Six have so far been built, introducing a new concept of an underwater battleship, capable of sustained combat using a variety of

weapons, its armament including 24 SS-N-19 SLCM, together with a large number of SS-N-15 and SS-N-16 missiles and torpedoes.

SSBNs

The Soviet Navy was as quick as the US Navy to see the potential of ballistic missiles launched from submarines. In particular, such a system offered a means of threatening the US homeland to counter the threat to the USSR posed by the large strategic bomber fleets of the USAF supplemented by naval bombers aboard the strike carriers. The first Soviet SLBM, the SS-N-4, a development of the German V-2 was mounted in the fin of various types of submarine. First was the Zulu V conversion (two missiles), followed by the first custom-designed SSB, the Golf I (three missiles). Both these had to launch their missiles from the surface, but the Golf II (three SS-N-5) was able to launch while submerged. The potential of the SLBM could only be matched by nuclear-propulsion and the Soviet Navy took the first step in this direction with the Hotel class SSBN in 1958, although this still featured four missiles (SS-N-4) mounted in the fin.

All of these were, however, interim measures pending finalisation of a design which would match the SSBNs then appearing in Western navies. This appeared in 1966 as the Yankee, a 9,600 ton submarine armed with sixteen SS-N-6 SLBMs mounted under a small 'turtleback' abaft the fin. The first of these boats took up station off the United States' Eastern seaboard in 1968, followed by a similar West coast deployment in 1971. The 33rd and last Yankee was launched in 1974, but the first of an enlarged version, designated the Delta, had already been launched in 1972. This design, which has progressed through I, II and III versions to the current IV is still in production in 1991.

Latest Soviet SSBN, the Typhoon class, is a true milestone in submarine development, being by far the largest underwater vessel ever built. It is armed with twenty SS-N-20 SLBMs. Production appears to have ceased with the sixth of class and it is open to question whether any navy will ever want to construct such a submarine ever again.

Post-War Soviet Submarines

DIESEL-ELECTRIC (SS)

Class	Displacement (tons)	In Service	Yards*	No
Stalinetz				
Series IXbis	1,090	1934-48	A	2
Series XVI	1,090	1945-47	D(3),E(3)	6
K Series XIV	2,095	1936-47	C(3),A(1)	4
Shch Series Xbis	705	1940-47	C	7
Malodki Series XV	351	1946-47	B	44
Zulu	2,500	1952-57	B(18),E(8)	26
Whiskey	1,355	1951-57	D,C,F	236
Quebec	510	1954-57	B	30
Foxtrot	2,500	1958-71	B,E	62
Romeo	1,800	1958-61	D	20
Tango	3,900	1972-82	D	22
Kilo	3,200	1979-?	F,D	14

ATTACK SUBMARINES, NUCLEAR-POWERED (SSN)

Class	Displacement (tons)	In Service	Yards*	No
November	5,300	1956-64	E	15
Victor				
I	5,100	1965-74	C	16*
II	5,900	1972-78	C	7
III	6,000	1978-?	C	26
Alfa	3,680	1979-83	B,E	7
Sierra	7,550	1983-?	D	4
Akula	10,000	1988-?	F	6
Mike	9,700	1986	E	1

BALLISTIC MISSILE, DIESEL-ELECTRIC POWERED (SSB)

Class	Displacement (tons)	In Service	Yards*	No
Zulu V	2,600	1956-58	E	6
Golf	2,850	1957-61	E,F	23

BALLISTIC MISSILE, NUCLEAR-POWERED (SSBN)

Class	Displacement (tons)	In Service	Yards*	No
Hotel	6,000	1958-62	E,F	9
Yankee	9,600	1967-74	E,F	34
Delta				
I	11,750	1973-76	E,F	18
II	12,750	1974-75	E	4
III	13,250	1972-82	E	14
IV	14,500	1985-?	E	5+
Typhoon	25,000	1977-90	E	6

GUIDED-MISSILE: DIESEL-ELECTRIC (SSG)

Class	Displacement (tons)	In Service	Yards*	No
Juliett	3,500	1962-69	D	16

GUIDED-MISSILE: NUCLEAR-POWERED (SSGN)

Class	Displacement (tons)	In Service	Yards*	No
Echo				
I	5,500	1960-62	E	5
II	6,000	1960-67	E,F	29
Charlie				
I	5,000	1967-73	D	12
II	5,500	1972-81	D	6
Papa	7,000	1970	D	1
Oscar				
I	14,500	1982-83	E	2
II	16,000	1984-?	E	4

MISCELLANEOUS

Class	Displacement (tons)	In Service	Yards*	No
Bravo	2,900	1968-70	F	4
India	4,800	1979-80	F	2
Lima	2,400	1978	C	1
X-Ray	500-700	1983	B	1
Uniform	2,000	1983	B	1
Beluga	2,500	1987	B	1

*Note: Particular submarine construction yards are identified in this table by the following letters: A: Ordzhonikidze Yard, Leningrad. B: Sudomekh Works, Leningrad. C: Marti Yard, Leningrad. D: Krasnaya Sormovo Yard, Gorki. E: Molotovsk Yard (to late 1950s) then 402 Yard, Severodvinsk. F: Yard 199, Komsomolsk.

Krab Class

(Minelaying submarine)

Displacement:
512 tons surfaced; 740 tons submerged
Performance:
Max speed 11.8kt surfaced; 7.1kt submerged
Range 1,700nm/7kt surfaced; 82nm/4kt
submerged
Maximum Operational Diving Depth:
150ft (45.7m)
Dimensions:
173ft 3in (52.8m) x 14ft 0in (4.27m) x 12ft 9in
(3.88m)
Machinery:
Four gasoline engines, 1,200bhp; two electric
motors, 400hp; two shafts
Complement:
50
Construction:
Naval Yard, Nikolayev. *Krab*. One boat.
Launched 1912.

Above: *The Russian submarine* Krab
*nearing completion at Nikolayev in 1915,
having been laid down in 1908.*

Below: Krab *was the first submarine
minelayer, a concept based on analysis of
the lessons of the Russo-Japanese War.*

Design: It was foreseen from the earliest
days of the submarine that it would serve
valuably in two roles. The first was that of
launching torpedoes at surface warships;
the second that of laying small,
clandestine minefields in naval choke-
points, such as narrow channels and
harbour entrances.

It was not until World War II that the
Germans developed a mine which could be
launched from a torpedo tube, following
which those navies wishing to lay mines
from submarines have used this method,
even though it means that mines can only
be carried at the expense of torpedoes.
Prior to this development all submarine
minelayers used separate launching devices
for their mines. The first such purpose-
built, submarine minelayer, the *Krab*, was
designed by a Russian railway engineer,
Mikhail Petrovich Nalyetov, for the
Imperial Russian Navy.

Nalyetov had been in the Far East during
the Russo-Japanese War and had observed
at first hand the destructive power of naval
mines. He immediately saw the
possibilities offered by a submarine to
deliver such effective weapons and being a
man of some determination he designed a
specialised minelaying submarine, the
construction of which was started in Port
Arthur. However, this vessel had to be
blown up before completion in order to

prevent its capture by the Japanese.

Nothing daunted, Nalyetov returned to
western Russia, where he quickly
persuaded the Admiralty of the value of his
proposals and a new boat was ordered in
1906. It was not actually laid down at the
Naval Yard in Nikolayev until 1908 and
construction was exceptionally slow, the
boat not being launched until September
1912, following which completion dragged
on until July 1915. The consequence of
these inordinate delays was that, although
when laid down she had been the first
purpose-built minelayer to be designed,
she was not the first such to enter service.
That honour fell to the German UC-I class
of small, 183 ton displacement boats,
whose design was started in October 1914.
Orders for these were placed one month
later and the first two boats were launched
in April 1915.

Having taken so long to build, once in
service *Krab* soon developed a reputation
for being particularly susceptible to
mechanical failures. The problem appears

Above right: *The designer Nalyetov's
horizontal minelaying system proved
very successful and had a much greater
capacity than the other system, which
involved vertical tubes mounted either in
the hull or in the ballast tanks. Krab
carried no less than 60 mines.*

to have lain in the fact that Nalyetov not only had an excellent concept for minelaying, but was also allowed the luxury of designing a complete submarine to take his system. It would almost certainly have been better if he had been directed to collaborate with an established designer in adapting an existing hull design to take the conveyor system.

Armament: Specialist submarine minelayers have traditionally used one of two methods to store and launch their mines. One stores the mines in a series of vertical (or near vertical) tubes, from which the mines may be dropped. A typical German World War I minelayer, the UC-III, for example, mounted six 100cm (39.4in) tubes, each containing three UC-200 mines.

Nalyetov's system, however, was the forerunner of the other type of minelaying system, in which the mines were stowed beneath the upper casing and moved aft on an electrically-driven conveyor belt to be laid over the stern. This enabled no less than 60 fairly large mines to be carried, a much more significant warload than for the other system.

In addition to her mines the *Krab* carried a heavy weapon load for her period. She had two 18in (457mm) torpedo tubes in the bow, with a further two torpedoes in Drzewiecki drop-collars mounted on the upper deck. She also mounted a 75mm gun and two machine-guns.

Service History: *Krab* spent her entire service career in the Black Sea. She was plagued by mechanical problems, but nevertheless took part in at least three minelaying operations between 1915 and 1918. In the first of these, mines were laid off the Turkish Straits, which damaged the Turkish gunboat *Isa Reis* (413 tons). A second minefield was laid in the same area in early 1916, but as far as is known this claimed no victims. In September 1916 she laid a minefield off Varna, which was subsequently entered by a group of Bulgarian torpedo boats; one of them, *Shumni*, was sunk and another, *Strogi*, damaged.

In the Revolution *Krab* was initially taken over by the Ukranians, but was then captured by the Germans. They, in turn, surrendered her to the British, who scuttled her on 26 April 1918. She was raised by the Soviet authorities in 1935 and scrapped.

Below: *The Nalyetov minelaying system involved two electrically-driven conveyor belts, mounted under the upper casing, which transported the mines aft and launched them over the stern. Krab suffered from a host of reliability problems whilst in service, but she did manage to lay several minefields in the Black Sea, which claimed several minor Turkish vessels.*

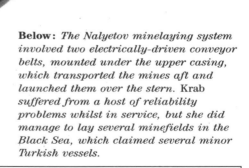

Amerikanskji Golland (AG) Class

(Patrol submarines)

Displacement:
355 tons surfaced; 433 tons submerged
Performance:
Max speed 12kt surfaced; 10kt submerged
Range 2,300nm/11kt surfaced; 100nm/5kt submerged
Maximum Operational Diving Depth:
200ft (61m)
Dimensions:
150ft 3in (45.8m) x 15ft 9in (4.8m) x 12ft 6in (3.8m)
Machinery:
Two NELSECO diesel engines, 960bhp; two electric motors, 640hp; two shafts
Complement:
30

Construction:
These submarines had one of the longest and most complicated construction and delivery processes of any class of submarine in history, which merits a special note. They were ordered in 1915 from the Electric Boat Company at a time when the USA was firmly neutral. To circumvent the neutrality problem, all parts of the submarine were manufactured in the USA in 1915-16 and then sent by railroad to the Vickers Yard at Montreal in Canada, where an American work force assembled the boats. This was an identical procedure to the H class boats ordered by the British and Italian navies except that these vessels were then sailed across the Atlantic, whereas the Russian boats had to be broken down again into major assemblies and sent by rail to the Canadian West Coast where they were transferred to ships for the voyage to Vladivostok. There they were transferred to rail yet again and sent via the Trans-Siberian Railway to the Baltic and Black Sea for final assembly, which took place at: Baltic Yard; Petrograd. *AG-11* to *AG-15*. 5 boats. Launched 1916 Naval Yard, Nikolayev. *AG-21* to *AG-26*. 6 boats. Launched 1917 to 1921

Design: Designed by the Electric Boat Company and following the principles laid down by John P Holland, this was a successful class. The boats for the Imperial Russian Navy were identical in every respect to the H class boats delivered to the US Navy (SS-28 to SS-30), the Royal Navy (*H-1* to *H-10*), and the navies of Italy (*H-1* to *H-8*) and Chile (*H-1* to *H-6*). They

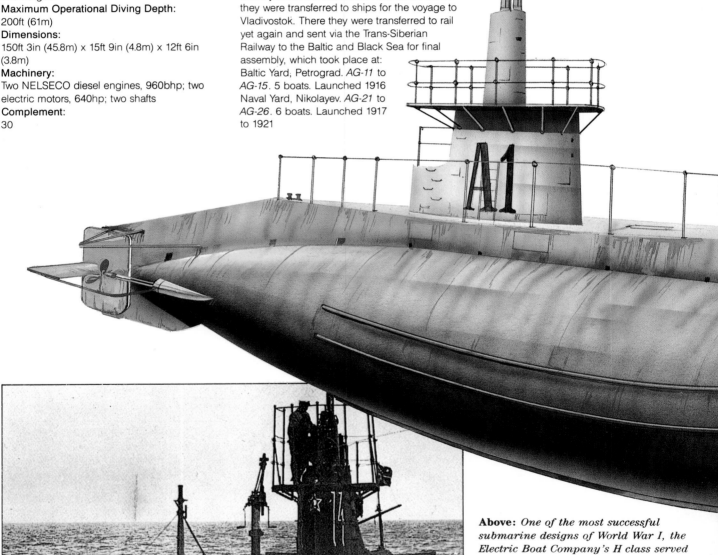

Above: *One of the most successful submarine designs of World War I, the Electric Boat Company's H class served in five navies, including the Imperial Russian Navy, where it was known as the Amerikanskji Golland (AG) class. This example was completed by the Soviets in the early 1920s as Trotzki (ex-AG-23), being redesignated No 12 in 1929 and A-1 in 1934. Main armament was four 18in (457mm) torpedo tubes; most also mounted a 47mm cannon as well.*

Left: *Seen here in 1930 is No 14, a submarine that was previously known as AG-25, becoming Marksist in 1923, No 14 in 1929, and A-3 in 1934. She was sunk by UJ-117 in November 1943.*

were of single-hull construction, with the pressure hull containing three watertight bulkheads, dividing the boat into four compartments. Forward was the torpedo room (which was also the officers' quarters), then the crew's quarters, the control room and finally the engine and motor room.

The original Russian orders were for 18 boats: *AG-11* to *AG-20* to be assembled in Petrograd and *AG-21* to *AG-28* in Nikolayev. However, following the outbreak of the Revolution in Russia the undelivered boats were purchased by the US Government and never reached Russia. These became US Navy *H-4* (SS-147) (ex-

AG-17), *H-5* (SS-148) (ex-*AG-18*), *H-6* (SS-149) (ex-*AG-19*), *H-7* (SS-150) (ex-*AG-20*), *H-8* (SS-151) (ex-*AG-27*) and *H-9* (SS-152) (ex-*AG-28*). There is some mystery over *AG-17*, which does not seem to have reached Russia and there is no evidence of it having been despatched.

Armament: Main armament comprised four 18in (457mm) torpedo tubes, which were mounted in the bow in two pairs, one above the other. They were the first boats in the Imperial Russian Navy to have such a heavy bow armament, and were unusual in not being fitted with either stern tubes or Drzewiecki drop collars. Most boats were fitted with a 47mm cannon, mounted on the foredeck.

Service History: The Baltic Fleet boats entered service in 1916, but achieved no noteworthy successes, except that both *AG-13* and *AG-15* sank accidentally in 1917 and were raised, refitted and returned to service. One boat, *AG-14*, was lost as a result of enemy action, being mined on 6 July 1917. All the remaining boats (*AG-11, AG-12, AG-13* and *AG-15*) were scuttled off Libau, Latvia on 3 April 1918 to prevent their capture.

Only one of the boats intended for the Black Sea Fleet was completed at Nikolayev in time to be commissioned into the Imperial Navy, all the others being completed by the new Soviet Navy in the early 1920. All underwent a complicated series of renaming and renumbering, except for *AG-22*, which became part of Wrangel's fleet, escaped abroad and was sold for scrap in 1924. *AG-21* shared the fate of most Black Sea submarines in 1918, being first captured by the Germans in May and then scuttled by the British in November. However, *AG-21* was raised by the Soviet Navy in 1928 and recommissioned in 1930. She was given a number for a short period (*16*) and then a name (*Metallist*) and was then renumbered in line with the rest of the class in 1934.

All were either lost to enemy action or stricken during World War II, except for *A-5* (ex-*AG-21*) which survived until 1948, when it was scrapped. One became a war loss, *A-3* (ex-*AG-25*) sunk by the German torpedo-boat *UJ-117* in the Black Sea. The others were all scuttled or stricken in mid-1942 to avoid capture by the advancing Germans.

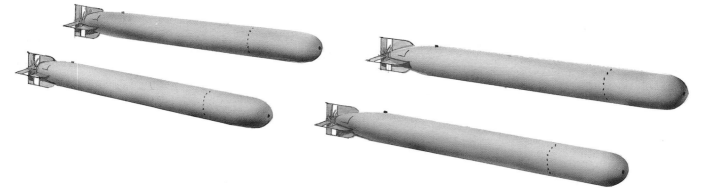

Leninetz Class

(Series II, XI, XIII, XIIIbis)
(Minelaying submarines)

Displacement:
Series II 1,040 tons surfaced; 1,335 tons
submerged
Series XI 1,100 tons surfaced; 1,400 tons
submerged
Series XIII/XIIIbis 1,123 tons surfaced; 1,414 tons
submerged

Performance:
Max speed
Series II/XI 14kt surfaced; 9kt submerged
Series XIII/XIIIbis 18kt surfaced; 10kt
submerged
Range
Series II/XI 6,000nm/9kt surfaced; 135nm/2kt
submerged
Series XIII/XIIIbis 14,000nm/9kt surfaced;
130nm/2kt submerged

Maximum Operational Diving Depth:
246ft (75m)

Dimensions:
Series II/XI 265ft 8in (81.0m) x 22ft 7in (6.9m) x
13ft 8in (4.18m)
Series XIII/XIIIbis 273ft 3in (83.3m) x 23ft 0in
(7.0m) x 13ft 5in (4.08m)

Machinery:
Series II Two diesel engines, 2,200bhp; two
electric motors, 1,050hp; two shafts
Series XI Two diesel engines, 2,200bhp; two
electric motors, 1,450hp; two shafts
Series Two diesel engines, 4,200bhp; two
XIII/XIIIbis electric motors, 2,400hp; two shafts

Complement:
50

Construction:
Series II Ordzhonikidze Yard, Leningrad. *L-1* to
(6 boats) *L-3*. 3 boats. Launched 1931.
Marti Yard, Nikolayev. *L-4* to *L-6.* 3
boats. Launched 1931
Series XI Prefabricated at Ordzhonikidze Yard,
(6 boats) Leningrad; assembled at Dalzavod
Yard, Vladivostok. *L-7* to *L-12.* 6 boats.
Launched 1935 to 1936
Series XIII Prefabricated at Ordzhonikidze Yard,
(7 boats) Leningrad; assembled at Dalzavod
Yard, Vladivostok. *L-13* to *L-19.* 7
boats. Launched 1937 to 1938
Series Prefabricated at Ordzhonikidze Yard,
XIIIbis Leningrad; assembled at Molotovsk
(6 boats) Yard. *L-20* to *L-22.* 3 boats. Launched
1939 to 1941
Prefabricated at Ordzhonikidze Yard,
Leningrad; assembled at Marti Yard,
Nikolayev. *L-23* to *L-25.* 3 boats.
Launched 1940 to 1941

Despite the study of *L-55* the Series II
were considered to be poorly designed,
with inadequate ventilation, low battery
capacity and a lack of stern torpedo tubes.

The Series XI consisted of six boats,
with minor improvements, intended for the
Pacific Fleet. The boats were fabricated at
the Ordzhonikidze Yard in Leningrad and
then moved in sections to Vladivostok,
where they were reassembled and
launched at the Dalzavod Yard. This was
no mean undertaking for boats of this size.

The Series XIII were a little larger and
were fitted with diesels and electric motors
of double the power of the previous boats.
There were also changes in the armament.
The Series XIIIbis incorporated further
minor improvements which did not
warrant a separate series number. All
seven Series XIII were constructed in a
similar manner to the Series XII, but the
Series XIIIbis were affected by the German
advances in the Crimea and were never

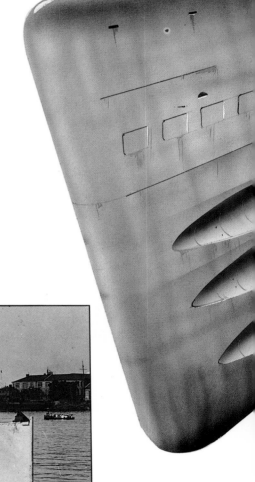

Design: In the first few years after the
Revolution the Soviet Navy concentrated
on keeping Tsarist submarines in service
and had little effort to spare for new
construction. However, in 1926 the design
of the Dekabrist class patrol submarines
was finalised and six boats were built;
three at the Ordzhonikidze Yard in
Leningrad (the former Baltic Yard) and
three at the Marti Yard in Nikolayev. They
were reported to have been developments
of the final design of the Tzarist-era
designer Bubnov, and were unsatisfactory
in many respects.

The Soviet Navy had sunk the British
submarine *L-55* off Kronstadt in June 1919
and it was decided to raise this boat in
order to examine Western construction
techniques. This was done in 1928 and,
the bodies of the crew having been
recovered and returned to the United
Kingdom with absolute correctness, the

boat was scrutinised closely before being
returned to service as *Bezbozhnik*
('Godless').

The lessons from *L-55* were first applied
to the design of the next series of boats to
be authorised under the 1926 Naval
Programme, the Leninetz (Series II)
minelayers. They also incorporated lessons
learned from the construction of the
Dekabrist class. Overall, the Leninetz class
consisted of three groups — Series II,
Series XI and Series XIII — together with
a modified version of the last, Series
XIIIbis.

The Series II were the largest
submarines built in Russia up to that time
(larger boats had been planned and some
even laid down, but none completed).

Below: *Leninetz class minelayers used a*
system developed directly from that used
on the pioneering Krab.

sent to the Pacific for final assembly. *L-20* and *L-23* were completed in Molotovsk and served with the Northern Fleet, while the remainder were completed in various Black Sea ports.

Armament: Designed principally as minelayers, all versions of the Leninetz class could lay between 14 and 20 mines

over the stern from tubes installed under the after casing. The minelaying mechanism was developed from the system which had previously been installed in *Krab*.

The Series II boats were fitted with six 21in (533mm) torpedo tubes, all in the bow, for which 12 torpedoes were carried.

It was unusual for boats of this period to mount only bow tubes and this was to prove unpopular with their crews. They also mounted one 100mm/52 calibre gun, together with one 45mm/46 calibre AA gun.

Armament on the Series XI was identical with that on Series II. However, the Series XIII and XIIIbis were fitted with an additional two stern torpedo tubes to answer criticism of the earlier design. A new model gun was also fitted (100mm/56 calibre), the 45mm/46 was retained and two 7.62mm machine-guns fitted.

Service History: In the late 1920s the Soviet Navy went through a period when submarines were given names, a system complicated by the fact that names were often changed to comply with current political trends. The first nine of these boats received names, but thereafter all were numbered in the 'L-' series. The names allocated were: *Leninetz* (*L-1*), *Stalinetz* (ex-*Marxist*) (*L-2*), *Frunzovetz* (ex-*Bolshevik*) (*L-3*), *Garibaldiyetz* (*L-4*), *Chartist* (*L-5*) and *Karbonari* (*L-6*), all Series II; and *Voroshilovetz* (*L-7*), *Dzherzhinetz* (*L-8*) and *Kirovetz* (*L-9*) of Series XI.

Three Series II boats (*L-1, L-2* and *L-3*) served in the Baltic, the other three in the Black Sea. All served in the war and three were lost. *Leninetz* (*L-1*) suffered the unusual fate for a submarine of being sunk by German field artillery while lying in the River Neva during the siege of Leningrad (October 1941). *L-2* was mined in the Baltic in 1941. *L-6*, the only boat of the class to be lost in the Black Sea, was sunk by a German submarine-hunter (*UJ-104*) off Costanza (18 April 1944). The remaining three boats survived and were eventually scrapped in the late 1950s.

All six boats of Series XI spent their operational lives in the Pacific Fleet. One boat (*L-7*) was lost in the war, cause unknown, while the remainder survived to be scrapped in the 1950s.

L-13 of Series XIII was sunk in the Pacific in 1941-42. Due to the pressure of events in the European theatre the Soviet Navy decided in 1942 to transfer two Leninetz and four Stalinetz class submarines from the Pacific to Northern Fleets. The six boats set off on this voyage on 25 September 1942, but, having successfully crossed the Pacific they were travelling on the surface some 500 miles (800km) off the US West Coast, heading south for the Panama Canal, when they were spotted by the Japanese submarine *I-15*. The Japanese boat had just one torpedo left, which it fired at *L-16*, scoring a hit. The Soviet submarine blew up, sinking with all hands, although the others continued, transited the Panama Canal and then crossing the Atlantic to reach the Northern Fleet in May 1943.

All three of the boats with the Northern Fleet (*L-20* to *L-22*) plus *L-15* survived the war and were scrapped in the 1950s. The three boats completed in the Black Sea, however, were all lost during the war. *L-23* was sunk by the German torpedo boat *UJ-106*, while both *L-24* and *L-25* were sunk by mines.

Above: *Soviet Navy Leninetz class, Series II. Armament comprised six torpedo tubes in the original Series II and XI, supplemented by a further two stern tubes in the Series XIII and XIIIbis,* *a modification made in reply to criticisms from operational crews. Main gun was a 100mm, and varying numbers of AA cannon and MGs were carried. The mine tubes carried a maximum of 20 mines.*

Stalinetz (S) Class

(Series IX, IXbis, XVI)
(Long-range patrol submarines)

Displacement:
Series IX 840 tons surfaced; 1,070 tons submerged
Series IXbis, XVI 856 tons surfaced; 1,090 tons submerged

Performance:
Max speed
Series IX 19.5kt surfaced; 9kt submerged
Series IXbis, XVI 18.85kt surfaced; 8.8kt submerged
Range 9,800nm/10.4kt surfaced; 148nm/3kt submerged

Maximum Operational Diving Depth:
263ft (80m)

Dimensions:
Series IX, IXbis 255ft 10in (77.98m) x 21ft 0in (6.4m) x 14ft 5in (4.44m)
Series XVI 255ft 1in (77.75m) x 21ft 0in (6.4m) x 13ft 4in (4.06m)

Machinery:
Early construction, two M.A.N. diesel engines, 4,000bhp; later construction, two Kolomna 1-D, 8-cylinder diesels, 4,200bhp.
All, two electric motors, 1,100shp; two shafts

Complement:
Series IX 46
Series IXbis, XVI 45

Construction:

Series IX (3 boats)	Ordzhonikidze Yard, Leningrad. *S-1* to *S-3*. 3 boats. Launched 1935-1936	
Series IXbis (39 boats)	Ordzhonikidze Yard, Leningrad. *S-4* to *S-6*. 3 boats. Launched 1936-1937	
	Krasnaya Sormovo Yard. *S-7* to *S-20*. 14 boats. Launched 1939-1941	
	Sudomekh Works, Leningrad. *S-21* to *S-24*, *S-101* to *S-104*. 8 boats. Launched 1938-1947	
	Marti Yard, Nikolayev. *S-31* to *S-37*. 7 boats. Launched 1939-1940	
	Dalzavod Yard, Vladivostok. *S-51* to *S-57*. 7 boats. Launched 1939-1940	
Series XVI (6 boats)	Krasnaya Sormovo Yard, Gorki. *S-46* to *S-48*. 3 boats. Launched 1947	
	402 Yard, Molotovsk. *S-25*, *S-52*, *S-27*. 3 boats. Launched 1945-1946	

Design: The Soviet Navy was not too happy with its early post-Revolution submarine designs and decided to take advantage of the working relationship established with the Germans resulting from the Rapallo Treaty, which had been signed on 16 April 1922. Accordingly, they commissioned a design by the Den Haag-based, German-owned, submarine design agency, *Ingenieurskantoor voor Scheepsbouw* (I.v.S). The result was an enlarged version of the I.v.S design A1, bearing a close relationship to the very similar Turkish *Gür* and German Type IA. The first three boats, the Series IX, were built at the Ordzhonikidze Yard in Leningrad in the remarkably short time (for Soviet yards) of eight months, supervised by German experts.

The design was subsequently refined in detail to produce the Series IXbis. One of the more visible modifications was that in the original version the gun was in a large, almost fully enclosed shield at the foot of the conning tower; this proved a hindrance and was removed. Later the streamlining of the sail was also improved. In the Series XVI the hulls were constructed of tensile steel and fabricated by welding rather than rivetting, and the gun was moved to the after casing.

The actual number of Series IXbis built is not known outside the USSR. Certainly at least 39 were completed, of which four were paid for by public subscription, a custom harking back to Tsarist days. At least five hulls were abandoned incomplete

or even destroyed on the ways in the face of German attacks and there may have been more. Some of the hulls which had been launched but were incomplete at the time of the German attack were transferred by inland waterways to other yards for completion.

All the boats constructed at the Krasnaya Sormovo Yard in Gorki were, in any case, transferred on pontoons to either Leningrad, Molotovsk (now Severodvinsk) or Nikolayev for fitting out and commissioning.

Armament: The armament of all these series was the same. They mounted six 21in (533mm) torpedo tubes (4 bow, 2 stern) for which 12 torpedoes were carried. Gun armament comprised one 100mm/56 calibre AA gun and one 45mm/46 cannon. Some boats also carried a 7.62mm MG.

Service History: These were the best of the Soviet pre-war boats. They were popular with their crews, and served with all major Soviet fleets during the war. One boat, *S-13*, conducted the most successful Soviet patrol of the war, sinking two large liners, the *Wilhelm Gustloff* (25,484 tons) and *General Steuben* (14,660 tons), in 1945, both of which were involved in transporting refugees from German East Prussia to evade capture by the advancing Red Army.

Four boats of this class made a notable voyage in 1942/43 in company with *L-15* and *L-16* (q.v.). These six boats were sent from the Pacific Fleet to the Northern

Above: *The Stalinetz class design was prepared by the German-owned I.v.S. and was very similar to that of the German Type IA. The original Series IX, shown* here, had the 100mm gun protected by a large shield, but this was discontinued. A 45mm cannon was also mounted. There were six 21in (533mm) TTs.

Above: *A Soviet Navy Stalinetz class submarine returns to her Northern Fleet base in 1945. This is* S-102, *one of the Series IXbis boats.*

Fleet via the Pacific Ocean, the Panama Canal and then across the Atlantic to the Barents Sea. *L-16* was lost off the US coast, but the remaining five boats reached the Barents Sea, where on the final leg of the voyage both *S-54* and *S-55* were lost. The other two boats, *S-51* and *S-56* (plus *L-15*) completed the voyage successfully. The two Stalinetz boats, after some years service in the Arctic, returned to the Pacific Fleet in 1950, but on this occasion via the Siberian route.

There were sixteen war losses, the first being *S-1* blown up to avoid capture on 24 June 1941. Six were lost to mines: five in the Baltic and one in the Black Sea. Four

were lost to German surface warships, all in the Baltic. Two were sunk by submarines: one in the Baltic by the Finnish *Vesihiisi* (ironically, another I.v.S design) — and the other in the Black Sea by an Italian midget submarine. Finally, there were the inevitable three 'lost, cause unknown'.

All three Series IX were sunk in 1940/41. Twelve of the Series IXbis survived the war, of which three were transferred to China in 1955 and the remainder scrapped in the 1950s and 1960s. The six Series XVI were completed in 1946/47, but were scrapped in the 1960s.

Victor I, II,II Class

(Nuclear-propelled attack submarines) (SSN)

Displacement:
Victor I 4,300 tons surfaced; 5,100 tons submerged
Victor II 4,500 tons surfaced; 5,900 tons submerged
Victor III 4,900 tons surfaced; 6,000 tons submerged

Performance:
Max speed (submerged)
Victor I,II 30kt
Victor III 29kt

Maximum Operational Diving Depth:
1,968ft (600m)

Dimensions:
Victor I 311ft 8in (95.0m) x 32ft 10in (10.0m) x 22ft 11in (7.00m)
Victor II 334ft 8in (102.0m) x 32ft 10in (10.0m) x 22ft 11in (7.00m)
Victor III 347ft 9in (106.00m) x 32ft 10in (10.0m) x 22ft 11in (7.00m)

Machinery:
Two pressurised-water nuclear reactors, steam turbines; one 5-blade propeller (except Victor III, see text); two small propellers for creep speeds; 30,000shp.

Complement:
Victor I, II 80
Victor III 85

Construction:
Victor I   Admiralty Shipyard, Leningrad. 16 boats. Commissioned 1968 to 1975
Victor II   Admiralty Shipyard, Leningrad. 7 boats. Commissioned 1972 to 1978
Victor III Admiralty Shipyard, Leningrad and Komsomolsk Shipyard. 21+ boats. Commissioned 1978 to 1988.

Design: Following World War II the Soviet Navy received a small number of Type XXIs which had been surrendered to the Allies. The Navy also ensured the completion of several more Type XXIs in yards which had been captured during their advance across Poland and eastern Germany. The lessons learned from these were incorporated into some of their post-war diesel-electric designs.

The first Soviet nuclear-powered attack submarine class, the November class, appeared in 1958. Like the early US Navy SSNs, this had a long, thin, traditional hull, developed from that of the Type XXI, which was fitted with two of the new nuclear propulsion units. The Novembers were not very satisfactory, having unreliable power units and a noisy, unmanoeuvrable hull.

In the 1950s the Soviet Navy became concerned by the appearance first of the US Navy's aircraft carriers with their nuclear bombers and then of the George Washington class SSBNs. As a result of the latter threat the Soviet Navy adopted an anti-submarine strategy, which led, in the case of the surface fleet, to the Moskva class helicopter cruisers and, in the case of the submarine fleet, to the Victor class SSNs, the first Soviet ASW submarines.

Above: *A Victor III with its pod. Thought at an early stage to house a new form of slow-speed propulsion system, it is now generally agreed to contain a winch for a towed sonar array.*

Below: *Victor IIIs are armed with a mix of nuclear-tipped SS-N-15 ASW missiles (1), ASW homing torpedoes (2), mines (3), SS-N-16 ASW missiles (4) or high-performance anti-ship torpedoes (5).*

The Victor class have a hull shape quite unlike that of preceding Soviet submarines, but it is by no means a copy of the Western Albacore hulls. The bow is bulbous, the hull somewhat rounder and the fin is lower and more streamlined, blending better into the hull form. It has been suggested from time-to-time that the Soviets have carried out extensive research into the hydrodynamics of whales and dolphins, and the shape of their SSNs, starting with the Victors, tends to support such a theory. Certainly the Victor is quieter than previous Soviet submarines and very much faster.

The first series, the Victor I, appeared in 1965 and 16 units were built at Leningrad. They were contemporaneous with the US Navy's Sturgeon (SSN-637) class and of a generally similar displacement and size. They are double-hulled and, despite many quietening measures, retain a large number of free-flood holes. They are also fitted with cruciform stern control surfaces, the first Soviet design to have them. They were thus the first Soviet boats for many years not to have stern torpedo tubes.

Another innovation in Soviet design was the use of a single main shaft with a large, slow-rotating, five-bladed propeller, which contributed to the noise reduction programme. They are also fitted with two unusual small propellers mounted on the horizontal stabilisers, which are used for very slow speed manoeuvring whilst operating in the 'hovering' mode during ASW operations.

Above: *Some Victor IIIs are fitted with twin, 4-bladed, co-rotating propellers.*

After some years a second version appeared, in which the hull was lengthened by some 23ft (7m) and without the pronounced hump on the forward casing. Seven of these Victor IIs were produced, joining the fleet in 1972, 1974, 1975, 1976 (two), 1977 and 1978.

Considerable excitement was caused in the West when the first Victor III appeared in 1978, as this introduced an

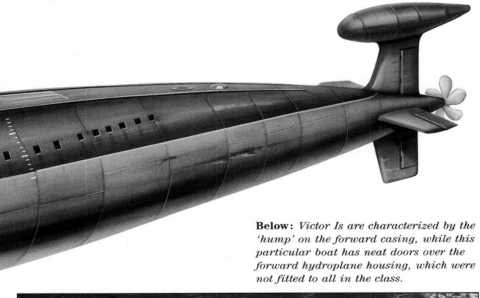

Below: *Victor Is are characterized by the 'hump' on the forward casing, while this particular boat has neat doors over the forward hydroplane housing, which were not fitted to all in the class.*

extraordinary, large, teardrop-shaped pod, mounted atop the vertical stabiliser. Two quite different explanations have been put forward as to the purpose of this pod. The first, that it houses a towed, passive, hydrophone array, the second that it is an entirely new form of 'creep' motor, using magneto-hydrodynamic propulsion. The former appears the more probable, particularly as the Victor III retains the two small propellers.

Some Victor IIIs are also fitted with a unique propeller, comprising two four-bladed propellers bolted together in tandem at an angle of 22.5° to form an 8-bladed device. Other Victor IIIs, however, use the more conventional five-bladed propeller.

Armament: Victor I is fitted with six 21in (533mm) torpedo tubes in the bow, for which torpedoes and SS-N-15 missiles are carried. In Victor II and Victor III two of the 21in (533mm) tubes are retained but four have been replaced by new 25.6in (650mm) tubes. A mix of torpedoes, SS-N-15 and SS-N-16 missiles is carried.

Service History: The Victor I entered service in 1968 and two per year then joined the Soviet Fleet until 1975. The first Victor II appeared in 1972, followed by one each in 1974 and 1975, two in 1976 and one each in 1977 and 1978. Victor III appeared in 1978, with a second production line being set up in Komsomolsk; by 1990 some 21 were in service.

Victor class SSNs have suffered a number of accidents. A Pacific Fleet Victor I collided with the carrier USS *Kitty Hawk* (CV-63) in 1984 in the Sea of Japan. Another Victor I hit a Soviet merchant vessel during an exercise in the Straits of Gibraltar, also in 1984, which resulted in some spectacular photographs of the damaged submarine lying alongside an auxiliary, her stove-in bow revealing elements of her sonar. In October 1983 a Victor III in the Caribbean managed to get her propeller snagged in the towed-array of a US frigate and had to be towed to Cuba for repairs.

Akula Class

(Nuclear-propelled attack submarines) (SSN)

Displacement:
7,500 tons surfaced; 10,000 tons submerged
Performance:
Max speed (submerged) 35kt
Maximum Operational Diving Depth:
1,300ft (396m)
Dimensions:
370ft 9in (113.0m) x 42ft 8in (13.0m) x 32ft 10in (10.0m)
Machinery:
Two pressurised-water nuclear reactors, steam turbines; one 7-bladed propeller, 40,000shp
Complement:
90+
Construction:
Komsomolsk Shipyard, Komsomolsk-na-Amur. 6 boats (as at early 1991). Commissioned 1984 to 1991.

Above: *A recent (1989) photograph of a Soviet Navy Akula class SSN running on the surface near her home port in northern Russia. The pod, which had first been seen on the Victor III, caused great debate among Western analysts. Note the long, low shape of the sail, quite unlike that of Western SSNs.*

Below: *The Akula class mounts six 25.6in (650mm) or 21in (533mm) tubes which are capable of launching a wide variety of torpedoes and missiles. Seen here are Type 65 torpedoes (1), anti-submarine homing torpedoes (2), SS-N-16 (3) and SS-N-15 (4) missiles, mines (5) and SS-N-21 cruise missiles (6).*

Design: Following the success of the early Victors the Soviet Navy set about the design of a small (3,680 tons) SSN, the Alfa class, powered by a revolutionary liquid-metal (lead-bismuth)-cooled nuclear reactor. With a titanium hull and a high degree of automation, the prototype caused some alarm in the West when it demonstrated an underwater speed of over 40kt and a maximum operating depth in excess of 2,300ft (701m). The prototype appeared in 1972 and was scrapped some two years later, but the Alfa was subsequently placed in limited production, six joining the fleet between 1979 and 1983.

In 1986 the Mike class (6,400 tons) appeared, apparently developed from the Alfa. This had a titanium hull and two liquid-metal cooled reactors; it had an operating depth similar to that of the Alfa, but its speed was a little less at 36kt. Only one was built and this was lost accidentally in the Norwegian Sea in 1989.

In the early 1980s two new classes of SSN were placed in production: the Sierra and Akula classes. The Sierra has a submerged displacement of 7,550 tons and is equipped with two 21in (533mm) and four 25.6in (650mm) torpedo tubes firing anti-ship and ASW torpedoes, as well as SS-N-15, SS-N-16 and SS-N-21 (land-attack) missiles. The Sierras are constructed at the Krasnaya Sormovo Yard at Gorki and transferred by barge to Severodvinsk for completion.

A totally different design of SSN is being produced at the Komsomolsk Yard in the Far East, which has been given the designation Akula by NATO. (*Akula*, the Russian word for shark, has been allocated because all the NATO letter designations from Alfa to Zulu have now been used up). The Akula is somewhat larger than the Sierra, with a submerged displacement of 10,000 tons, although both designs have the same weapons and are fitted with the same towed sonar array mounted in a large

'tear-drop' atop the vertical rudder.

The Akula, however, has a more streamlined shape than the Sierra, with the sail, which has similarities to that of the Alfa, carefully faired into the hull. The forward hydroplanes are not visible in photographs, which means that they must be located on the horizontal centre-line of the hull, as on the Alfa class.

Armament: The Akula is fitted with six bow tubes, probably two 21in (533mm) and four 25.6in (650mm), as in the Sierra. These are capable of launching anti-ship and anti-submarine torpedoes, as well as SS-N-15, SS-N-16 and SS-N-21 missiles.

Service History: The first Akula class SSN was launched in July 1984 and the second in 1986, but the rate has since increased, with six in service by early 1991. It would appear that the success of the Akula, coupled with the need to replace obsolescent SSNs could well lead to a force of some 20 of these highly capable submarines by the mid-1990s.

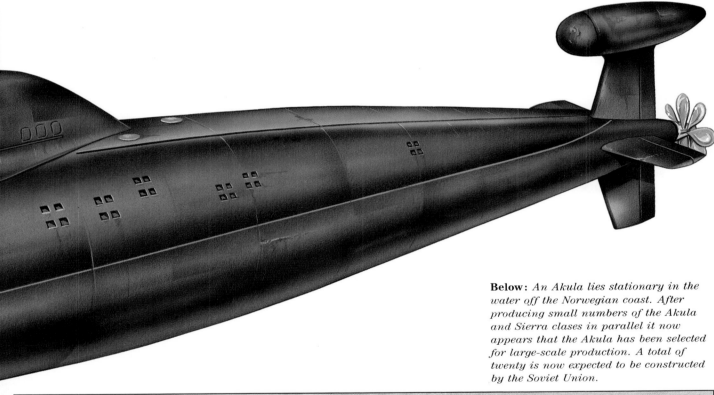

Below: *An Akula lies stationary in the water off the Norwegian coast. After producing small numbers of the Akula and Sierra clases in parallel it now appears that the Akula has been selected for large-scale production. A total of twenty is now expected to be constructed by the Soviet Union.*

Oscar Class

(Nuclear-propelled cruise-missile submarines)
(SSGN)

Displacement:
11,500 tons surfaced; 14,500 tons submerged
Performance:
Max speed (submerged) 33kt
Maximum Operational Diving Depth:
Not known
Dimensions:
Oscar I 479ft 0in (146.0m) x 59ft 1in (18.0m) x 32ft 10in (10.0m)
Oscar II 511ft 10in (156.00m) x 59ft 11in (18.0m) x 32ft 10in (10.0m)
Machinery:
Two pressurised-water nuclear reactors, steam turbines; two 7-bladed propellers, 30,000shp
Complement:
150
Construction:
Oscar I   Severodvinsk, Shipyard No 402. 2 boats. Commissioned 1982 to 1983
Oscar II   Severodvinsk, Shipyard No 402. 4+ boats. Commissioned 1982 to —

Design: The Soviet Navy concluded in the mid-1950s that one of the most serious threats to their territory was from US Navy carrier task forces operating in the Pacific and North Atlantic Oceans. One of their principal responses has been to develop a force of submarines armed with cruise-missiles, whose mission is to attack the carriers before they can get within aircraft range of the USSR.

The first class intended for this role was the Echo II, a group of 29 nuclear-powered submarines armed with eight SS-N-3A anti-ship missiles. The missiles were mounted in four pairs in elevating bins with large thrust-deflecting recesses behind each missile, resulting in a very noisy hull. The missiles could not be launched while the submarine was submerged and the entire preparation/launch/guidance sequence required an Echo II to remain on the

Above: *An Oscar I returning to base with many of its anechoic tiles missing.*

surface for some 40 minutes, during which time it could scarcely have escaped detection by a task force's screen.

Concurrently with the Echo II SSGN, 16 diesel-electric-powered Juliett class SSGs were built, armed with four SS-N-3A missiles. The force of Echo II and Juliett class boats was split between the Northern and Pacific Fleets.

These first-generation anti-carrier classes were succeeded by the much more sophisticated Charlie class SSGNs, which had a much better designed hull and were armed with SS-N-7 anti-ship missiles. The eight missiles were mounted in fixed-angle launch bins in the bows and the large, noisy thrust-deflecting recesses were done away with. The SS-N-7 had one major tactical advantage over the SS-N-3A in that it was launched while the submarine was submerged, although its range was much shorter.

Following the Charlie was the single Papa class SSGN, armed with ten SS-N-9 SLCMs, which was commissioned in 1970. This boat remains in service, although it has undergone two lengthy refits and has made few operational deployments.

Then, after a long gap the new Soviet SSGN emerged, the mighty Oscar class, with a submerged displacement of 14,500 tons and armed with twenty-four SS-N-19 SLCM. This very large submarine has a central pressure-hull of some 30ft (9.1m) diameter with a row of twelve missile bins along either side. The result is a very broad, squat outer hull topped by a long, low sail. The bow is virtually hemispherical in shape, while abaft the aftermost missile bin the hull tapers rapidly to the cruciform after control surfaces and the twin, 7-bladed propellers. The hull is covered in anechoic tiles.

The second Oscar built was similar externally to the first, but one noticeable difference was the fitting of a towed-array dispenser tube at the top of the vertical rudder. The third and subsequent boats have been lengthened by the insertion of a 32ft 10in (10m) plug abaft the sail and are designated Oscar II.

A notable innovation in the Oscar class is a rescue chamber housed in the sail. This chamber is accessible to the crew from inside the submarine and in the event

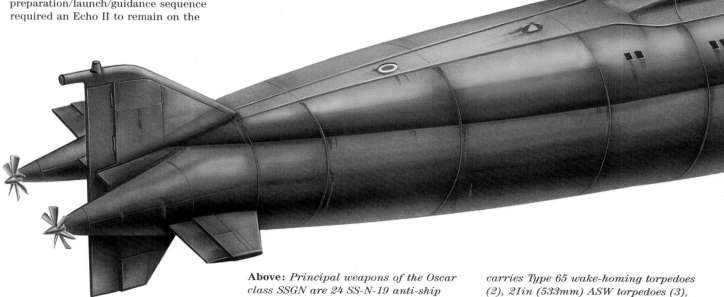

Above: *Principal weapons of the Oscar class SSGN are 24 SS-N-19 anti-ship missiles (1), launched from the angled bins on either side of the sail. It also*

carries Type 65 wake-homing torpedoes (2), 21in (533mm) ASW torpedoes (3), SS-N-15 nuclear-tipped ASW missiles (4), SS-N-16 conventional ASW missiles (5).

of a disaster they would enter, seal it and then release it to rise to the surface. This is conceptually similar to the IKL 'Rescue Sphere', fitted to some of the larger versions of the German Type 209 submarine, such as the Indian Navy's SSK-1500s.

Armament: Primary weapons system of the Oscar class is the SS-N-19 anti-ship cruise missiles. Twenty-four missiles are mounted in tubes mounted at a fixed-angle either side of the fin. These missiles carry either a nuclear or a conventional warhead and have a range of some 300nm (555km). Targetting information for the SLCMs is received via a satellite link, using the Punch Bowl antenna, which is housed beneath a large semi-circular hatch in the sail.

There are eight torpedo tubes, a mix of 21in (533mm) and 25.6in (650mm). The 21in (533mm) tubes fire conventional anti-ship and ASW torpedoes and SS-N-15 missiles, while the 25.6in (650mm) tubes fire Type 65 wake-homing torpedoes and SS-N-16 ASW missiles. The large volume of the hull makes it likely that 24-30 torpedoes and missiles can be carried.

Service History: All six Oscars have been allocated to the Northern Fleet up to 1991,

operating out of the new base at Zapadnaya Litsa. The war role for which they were designed was to sortie out into the Norwegian Sea to attack advancing US Navy carrier task groups. With the demise of the Superpower confrontation, however, it appears that such a role is redundant and there is no other naval power which might threaten the Soviet motherland, at least in the foreseeable future.

Above: *Only the Soviet Typhoon and US Ohio class SSBNs are larger than the Oscar class SSGN. They were designed to attack US Navy carrier-based task groups, a threat which has now reduced.*

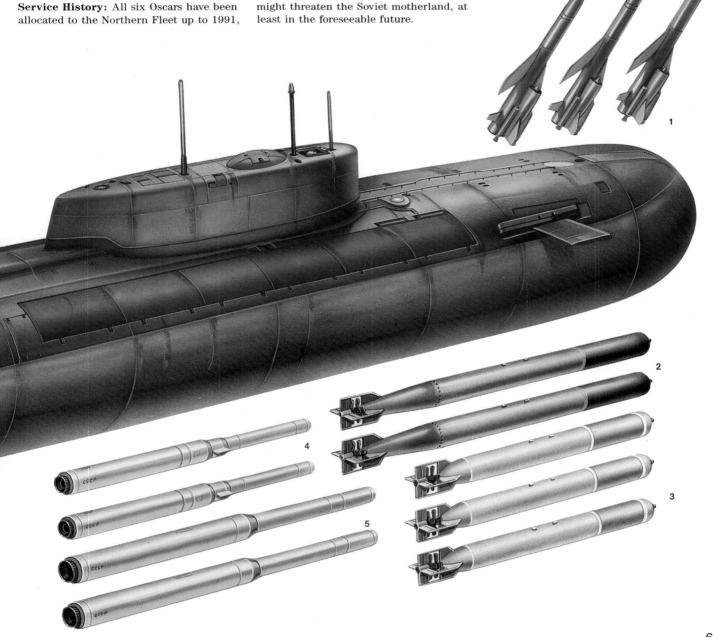

Typhoon Class

(Nuclear-propelled ballistic-missile submarines) (SSBN)

Displacement:
18,500 tons surfaced; 25,500 tons submerged
Performance:
Max speed (submerged) 25kt
Maximum Operational Diving Depth:
Not known
Dimensions:
561ft 0in (171.0m) x 78ft 9in (24.0m) x 41ft 0in (12.5m)
Machinery:
Two 330 to 360 MW pressurised-water nuclear reactors, steam turbines; two 7-bladed propellers, 75,000shp
Complement:
150
Construction:
Severodvinsk, Shipyard No 402. 6 boats. Commissioned 1983 to 1989

Design: Russians have long been fascinated by sheer size in military equipment; they currently operate the largest military aircraft, the six-engined Antonov An-225 (Cossack), for example. It is thus no surprise that the efforts spent on expanding the Soviet Navy's submarine fleet should eventually lead to the Typhoon class, by far the largest underwater vessels ever constructed. Photographs of Typhoon at sea rarely have any other object in view to enable the viewer to gauge the sheer size of these huge submarines. To try to put them into perspective, they make an interesting comparision with HMS *Belfast*, the largest British cruiser of World War II, now moored in the Thames in London, England:

	HMS *Belfast*	Typhoon
Length	579ft	561ft
	(176.5m)	(171.0m)
Beam	63ft 4in	78ft 9in
	(19.3m)	(24.0m)
Draught	21ft 3in	41ft
	(6.48m)	(12.5m)
Displacement	13,175 tons	18,500 tons surfaced

The first Soviet true SSBN was the Yankee class, which appeared in the early 1960s. These were very similar to the United States SSBNs, having a displacement of 9,600 tons (submerged) and mounting sixteen SS-N-6 missiles in two rows of eight abaft the fin. Various versions of the Yankee appeared, leading eventually to the Delta class, which was, in many respects, simply a modified and enlarged version of the later Yankees.

The Delta I (11,750 tons) entered service in 1972, armed with 12 SS-N-8 SLBM; 18 were built. This was followed by the Delta II (13,250 tons) in 1974, of which four were built, lengthened by 50ft 10in (15.5m) to enable the missile armament to be increased to 16 SS-N-8. Next to appear was the Delta III (13,250 tons) in which a raised turtle-deck enabled sixteen of the longer and more capable SS-N-18 missiles

to be carried. Fourteen were built between 1975 and 1982.

The first Typhoon was launched in 1980 and it was thought in the West that this would supersede the Delta class in production, but there was some surprise when a new version, the Delta IV, appeared in 1984. Delta IV has continued in production in parallel with the Typhoon and will apparently continue to be built well into the 1990s. This latest version of the long-lived Delta is armed with 16 SS-N-23 missiles and is optimised for under-ice operations.

In the late 1970s, at the height of the Cold War and a time when the United States Navy was constructing the first of the 18,000 tons Ohio class SSBNs, rumours began circulating in Western naval circles concerning an even larger vessel under construction in a Soviet yard. Despite this advanced warning, the sheer size of the Typhoon came as a complete surprise, as did many features of its design.

No Westerner has ever seen inside a Typhoon and there has thus been intense and protracted speculation about its construction. However, there is now a consensus that the Typhoon is constructed of two parallel pressure hulls, each some 29ft 6in-32ft 10in (9-10m) in diameter. At their after ends each of these hulls contains a complete power-train consisting of a pressurised-water nuclear reactor, turbines, gears, shaft and propeller. Forward, the two hulls narrow considerably. Such a multi-hull concept is reminiscent of the Dutch Dolfijn class of the 1950s (q.v.).

The missiles are housed in twenty vertical tubes mounted between the two pressure hulls and forward of the sail. The torpedo tubes are mounted in the bows. Again, the precise layout is uncertain, as the tubes may be either in a separate pressure hull mounted between the two main pressure hulls or they may be at the

forward ends of the two hulls. In the latter case it would seem likely that the 21in (533mm) tubes would be in one hull and the 25.6in (650mm) tubes in the other.

The command and information centre (CIC) is mounted in a separate pressure-hull, situated above and between the two main hulls, with the fin and the sensor masts above.

In the Yankee and Delta classes the Soviet Navy followed US Navy design practice and sited the forward hydroplanes on the fin. However, in the Typhoon class the hydroplanes are mounted in the bows and are retractable. This, together with the sturdy construction of the fin and vertical rudder, suggest that the Typhoon is designed primarily for under-ice operation, the strength of the upper works being used to break through the ice prior to the launch of the missiles.

Among the many interesting features of the Typhoon are two large triangular hatches on the rear deck, which probably contain closed-circuit TV cameras (CCTV).

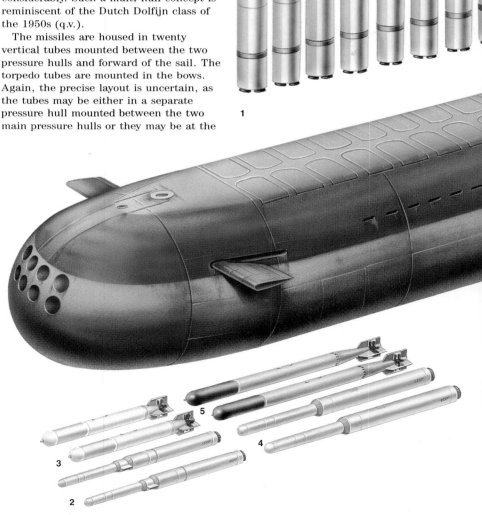

These could be used for a variety of purposes, including monitoring the deployment of VLF buoys just ahead of the cameras, observing the underside of *polnyas* (thinner patches of ice) immediately prior to surfacing and also giving an external view of the hull before ordering the launch of the missiles.

Armament: The Typhoon's primary weapons system is the SS-N-20 SLBM, for which there are 20 launch tubes, mounted in two rows of ten forward of the sail. These missiles carry 6-9 MIRV warheads and have a maximum range of some 4,300nm (7,965km).

Like all combat submarines the Typhoon also carries torpedoes, although the precise number and type of tubes is not yet certain. It is estimated that there are six or eight tubes, of which some are standard 21in (533mm) and the remainder 25.6in (650mm) diameter, the latter being used to launch Type 65 anti-ship torpedoes or SS-N-16 ASW missiles.

The size of the hull is such that space is unlikely to be at a premium and thus as many as 40 torpedoes/missiles could be carried.

Service History: The first of class was laid down at the Severodvinsk Yard in 1977 and launched in September 1980, joining the fleet in 1982. The second was commissioned in 1983, the third in 1984, fourth in 1985, fifth in 1987 and sixth in 1989.

There have been suggestions in the Western Press that the Soviet Navy is not too happy with these enormous boats, whose size, complexity and crewing requirements must place a heavy load on the submarine service. Further, with the ending of the East-West confrontation their *raison d'être* is at least questionable, even if it has not totally disappeared.

It may be, therefore, that the building rate will slow down even further; having started at one per year, it is now one every two years. It may even cease altogether, as the fourth Oscar II was built on the building way previously used for the

Typhoons, although such an enormous programme cannot be 'switched-off' overnight and would need to be wound-down gradually.

When they originally entered service the Typhoons were the first Soviet Navy SSBNs to use the western pattern of two (Blue and Gold) crews to increase the submarines' sea-time. Whilst efficient in the use of the hulls this may prove increasingly difficult to sustain in the light of the reduction of the threat and of the increasing manning difficulties of the Soviet Navy.

All the boats so far built operate from two bases on the Kola Peninsula: one is at Zapadnaya Litsa, the other at Gremikha. The latter appears to have been constructed specifically for the Typhoons and includes huge submarine pens blasted out of granite to provide what is, perhaps, the ultimate in survivable facilities. No Typhoons are known to have deployed outside Arctic waters and none serve with the other SSBN force in the Pacific Fleet.

Above: *The Typhoon class SSBN has twenty launch tubes forward of the sail for its SS-N-20 solid fuel, ballistic missiles (1), each of which carries 6-9 MIRVed nuclear warheads. It also carries SS-N-15 ASW missiles (2) and homing torpedoes (3), both of which are 21in (533mm) weapons, together with the 25.6in (650mm) SS-N-16 missiles (4) and Type 65 wake-homing anti-ship torpedoes (5). Six of these huge boats have been built and production may well have now ceased.*

Right: *The eight men on the bridge reveal the colossal size of the Typhoon, the largest submarine ever built.*

GERMANY

In common with numerous other countries there is a long history of German inventors pestering the authorities with their design proposals for submersible craft. The earliest known is a man named Keyser, who is said to have designed a submersible in Nürnberg in the 15th Century. In the 1690s the Landgraf von Hessen financed the building of a design submitted to him by a French professor at the University of Marburg and at least one successful dive was undertaken.

It was not until the 19th Century, however, that a practicable design (the *Brandtaucher*, literally 'Incendiary Diver') was produced by Wilhelm Bauer (1822-75). Bauer made several working scale models of his designs before constructing his first boat, which was completed on 18 December 1850. Unfortunately, shortage of funds had forced Bauer to compromise in certain areas, particularly in the strength of the frame and the thickness of the hull. On her second trip she sank with her crew of three: Bauer in charge and two volunteer assistants, a blacksmith and a carpenter. As she lay on the bottom at a depth of 53ft (16.2m) Bauer kept his crew calm in the stygian darkness and made them wait for six-and-a-half hours for the internal and external pressures to equalise, which he had, quite correctly, worked out to be necessary for a safe escape. When he was satisfied, Bauer opened the hatch and all three floated to the surface, to their relief and the very considerable surprise of onlookers, who had long since given them up for dead. *Brandtaucher* was subsequently recovered and has been on exhibition in the Dresden War Museum since 1972.

Bauer prepared many further designs but none was constructed. Plans were also prepared by other pioneers. Friedrich Vogel's steam-driven submarine sank on her first trial in 1870, while the firm of Howaldtswerke built a boat in 1891, but nothing is known of her performance. The next German submarine to be built was designed by Karl Leps and built by Howaldtswerke in 1897. This 47ft (14m) long craft was propelled by an accumulator-driven electric motor and had a crew of three. She is known to have carried out surface trials, but whether she dived or not is not known.

A Spanish engineer, Raymondo d'Equivilley-Montjustin, who had worked with the French submarine designer Maxime Laubeuf, submitted a design to the German firm of Krupps, which had just taken over the Germaniawerft shipyard. The Germans were impressed by the design and it was built at the Germaniawerft yard, being completed in June 1903. Named *Forelle* (Trout) she was powered by a 65hp electric motor with a fixed-speed, variable-pitch propeller and displaced 15.5 tons. She was fitted with a periscope, one of the first to be so equipped, and was designed to carry two 17.7in (45cm) torpedoes in single tubes mounted either side of the hull.

Trials were very successful. Two Imperial Russian Navy officers were so impressed that they placed orders for three much larger submarines (Karp class) and also bought *Forelle* herself and had her shipped to Vladivostok for employment against the Japanese. *Forelle* also impressed the Imperial German Navy and led to an order for the first boat for Germany, *U-1*.

Having come later on the submarine scene than the other major navies, the Imperial Germany Navy quickly saw the potential of this new weapon, but principally in the *defensive* role, secondary in importance to the mighty High Seas Fleet. In 1912 a plan was produced for a force of 70 submarines, to be completed by 1919: 36 boats would be stationed in the Heligoland Bight, defending the main bases of the surface fleet, 12 boats defending Kiel Bay, 12 for offensive operations in the North Sea, and 10 in reserve. When war broke out in August 1914, there were only 20 boats ready for operations and a further 15 working-up or under construction.

Between the commissioning of *U-1* and the outbreak or war, no less than twelve classes were built, either by the Danzig Naval Yard or by Germaniawerft, Kiel, with the sole exception of *U-2*, which was built at the Kiel Naval Yard. Each new class was an improvement, of which perhaps the most significant was the introduction of diesel engines in the U-19 class of 1912. In common with several other navies, the Imperial German Navy was impressed by Italian submarine technology and ordered a Fiat-Laurenti boat in 1913; the number of *U-42* was allocated, but the Italians requisitioned her hull on the outbreak of war and when completed she was commissioned into the Italian Navy as the *Balilla*.

World War I

On the outbreak of war U-boat operations began. On 9 August *U-15* was lying stationary on the surface carrying out repairs when she was spotted by the cruiser HMS *Birmingham*, which rammed and sank her, the first German submarine to be lost in combat. Three days later *U-13* became the first to suffer another fate, failing to return from patrol for reasons unknown. However, the U-boats also scored successes: *U-21* accounted for the cruiser HMS *Pathfinder* on 5 September 1914 off the Firth of Forth, while, in a deservedly famous encounter, *U-9* sank the cruisers HMS *Aboukir, Cressy* and *Hogue* within an hour of each other on 22 September, with a loss of 62 officers and 1,397 sailors of the Royal Navy. *U-9* struck again on 15 October, sinking another cruiser, HMS *Hawke*.

These sinkings signalled the arrival of the submarine as a weapon to be feared by surface fleets, but another, and equally significant event a few days later attracted rather less attention. This was the sinking on 20 October of the British merchantman SS *Glitra* (866 tons) by *U-17*. The U-boat captain observed the contemporary rules of engagement to the letter, boarding the steamer and ensuring that the crew were all in the lifeboats before the sea-cocks were opened. He even towed the lifeboats to within a few miles of the Norwegian shore.

As the British naval blockade of Germany began to become really effective the Germans looked with increasing urgency for ways either to break or counter it. The High Seas Fleet could do neither, because it was confined to the North Sea by the more powerful British Grand Fleet, and, while U-boats could attack British warships, they were unlikely to do so in sufficient numbers to break the blockade. It became increasingly obvious, however, that what the U-boats could do was to impose a counter-blockade on Britain by sinking merchant ships. A German Naval estimate was that some 200-250 U-boats would be needed to make such a blockade effective, but by February 1915 the navy possessed precisely 36 operational boats (*Frontboote*) in service, with a further 29 under construction.

Several steps were taken to speed the delivery of U-boats to the navy for what was still estimated to be a short war. A

Below: U-1, *first submarine of the Imperial German Navy, launched in 1906.*

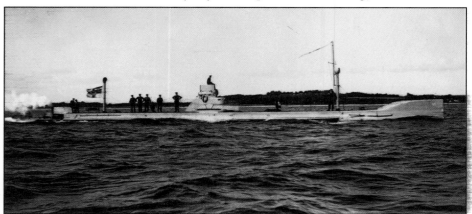

Above: *Having sunk three British cruisers on 22 September 1914, U-9 returns to base.*

Below: *The UC-16 class minelayer UC-27 sank 52 merchantmen in World War I.*

series of 'Mobilization' (Ms) programmes consisted of progressive improvements to classes already constructed. Thus, the U-51 class was based on the *U-41*, itself the last of the U-31 class, while the U-57 class was based on the U-51 class, and so on. This enabled the shipyards to make rapid progress in producing hulls, but it proved much more difficult to speed up delivery of diesel engines.

The second step was to impress boats under construction for foreign navies. This only accounted for one boat, the last of five ordered by the Norwegian navy, which was impressed as *U-A*. The third step was to produce new, small and simplified designs, which led to the U-B series of coastal attack submarines and the U-C series of coastal minelayers. The UB-1 class, for example, had a submerged displacement of 142 tons, a single shaft (thus needing only one of the scarce diesel engines) and mounted two torpedo tubes, for which four torpedoes were carried. The UC-1 minelayers were a little larger, having a displacement of 183 tons, but they, too, had only a single shaft; they carried 12 mines, but had no torpedo tubes. As always happens, both the UB- and UC- series grew in size and complexity during the war, but even the final classes were still smaller than the U-series boats.

The growing demands of the Naval Staff to attack Allied merchantmen at ever greater ranges from German ports led to larger U-boats. The U-93 class of 1916 had a submerged displacement of 1,000 tons, whilst the largest cruiser submarines actually to see service during the war were the four boats of the U-139 class, with a displacement of 2,489 tons and armed with six 19.7in (50cm) torpedo tubes (19 torpedoes) and two 5.9in (15cm) guns.

There was also an interesting attempt to break the blockade by building the seven-strong Deutschland class of submersible

merchant freighters (1,875 tons). However, only two commercial voyages were ever undertaken. The first by *Deutschland* was a success: she delivered 163 tons of dye to the USA and returned to Germany with 782 tons of urgently needed rubber, tin and nickel. The second by *Bremen* was a failure, however, as the submarine disappeared on her outward voyage. Once the USA entered the war, the purpose of these boats disappeared and the remaining boats were either converted to, or completed as warships, with two 5.9in (15cm) guns and two 19.7in (50cm) torpedo tubes. They remain, however, the only commercial trading submarines ever built.

The U-boat offensive against British shipping can be split into several phases. The first phase lasted from February to September 1915 and accounted for 365 ships (532,116grt), but was eventually called-off, primarily because Germany wanted to avoid provoking the United States into joining the war. However, spectacular results had been achieved by a very small number of U-boats. On average, less than nine were at sea on any one day during this period.

The second major phase began in February 1916 with the U-boats subjected to severe operational limitations to avoid aggravating the USA. However, on 24 March a French cross-Channel steamer was sunk off Dieppe, with the loss of 50 lives including some US citizens. Thereafter, even more stringent limits were placed on the captains; they proved so restrictive that the offensive was called off in April.

From October onwards U-boat operations re-gathered strength, and then on 1 February 1917 an unrestricted campaign began in earnest. Allied losses were appalling: 1,945,243 tons in all, of which 1,931,102 tons (977 ships) were British, in just the first three months. This onslaught

was one of the primary reasons for the US Declaration of War on 6 April 1917. Allied technical counter-measures were inadequate and, despite the best efforts of the many ASW ships, the war against the U-boats was being lost. In the end, the one counter that was effective was tactical rather than technical: the introduction of convoys, to which the Germans never found an effective answer.

The German submarine offensive was not confined to the Atlantic and North Sea, although these were the most important strategic theatres of war. A large number of small UB- and UC- types operated in the southern North Sea and the Channel, inflicting losses with both torpedoes and mines. A number of boats also operated in the Mediterranean in co-operation with the Imperial Austro-Hungarian Navy, while a flotilla operated out of Constantinople.

By the end of the war there were 179 submarines in service, with another 149 under construction. The U-boats had proved the extraordinary strategic value of the submarine, it had wrought slaughter on the high seas in an unprecedented way, particularly against the merchant marine, and had brought Great Britain to the verge of defeat. The grand total of British, Allied and neutral merchant shipping sunk by U-boats was 5,282 vessels (12,284,757grt), and *U-35* of the U-31 class remains to this day the highest scoring submarine in any navy. The cost to Germany had been 178 U-boats, 511 officers and 4,576 ratings. Unfortunately, for the Germans, the U-boat had also been one of the major causes of the United States' entry into the war, which, in the end, led to Germany's defeat.

U-Boat Losses in World Wars I and II		
CAUSE	1914-18	1939-45
Warships	61*	252
Submarines	18	25
Aircraft	1	382
Shared by aircraft and warships	—	51
Mines	34	34
Other fixed ASW defences	2	—
Merchant ships	6	—
Accidents	19	45
Unknown	37	15
Shore batteries	—	1
Totals	**178**	**805**

*Includes 11 sunk by Q-ships.

The Inter-War Years

At the conclusion of the war the Allies were determined to eliminate the U-boat menace completely and after the Armistice 176 boats were surrendered, seven foundered on their way to surrender, 149 boats under construction were broken up on the ways and 10 old boats scrapped. The surrendered boats were allocated to the Allied navies (UK, 105; France, 46; Italy, 10; Japan, 7; US, 6; Belgium, 2), although all except the French scrapped their prizes within a few years.

Despite an Allied prohibition a German submarine office was established in Den Haag, The Netherlands in July 1922, under the cover-name *NV Ingenieurskaantor voor Scheepsbouw* (IvS). Staffed by a mixture of civilians from former German submarine yards and

a naval officer, IvS was responsible for keeping its staff abreast of foreign submarine development, and they dealt with a similar clandestine office in Berlin. Although many designs were prepared, only a small number of boats were actually built in foreign yards (one in Spain and one in Finland). However, commercial success was not the object and when the time came to re-arm in 1935, the plans for renewed production in Germany were ready and new U-boats were speedily in service. The most successful of these initial designs was the Type II.

At first the size of the U-boat fleet was governed by two Naval Agreements with the United Kingdom. In the first (signed on 18 June 1935) the German Navy was limited to 35 per cent of the total tonnage of the British Commonwealth, except in submarines where she was allowed to build to 100 per cent of the tonnage, but with an agreement not to exceed 45 per cent 'unless special circumstances arise'. The second (signed 17 July 1937) reaffirmed the 1935 agreement, but went on to limit the largest U-boats to 2,000 tons and the largest U-boat gun to 5.1in (130mm).

By late 1938 Germany had reached the 45 per cent figure and at that point decided to press on with construction in order to reach parity within several years. When they informed the United Kingdom of this intention, the British accepted that it was within the terms of the agreement and let the matter rest. Hitler, however, then repudiated both treaties on 29 April 1939 and building carried on at an increasing pace under the programme known as 'Plan Z'.

World War II

On 3 September 1939 the *Kriegsmarine* disposed of 39 *Frontboote*, plus 18 in the training organisation or running trials and another six that were in the final stages of construction. The 57 in commission were grossly inadequate for the task intended for them and, in fact, on the day war was declared only 18 were at sea. Despite strict orders from Hitler for complete obedience to the Prize Regulations, *U-30* — a Type VIIA boat — sank the passenger liner *Athenia* on the very first day of the conflict, leading to the British to implement a system of convoys at once. Notwithstanding the shortage of boats, unreliable torpedoes and the

Above: *U-boats fitting-out at Krupp's Germaniawerft, Kiel in the late 1930s.*

implementation of tactics little changed from 1917, the U-boats scored successes, sinking 242 merchant ships (802,813grt) by 31 May 1940.

The period between June 1940 and March 1941 became known as the 'happy time' to German submariners when huge numbers of Allied ships were sunk. Crucial to these successes was the acquisition of forward bases on the French Atlantic coast (Brest, Lorient, St Nazaire, La Rochelle and Bordeaux) and in Norway. These bases acted, in modern parlance, as 'force multipliers' cutting out lengthy and dangerous transits around the British Isles, and effectively increasing the number of boats in the operational areas by some 25 per cent.

Operational U-Boats Commissioned 1935-45					
Type	Role	Displacement (submerged)	Commissioned	Numbers Sub-type	Total
Type IA	Atlantic	983	1936	2	2
Type IIA	Coastal	303	1935	6	
IIB	Coastal	328	1935-40	20	
IIC	Coastal	341	1938-39	9	
IID	Coastal	364	1940	15	50
Type VIIA	Atlantic	745	1936-37	10	
VIIB	Atlantic	857	1938-41	24	
VIIC	Atlantic	871	1940-44	567	
VIIC/41	Atlantic	871	1943-44	92	
VIIC/42	Atlantic	1,099	1943	2	
VIID	Minelayer	1,080	1941	6	
VIIF	Torpedo re-supply	1,181	1943	4	705
Type IXA	Atlantic	1,153	1938-39	8	
B	Atlantic	1,178	1939-40	14	
C	Atlantic	1,232	1940-42	30	
C/40	Atlantic	1,257	1942-44	111	
D/41	U-cruiser	1,799	1941-42	2	
D/42	U-cruiser	1,804	1941-44	29	194
Type XB	Minelayer	2,177	1941-43		8
Type XIV	Tanker	1,932	1941-42		10
Type XXI	Atlantic elektroboot	1,819	1944-45		123
Type XXIII	Coastal elektroboot	256	1944-45		35
Estimated commissioned in 1945*			1945		65
Total					1,192

*Due to the chaotic conditions in Germany in early 1945 and the destruction of records, the actual numbers commissioned and their individual types has never been reliably established.

The U-boats sought to counter British convoy tactics by operating in 'wolf-packs', which, under favourable conditions, could wreak havoc. However, it is important to realize that throughout this period the U-boats' favoured tactic was to attack *on the surface* and only to submerge if forced to do so by Allied surface escorts or aircraft. The fact was that, like all contemporary submarines, the U-boats' underwater speed and endurance were extremely limited and they were still effectively submersible torpedo boats. Transits were also carried out on the surface, as far as possible. For example, *U-123* travelled from Lorient, France to the US eastern seaboard between 23 December 1941 and 9 January 1942; during that time she covered 2,597nm, of which just 50nm (1.93 per cent of the total distance) were submerged.

The brunt of the U-boat war was borne by the two classes of 'Atlantic boats': the Type VII and the slightly larger Type IX. These were supported by the much smaller Type IIs, diminutive boats which, despite their size and light armament, fought a very hard war. Just eight of the large (2,177 tons submerged displacement) Type XB minelayers were built, of which six were lost in action, one was transferred to Japan and one survived the war to be surrendered to the Allies.

The *Kriegsmarine* also sought to replenish their U-boats at sea in order to extend their time in operational areas. The Type VIIF was developed to deliver torpedoes, whilst a new class of submarine tanker, Type XIV (1,901 tons), was produced, with a capacity of 432 tons of fuel oil. All ten built became war losses, virtually all of them destroyed with the invaluable assistance of the codebreakers who had penetrated the German Navy codes, particularly those using the Enigma machine.

The submariners of the *Kriegsmarine* prosecuted the U-boat war on an almost global basis. The primary theatre was, as in World War I, the North Atlantic, but a major campaign was fought on the East Coast of the United States. Lesser, but nevertheless fiercely fought, campaigns took place in the Mediterranean, the Black Sea, the Arctic, the South Atlantic and the Indian Ocean. A German U-boat base was even established at Penang in Malaya to provide the proper facilities for boats operating in Far East waters.

The first response to growing Allied mastery over the U-boats was a series of countermeasures. Radar detectors enabled U-boats to know when searching Allied ASW aircraft or surface ships were in the area, and the schnorkel, a Dutch invention perfected by the *Kriegsmarine*, enabled boats to recharge their batteries whilst still remaining at periscope depth. Increased anti-aircraft armament, such as quad 20mm guns, helped defend against attacking aircraft but had a devastating effect on underwater hydrodynamic resistance, and thus on speed and manoeuvrability.

It was realised by 1941 that the answer lay in developing a real submarine which could remain submerged for protracted

Above: *Type XB minelayer, U-118, about to be sunk by aircraft from USS* Bogue *off the Canary Islands, 12 June 1943.*

periods and which had a much better underwater performance. Professor Helmuth Walter sought for years to perfect an air-independent propulsion system, using hydrogen peroxide as the fuel. His first submarine using this system, designated *V-80*, was launched in January 1940 with encouraging results, which led to further trials boats and finally to the Type XVIIB. Only three of these were completed and were not operational at the war's end.

The other development lay with radical improvements to the diesel-electric submarine itself and this led to the remarkable Type XXI *Elektroboot* and the smaller, coastal Type XXIII. Fortunately for the Allies neither of these classes reached operational status in significant numbers before the end of the war.

During World War II U-boats sank 2,927 Allied merchant ships (14,915,921grt). They also sank a large number of warships, the most notable of which were the battleships HMS *Barham* and *Royal Oak*, the aircraft carriers HMS *Ark Royal, Courageous* and *Eagle*, and the escort carriers HMS *Audacity, Avenger* and SS *Block Island*.

This was achieved for a total loss (from all causes) of 805 U-boats. Some 40,000 officers and men served in the *Frontboote*, of which 28,000 — an astonishing 70 per cent — died. The most successful commander was *Korvettenkapitän* Otto Kretschmer, who sank 44 merchant ships (266,629grt) whilst in command of *U-23* and *U-99*. He was closely followed by

Wolfgang Lütz with 43 ships (225,713grt), who commanded no less than five boats. The most successful submarine was *U-48*, a Type VIIB, which, during the period September 1939 to June 1941, carried out 13 patrols (291 days at sea), during which she sank 51 merchant ships (310,407grt).

German U-Boats: Wartime Record			
GAINS		1914-18	1939-45
In commission at outbreak of war		28	57
Commissioned during the war		345	1,135
Foreign boats impressed		1	18
	Totals	374	1,210
LOSSES			
War losses		178	805
Scuttled		14	14
Interned		6	2
Ceded to other navies		5	—
	Totals	203	821

The Cold War

In 1945 the Allies were very keen once again to dispose of Germany's U-boat arm, whilst also availing themselves of the latest technology of their erstwhile foe. Consequently, the U-boats were taken over by the Allies, less those that had been scuttled by their defiant crews in the final days. One boat, *U-977*, even sailed from Norway to Argentina to avoid surrendering to the Allies, a continuously submerged passage of 66 days, under her captain, *Oberleutnant zur See* H. Schäffer. A small number were shared out and most of the remainder were assembled at Lisahally in Northern Ireland and taken out into the Atlantic where they were scuttled (Operation Deadlight).

For a time the German nation had no interest in naval matters, but with the intensification of the Cold War in the early 1950s, a new navy, the *Bundesmarine*, was created. On 15 August 1957 the former *U-2365*, a Type XXIII boat which had been raised from the bottom of the Kattegat in 1956 and refurbished, was recommissioned as the *Hai* ('Shark'), followed a month later by the similar *Hecht* ('Pike'). A Type XXI boat (*U-2540*) was also raised, which was refitted, renamed *Wilhelm Bauer* and then used for trials and training; she was registered as a civilian vessel but never became operational.

Since that time the *Bundesmarine* has developed and put into service a number of classes of U-boat, which have taken their place alongside their NATO allies, patrolling primarily in the Baltic and the North Sea. The first post-war design was the Type 201, which led to the Type 206, which will be replaced by the Type 211 in the 1990s.

The Federal Republic has also achieved remarkable successes in foreign markets. A very few submarines had been sold to overseas navies prior to 1940, but exports had never been a major consideration. In the 1960s, however, German designers entered the export market at a time when numerous smaller navies either wanted to start a submarine arm or else had such an arm which was equipped with elderly boats which needed replacing. As a result a large number of submarines have been sold abroad, principally the Type 209.

Merchant Ship Sinkings by U-Boats 1939-1945								
War Zone	1939	1940	1941	1942	1943	1944	1945	Totals
Atlantic, North Sea	147 (509,321)	513 (2,435,586)	431 (2,224,941)	1,000 (5,385,700)	310 (1,860,212)	61 (313,720)	54 (231,030)	2,516 (12,960,510)
Arctic	—	—	5 (10,733)	43 (233,858)	14 (48,750)	12 (57,978)	6 (38,494)	80 (389,813)
Mediterranean	—	5 (15,058)	18 (49,979)	58 (211,016)	66 (236,848)	12 (72,415)	—	159 (585,316)
Baltic	—	—	2 (7,304)	—	—	4 (1,650)	1 (640)	7 (9,594)
Indian Ocean	—	2 (12,223)	1 (5,757)	54 (318,899)	62 (364,494)	36 (217,545)	2 (14,312)	157 (933,230)
Pacific Ocean	—	—	—	—	—	1 (7,180)	—	1 (7,180)
Black Sea	—	—	1 (1,975)	—	5 (26,453)	1 (1,850)	—	7 (30,278)
Totals	147 (509,321)	520 (2,462,867)	458 (2,300,689)	1,155 (6,149,473)	457 (2,536,757)	127 (672,338)	63 (284,476)	2,927 (14,915,921)

Below: *The Brazilian submarine* Tupi, *built 1985-88, is one of a great number of German-designed submarines now serving in many overseas navies.*

U-1 Class

(Experimental submarine)

Displacement:
238 tons surfaced; 283 tons submerged
Performance:
Max speed 10.8kt surfaced; 8.7kt submerged
Range 1,500nm/10kt surfaced; 50nm/5kt
submerged
Maximum Operational Diving Depth:
98ft (30m)
Dimensions:
138ft 9in (42.3m) x 12ft 6in (3.8m) x 10ft 6in
(3.2m)
Machinery:
Two Körting kerosene engines, 400bhp; two
electric motors, 400shp; two shafts
Complement:
2-3 officers; 10-19 ratings
Construction:
Germaniawerft, Kiel. *U-1*. 1 boat. Launched
1906.

Above: *The Imperial German Navy's first U-boats; U-1 on the left, with U-2, U-3 and U-4 inboard. These four boats were the progenitors of the U-boat fleets which twice came within sight of a strategic victory over Allied shipping in the Atlantic.*

Below: *The two electric motors and the power distribution panel in U-1's engine-room. U-1 is preserved at the Deutsches Museum in Munich, where she has been cut in half to show just how cramped and harsh were the conditions in which the early submariners worked.*

Design: A number of submarines were designed and built in Germany during the 19th Century, but they were regarded as irrelevances by the German Naval Staff, which was intent on constructing a surface fleet to challenge the British. In 1902 the Germaniawerft, a shipyard newly bought by the steelmaker Krupp, started designing submarines. Their first boat, *Forelle*, a midget of only 17 tons submerged displacement, was demonstrated on several occasions to the Imperial German Navy, but to no avail. She was then sold to the Imperial Russian Navy, which was desperately buying submarines to defend her Pacific ports in the Russo-Japanese war, which had just started. They also ordered three larger boats from Germaniawerft, designated the Karp class.

The Imperial German Naval Staff and the State Secretary of the *Reichsmarineamt*, Admiral von Tirpitz, remained unconvinced of the value of this new weapon until well after other major navies had recognised its significance. Thus, for example, by the time the German Navy placed its order for an experimental boat on 4 April 1904, their main rivals, the Royal Navy, already had five Hollands and six A class in service, with more As building and the B class already on order.

This first submarine for the Imperial German Navy was designed by a Spanish submarine engineer, Raymondo d'Equevilley-Montjustin (who had worked with the French submarine pioneer Maxime Laubeuf) and built under the direction of the distinguished German naval engineer, Gustav Berling, at the Germaniawerft, Kiel. The design was based closely upon that of the Russian Karp class, which were being built in the same yard at the same time. In fact, the Russians complained bitterly about the length of time it took for their boats to be completed, claiming that this was due to priority being given to the German boat.

The German Naval Staff had taken note of the reports from abroad of numerous

accidents in submarines fitted with petrol engines. Accordingly, they insisted that their early classes were to be powered by kerosene (paraffin) engines; such engines were manufactured by Körting (*U-1* and *U-3* to *U-18*) and Daimler (*U-2* only). These were safer than the petrol engines, but their fuel was much more pungent and there was a major tactical penalty, as the boats left a vast white smoke trail, which could be seen for many miles, when running on the surface. Thus, from *U-19* onwards diesel engines were fitted, instead.

The particular type of kerosene engines fitted into *U-1* could not be reversed, nor their power output regulated. As a result controllable-pitch propellers were fitted, which continued to turn even when the boat was motionless.

Armament: Not surprisingly, *U-1*'s armament was very simple, being equipped with just one 17.7in (450mm) torpedo tube in the bow. One torpedo was in the tube and two reloads were carried. No other armament was ever fitted, as she was never seriously considered to be an operational boat.

Above: *Having heard of accidents abroad with petrol engines, the German Naval Staff insisted that the early U-boats were powered by the safer kerosene (paraffin) engines. One disadvantage of these, however, was that they emitted a dense white exhaust, as shown here.*

Service History: It was not until 1906 that the Imperial German Navy commissioned its first submarine, designated *Unterseeboot-1* (submarine number 1), thereby introducing a new (and ominous) word — U-Boat — into the international vocabulary. However, there was no premonition of the notoriety to come when the new boat was tested on 4 August 1906, being lowered from a floating crane to a depth of 98ft (30m) twice, first without and then with its crew. Trials started in September 1906 and were completed with the boat's commissioning on 14 December at Kiel, her first

Below: *The German submarine* U-1 *was designed by a Spaniard, Raymondo d'Equevilley-Montjustin, who had previously collaborated with Maxime Laubeuf, the French submarine pioneer. U-1's design was based on that of the Karp class, which Germaniawerft was building for the Imperial Russian Navy. At the time of* U-1*'s launch in 1906 the Royal Navy already had twenty-five submarines in service.*

commanding officer being Kapitän-Leutnant von Böhm-Bezing, IGN.

U-1 was used for many trials. In September 1907 she travelled, in bad weather, from Wilhelmshaven to Kiel, around the Skagerrak, a distance of some 487nm (900km). In 1910 *U-1* was used, in conjunction with *U-3* and *U-4*, in what were probably the first-ever tactical trials of submarines working together, a precursor of the 'wolf-pack', a tactical concept which was to reach maturity in World War Two. After many such trials *U-1* was relegated to training duties until 1919.

When she was stricken in 1920 her manufacturers, Germaniawerft, were sufficiently perceptive, despite the chaos then prevailing in post-war Germany, to buy her and present her to the Deutsches Museum at Munich. *U-1* resides in that museum to this day, cut-away to reveal her interior, one of only a few such memorials to the extraordinary hazards and dire conditions endured by the early submariners. Indeed, any observer can only be astonished by the extreme fragility and lack of sophistication of these early boats.

U-31 Class

(Patrol submarines)

Displacement:
U-31 to *U-36* 685 tons surfaced; 878 tons submerged
U-37 to *U-41* 685 tons surfaced; 824 tons submerged
Performance:
Max speed 16.4kt surfaced; 9.7kt submerged
Range 7,800nm/8kt surfaced; 80nm/5kt submerged
Maximum Operational Diving Depth:
164ft (50m)
Dimensions:
212ft 3in (64.7m) x 20ft 8in (6.3m) x 11ft 10in (3.6m)
Machinery:
Two Germaniawerft 6-cylinder, 2-stroke diesels, 1850bhp; two electric motors, 1200shp; two shafts
Complement:
4 officers; 31 ratings
Construction:
Germaniawerft, Kiel. *U-31* to *U-41*. 11 boats Launched 1914

Above: *U-33 of the U-31 class, pictured prior to the installation of a deck gun. Note the two masts to support the radio antenna and the long periscope. She survived the war to be broken up, with all other surviving U-boats, in 1919.*

Below: *Despite the Turkish flag, U-38 was serving in the Imperial German Navy when this World War I picture was taken. The animal carcasses and the sacks of rice suggest that she is setting out on a long patrol.*

Design: The U-31 class was the last of the pre-war designs and was the latest in a series of incrementally improved designs. The greatest distinction of the class is that one of its number, *U-35*, remains to this day the highest scoring submarine of any nation, while the class collectively sank an astonishing 801 enemy vessels.

On the outbreak of war the Imperial German Navy possessed precisely 20 combat-ready submarines, with a further 15 either under construction, or in commission but not yet fully operational. A hasty 'mobilization programme' was set in train to increase production rates for the anticipated short war and a number of small minelayer types were designed and built. As the U-boat campaign against Allied merchant shipping gathered momentum, however, larger types were designed and built.

Following the successful trials of *U-1*, each following class introduced improvements. The smoke-producing Körting kerosene engines were replaced by diesel engines in the U-19 class (launched 1912-1913), these new engines being built by either M.A.N. or Germaniawerft. The latter suffered from numerous problems, although these were eventually solved.

Speeds (both surfaced and submerged) were gradually increased and range extended, although underwater endurance remained very limited: in the U-31 class, for example, which was typical for its time, it was just 80nm (148km) at 5kt. There were also other less dramatic but nevertheless important improvements, such as the introduction of longer periscopes from *U-27* onwards, which greatly eased captains' problems in maintaining periscope depth.

The U-31 class was identical in dimensions to the four-strong U-23 class, apart from slightly deeper draught due to a greater displacement. All were built at

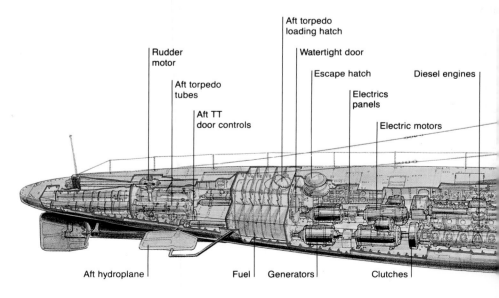

Rudder motor
Aft torpedo loading hatch
Watertight door
Aft torpedo tubes
Escape hatch
Diesel engines
Aft TT door controls
Electrics panels
Electric motors
Aft hydroplane
Fuel
Generators
Clutches

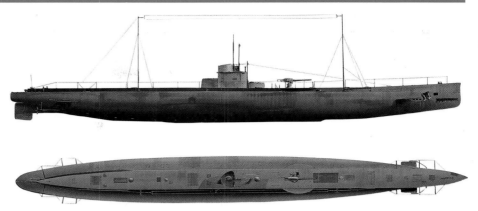

Above: U-35, *highest scoring submarine in any navy, sets out on a Mediterranean patrol in 1917. She sank 224 Allied ships, most of them while under the command of Kapitän-Leutnant Lothar von Arnauld de la Perière.*

Germaniawerft, although they were all at least six months late in delivery due to the engine problems.

Armament: Primary armament of all U-boats was the torpedo. The 17.7in (450mm) was installed from the U-1 to the U-17 classes, being replaced from the U-19 class onwards by the more powerful 19.7in (500mm). The U-19s were also the first to be fitted with stern tubes. The U-31 class was armed with four 19.7in (500mm) torpedo tubes, two in the bow and two in the stern, with a total of six torpedoes carried.

Most pre-war naval doctrine foresaw submarines being used against warships, for which torpedoes were the only practicable weapon. However, deck guns were introduced into U-boats in 1914, in order to enable them to comply with the prevailing tactical orders to halt merchant ships on the surface and allow their crews time to take to their boats. Most German

Above: *The U-31 class was armed with four 19.7in (500mm) torpedo tubes (two bows, two stern).*

boats mounted one 3.45in (88mm) KL/30 gun on a 'wet' mounting, while those which would not be rendered unstable by such provision even had two such guns. Later in the war some boats mounted 3.93in (100mm) or larger guns.

Early boats of the U-31 class had no guns, but one 3.45in (88mm) gun was added soon after commissioning. From 1916 onwards, as the campaign against Allied merchant shipping gathered pace, all surviving boats had the 88mm replaced by a 105mm (4.13in) KL-45.

Service History: This class had a busy war, with only four out of the eleven surviving to be broken up in 1919-1921 (*U-33*, *U-35*, *U-38* and *U-39*). The class as a whole destroyed 801 Allied merchantmen, with a total tonnage of 1,917,146, a significant contribution to the German naval effort.

U-35 achieved the distinction of being the highest scoring submarine of all time, sinking no less than 224 ships (535,900 gross registered tons (grt)) in the course of 25 patrols off the British and West African coasts, and in the Mediterranean. She served under four highly skilled commanding officers: Waldemar Kophamel, Ernst von Voigt, Heino von Heimberg, and Kapitän-Leutnant Lothar von Arnauld de la Perière. Kophamel sank 35 ships with a total tonnage of 89,192grt while in

command from 3 November 1914 to 17 November 1915, but his successor, de la Perière became (and remains) the highest scoring submarine captain in any navy, sinking no less than 194 ships (453,716 tons). In one three week cruise in the Mediterranean in *U-35* he sank 54 ships (91,000grt), which he achieved with the expenditure of 900 rounds of ammunition and four torpedoes! He commanded *U-35* from 18 November 1915 to March 1918, being awarded Germany's highest gallantry award, *Pour le Merite*, in October 1916, whilst still in command of *U-35*. Despite these exceptional exploits *U-35* survived the war to be broken up in 1920.

The next three most successful U-boats of World War I were also of this class:

U-39	151 ships	398,564grt
U-38	136 ships	292,977grt
U-34	120 ships	258,990grt

Of the eleven boats in the class, just four survived to the end of the war, one having been interned in El Ferrol in May 1918 and the other three surrendered after the Armistice; all were scrapped in the early 1920s. *U-37* was sunk in the Dover Barrage in 1915, while *U-32*, *U-36* and *U-41* were all sunk by British surface warships and *U-40* by a British submarine. The remaining two failed to return from patrols: *U-31* in the North Sea and *U-34* in the Mediterranean.

Below: *This cutaway of* U-31 *shows what dramatic advances had been achieved since* U-1*'s launch eight years earlier.*

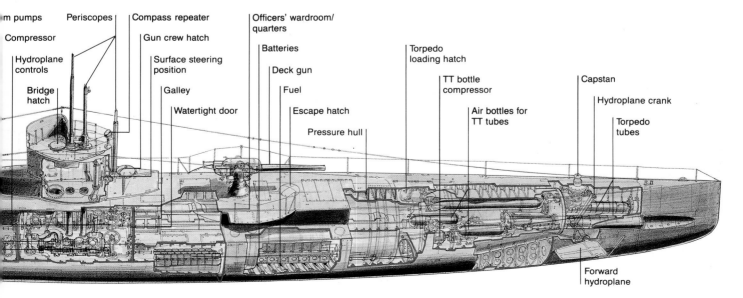

m pumps   Periscopes   Compass repeater   Officers' wardroom/quarters

Compressor   Gun crew hatch

Hydroplane controls   Surface steering position   Batteries   Torpedo loading hatch

Bridge hatch   Galley   Deck gun   TT bottle compressor   Capstan

Watertight door   Fuel   Air bottles for TT tubes   Hydroplane crank

Escape hatch   Torpedo tubes

Pressure hull

Forward hydroplane

Type II

(Coastal patrol submarines)

Displacement:
Type IIA 253.8 tons surfaced; 303.1 tons submerged
Type IIB 278.9 tons surfaced; 328.5 tons submerged
Type IIC 291 tons surfaced; 341 tons submerged
Type IID 314 tons surfaced; 364 tons submerged

Performance:
Max speed
Type IIA/B 13kt surfaced; 7kt submerged
Type IIC 12kt surfaced; 7kt submerged
Type IID 12.7kt surfaced; 7.4kt submerged
Range
Type IIA 2,000nm/8kt surfaced; 71nm/2kt submerged
Type IIB 3,900nm/8kt surfaced; 83nm/2kt submerged
Type IIC 4,200nm/8kt surfaced; 81nm/2kt submerged
Type IID 5,650nm/8kt surfaced; 100nm/2kt submerged

Maximum Operational Diving Depth:
262ft (80m)

Dimensions:
Type IIA 135ft 0in (41.19m) x 13ft 6in (4.1m) x 12ft 8in (3.85m)
Type IIB 140ft 0in (42.67m) x 13ft 6in (4.1m) x 12ft 10in (3.92m)
Type IIC 144ft 10in (44.16m) x 13ft 6in (4.1m) x 12ft 7in (3.85m)
Type IID 145ft 1in (44.23m) x 16ft 2in (4.92m) x 12ft 9in (3.89m)

Machinery:
Two Motoren Werke Mannheim (MWM) diesels, 700bhp; two electric motors, 360shp (Type IIA and IIB), 410shp (Type IIC and IID); two shafts

Complement:
3 officers; 22 ratings

Construction:

Type IIA (6 boats)	Deutsche Werke, Kiel. U-1 to U-6. 6 boats. Launched 1935	
Type IIB (20 boats)	Germaniawerft, Kiel. U-7 to U-12. U-17 to U-24. 14 boats. Launched 1935 to 1936	
	Deutsche Werke, Kiel. U-13 to U-16. 4 boats. Launched 1935 to 1936.	
	Flender Werft, Lübeck. U-120 to U-121. 2 boats (requisitioned from Chinese order). Launched 1939 to 1940	
Type IIC (8 boats)	Deutsche Werke, Kiel. U-56 to U-63. 8 boats. Launched 1937 to 1940	
Type IID (16 boats)	Deutsche Werke Kiel. U-137 to U-152. 16 boats. Launched 1939 to 1941	

Design: From the moment that the victorious Allies deprived Germany of her U-boats in 1918/19 the new navy, the *Kriegsmarine*, was determined to regain a force of the warships which had so nearly brought them victory in 1916-17. The Type II was the second in the *Kriegsmarine's* initial building plan of the early 1930s. The Type IIA was a development of the Finnish Vetehinen class design, which had, in its turn, been developed from the Type UB III of 1918. Concealed under the design code of MVB-II, once the order to proceed was given by Hitler the Type IIAs were built rapidly and *U-1* was commissioned on 29 June 1935, just *eleven* days after the signing of the Anglo-German Naval Treaty, thus making obvious just how much clandestine work had been going on.

The Type IIs, small boats which were known throughout the *Kriegsmarine* as *Einbäume*, or 'dug-out canoes', were developed through four versions, each having greater range and all intended for coastal operations in the North Sea, English Channel and Baltic areas in war. The Type IIB was simply a slightly lengthened version of the Type IIA, while the Type IIC was again enlarged to accommodate more communications equipment and to increase bunker space. The Type IID was very slightly larger again, also to provide greater bunkerage for increased range.

Armament: All boats in this class were armed with three bow-mounted 21in (533mm) torpedo tubes. They carried either five torpedoes or 18 tube-launched mines. They were originally not armed with guns, but in 1942 a single 20mm AA cannon was fitted, which was replaced in

May 1943 by a quadruple 20mm mounting, to counter the ever-increasing air threat.

Service History: The original Type IIAs were urgently required as the Navy had set up the *U-bootabwehrschule* (U-Boat Defence School) on 1 October 1933 to train the crews for the new U-boat arm, but without any boats in which to train. Once built, a number of Type IIs were always in the training flotillas in the Baltic, but many of them also saw active service during World War Two in the planned arenas of the North Sea, the English Channel and the Baltic.

In the early summer of 1942 it was decided to send three Type IIB boats (*U-9, U-19* and *U-24*) to the Black Sea. They were completely dismantled at Kiel and sent by barge through the Kiel Canal and

Below: U-58, a Type IIC. The very small Type IIs were known, somewhat disparagingly, as Einbäume (dug-out canoes) in the Kriegsmarine, but they had a good wartime operational record.

then down the river Elbe to a point near Dresden. There they were transferred to road transporters and taken along the autobahns to Ingolstadt on the Danube. At Ingolstadt they were transferred once more to barges and then moved to Linz, where they were reconstructed (except for the ballast keel) and then towed to Constanza. The entire operation took some four months, being completed in October 1942.

Hitler then ordered another three to be sent; these followed the same route, but with the additional hazard of winter to contend with! These boats (*U-18, U-20* and *U-23*) operated out of Feodosia, a captured Soviet naval base in the Crimea.

Of the fifty boats in this class, only eleven were lost in World War Two due to enemy action. Three struck mines, four were sunk by depth-charges from British ASW warships and two were sunk in harbour by aircraft bombs. Finally, two were sunk by Allied submarines, one of which, *U-144* was sunk by the Soviet submarine *Shch-307* in the Gulf of Finland (9 August 1941), one of the few to be sunk by a Soviet submarine during World War Two. Another four were lost in accidents, all due to collisions in the Baltic, a reflection of their training role.

Of the six boats in the Black Sea flotilla, one was sunk by Soviet aircraft and another two damaged, being blown up by their crews four days later as the port was being abandoned (24 August 1944). The other three boats were offered for sale to Turkey, but when this was declined they were scuttled off the Turkish coast (2 September 1944).

A number of boats were placed into reserve or scrapped in 1944 and early 1945. Others remained until May 1945 and were then either scuttled or surrendered.

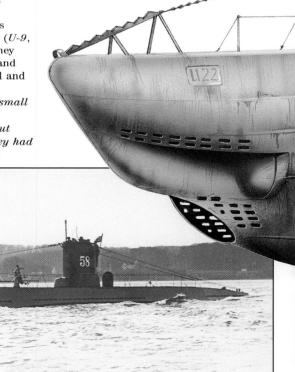

Above: U-2, *second of the Type IIA class proceeding to sea soon after her commissioning in 1935. The design was based on that of the Finnish* Vetehinen, *which in turn had been based on that of the German World War I Type UB III.*

Right: U-9 *and* U-24 *lying in a partially dismantled state on barges during their four-month transportation from Germany to the Black Sea. Three Type IIs were sent to Constanza in 1942 and a further three to Feodosia in 1943.*

Below: U-9, *a Type IIB, was armed with three bow 21in (533mm) torpedo tubes. Originally unarmed with guns, the Type IIs were later fitted with a single 20mm AA cannon (as shown here) and some even had a quad 20mm.*

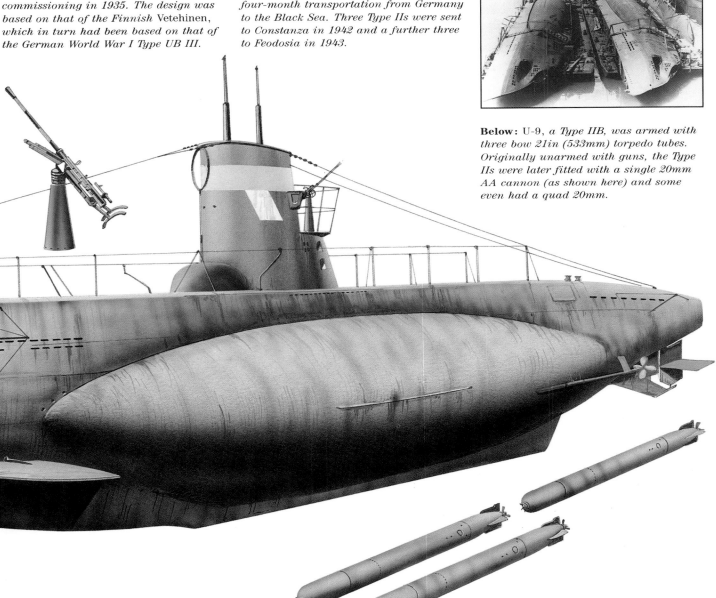

Type VII

(Ocean-going patrol submarines)

Displacement:
Type VIIA 626 tons surfaced; 745 tons submerged
Type VIIB 753 tons surfaced; 857 tons submerged
Type VIIC/C-41 769 tons surfaced; 871 tons submerged
Type VIID 965 tons surfaced; 1,080 tons submerged
Type VIIF 1,084 tons surfaced; 1,181 tons submerged

Performance:
Max speed 16.7-18.6kt surfaced; 7.3-8.0kt submerged
Range
Type VIIA 6,800nm/10kt surfaced; 130nm/2kt submerged
Type VIIB 9,400nm/10kt surfaced; 110nm/2kt submerged
Type VIIC/C-41 9,700nm/10kt surfaced; 130nm/2kt submerged
Type VIID 13,000nm/10kt surfaced; 127nm/2kt submerged
Type VIIF 13,950nm/10kt surfaced; 130nm/2kt submerged

Maximum Operational Diving Depth:
Type VIIA/B/C/C-41 328ft (100m)
Type VIIC-41 394ft (120m)
Type VIID/F 328ft (100m)

Dimensions:
Type VIIA 212ft 11in (64.89m) x 19ft 4in (5.88m) x 14ft 5in (4.39m)
Type VIIB 219ft 5in (66.88m) x 20ft 6in (6.24m) x 15ft 7in (4.74m)
Type VIIC/C-41 221ft 5in (67.49m) x 20ft 6in (6.24m) x 15ft 7in (4.74m)
Type VIID 252ft 4in (76.90m) x 20ft 11in (6.37m) x 16ft 5in (4.99m)
Type VIIF 256ft 2in (78.08m) x 23ft 11in (7.30m) x 16ft 1in (4.91m)

Machinery:
Two diesels (various types) (Type VIIA — 1,160bhp; Type VIIB/C/C-41/D/F — 1,400bhp); 2,800bhp; two electric motors, 375shp, two shafts

Complement:
4 officers; 40-42 ratings

Construction:
Type VIIA Total 10 boats. Deschimag, Bremen (6); Germaniawerft (4)
Type VIIB Total 24 boats. Germaniawerft, Kiel (15); Vulkan, Bremen (4); Flenderwerft (5)
Type VIIC/C-41 Total 675 boats. Blohm & Voss, Hamburg (181); Vulkan, Bremen (70); Schichau Werft, Danzig (64); Germaniawerft, Kiel (61); Danziger Werft (42); Flenderwerft (36); Howaldtswerke, Hamburg (33); Howaldtswerke, Kiel (32); Deutsche Werke, Kiel (30); Nordeseewerke, Kiel (30); Kriegsmarine-Werft, Wilhelmshaven (29); Flensburger Schiffbau (28); Stülcken, Hamburg (26); Neptun Werft, Rostock (10); Oder Werke, Stettin (2); Vulkan Werke, Stettin (2)
Type VIID Total 6 boats. Germaniawerft, Kiel (6)
Type VIIF Total 4 boats. Germaniawerft, Kiel (4)

Design: Once the Types I and II had been selected for production, thoughts turned to what other types would be required and designs for Types III to VII were produced. However, in late 1934 attention concentrated on a medium-sized boat developed from the Finnish *Vetehinen*, a single-hull, saddle-tank, 550 ton design with a range of 6,000nm (11,112km) at 8kt. This boat — the Type VII — was eventually produced in seven major sub-types and some 719 were commissioned between 1936 and 1945, making it one of the great submarine designs of all time.

The first Type VIIA, *U-33,* was commissioned on 25 July 1936, but the new head of the U-boat arm, Kapitän zur See Dönitz, requested improvements, which led to the Type VIIB. Priority was given to improving surface range, surface speed and torpedo-carrying capability. The hull was lengthened by 6ft 7in (2.00m), which enabled larger tanks to be fitted and the diesel engines were given superchargers, which increased the speed by 1kt, although the installation took up more internal space. Finally, twin rudders were fitted, which both improved the turning radius and also enabled the stern torpedo tube to be moved inside the pressure hull.

In a programme of continuous development the next version, Type VIIC, was slightly longer than the Type VIIB, the first being commissioned in 1940. The Type VIIC-41 was very similar to the Type VIIC, but had a strengthened hull, giving a 66ft (20m) increase in maximum operational depth to 394ft (120m).

At the start of the war it was decided to develop a specialised minelayer from the Type VIIC by adding a 32ft 2in (9.8m)

Below: *The excellent Type VIIC was the workhorse of the German submarine service throughout World War II. All versions were armed with five torpedo* tubes, four in the bow and one in the stern. Gun armament varied, but by the end of the war most had an 88mm gun and four 20mm flak in a quad mounting.

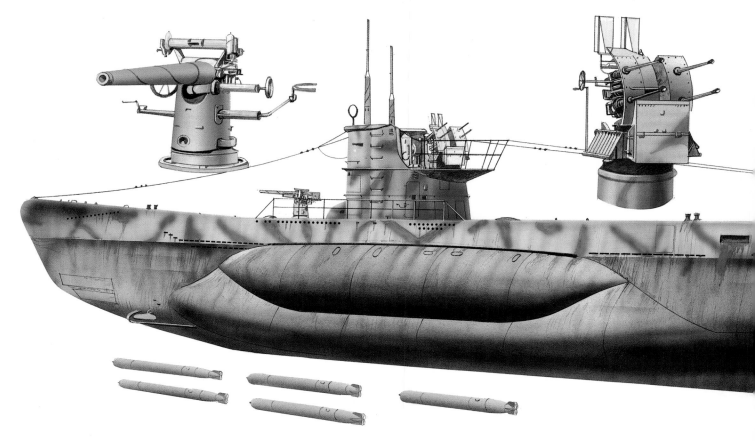

centre section to house five vertical mine tubes, each containing three SMA mines. As a bonus, this also enabled additional fuel to be carried, extending the surface range. Although the same propulsion was used as in the Type VIIC, speed was affected very little.

U-boats operating in distant waters frequently needed resupply of both fuel and torpedoes. In the early years of the war, it was occasionally possible for U-boats returning to base to transfer unexpended torpedoes at sea to an outward-bound boat, but this could only be done on an opportunity basis. So, a requirement was stated for specialised torpedo resupply boats to match the fuel supply boats (Type XIV) then being produced. The resulting Type VIIF was based on the Type VIID, but with the extra space in the centre of the boat devoted to a cargo of 21 torpedoes instead of mines (this did not affect the boat's own combat load of fourteen torpedoes). It also had rather wider saddle-tanks to increase fuel stowage for extra range and a specially widened after-deck to accommodate the working parties during the at-sea transfer process.

At least two other versions of the ubiquitous Type VII were planned. The Type VIIC-42 was a development of the Type VIIC-41, with greater length, displacement and range. A reinforced hull gave a maximum safe operating depth of no less than 920ft (280m), while an armour-plated conning-tower and numerous cannon improved anti-aircraft protection.

Above: An early Type VII at sea. 719 Type VIIs of six sub-types were commissioned between 1936 and 1945.

Armament: All versions of the Type VII were fitted with five 21in (533mm) torpedo tubes, four in the bow and one in the stern. The Type VIIA was fitted with a single rudder and thus the stern torpedo tube had to be mounted in the upper casing above the waterline. This meant that it could not be reloaded or maintained while submerged, nor could it be fired on the surface. However, the Type VIIB and all later versions had twin rudders, which enabled the stern tube to be mounted inside the hull.

The Type VIIA carried eleven torpedoes, but this was increased to fourteen in the Type B, all versions of the Type C and the Type F, although the Type D carried only twelve. The Type F also carried 21 torpedoes as freight for resupply to other U-boats.

Virtually all German U-boats could carry TMA or TMB mines (when they came into service) in place of torpedoes. Loads were: Type VIIA, 33; Type VIIB/C/C-41/D, 39; Type VIIC-42, 14. The Type VIID, which was built as a minelayer, carried 15 SMA mines. The Type VIIF carried no mines.

The original deck weapons fit was one 37mm Flak and one 20mm Flak twin. However, with wartime experience this was steadily increased. 88mm guns were mounted, flak twins were converted to quads and extra bridge-mounted machine-guns were also to be found.

Service History: Seven Type VIIAs deployed to Spain during the Civil War, but saw no action. The first sinking of a merchant vessel in World War Two was carried out by a Type VIIA when, in a notorious incident, *U-30* (Lemp) sank the British passenger liner *Athenia* (13,581grt) on 4 September 1939. The liner, en route from Liverpool to Montreal with 1,400 passengers, sank with the loss of 120 lives.

Two weeks later on 17 September *U-29* chanced upon the aircraft carrier HMS *Courageous* (27,560tons), accompanied by four destroyers. Evading the escorts, *U-29* torpedoed the carrier, which sank immediately with the loss of 515 lives.

On the outbreak of war the eight Type VIIB boats in commission were grouped in U-Flotille VII. They were quickly in the thick of the action and were used in the earliest attempts at 'wolf-pack' tactics. *U-47* (Prien) achieved one of the most notable early successes when he penetrated the British Naval base at Scapa Flow on the night of 13/14 October 1939 and sank the battleship HMS *Royal Oak* (31,250tons). Of the 24 boats in this group only four survived to the war's end and of those three were scuttled prior to capture, leaving just one, *U-101*, to surrender.

U-48, a Type VIIB, was the most successful submarine of World War Two. Between September 1939 and June 1941, when it left operational service, it undertook 13 operations, spending 291 days at sea under three captains, during which it sank 51 ships with a total displacement of 310,407 tons.

It was the Type VIIC which bore the lion's share of Germany's U-boat war, with 675 VIICs and VIIC-41s being commissioned; greater in number, by far, than any other type in submarine history. It was continuously modified in service, with schnorkels being added, *Balkon Gerät* (an early sonar device) being added under the bow, increasingly sophisticated radars and, inevitably, more anti-aircraft weapons.

Of the six Type VIIDs only one boat, *U-218*, survived to surrender in 1945. Two boats were sunk on their first operation, the others survived slightly longer. The four Type VIIFs did not have a very successful war, either. All four were located and attacked on their first patrols: three were sunk and one was able to struggle into a Norwegian port where she remained for the rest of the war.

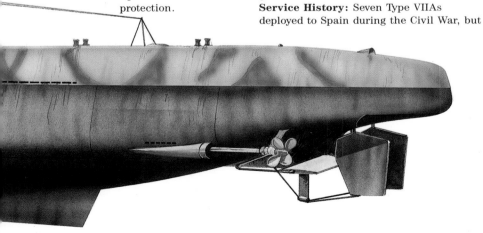

Type XXI

(Ocean-going patrol submarines)

Displacement:
1,621 tons surfaced; 1,819 tons submerged
Performance:
Max speed 15.6kt surfaced; 17.18kt submerged
Range 15,500nm/10kt surfaced; 365nm/5kt submerged
Maximum Operational Diving Depth:
443ft (135m)
Dimensions:
251ft 8in (76.70m) x 21ft 8in (6.60m) x 20ft 6in (6.24m)
Machinery:
Two M.A.N. diesels, 2,000bhp; two electric motors, 2,500shp; two 'creep' electric motors, 113shp; two shafts
Complement:
5 officers; 52 ratings
Construction:
The number of boats completed differed greatly from the number actually commissioned, as described in the Design Notes, below. However, the boats to enter service were:
Blohm & Voss, Hamburg. 262 boats ordered (*U-2501* to *U-2762*), of which 48 were completed: *U-2501* to *U-2546*; *U-2548*; *U-2551* to *U-2552*
Deschimag, Bremen. 295 boats ordered (*U-3001* to *U-3295*), of which 41 were completed: *U-3001* to *U-3041*, *U-3044* to *U-3046*
Schichau, Danzig. 195 boats ordered (*U-3501* to *U-3695*), of which 30 were completed: *U-3501* to *U-3530*.

Above: *The clean lines of the Type XXI are shown in this shot of* Wilhelm Bauer, *(ex-U-2540), which was raised after the war and recommissioned as a trials boat.*

Above: *Revolutionary prefabrication methods were used to speed construction of the desperately-needed Type XXI.*

Design: The Type XXI was one of the truly great submarine designs, which revolutionised submarine design and tactics. It was developed and constructed entirely during the war, a remarkable achievement, which was not paralleled by any of the other combatant nations who, for their own good reasons, stayed with tried and tested designs. Unfortunately for the Germans, after all the effort and the production of a significant number of Type XXIs, only one actually carried out a combat patrol before the war ended.

By the middle of 1943 German submarine losses were reaching unacceptable levels as a result of Allied improvements in ASW equipment and techniques, and it appeared to Admiral Dönitz that sonar and radar, together with the ever more effective use of ships and aircraft, were proving too much for his captains. To a large extent he was correct, although he was not to know that electronic warfare, and in particular the breaking of the Enigma code, was having a major influence in enabling the Allies to place ships and aircraft in the right place at the right time. What was needed, in the German view, was a true submarine which would be able to operate for protracted periods under water and to avoid detection by radar or sonar. It would also improve survivability if the boats could operate at considerably higher speeds and so be able to outrun surface hunters.

Professor Walter had been experimenting for some years with both streamlining and new means of propulsion, but his hydrogen peroxide powerplants proved to be too unreliable for operational use. The only alternative was to streamline the hull, reduce all protrusions to limit hydrodynamic drag, and vastly increase the battery power of the traditional diesel-electric boats. This, coupled with the schnorkel tube, anti-radar hull coatings and new sonars, resulted in a truly outstanding design, which, however, appeared too late to have any effect on the outcome of the war. This was extremely fortunate for the Allies as they had no antidote to this extraordinary design.

Armament comprised six bow torpedo tubes, with a total of 23 torpedoes. Among the many innovations was a rapid-reloading device, which enabled eighteen torpedoes to be fired in twenty minutes, if required, an unheard-of rate of fire up to that time.

The new design was based on the outer shape of the Type XVIII, but with diesel-electric propulsion. Surface propulsion was by two M.A.N supercharged six-cylinder diesels. Subsurface propulsion was by two new and powerful electric motors with an output of 2,500shp each.

Another unusual feature was the installation of two 'creep' electric motors, although this was not the first such, since a similar idea had been incorporated into the revolutionary British R-class hunter-killer submarine of 1918.

It was in their underwater performance that these boats were unique. Their designed underwater maximum speed was 17.18kt for 1 hour, but they were also capable of 110nm (204km) at 10kt, 170nm (315km) at 8kt or 365nm (676km) at 5kt. All of this was a vast increase on any contemporary submarine; the British A class, for example, could only achieve 16nm (30km) at 8kt or 90nm (167km) at

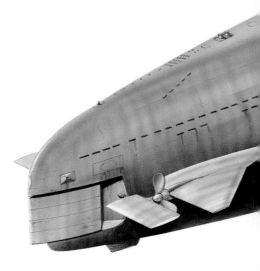

3kt. This exceptional performance by the Type XXI would have posed almost insuperable problems for Allied surface ASW warships had the German submarines reached operational status.

The construction methods also broke totally new ground. The Type XXIs were constructed in ten separate sections which were delivered to one of three yards complete, except for Section 3, which still required the diesel engines to be installed. Quite how the materials for this huge fleet of 752 boats would have been found, let alone the crews selected and trained is open to question. On top of that were the problems of regular air raids by Allied bombers, which destroyed and disrupted work at the main yards and at the many construction plants involved, as well as on the railways, roads and canals linking them.

The records for the completion and commissioning of the Type XXIs are incomplete, due to the chaotic state of the shipyards in the final stages of the war. As a result there is some disagreement on the actual numbers involved. However, it is generally accepted that some 119 submarines were launched prior to the end of hostilities (48 by Blohm & Voss, 41 by Deschimag and 30 by Schichau), with possibly some more being completed after the war in yards overrun by the Soviet Army. Of the 119, 93 are believed to have been commissioned.

Armament: There were six 21in (533mm) torpedo tubes, with no less than 17 reloads. All or part of the torpedo load could be replaced by tube-launched mines; typically, 17 torpedoes plus 12 mines. Since the Type XXI was designed to live and fight submerged, there were no deck guns, surface weaponry being confined to four 20mm or 30mm AA cannon in streamlined turrets at either end of the fin.

Service History: The pressure to get these marvellous new boats into service was intense and all concerned worked furiously over the last months of the war to achieve this. The first problem was the slowing down of German industry as Allied forces tightened their grip on the country; raw materials failed to arrive, coal supplies diminished to virtually zero and then the Russians overran the Schichau yards at Danzig. There were also regular air raids on the yards, which were increasingly successful, especially in February/March 1945, when large numbers of Type XXIs were destroyed or damaged beyond repair.

It took much longer than had been expected to train the crews, since just about everything was novel and it took a long time to integrate all the systems and work each boat and its crew up to an acceptable standard for operations. In the end precisely one Type XXI carried out an operational voyage, U-2511, and she carried out one mock attack only, because the war had ended.

Twelve of those that had been commissioned were destroyed by aircraft whilst in port: five in Hamburg, four in Kiel and one each in Bremen, Lübeck and Wilhelmshaven. Another four were so severely damaged in raids that they had to be scuttled.

Seven submarines were destroyed by aircraft whilst at sea in the Baltic and the Kattegat. Mines also accounted for three, all in the Baltic. 61 were scuttled, leaving only eleven boats to be surrendered in May 1945.

Naturally, the victorious Allies were intensely curious about these impressive new boats. In the division of spoils four went to the Royal Navy, four to the USSR, two to the US Navy and one to France. U-2540, which had been sunk in an air attack, was later raised by the new West German Navy, rebuilt and recommissioned as the *civilian* trials submarine *Wilhelm Bauer*. Another, U-3503, was raised and very carefully examined by the Royal Swedish Navy before being scrapped.

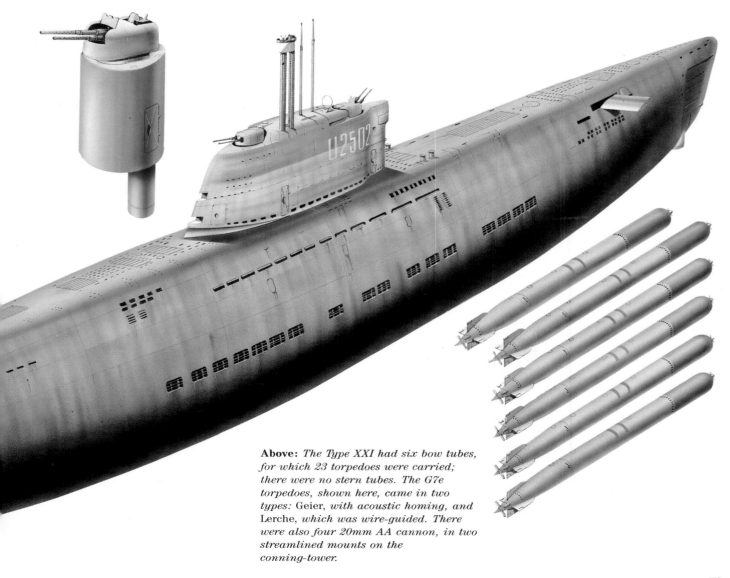

Above: *The Type XXI had six bow tubes, for which 23 torpedoes were carried; there were no stern tubes. The G7e torpedoes, shown here, came in two types:* Geier, *with acoustic homing, and* Lerche, *which was wire-guided. There were also four 20mm AA cannon, in two streamlined mounts on the conning-tower.*

Type 206

(Ocean-going patrol submarines)

Displacement:
German 450 tons surfaced; 500 tons submerged
Vickers 420 tons surfaced; 600 tons submerged

Performance:
Max speed 10kt surfaced; 17.5kt submerged
Range 4,500nm/5kt surfaced (schnorkel);
200nm/5kt submerged

Maximum Operational Diving Depth:
492ft (150m)

Dimensions:
German 159ft 6in (48.64m) x 15ft 0in (4.6m) x 14ft 0in (4.3m)
Vickers 147ft 8in (45.0m) x 15ft 5in (4.7m) x 12ft 6in (3.8m)

Machinery:
German Two MTU 12V493AZ diesels, 1,200bhp; one Siemens electric motor, 2,300shp; one shaft
Vickers Two MTU 12V493TY60 diesels, 1,200bhp; one AEG generator; one Siemens electric motor, 1,800shp; one shaft.

Complement:
German 4 officers; 17 ratings
Vickers 4 officers, 18 ratings

Construction:
Howaldtswerke-Deutsche Werft, Kiel. 8 boats. *U-13, U-15, U-17, U-19, U-21, U-25, U-27, U-29.* Launched 1971 to 1973.
Rheinstahl-Nordseewerke, Emden. 10 boats. *U-14, U-16, U-18, U-20, U-22, U-23, U-24, U-26, U-28, U-30.* Launched 1972 to 1974.
Vickers, Barrow, UK. 3 boats. *Gal, Tanin, Rahav.* Launched 1975 to 1977.

Design: When submarine construction was permitted to the post-war *Bundesmarine* an upper limit of 350 tons was initially imposed. This constraint taxed the ingenuity of the designers who were compelled to rethink submarine constraints *ab initio,* although, of course, experience gained with the wartime submarines was of great value.

The operational requirement was prepared with great care. As the new submarines were intended primarily for operations in the Baltic, endurance assumed a low priority, while the poor acoustic conditions in these shallow waters meant that high-powered, long-range sensors would be of limited value. What was needed was a small, agile submarine capable of operating submerged for long periods and with a powerful battery of torpedoes to cope with the multiple targets which were expected in the event of a Warsaw Pact amphibious landing.

The first post-war design, the Type 201, was constructed of a special anti-magnetic steel, but this was quickly found to suffer from serious corrosion and the last nine boats of the class were therefore rebuilt under the new designation, Type 205. Two boats, known as the Improved Type 205, were built in Denmark as the Narvhalen class.

In 1962 the upper limit for tonnage was raised to 450 tons and the *Bundesmarine* embarked on the design of an improved

class, the Type 206, which would take into account experience with the earlier boats and also incorporate improvements in sensors and weapons. Design work was undertaken in Ingenieurkonto Lübeck (IKL). The hull was based on that of the earlier types and the need to keep displacement within the 450 ton limit resulted in a single-hull design with the main ballast tanks at the fore and after ends of the submarine. The large fin, with a prominent bridge at its forward end, was in part a concession to the need for surface transits in peacetime, but was also needed to accommodate the full complement of retractable masts. The near circular bow accommodated no less than eight 'swim-out' tubes, a launch method which saved weight. Eight reloads were carried.

A single-deck layout was used in the forward part of the boat, with the control-room directly abaft the crew spaces and the battery compartments beneath. The silver-zinc battery cell has twice the capacity of other cells of the period and a very fast reload cycle, which requires shorter schnorkelling periods, thus reducing demands on the crew and making the submarine more difficult to detect.

A particulary ingenious solution was adopted for the provision of quick-reaction control surfaces. The forward hydroplanes

are curved and fully retractable, being used alternatively, one to produce a bow-up and the other a bow-down attitude. The after planes are integrated with the stabilisation fin, with the rudder abaft the single propeller.

Three boats to a slightly modified design were produced by the British firm of Vickers for the Israeli Navy. There were small differences in the specification and in the armament.

Armament: The eight bow tubes are of 26in (660mm) diameter, but fire 21in (533mm) torpedoes. Early German post-war torpedoes were of the free-running type, but the Type 206 was designed to fire a new generation of wire-guided torpedoes. *Seeal*, a heavyweight anti-ship torpedo was 21ft (6.4m) long and had a range of 7nm (13km) at 35kt. *Seeschlange*, a wire-guided anti-submarine torpedo based on the US Navy's Mark 37, was also used. Both were later superseded by the SUT (Surface/Underwater Target) heavyweight torpedo, which has a length of 22ft (6.7m) and can be fired against both surface ships and submarines. In addition to the torpedoes the Type 206 can carry 24 mines in GRP containers strapped around the hull.

The Vickers-constructed boats for the Israeli Navy are also equipped with eight

Above: U-12, *a Type 205 submarine of the Federal German Navy. Early boats of this class were built of poor anti-* *magnetic steel and had short lives. The remaining boats are constructed of a new, more satisfactory steel.*

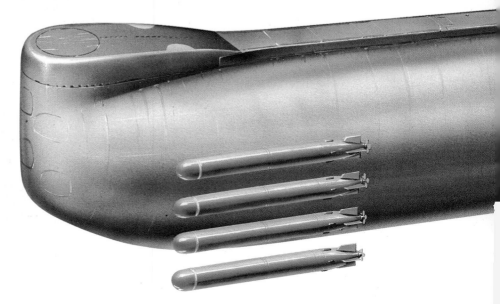

bow tubes, but these are designed to launch US-supplied NT-37E torpedoes and the Sub-Harpoon missile. These boats were fitted to take the Vickers Submarine-Launched Air-Defence Missile (SLAM) system, which features a quadruple Blowpipe launcher mounted in the fin. However, no such launchers have actually been mounted.

Service History: Eighteen Type 206 submarines were built for the *Bundesmarine*, construction being shared between Howaldtswerke, Kiel (eight boats) and Rheinstahl-Nordseewerke, Emden (ten boats). The first was commissioned on 19 April 1973 and the last on 13 March 1975.

A modernisation programme for twelve out of the eighteen German boats was started in 1987 and will be completed in 1992. The resulting boats, designated Type 206A, have the combat system replaced by a modern development and they are also fitted for the new DM 2A3 torpedo. Masts and antennas are being replaced and the Combat Information Centre (CIC) laid out in a more ergonomic fashion.

The Israeli boats have also been modernised and are likely to remain in service well into the next century. This is despite the announcement that they were to be supplemented by new construction boats in the 1990s.

Above: U-29, *a Type 206. The large bow sonar dome is mounted on top of the torpedo tubes. The design of these boats has been optimised for NATO operations in the Baltic and North Seas.*

Below: U-10, *a Type 205, photographed in 1981. Once the problems with the original anti-magnetic steel in the early boats had been resolved, this class has proved successful in service.*

Above: U-16, *the fourth Type 206 to be completed. These submarines are armed with eight tubes, for which 16 torpedoes are carried. Tube-launched mines can be carried instead of torpedoes, but a new 'mine-belt' has been developed to enable 24 mines to be carried as well as the normal complement of torpedoes.*

Type 209

(Ocean-going patrol submarines)

Displacement:
Argentina, Greece, Peru 980 tons surfaced;
1,230 tons submerged
Indonesia 980 tons surfaced; 1,440 tons
submerged
Colombia, Turkey, Venezuela 990 tons surfaced;
1,290 tons submerged
Chile, Ecuador 1,285 tons surfaced; 1,390 tons
submerged
Brazil 1,400 tons surfaced; 1,900 tons
submerged
India 1,450 tons surfaced; 1,860 tons
submerged

Performance:
Maximum Speed
Argentina 11kt surfaced; 23kt submerged
Brazil, Colombia, Peru, Turkey, Venuzeula 11kt
surfaced; 21.5kt submerged
Chile, Ecuador, Indonesia 10kt surfaced; 22kt
submerged
Greece 12kt surfaced; 22kt submerged
India 11kt surfaced; 22.5kt submerged
Range
Argentina 6,000nm/8kt (schnorkel) surfaced;
230nm/8kt submerged
Brazil, Colombia, Chile, Ecuador, Greece,
Indonesia, Peru 8,200nm/8kt surfaced;
400nm/4kt submerged
India 13,000nm/10kt surfaced; 524nm/4kt
submerged
Turkey, Venezuela 7,800nm/8kt surfaced;
400nm/4kt submerged

Maximum Operational Diving Depth:
820ft (250m)

Dimensions:
Argentina 183ft 5in (55.9m) x 20ft 4in (6.2m) x
18ft 0in (5.5m)
Brazil, Chile, Indonesia 200ft 2in (61.0m) x 20ft
4in (6.2m) x 18ft 0in (5.5m)

Ecuador 195ft 3in (59.5m) x 20ft 4in (6.2m) x
18ft 0in (5.5m)
Greece (1st 4) 180ft 5in (55.0m) x 21ft 8in (6.6m)
x 19ft 4in (5.9m)
(2nd 4) 184ft 1in (56.1m) x 21ft 8in (6.6m) x 19ft
5in (5.9m)
India 211ft 3in (64.4m) x 21ft 4in (6.5m) x 20ft 4in
(6.2m)
Peru 178ft 6in (54.4m) x 20ft 4in (6.2m) x 18ft
0in (5.5m)
Colombia, Turkey, Venezuela 184ft 7in (56.1m) x
20ft 4in (6.2m) x 18ft 0in (5.5m)

Machinery:
Four MTU 12V493TY60 diesels, 1,200bhp; four
405kw generators, one Siemens electric motor,
(Indian and Indonesian boats, *two* electric
motors) 5,000 shp; one shaft

Complement:
Argentina, Colombia, Chile, Ecuador, Greece,
Peru, Venezuela 5 officers, 26 ratings
Brazil 5 officers, 25 ratings
India 8 officers, 28 ratings
Indonesia 6 officers, 28 ratings
Turkey 6 officers, 27 ratings

Construction:
Howaldtswerke-Deutsche Werft, Kiel. 30 boats.
Argentina: *Salta, San Luis.* Launched 1972/73
Brazil: *Tupi.* Launched 1987
Chile: *Thomson, Simpson.* Launched 1982/83
Colombia: *Pijao, Tayrona.* Launched 1974
Ecuador: *Shyri, Huancavilca.* Launched 1977/78
Greece: *Glavkos, Nereus, Triton, Proteus.*
Launched 1971 to 1972.
Poseidon, Amphitrite, Okeanos, Pontos.
Launched 1979 to 1980.
India: *Shishumar, Shankush.* Launched 1984.
Indonesia: *Cakra, Nanggala.* Launched 1980.
Peru: *Casma, Antofagasta, Pisagua, Chipana,
Islay, Arica.* Launched 1973 to 1981.
Turkey: *Atilay, Saldiray, Batiray.* Launched 1974
to 1977.
Venezuela: *Sabalo, Carite.* Launched 1975.
Ast Ilha das Cobras, Rio. Three boats. *Tamoio,
Timbira, Tabajos.* Launched 199?
Mazagon DY, Bombay. Two boats. To be
launched 1991.
Gölcük, NSY, Turkey. Four boats. *Yildiray,
Doganay, Titiray, Dolunay.* Launched 1979 to
1990.

Design: The Type 209 is similar in shape
and layout to the Type 205, but has
increased dimensions, greater battery
capacity and more powerful propulsion.
The hull is exceptionally smooth, with
retractable hydroplanes mounted low on
the bows, cruciform after control surfaces
and a single propeller. Careful hull design
and powerful motors result in an
astonishing 'burst' speed of 23kt. They are
designed for patrols of up to 50 days'
duration.

The Type 209 has proved very attractive
to some eleven navies to date, many of
which have placed repeat orders. At heart,
of course, it is a very effective design. It is
also a very flexible design and the
variations in the specifications above show
how IKL have been able to tailor the
design to the specific needs of each navy.
Just one example is that the boats for
Chile have a fin and masts some 1ft 8in
(0.5m) taller than normal to cope with the
heavy seas encountered in the Chilean
Navy's operating areas.

The boats for the Indian Navy have a
central bulkhead, dividing the hull into
two watertight compartments. They are
also fitted with the IKL-developed 'crew
rescue sphere', which enables up to 40
men to escape simultaneously from a
stricken submarine.

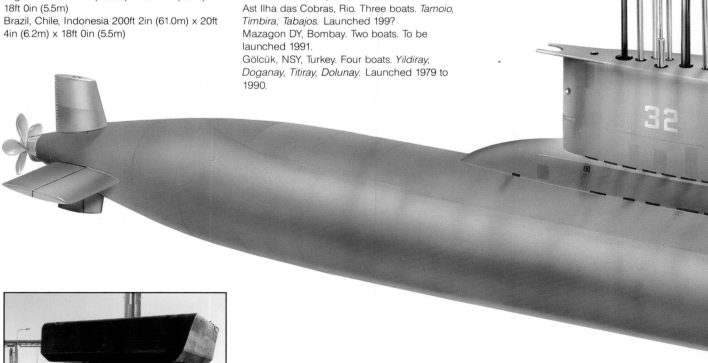

Left: *The Gabler rescue sphere enables 40
men to escape from a sunken submarine
and is fitted in the Indian Navy's
Shishumar (Type 209-SSK 1500) class.*

Above: San Luis *of the Argentine Navy.
The Type 209 has eight swim-out tubes
capable of firing any torpedo of 21in
(533mm) diameter (SST-4 shown here).*

Above: *The Type 209 has exceptional underwater performance and requires only a crew of about 30, making it an attractive proposition for small navies.*

Below: *Tupi (S-30) of the Brazilian Navy running trials. The first of class was built in Germany, while the remainder are being built in Brazil to establish a submarine-construction capability.*

Above: *The German-designed Type 209 is the most successful post-war diesel-electric submarine and has been exported to many countries in Europe, the Far East and Latin America.*

A further attraction is IKL's espousal of 'technology transfer', enabling countries to construct their own boats, usually from sections and components supplied by Howaldtswerke.

Armament: The Type 209 is armed with eight 21in (533mm) torpedo tubes, all mounted in the bow. The launch system employs the 'swim-out' technique, which is lighter, takes up less space, is easier to operate, creates less noise and most importantly, does not produce an air-bubble, which could disclose the submarine's position. Most navies use the German SUT dual-purpose torpedo, together with the US NT-37E. The Chilean Navy also uses the Whitehead A-184. The Brazilian Navy uses none of these, equipping its boats solely with the British Mark 24 Mod 1 Tigerfish, instead.

As far as is known no Type 209 has been adapted to take the US Navy Sub-Harpoon, although there is no technical reason why this weapon could not be launched.

Service History: The Type 209 submarines have already been taken into service by eleven navies and the number may well increase. The first country to place an order, Argentina, is the only one to have used the type in actual combat, when the *San Luis* was deployed against the British Task Force in the South Atlantic during the 1982 Falklands War. She reportedly managed to approach very close and launched several torpedoes, but without scoring any hits. The same reports suggest that the reason for the misses was that the submarine was deeper than the maximum operating depth of the torpedoes, but this has never been confirmed. Even though she scored no hits the presence of the submarine was known to the Task Force and forced the Royal Navy to expend a great deal of effort on ASW operations.

All navies operating the Type 209 update them regularly, installing new electronics and weapons systems to keep them abreast of the latest advances in technology.

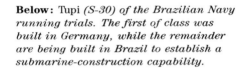

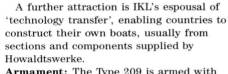

BRITAIN

In the 19th Century Great Britain possessed the most powerful navy in the world, the strength of which in the latter half of the century, lay predominantly in its large fleet of battleships: huge, armoured monsters armed with large calibre guns. To such a strategic force the concept of a small vessel, crewed by a few men and which could approach a fleet stealthily underwater, was bound to be anathema, because it threatened their very existence. Thus, the whole concept of submarine warfare was treated with contempt and pioneers such as Holland, Nordenfelt and Garrett dismissed out of hand.

Interest began to increase in the 1890s and a wary eye was kept on developments abroad, particularly those in France, although nothing was done to encourage any development work in Britain itself. Then John P Holland produced a viable craft and the Admiralty was forced to take a real interest. Events then moved with surprising rapidity, so much so that by the time of the outbreak of World War I, no less than 87 submarines of six different classes had been produced.

The Holland boats were constructed in the USA by the Electric Boat Company and their first order from the US Navy was placed in April 1900. The British firm of Vickers obtained a 25-year licence to produce the Holland submarines and five boats were ordered for the Royal Navy, being commissioned in 1903 as the Holland class. Armed with one 18in (457mm) torpedo tube and with a crew of two officers and six ratings, they were highly effective. None was lost during its service life, although *No 1* sank under tow to the scrapyard in 1913; however, she was raised in 1981 and today lies at the Royal Navy Submarine Museum in Gosport, a proud reminder of the days when submarines were considered dangerous toys by most admirals.

The much improved A class was ordered in late 1901, thirteen boats being delivered in 1902-03. The B class (316 tons) of

Above: *Royal Navy submarine No 2, one of five built by Vickers in 1901/02.*

1905-06 was armed with two torpedo tubes and was the first to be equipped with both forward and after hydroplanes, giving much improved control; eleven were built. No less than 38 C class were delivered between 1906 and 1910, with, for the first time, some being built at a yard other than Vickers at Barrow: Chatham Dockyard. However, even this class was still only considered suitable for harbour and (perhaps) coastal defence tasks, and they were still powered by dangerous and unpopular petrol engines.

By 1905 the Royal Navy had started to think of using submarines in a more positive manner and wanted a vessel which could take the war to the enemy. This role required a larger, more seaworthy, more reliable and more habitable boat, with a heavier armament. The result was the D class (620 tons), with a surface range of 2,500nm (4,630km) at 10 knots, armed with three torpedo tubes (two bow, one stern) and powered by two diesel engines. But, so rapid were developments that only eight D class submarines were built before production ceased and a new and even better type, the E class, was being produced.

Below: *The growth in size is clearly shown by (from right to left) HM Submarines A-5, B-1, C-35, D-2 and E-1.*

World War I

The efforts of the Submarine Service in World War I were marked by adventurous and aggressive tactics, many days of frustrating patrols, unreliable torpedoes and high losses. The Admiralty's highest priority task was submarine patrols in the North Sea watching for the German High Seas Fleet, which resulted in a large number of boats carrying out many fairly frustrating patrols, although over half the total submarine losses of the war were incurred in those restricted waters. Repeated efforts were made to find a way of direct co-operation between the Grand Fleet and 'fleet submarines', but all concerned eventually admitted that this was an impracticable dream.

Far greater success was achieved by a very small force of four C class and five E class boats in the Baltic, operating out of Kronstadt in co-operation with the Imperial Russian Navy. They achieved some major successes, particularly against the iron-ore traffic running from Sweden to Germany, but in the end the surviving seven boats had to be scuttled to avoid them falling into the hands of the Communist forces, following the Russian Revolution.

In the Middle East a small force of nine British and four French submarines operated against Turkey from 1914 to early 1916, sinking one elderly battleship, one destroyer, 11 transports, 44 merchantmen and no less than 148 sailing vessels. These operations were carried out in the Sea of

Marmora from bases in the Aegean, which meant that the submarines had to run the gauntlet of the heavily defended Dardanelles twice on every patrol.

At the start of the war the submarine was an untested weapon in the Royal Navy, although front-line strength was no less than 78 boats. By the end of the war they were an established component of naval strength. However, despite heroic endeavours in home waters, their major contributions in the war were in two relatively distant theatres: the Baltic and the Middle East.

The development of submarines during the war followed an erratic and wasteful path, due in part to the dynamic First Sea Lord, Fisher, whose misguided enthusiasms were difficult for his subordinates to control. The navy felt a desire to test foreign designs and two types were built one to an Italian Fiat-Laurenti design (S class, three built) the other to a Laubeuf design from France (W class, four built). Both classes were complete failures in British service.

Two other 'one off' designs, *Nautilus* and the steam-driven *Swordfish* never even reached operational status, while the V class (486 tons), double-hulled, harbour-defence boats, were barely adequate in service and only four were built.

The M class monitors, of which three were eventually completed, were armed with a 12in (305mm) gun in response to a proposal from the powerful Admiral Fisher. They proved to be failures, not least because nobody could define a role for them.

There were successes, however. When war broke out in August 1914 Admiral Fisher encouraged the First Lord of the Admiralty, Winston Churchill, to introduce the 'War Emergency Programme' in November 1914, which required a large number of submarines to be built within two years. Thirty-eight more E class were ordered and orders were placed with Bethlehem Steel in the US for 20 H class submarines, which were delivered in just seven months. So good was the design that another 33 were constructed in Britain (H 21 class). These boats remained in service for many years, nine still being operational on the outbreak of World War II.

The L class, an all-round improvement on the E class was built between 1917 and

Top: *The British K class was one of many attempts to design a submarine capable of operating with the surface fleet.*

Above: *The exceptional British R class of 1917 was the progenitor of all modern high-speed ASW submarines.*

1925. Group I had six 18in (457mm) tubes, four in the bow and two amidships, as in the E class. Group II boats achieved a very odd compromise with a bow battery of four of the new 21in (533mm) tubes, while retaining two beam 18in (457mm) tubes. Finally, the overriding value of the heaviest possible bow salvo was at last identified and the Group III boats had an armament of six 21in (533mm) tubes, all in the bow.

A curious mix of torpedo calibres was installed in the G class (837 tons) overseas submarines, fourteen of which had been ordered in November 1914. These had four 18in (457mm) tubes (two bow, two beam), but with a single 21in (533mm) stern tube. They were not a great success during the war, although they sank two U-boats in the North Sea for the loss of three of their own number.

By the start of the war all new British overseas submarines were being fitted with guns during construction, although for some time these were on complex and heavy 'disappearing' mounts. Later it was realised that the 'wet' gun on a fixed mount could be brought into action more quickly and also saved vital top-weight.

A role was sought for submarines in support of the battlefleets, which led to the 'fleet-submarine', intended to have the range and speed to keep up with battleships, as well as a strong armament to play a useful role in any engagement. The Royal Navy was not alone in this, the United States' and Japanese navies both pursuing this same, elusive goal.

The first fleet submarines were six J class, completed in 1916, with three diesels and three propellers. The fastest diesel-propelled submarines of the war they could still only achieve 19kt, instead of the 21 required. Displacing 1,820 tons and with a surface range of 5,000nm (9,260km) at 12.5kt they were the largest submarines yet built for the Royal Navy and with the longest range.

Nevertheless, they could not perform their intended role and were redesignated 'overseas submarines'.

The K class were even larger, displacing 2,565 tons, mounting ten 18in (457mm) torpedo tubes, two 4in (102mm) and one 3in (76mm) guns and with a surface speed of 24kt, which was achieved by using steam propulsion on the surface. They were very unsatisfactory, being poor sea-boats, with unbearably hot engine-rooms, slow to dive and suffering numerous minor problems. They were not very manoeuvrable, were difficult to see (especially at night) and suffered from limited visibility. In the disastrous 'Battle of May Island' (31 January 1918) two flotillas of K boats, part of a force of some 40 ships of the Grand Fleet, departed the Forth at night on exercise. In a series of complicated rammings two K-boats were sunk and three were badly damaged, together with a light cruiser. Over one hundred men died in what, with hindsight, was an avoidable tragedy.

The German Navy developed submarine minelayers and the British followed with six converted E class, which had ten vertical tubes in each ballast tank, one mine in each tube. There were also six converted L class, also with vertical tubes, but these were too late for the war and, since the preferred method of minelaying had changed to horizontal conveyor belts, as in the Russian *Krab*, they were never employed in the role, either.

British Submarine Losses 1914-1918						
CAUSE	1914	1915	1916	1917	1918	Totals
Aircraft					1	1
Surface ships	1		1		1	3
Submarines	1	2	1	2	1	7
Mines	1	4	4	1	2	12
Shore guns					1	1
Operational losses		1	1	2	3	7
Interned		1	1			2
Scuttled to avoid capture		1		1	7	9
Sunk in error Airship					1	1
Surface ship				1	1	2
Unknown	1	1	3	1	3	9
Totals	**4**	**10**	**11**	**8**	**21**	**54**

Inter-War Years

The two major events of the inter-war years for navies were the two naval conferences: in Washington in 1922 and in London in 1930. The British made strenuous efforts at both to get submarines banned altogether, a ploy which no other nation was prepared to concede, although some minor limits in size and weapons were agreed.

Despite these proposals the British continued to build submarines, concentrating on a series of very similar boats, intended primarily for long-range patrols on the China Station, each class representing a minor imrpovement on the previous class. This started with *Oberon* (1,892 tons) in 1927, followed by two of the very similar Otway class for Australia (given to the Royal Navy as free gifts in 1931). Then came six Odin class (2,038 tons) in 1929-30, with six virtual repeats in 1930-31, the Parthian class, and another very similar series, the four-boat Rainbow class in 1930-32.

Attention in the 1930s turned more towards Europe and a slightly smaller series of patrol submarines was started with the Swordfish class (927 tons), the first of which was completed in 1932 and which led into the very successful 'S' series, of which 62 were eventually built. These were intended for operations in the North Sea and the Mediterranean, but, as so often happens in British military equipment, ended up much further afield!

Like many other navies the British also produced a number of experimental submarines in the inter-war years as they sought to derive maximum benefit from the experiences of World War I. Early in the 1920s the *X-1* cruiser submarine was produced, but she was not only extremely unreliable but also failed to find a role and quietly disappeared. Despite the experiences with the K class during the war one more, *K-26*, was completed in 1923 and served until 1931. Two of the M class were converted, *M-2* being given a hangar to carry a small seaplane, but was lost with all hands in 1926.

M-3 became a prototype minelayer, but, although her minelaying gear worked reasonably well, she had such appalling diving characteristics as to be positively dangerous; she was quickly disposed of. However, the trials with *M-3* led to a purpose-built minelayer, *Porpoise* (2,053 tons), which was followed by five boats of the Grampus class (2,157 tons). Of these six minelayers no less than five were lost in the war.

World War II

The Royal Navy entered World War II with 57 submarines and, as in the previous conflict, numerical deficiencies had to be made good by emergency programmes, with 168 new boats being constructed during the war. The submarines operated in home waters (mainly the North Sea), the Atlantic, the Mediterranean and the Pacific, but it was only during the German invasion of Norway and in the Mediterranean that targets were at all plentiful. British submarines sank 105 enemy warships, 475 merchantmen and approximately 400 small craft for a loss of 78 of their own number, of which no less than seven were sunk in error by friendly (!) forces.

As with the US Navy, the Royal Navy concentrated on building existing, pre-war designs, although obviously incorporating improvements gained from war experience. Indeed, just two of the purely wartime design, the A class, were completed before VJ-day. There were few technical innovations during the war, apart from the fitting of radar, and the introduction, later in the war, of all-welded hulls. Most submarines were fitted with Asdic (sonar), but this was a continuation of a pre-war programme. One distinct advantage was that British submarines had an effective and reliable torpedo, the Mark VIII, thus avoiding the problems incurred by their predecessors in World War I and which

were to dog the German and United States navies during the early years of World War II.

In the early 1930s the O and P class boats were judged to be less than satisfactory and work was started on the T class, a smaller, cheaper and simpler design. Fifty-three were built altogether in three groups: (Group I, 15, completed 1938-40; Group II, 7, completed 1941-42; Group III, 31, completed 1942-45.) The early boats were all rivetted, those in the middle of the programme were part-welded, but the final boats were all-welded. The T class served with distinction in all theatres during the war, 15 being lost. After the war only the

surviving Group III boats were retained.

The 1930s saw a great resurgence of interest in ASW in the Royal Navy, and it was necessary to replace the elderly H class boats, which were used as ASW targets. Accordingly, the Undine class (730 tons) was designed; this was originally to have been unarmed, but at a late stage it was decided to install torpedo tubes so that, in case of war, they could be deployed in the North Sea and the Mediterranean. Three boats were completed in 1938, but on the outbreak of war twelve boats of a slightly altered version — the U class, Group I — were ordered, joining the fleet in 1940-41. These were extremely successful, particularly in the Mediterranean, where *Upholder*, commanded by Lieutenant-Commander David Wanklyn, VC, DSO, sank two submarines and one destroyer, and damaged one cruiser, together with eleven merchantmen sunk and three damaged (112,000grt), the highest score for any British submarine commander. Group II was completed in 1941-43, 34 boats of an improved design, of which nine were lent to allied navies. Overall war losses for the U class boats were heavy: of the 49 built, 20 were lost.

The V class was virtually a continuation of the U class. Twenty-two were completed between 1943 and 1945, at a time when their intended theatre, the Mediterranean,

British Submarines 1939-1945

LARGE PATROL SUBMARINES

Class	Lead Boat	Displacement (tons)	In Service	Built (no)	War Losses	Remarks
Oberon	—	1,892	1927	1	—	
Oxley	—	1,872	1927	2	1	Ex-RAN
Odin	Osiris	2,038	1929	6	4	
Parthian	Perseus	2,040	1930	6	4	
Rainbow	Regent	2,015	1930	4	3	
T Group I	Triton	1,573	1938	15	9	*Thetis* lost in accident 1939. Re-commissioned 1940 as *Thunderbolt*
Group II	Thrasher	1,571	1941	7	5	
Group III	P-311	1,571	1942	31	2	
A	Amphion	1,620	1945	2	—	14 completed after end of war

MEDIUM PATROL SUBMARINES

Class	Lead Boat	Displacement (tons)	In Service	Built (no)	War Losses	Remarks
S Group I	Swordfish	927	1932	4	3	
Group II	Sealion	960	1934	8	5	
Group III	Safari	814-890	1942	50	10	

SMALL PATROL SUBMARINES

Class	Lead Boat	Displacement (tons)	In Service	Built (no)	War Losses	Remarks
H-21	—	500	1918	9	2	24 built, 9 still in service in 1939
Undine	—	730	1938	3	1	
U Group I	Utmost	732	1940	12	9	
Group II	Uproar	740	1941	34	10	
V	Venturer	740	1943	22	0	

FLEET SUBMARINES

Class	Lead Boat	Displacement (tons)	In Service	Built (no)	War Losses	Remarks
Thames	—	2,723	1932	3	1	

MINELAYING SUBMARINES

Class	Lead Boat	Displacement (tons)	In Service	Built (no)	War Losses	Remarks
L	L-14	1,065	1918	2	—	6 built, 2 remained to serve in the war
Porpoise	—	2,053	1933	1	1	
Grampus	Narwhal	2,157	1936	5	4	

British Submarine Losses 1939-1945

CAUSE	1939	1940	1941	1942	1943	1944	1945	Totals
Aircraft		2		2			2	6
Surface ships		10	4	9	7	1	1	32
Submarines		3			1			4
Mines		3	3	1	2			9
Captured		1						1
Operational losses		2	2			1		5
Sunk in error								
Submarine	1							1
Surface ship				1				1
Aircraft				1				1
Unknown	1	2	2	4	4	4	3	20
Totals	2	23	11	18	14	6	6	80

no longer needed them. Eleven were lent to foreign navies and most of the others saw out their service as ASW targets in home waters and in the Far East. One of the class, *Venturer*, was very successful, sinking five surface vessels and two U-boats, but it was the second of these, *U-864*, a Type IX-D, which represented the truly remarkable achievement. In an engagement lasting 2 hours and 40 minutes the submerged *Venturer* used only her sonar to detect and then pinpoint her target, which was also submerged throughout. The unsuspecting *U-864* was then sunk by a salvo of four torpedoes. It was the first (and is still the only) sinking of one submarine by another, where both boats have remained fully submerged throughout the engagement.

The British government was determined to play as full a role as possible in the Pacific campaign and submarines were sent out to that theatre from 1942 onwards. However, none was really suitable, especially in terms of range and habitability. Accordingly, the A class was designed specifically for the Far East; 46 were ordered but only 20 completed, only two of them before VJ-day.

The Royal Navy operated a number of foreign submarines during the war. Two out of four boats ordered by Turkey were taken over, of which one was lost in the war and the other given to Turkey in 1945. The US Navy lent three R class and six S class, all very elderly, which were used for training. One captured U-boat, *U-570*, was commissioned as *Graph* and served for a period under the White Ensign.

Post-War Developments

After the war there was the inevitable large-scale scrapping of worn-out and outdated submarines, accompanied by detailed examination of the latest German submarines, particularly the Type XXI and Type XXIII *Elektroboote*, and the Walter hydrogen-peroxide design system. This latter caused intense interest in the Royal Navy as it seemed to offer a relatively cheap method of obtaining extended underwater endurance. The surrendered *U-1407*, a Type XVIIB, was overhauled and commissioned as *Meteorite* and two new boats were later constructed with a

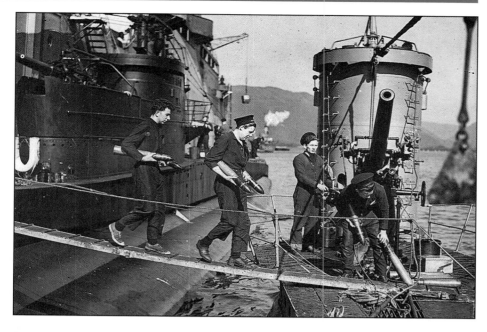

Above: *Royal Navy submarine crew load ammunition for the deck gun, in preparation for a World War II patrol.*

development of the propulsion system. After a lot of effort and expense (and some danger to the crews) it was finally recognised that this was a dead-end and all further development ceased in the mid-1960s.

Meanwhile surviving T and A class boats were given similar treatment to the United States Guppy programme, with hulls and fins being streamlined, protruding fittings eliminated or made retractable, more powerful batteries installed and schnorkels fitted. This was, however, only an interim measure pending the arrival of submarines designed from the start to the new standards. These took some time, the first of the eight-boat Porpoise class (2,100 tons) only being completed in 1958, closely followed in the 1960s by the virtually indentical Oberon class. These served for many years and it seemed likely that they would be the final class of diesel-electric

Below: *The ultimate in strategic power, HMS* Resolution, *one of four British Polaris submarines currently in service.*

submarine in the Royal Navy. However, in the 1970s it was decided to build the new Upholder class, named after the most successful British boat of World War II.

Meanwhile the Royal Navy had also turned to nuclear-propulsion, the first boat, *Dreadnought*, being completed in 1963. Since then three further classes of SSN have been produced, with a fourth class (SSN-20) due in the late 1990s. A British SSN, *Conqueror*, sank an Argentine warship in 1982, the only SSN to have sunk an enemy ship in combat.

Even more important than the SSNs are the SSBNs, the first of which, *Resolution*, became operational in 1967, since when at least one of the four Polaris submarines have been on constant deterrent patrol. The Vanguard class of Trident-armed SSBNs is now being constructed, the first-of-class being due to enter service in 1994.

Following the end of the Cold War the British government carried out a review of future defence commitments, which was published in mid-1990. This proposes a future British submarine fleet of four SSBNs, twelve SSNs and four SSKs. These will form a very capable force, but their numbers, especially of SSNs and SSKs are worryingly meagre.

E Class

(Overseas submarines)

Displacement:
Group I 652 tons surfaced; 795 tons submerged
Groups II, III 662 tons surfaced; 807 tons submerged

Performance:
Max speed 15.25kt surfaced; 9.75kt submerged
Range 3,225nm/10kt surfaced; 10nm/5kt submerged

Maximum Operational Diving Depth:
100ft (30.5m)

Dimensions:
Group I 176ft 0in (53.65m) x 22ft 6in (6.86m) x 12ft 0in (3.66m)
Groups II, III 180ft 0in (54.86m) x 22ft 6in (6.86m) x 12ft 6in (3.81m)

Machinery:
Two Vickers-Admiralty diesel engines, 1,600 bhp; two electric motors, 840shp; two shafts

Complement:
3 officers, 28 ratings

Construction:

Group I (10)	HM Dockyard, Chatham. *E-1, E-2, E-7, E-8*. Four boats. Completed 1913-14.
	Vickers, Barrow. *E-3* to *E-6. AE-1, AE-2*. Six boats. Completed 1913-14.
Group II (12)	Vickers, Barrow. *E-9* to *E-11, E-14* to *E-20*. Ten boats. Completed 1914-15.
	HM Dockyard, Chatham. *E-12, E-13*. Two boats. Completed 1914.
Group III (35)	Thirteen different yards. *E-21* to *E-27, E-29* to *E-56*. Thirty-five boats. Completed 1915-17. See Notes.

Design: The 57 'overseas' submarines of the E class were the Royal Navy's first truly formidable and reliable submarines, and became that Service's workhorse during World War I. The class was the outcome of a progressive development programme stretching back to the Holland class at the turn of the century.

The E class were enlarged and improved versions of the D class, of which ten had been built between 1908 and 1912. This had shown itself to be an excellent design, the strong hull and transverse watertight bulkheads (the first in British submarines) achieving new standards of integrity. This was proved repeatedly in the war, one boat going as deep as 245ft (74.7m) to escape from a Turkish anti-submarine net, exceeding the recommended maximum operational depth of 100ft (30.5m) by a very handsome margin!

Like all early British submarines they could dive quickly, although they still suffered from the deplorable habit of diving suddenly and totally unexpectedly when travelling at high speed on the surface. Their Vickers-Admiralty diesels, though less sophisticated than their German contemporaries, were very reliable for the time.

The E class was to have been succeeded by the yet larger G class, but these took longer to build and on the outbreak of war in 1914 it was decided to order more E class to build up the British submarine force as quickly as possible. The first eighteen boats had each taken 20-30 months to build, but *E-19*, ordered in

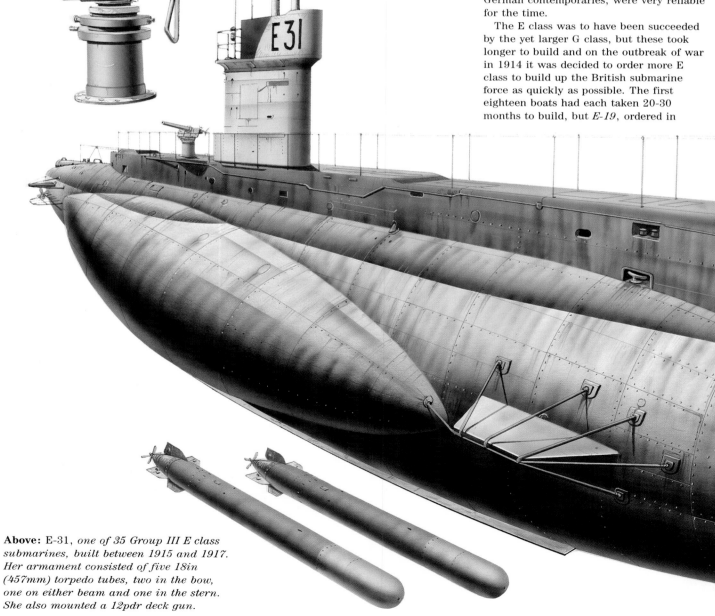

Above: *E-31, one of 35 Group III E class submarines, built between 1915 and 1917. Her armament consisted of five 18in (457mm) torpedo tubes, two in the bow, one on either beam and one in the stern. She also mounted a 12pdr deck gun.*

November 1914 took just eight months to build, fit-out and hand over to the navy!

Two Group I boats were built for the Royal Australian Navy, numbered *AE-1* and *AE-2*. Two others, *E-25* and *E-26* were originally ordered by Turkey, but were taken over by the Royal Navy during construction. Six of the Group III boats were converted into minelayers while under construction.

All British submarines up to and including the E class Group II had been built at either the Vickers Yard at Barrow or HM Dockyard, Chatham. There was, however, a clear need to broaden the

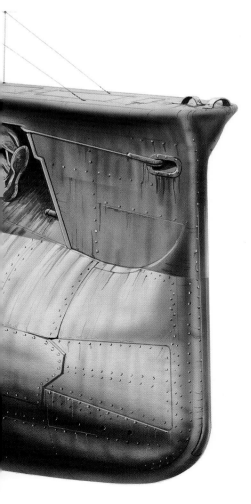

Above: *HM Submarine* E-14 *departs on patrol in April 1915. Note the high frequency (HF) radio antenna and the lack of any form of deck gun.*

production base and most of the Group III boats were built at other yards, all of them constructing submarines for the first time. Their names read like a roll-call of the British shipbuilding industry that once existed: Armstrong-Whitworth, 2; Beardmore, Dalmuir, 6; John Brown, Clydebank, 3; Cammell Laird, Birkenhead, 4; Denny, Dumbarton, 3; Fairfield, Govan, 2; Palmer, Jarrow, 2; Scotts, Greenock, 2; Swan-Hunter, Wallsend, 3; Thornycroft, Woolston, 2; Vickers, Barrow, 4; White, Cowes, 1; Yarrow, Scotstoun, 1.

Armament: Group I boats were fitted with four 18in (457mm) torpedo tubes, one in the bow, one in the stern and two in the beam, spanning the bulged lateral tanks, one firing on either beam. This latter innovation was at the urgent request of the Submarine Service who were concerned at the danger of collision with targets after firing torpedoes from the bow-tube at the very short ranges then necessary. Nevertheless, the single bow-tube was found to be a tactical disadvantage and in the Group II and III boats a second bow-tube was installed. Provision was made for one reload torpedo per tube. However, enterprising captains often lashed additional spare torpedoes to the upper casing.

Although not fitted during construction to the earlier boats, all E class boats were armed with a deck gun from about 1915 onwards. The standard weapon was a 12-pounder/40, QF (76mm), which in later boats was on a disappearing mount, although some boats had other gun types fitted. Some even mounted an additional single 2-pounder pom-pom.

The six minelayers were fitted with 20 vertical tubes mounted in the side ballast tanks, each containing one mine. These displaced the beam torpedo tubes.

Service History: The E class fought from start to finish of World War I. On the outbreak of hostilities all those then in commission were based at Harwich on the

East Coast, their operational area being the North Sea. However, some were quickly deployed to the Mediterranean where they played a very distinguished part in the campaign against Turkey. E class submarines also served in the Baltic and in the Atlantic.

Their successes included a large number of enemy warships: one battleship, three cruisers, five submarines, four torpedo boats and three gunboats, their captains earning no less than three Victoria Crosses. The price paid was equally high, 26 (46 per cent of the class) were lost during the war. Four were sunk by German U-boats, five were mined, three were sunk by gunfire from enemy warships, two were stranded on hostile shores after battles with enemy surface warships, six were lost 'causes unknown' and four of the Baltic flotilla had to be scuttled to avoid capture, following the Russian Revolution. The remaining two were operational losses, one of them being rammed by another E class submarine, the other being wrecked off the German coast. The survivors were quickly sold for scrap in the early 1920s, only *E-48* surviving (as a target) to 1928.

The two boats for the RAN were sent to Australia under their own power, by far the longest journey yet attempted by submarines. Unfortuantely, *AE-1* was lost due to unknown causes in the Bismarck Archipelago. *AE-2* returned to the Mediterranean in early 1915, where she had to be scuttled after being damaged by gunfire from a Turkish MTB.

In early 1916 German Zeppelin raids on England were causing great alarm. In an attempt to intercept them before reaching the coast two Sopwith Schneider floatplanes were mounted on *E-22*'s upper casing, the idea being that she would put to sea and then partially submerge to enable the aircraft to float off, reversing the procedure on their return. The experiment was not a success, but although she was unable to submerge, this was the first British attempt to combine submarines and aircraft, a concept which, although tried by several navies, only the Japanese were to develop into a workable proposition.

X-1 Class

(Experimental cruiser submarine)

Displacement:
3,050 tons surfaced; 3,600 tons submerged
Performance:
Max speed 20kt surfaced; 9kt submerged
Range 18,700nm/8kt surfaced; 50nm/4kt
submerged
Maximum Operational Diving Depth:
350ft (106.7m)
Dimensions:
363ft 6in (110.8m) x 29ft 10in (9.09m) x 15ft 9in
(4.8m)
Machinery:
Two Admiralty diesel engines, 6,000bhp; two
auxiliary M.A.N diesel engines, 2,600bhp; two
G.E.C electric motors, 2,400shp; two shafts
Complement:
109
Construction:
HM Dockyard, Chatham. X-1. One boat.
Completed 1925.

Design: The submarine, as a weapon of
war, reached a rapid maturity during
World War I, its most dramatic
manifestation being its use by the Imperial
Germany Navy as a strategic weapon
against the Trans-Atlantic supply routes.
The principal type of submarine both
before and during the war was the attack
submarine (usually called a 'patrol' or
'overseas' submarine in those days) armed
with torpedoes and guns, whose role was
to seek and destroy enemy warships and
merchant shipping. A second type had
appeared at the beginning of the war: the
minelayer. Pioneered by the Russians with
the *Krab,* the idea had been seized upon
and expanded first by the Germans and
then by the British.

As with any new weapon, however, once
the submarine had shown its practicability
people began to become excited by its
possibilities and a whole host of new roles
began to be dreamt up. In 1918/19 the
Royal Navy had produced the R class, the
first anti-submarine hunter/killer
(although it was not given that more
modern name then). She was also the first
submarine to be faster submerged than on
the surface. The Royal Navy, too,
experimented with the idea of a 'big gun'
(or, monitor) submarine, the M class
(1,950 tons) of 1917 being armed with one
12in (305mm) main gun, one 3in (76mm)
secondary gun and four torpedo tubes.
Conceived by the dynamic Admiral Fisher,
who was fascinated by large guns, the role
of the M class was never clear and only
three were completed.

During World War I the Germans had
introduced the idea of a 'cruiser'
submarine, of which two main types were
produced. First was the U-139 class (2,483
tons), with a surface range of 17,750nm
(32,875km) at 10kt, and armed with two
5.9in (150mm) guns and six 19.7in
(500mm) torpedo tubes with 13 reloads.
The Deutschland (U-151) class (1,875
tons), which had originally been built as
submarine freighters were also converted
to the cruiser role in 1917, armed with
two 5.9in (150mm) guns, two 3.45in
(88mm) guns and two 19.7in (500mm)
torpedo tubes. These were expected to
carry out very long-range patrols
harrassing enemy merchant shipping,
which would not only sink ships but would
also cause the enemy to dissipate its anti-
submarine resources over a much wider
area.

Such a concept of the lone submarine
roaming the world's sea-lanes, causing
havoc to enemy shipping had its attractions
and the British decided to pursue it,
ordering the *X-1* in 1921. The operational
requirement stated that the submarine
must be able to defeat any destroyer or
armed merchantman by gunfire. There
were secondary motives in the plan,
including a desire to study the underwater

Above: *When she was launched in 1925,*
X-1 *was the world's largest submarine,*
displacing 3,600 tons and designed to
defeat enemy destroyers by gunfire.

behaviour of really large submarines and
to gain experience with operating a
multiple, heavy gun armament aboard a
submarine.

Armament: *X-1*'s primary armament was
four 5.2in/42, QF, Mk 1 (132mm), which
were installed in two twin turrets, one
mounted before the bridge, the other aft,
both with unarmoured shields. A director
tower was mounted in the forward part of
the bridge, with a 9ft (2.74m) base
rangefinder just behind it; in action they
could be raised 2ft (61cm) and 9ft (2.74m)
respectively. There were elaborate
arrangements for ammunition supply,
which were never very satisfactory and the
design rate-of-fire of 6 rounds per minute
per gun was never attained in practice.

There were six 21in (533mm) torpedo
tubes with six reloads.

Interestingly, *X-1* was one of the first
submarines to be fitted with the then
highly secret Asdic device for detecting
submerged submarines.

Service History: *X-1* was laid down in
November 1921 and completed in
September 1925. She proved to be an
excellent sea-boat on the surface and
provided a stable gun platform, with the
turrets well clear of the waterline. She was
also rather better underwater than had

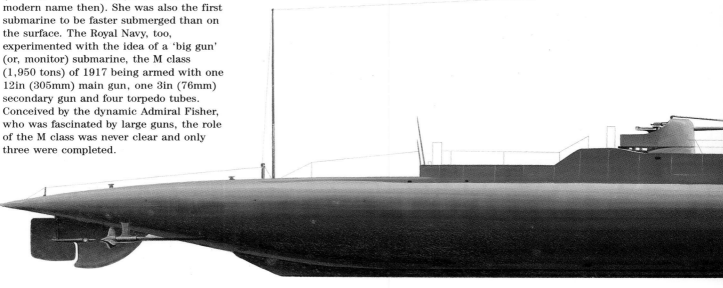

been expected, being very manoeuvrable and responsive to controls.

Unfortunately, these good qualities were offset by a number of problems. One was that she had incurable leaks in her external fuel tanks, which enabled her position and direction to be established with some accuracy by surface observers. This was a relatively common problem with rivetted submarines, but *X-1* proved to be an extreme case. In the event, this was less critical than some of her other problems, but would have been serious had she ever had to go to war.

X-1 suffered from never-ending mechanical problems with all three sources of power. Her Admiralty main diesels were a poor design, seeking to obtain far more power per cylinder than was practicable with contemporary technology; as a result they never delivered anything like the design power output. The electric motors, too, were barely adequate and needed a huge development effort even to reach that stage. She was also fitted with two auxiliary diesels for battery-charging, German M.A.N engines which had been obtained from the surrendered *U-126* and even these, despite the high reputation of German diesels, proved incapable of producing their design power output! Because of these problems the machinery proved to be extremely unreliable and breakdowns were depressingly frequent.

Above: X-1 *has a purposeful look about her, but she never saw any action and was the first British boat built since the end of World War I to be scrapped.*

On trials the gunnery arrangements proved to be good, although it was the general consensus that the basic concept was unsound and the idea of undertaking a gun duel with a destroyer was considered to be very hazardous. The only remaining mission was that of commerce-raiding, which in the case of Great Britain in the first half of this century, was a very unlikely role; other nations were far more likely to prey on Britain's world-wide commercial traffic rather than the other way around!

X-1 carried out two years of trials (1924-26) and then undertook an operational deployment with the Mediterranean Fleet for four years. She was then sent back to Britain for a refit, following which she was placed in reserve. Then, uncertain of her role and plagued by unending mechanical problems, *X-1* was stricken in 1935 and scrapped in 1936.

The British never returned to the idea of a big-gun, cruiser submarine, but the French Navy developed a similar concept in the *Surcouf*, which not only mounted a heavy gun armament, but also carried a small aircraft for reconnaissance and target spotting. However, as with *X-1* the basic concept proved unsound and no other navy pursued it further.

Below: X-1 *was a good gun platform and was quite manoeuvrable underwater, but the concept was seriously flawed. In 1935 the British Navy finally abandoned the idea of a 'big-gun' submarine.*

Above: X-1 *enters Grand Harbour, Malta, where she was based 1926-1930. The bar-like object on her bridge is the range-finder, which was raised in action for use in directing the fire of the guns.*

S Class

(Medium patrol submarines)

Displacement:
Group I 730 tons surfaced; 927 tons submerged
Group II 768 tons surfaced; 960 tons submerged
Group III 865 tons surfaced; 990 tons submerged

Performance:
Max speed
Groups I/II 13.75kt surfaced; 10kt submerged
Group III 14.75kt surfaced; 9kt submerged
Range
Group I 3,700nm/10kt surfaced; 106nm/4kt submerged
Group II 3,800nm/10kt surfaced; 106nm/4kt submerged
Group III 6,000nm/10kt surfaced; 100nm/4kt submerged

Maximum Operational Diving Depth:
300ft (91.44m)

Dimensions:
Group I 202ft 6in (61.72m) x 24ft 0in (7.3m) x 11ft 11in (3.63m)
Group II 208ft 8in (63.60m) x 24ft 0in (7.3m) x 11ft 10in (3.60m)
Group III 217ft 0in (66.14m) x 23ft 9in (7.24m) x 13ft 3in (4.04m)

Machinery:
Two Admiralty diesel engines, 1,550bhp (Group III 1,900 bhp); two electric motors, 1,300shp (Group II 1,440shp); two shafts

Complement:
Group I 4 officers, 34 ratings
Group II 5 officers, 35 ratings
Group III 5 officers, 43 ratings

Construction:
Group I (4 boats)   HM Dockyard, Chatham. *Sturgeon, Swordfish, Seahorse, Starfish.* Four boats. Completed 1932-33.

Group II (8 boats)   Cammell Laird, Birkenhead. *Salmon, Sealion, Spearfish.* Three boats. Completed 1934-36.
Scott's, Greenock. *Seawolf.* One boat. Completed 1936
HM Dockyard, Chatham. *Shark, Snapper, Sterlet, Sunfish.* Four boats. Completed 1934-38.

Group III (50 boats)   Cammell Laird, Birkenhead. Thirty-two boats. Completed 1942-45
Scott's, Greenock. Ten boats. Completed 1943-45
Vickers-Armstrong. Five boats. Completed 1942-43
HM Dockyard, Chatham. Three boats. Completed 1942-44

Design: Following construction of the *X-1* in the early 1920s the Royal Navy produced a series of numerically small classes of large submarines for 'overseas patrol' tasks. They also made one final attempt to develop the long-desired 'fleet submarine' — the Thames class of 1932-35 — only to find that battleship speeds had increased to some 30kt. Instead of the planned twenty boats, construction ceased with the third, and the 'fleet' dream was abandoned for ever.

Meanwhile, the remaining boats of the World War I H class, continued to serve in the North Sea and other coastal areas, and there was a pressing need for a new medium-range submarine to replace them. The result was the Swordfish class, subsequently known as the S class, Group I, as it turned out to be the precursor of the largest single class of submarine ever

to serve in the Royal Navy. The Swordfish class had a rivetted hull, reasonable speed both on the surface and submerged, good range and a heavy armament. The only major drawback of these boats was that the internal arrangements were somewhat cramped and complicated, making them unpopular with their crews.

First-of-class, *Swordfish*, was commissioned in November 1932 and early experience with her led to small changes in the design for the Group II boats (also known as the Shark class), the first of which was laid down in June 1933. The main change was that the pressure hull was lengthened, enabling the internal

Below: *An S class submarine flying the traditional 'Jolly Roger'. With 62 units built over 15 years, this was the largest class ever built for the Royal Navy.*

arrangements to be revised, resulting in an improvement in working conditions for the crew.

When war broke out in 1939 an obvious need existed for more submarines and this was met in part by placing the tried and tested S class into full-scale production. In fact, orders were placed every year for five years: 1939, 5; 1940, 20; 1941, 15; 1942, 12; and 1943, 9 (although some of the last year's orders were cancelled). Group III boats were somewhat longer and had a slightly greater displacement. Their production spanned the period of changeover in British shipyards from rivetting to welding. As a result the early boats were partly welded, although the pressure hull was still rivetted, but all but two of those boats ordered in 1942 and all of those ordered in 1943 were fully welded throughout.

Nothing about the design of the S class was revolutionary or striking, but everything seemed to come together in a harmonious way to produce a submarine which was effective, reliable, safe, manoeuvrable, with sufficient armament and a very acceptable performance. Thus, the Admiralty's decision to stick with a well-proven design whose snags had been identified and eliminated during peacetime made a great deal of sense, although their later decision to send submarines of this class to the Far East towards the end of the war was, perhaps, trying both boats and crews a trifle too far.

Armament: Armament of the Group I boats was six 21in (533mm) torpedo tubes, all in the bow, with six reloads. The first two boats had a 3in (76.2mm) gun on a disappearing mounting, which folded away into a casing built onto the forward end of the conning-tower. This proved very unsatisfactory and was changed for a more conventional fixed mount, which was used in all subsequent boats.

The armament in the Group II boats was identical, but in most of the Group III one additional, external torpedo tube was installed in the stern, although this could not be reloaded at sea. Most boats could carry twelve M2 mines as an alternative to torpedoes.

As the war progressed there were many changes to armament. Some of the later Group III boats were fitted with a 4in/40 (102mm) gun in place of the 3in (76.2mm) and in such boats the stern torpedo tube had to be removed to compensate for the increased weight. Many boats were also given a 20mm AA cannon, which was mounted on a platform at the after end of the conning-tower.

Service History: These boats had a hard-fought war, serving in the Atlantic, North Sea, Arctic, Mediterranean and eventually in the Far East. They sank a large tonnage of merchant shipping, as well as seven enemy submarines and two destroyers.

Eighteen of the 62 boats in the three groups were lost during the war whilst under the White Ensign. Eight were lost in action against surface ships, although some of these were scuttled by their own crews after damage in gunfights. Six were mined, two were lost to a combination of aircraft and ships, one was lost to a submarine and one, inevitably, disappeared 'lost, causes unknown.'

A particularly poignant loss was that of the former *Sunfish*, which had been transferred on loan to the Soviet Navy in 1944 as *V-1*. On her delivery voyage she was sighted by a patrolling RAF aircraft when well off her agreed track and then contravened the agreed procedure by diving instead of remaining on the suface and giving the recognition signal. The aircraft had no alternative but to consider her hostile and sank her with depth-charges.

After the war the three surviving Group I and II boats were all scrapped, but the Group III boats served on for a little longer. Five were sold abroad: three to Portugal and two to Israel. A further four were lent to France in the 1950s for use in ASW training, of which one sank in an accident; the remaining three were later returned to be scrapped.

In 1944 there was an urgent need to train ships and crews for the impending ASW engagements against the new German Type XXI submarines, and three S class boats were converted into high-speed targets. Fortunately for the Allies only one Type XXI carried out an operational patrol, but by 1946 the USSR was seen to be the next threat and it was known that she had obtained a number of Type XXIs. So, the need for such training remained and a further five S class boats were converted in the late 1940s. The boats were streamlined, guns were removed and better batteries and motors installed, increasing underwater speed to about 12kt for short periods.

One of these, *Seraph*, was also given extra protection for use as a target for torpedoes with inert warheads, an experiment that was also being tested in the USA and USSR at that time. Another, *Sidon*, was used to test a new type of torpedo which used high-test peroxide (H_2O_2) as a fuel. Notorious for its instability, one exploded while the submarine was lying alongside in Portland in 1955 and, after a brief interval, she sank with the loss of thirteen lives. By now, the day of these excellent boats was over and they were progressively sold off for scrap, the last to be stricken being *Sea Devil* in 1962.

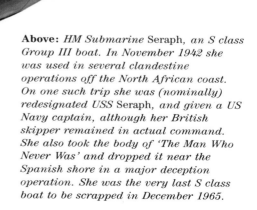

Above: *HM Submarine* Seraph, *an S class Group III boat. In November 1942 she was used in several clandestine operations off the North African coast. On one such trip she was (nominally) redesignated USS* Seraph, *and given a US Navy captain, although her British skipper remained in actual command. She also took the body of 'The Man Who Never Was' and dropped it near the Spanish shore in a major deception operation. She was the very last S class boat to be scrapped in December 1965.*

Upholder Class

(Diesel-electric powered hunter/killer submarine) (SSK)

Displacement:
2,185 tons surfaced; 2,400 tons submerged
Performance:
Max speed 12kt surfaced; 20kt submerged
Range 10,000nm plus surfaced; not known submerged
Maximum Operational Diving Depth:
820+ft (250+m)

Dimensions:
230ft 6in (70.26m) x 24ft 11in (7.6m) x 18ft 0in (5.5m)
Machinery:
Two Paxman-Valenta 16 RPA 200SZ diesel generators, 4,070bhp; two GEC alternators, 5,000kW; one shaft
Complement:
7 officers, 37 ratings
Endurance:
49 days
Construction:
Vickers (VSEL), Barrow. *Upholder* (S-40). One boat. Completed 1988
Cammell Laird, Birkenhead. *Unseen* (S-41), *Ursula* (S-42), *Unicorn* (S-43). Three boats. Completed 1991 to 1993?

Above: *HMS* Upholder, *nameship of her class is launched at the Vickers' yard, Barrow-in-Furness on 2 December 1986.*

Bottom left: *A fine view of* Upholder *at her launch. The bulge around her bow is a cover fitted to hide her sonar dome from curious eyes during the launch ceremony; the platform on the bows and the railings along the deck are also temporary. Current plans call for a total of four boats.*

Design: After World War II there ensued a considerable hiatus in submarine construction by the Royal Navy, apart from some experimental types, until the Porpoise class (eight boats) and the very similar Oberon class (thirteen boats) were constructed between 1956 and 1966. Production of these two very successful classes for the Royal Navy ended when *Onyx* (S-21), the final boat of the Oberon class, entered service in 1967. It was stated at that time that she would be the last-ever diesel-electric submarine. In the 1970s, however, the navy came to the conclusion that, while SSNs may have many advantages, there was still a need for conventional types. Accordingly, the decision was made in 1983 to procure the new Upholder class.

The design is based on the Vickers Type 2400, a private venture offered to several foreign navies in the late 1970s. The single-hull form is similar to that of British SSNs and has a high beam-to-length ratio, with a pressure hull constructed of NQ-1 steel (equivalent to HY-80). Internally, the hull is sub-divided by two main bulkheads, with the two forward watertight

Above: *The stubby hull lines of* Upholder *are typical of modern high-speed submarines. She is shown here with a conventional 7-bladed propeller, but is believed to have been fitted with a shrouded 'pump-jet', which reduces the noise created by open blades, even when they are rotating very slowly. Weapons may include Tigerfish Mod 2 (1) or Spearfish (2) torpedoes, canister-launched (3) Sub-Harpoon missiles (3A) or Stonefish mines (4). Spearfish is reported to be extremely fast.*

Above: Upholder *at sea. Note the retractable sonar dome on the foredeck and the very high sail.*

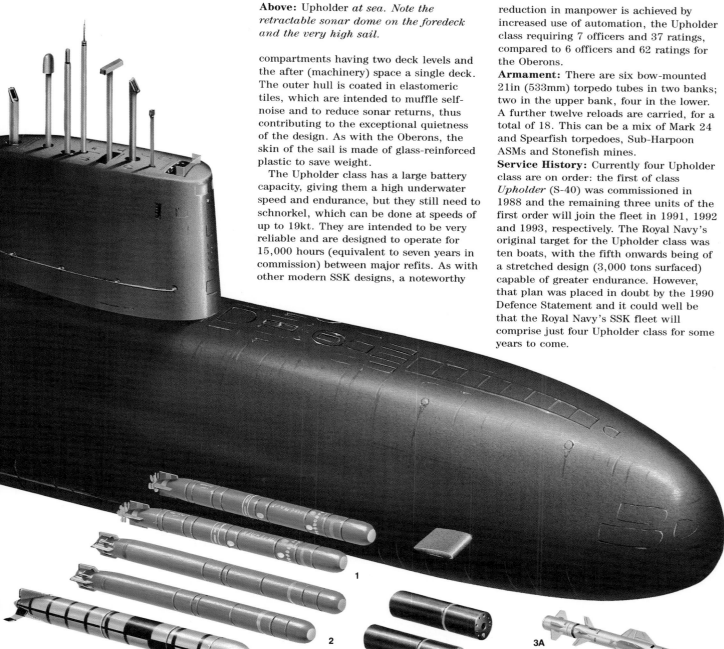

compartments having two deck levels and the after (machinery) space a single deck. The outer hull is coated in elastomeric tiles, which are intended to muffle self-noise and to reduce sonar returns, thus contributing to the exceptional quietness of the design. As with the Oberons, the skin of the sail is made of glass-reinforced plastic to save weight.

The Upholder class has a large battery capacity, giving them a high underwater speed and endurance, but they still need to schnorkel, which can be done at speeds of up to 19kt. They are intended to be very reliable and are designed to operate for 15,000 hours (equivalent to seven years in commission) between major refits. As with other modern SSK designs, a noteworthy reduction in manpower is achieved by increased use of automation, the Upholder class requiring 7 officers and 37 ratings, compared to 6 officers and 62 ratings for the Oberons.

Armament: There are six bow-mounted 21in (533mm) torpedo tubes in two banks; two in the upper bank, four in the lower. A further twelve reloads are carried, for a total of 18. This can be a mix of Mark 24 and Spearfish torpedoes, Sub-Harpoon ASMs and Stonefish mines.

Service History: Currently four Upholder class are on order: the first of class *Upholder* (S-40) was commissioned in 1988 and the remaining three units of the first order will join the fleet in 1991, 1992 and 1993, respectively. The Royal Navy's original target for the Upholder class was ten boats, with the fifth onwards being of a stretched design (3,000 tons surfaced) capable of greater endurance. However, that plan was placed in doubt by the 1990 Defence Statement and it could well be that the Royal Navy's SSK fleet will comprise just four Upholder class for some years to come.

Trafalgar Class

(Nuclear-powered hunter/killer submarines)
(SSN)

Displacement:
4,730 tons surfaced; 5,208 tons submerged
Performance:
Max speed 30kt submerged
Maximum Operational Diving Depth:
Operating 984ft (300m)
Maximum 1,640ft (500m)
Dimensions:
280ft 1in (85.38m) x 32ft 3in (9.83m) x 27ft 1in (8.25m)
Machinery:
One PWR-1 pressurized-water cooled nuclear reactor, two General Electric turbines, 15,000shp; one Paxman auxiliary diesel, 400hp; one shaft, shrouded pump-jet
Complement:
97
Endurance:
85 days
Construction:
Vickers, Barrow-in-Furness. *Trafalgar* (S-107), *Turbulent* (S-110), *Tireless* (S-117), *Torbay* (S-118), *Trenchant* (S-91), *Talent* (S-92), *Triumph* (S-93). Seven boats. Completed 1983-91.

Design: The Royal Navy became the second navy to operate nuclear-powered submarines when its first SSN, *Dreadnought* (S-101) was commissioned in 1963. She was powered by a Westinghouse S5W nuclear reactor, bought from the United States in order to speed up the programme. Since then the Royal Navy has followed a policy of steady improvement and refinement in its SSNs, producing a new class of some 5-7 submarines at approximately ten year intervals.

Dreadnought was followed by the five-boat Valiant class, the first of which was completed in July 1966. The Valiants, which entered service between 1967 and 1971, are generally similar to the *Dreadnought*, but are 19ft (5.8m) longer and have a somewhat larger crew (103 as opposed to 88 officers and men).

The third class of British SSNs was the Swiftsure class, the first of which joined the fleet in April 1973. These boats are 13ft (4m) shorter than the Valiant class, with a flat upper deck giving a different appearance from the humped-back of the earlier British SSNs. This new shape suggests greater internal volume, giving more space and better living conditions. The sail is lower than on earlier classes, suggesting a slight reduction in periscope depth. On the Valiant class, the forward hydroplanes are mounted virtually at the

top of the casing, but in the Swiftsure and later classes they have been moved down to some 6ft (1.8m) below the waterline; as a result they are not visible when the submarine is running on the surface.

The Swiftsure class SSNs are renowned for being particularly quiet and some, if not all, are coated with anechoic tiles made of an elastomeric material to reduce the submarine's acoustic signature, or as it is euphemistically termed, 'improve the noise hygiene'. It has been reported that, in addition, some of this class are also fitted with the British-invented, shrouded pump-jet rather than conventional 'open-blade' propeller. This device reduces the noise signature yet further and also gives a higher top speed than a conventional propeller, but at half the revolutions.

The SSN class of the 1980s is the Trafalgar class, consisting of seven boats, which joined the fleet between 1983 and 1991. These are a development of the Swiftsure class and all are coated with a layer of rubber-compound anechoic tiles to reduce radiated and reflected noise. All except the first-of-class *Trafalgar* are fitted with the shrouded pump-jet propulsion system.

The next class of British SSN will be the 'SSN-20' class, powered by the Rolls-Royce PWR-2 reactor. The first order was due to be placed in 1990, but may well be delayed

Above: *The Trafalgar class SSN is fitted with five 21in (533mm) torpedo tubes. These can launch Mark 24 Tigerfish torpedoes (1), Sub-Harpoon missiles (2), shown here with their launch canisters, Stonefish mines (3) and Sea Urchin programmable mines (4). They will also be used to launch Spearfish torpedoes (not shown), when these come into service in the late 1990s.*

Left: Turbulent, *seen here, is reported to be the first fitted with a pump-jet, rather than a conventional propeller. British SSNs have given excellent value in service although many boats of earlier classes are being stricken.*

due to the defence cuts announced in 1990. SSN-20 will be a radically new design, with, among other features, a sail virtually in the bow, suggesting that the torpedo room will be moved to the amidships position, as in most modern US Navy SSNs.

Armament: *Dreadnought* and the Valiant class were all fitted with six torpedo tubes in the bow. The third boat of the Valiant class, *Churchill*, was used for trials with the US Navy's Sub-Harpoon system in 1980, following which all existing British SSNs (except *Dreadnought*) were modified to fire this

weapon. The Valiant class carries 26 missiles, a mixture, depending on the tactical requirements, of Mark 8 and Mark 24 torpedoes, and Sub-Harpoon.

In the Swiftsure class the number of torpedo tubes was reduced to five and the total load of missiles carried to twenty. The Trafalgar class has a similar weapons fit, except that they do not carry the 50-years old Mark 8 torpedoes.

Service History: *Dreadnought* was launched in 1960 and after extended trials served as a normal operational submarine. She subsequently had a major refit from 1968 to 1970, when the reactor core was renewed, but was taken out of service in 1981 and has since been stricken.

The Valiant class entered service between 1966 and 1971. *Valiant* herself travelled 10,000nm (18,500km) submerged from Singapore to Portsmouth in 28 days in 1967 in a demonstration of SSN capability. A further and more lethal demonstration was given by the *Conqueror* when, during the 1982 Falklands War, she

sank the Argentine cruiser *General Belgrano*, thus changing the naval balance of power in the South Atlantic. It is reliably reported that the weapon used was the rather elderly Mark 8 torpedo, rather than one of the more modern types which *Conqueror* can be assumed also to have been carrying.

The Swiftsure class also underwent major refits in the mid-1980s which involved them in receiving a much more powerful Type 2020 sonar, together with the new Type 2040 towed array, a new decoy system and new reactor core with a life of twelve years.

With the commissioning of *Triumph* (S-93), the last-of-class in 1991, the Royal Navy has eighteen SSNs in service. However, the plans announced in 1990 for reductions in the British armed forces state that the submarine force (excluding the SSBNs) will be cut from 27 to 16 boats, which means a reduction of six SSNs. This will result in the complete Valiant class being paid off, plus one of the Swiftsure class, and may well also lead to a more ambitious update of the other five Swiftsure class than had perhaps been planned.

1

2

3

4

JAPAN

Commodore Perry, USN, negotiated the Treaty of Kanagawa with Japan on 31 March 1854. The effect of this was to open the country to foreign ideas for the very first time, and to bring about regular political and economic dealings between Japan and the major Western nations. It was not until 1869 that modernisation really began, but by the outbreak of the Russo-Japanese War in 1904 the Imperial Japanese Navy was a thoroughly capable and modern force, which played a vigorous role in the war, culminating in the defeat of the Russian Fleet at Tsushima on 27 May 1905.

Early Years

On the outbreak of the Russo-Japanese War both combatants ordered submarines from the USA: Russia from Lake, Japan from Holland. The five boats for the IJN (Imperial Japanese Navy) were shipped to Japan for assembly. They then constructed two smaller boats in their own yards to a modified Holland design, one of which (*No 6*) was fitted with the first-ever schnorkel device. She was carrying out an underwater test with her petrol engine when she flooded and sank with the loss of all hands. She was later raised and returned to service and is now a memorial at Kure Naval Station.

Next came two much larger boats designed by Vickers in England, the C1 class (321 tons), which were also built by Vickers. These were followed by three boats of the C2 class (326 tons), which, like the Holland boats, were fabricated abroad and shipped in sections to Japan for assembly. They entered service in 1909-11, serving until 1929. Again, modified versions were constructed in Japan; first, a single boat of the 'Modified Vickers class' (340 tons), completed in 1912, then two of the 'Improved Vickers' or C3 class (326 tons) completed in 1916-17. A long association with Vickers ended with the construction of six boats of the L1/L2 type (1,195 tons), followed by the very similar L3 class, all of them based upon the British L class.

Still searching for suitable designs the IJN next turned to France, ordering two Schneider-Laubeuf boats in 1913. The first, *No 14*, was taken over by the French Navy as *Armide*, but *No 15* was completed and delivered according to contract. The IJN then obtained a licence to build a modified boat as a new *No 14*, which was completed in 1920, by far the largest submarine constructed in Japan up to that date. Next, plans for a new type were obtained from Fiat-Laurenti of Italy and two submarines of the F1 class were completed by the Kawasaki Yard in 1920. These were the IJN's first submarines to exceed 1,000 tons displacement and were also their first true ocean-going boats, having a surface range of 3,500nm

Top: *No 6, a modified Holland design, was the first submarine ever to be fitted with a schnorkel device. She sank in 1910 with the loss of all hands.*

Above: *No 12, the third of the C2 class, built in England and shipped to Japan for assembly at Kure.*

(6,480km) at 10kt. Three boats were then built to a modified design, the F2 class, but these were unpopular with their crews and had a brief operational career.

During World War I Japan aligned herself with the Allies, carrying out a number of operations, which included deploying a destroyer squadron to the Mediterranean. As a result she was allocated a share of the booty, including seven ex-German submarines, which, because of growing British and American concern about Japanese strategic intentions, were stipulated to be specifically for experimental purposes; she was not allowed to take them into service.

The Inter-War Years

The USA was seen by Japan as the main threat and the cornerstone of IJN strategy was to attack an advancing US fleet as far east as possible. Submarines were essential to this mission; under the command of the surface fleet commander they would report enemy movements and sink as many warships as possible prior to the engagement of the main battlefleets. The German World War I U-boat campaign in the North Atlantic was given scant attention and no consideration was given to attacks on merchantmen, even those in

the fleet-train of the advancing battlefleets.

The Washington Naval Conference of 1922 acknowledged the IJN as the third great navy (after the British and US), but nevertheless allocated the IJN less tonnage than the Naval Staff thought necessary. The London Naval Conference of 1930 was even worse from the Japanese point-of-view and they withdrew from the treaty in December 1936.

Early post-war development efforts centred on long-range submarines with high surface speed, good communications and heavy armament. Initially there were two types: one specialising in reconnaissance, *junsen* type (*junyo sensuikan* (J) = cruiser submarine), the other in attack (*kaigun dai* (KD) = large navy design). The main difference was that the KD type would be expected to operate together in squadrons, whereas the J type would work more as individual units on their scouting tasks.

In the mid-1930s this doctrine was amended slightly. The two previous types were retained, but now termed Type B (reconnaissance submarines) and Type C (attack boats). These were to be commanded at sea by an admiral, exercising command from a new type of command submarine (Type A) a concept unique to the IJN. During the war a new category (Type D) was added; these were transport submarines required to replenish the outlying island garrisons.

There was one divergence from these neat plans: the KRS class (*kirai sensuikan* = minelaying submarine) which were built in the 1920s. Displacing 1,768 tons, they were developed from the German *U-125* minelayer.

A number of navies investigated the possibility of submarine aircraft-carriers in the interwar years, but only the IJN made a success of it, the concept becoming an integral part of their war plans. Numerous submarines were able to carry one aircraft, with the STo class carrying three. This concept proved effective in 1941-43, but increasing use of radar by the Allies made these submarines very vulnerable during launch and recovery operations, due to the time they had to stay surfaced.

The KD attack boats and J scouts were developed progressively through a series of sub-classes (KD1, KD2, KD3A/B, etc). The J boats were the larger, the final version (J3) having a displacement of 3,583 tons, a range of 14,000nm (25,930km), a heavy armament and one floatplane. Development of the J class ended in 1938 as the new A, B and C class boats were introduced, but one more in the KD series appeared (KD7) in 1942.

Four HQ submarines were built; three of the A1 class in 1941-42 and one of the similar, but lower powered, A2 class in 1944. All were very large, with a heavy armament and a floatplane, as well as extra space and communications for the admiral and his staff. All were sunk: two by USN warships and two lost to 'causes unknown'.

There were three classes of Type B scouting submarines, 29 boats in all, of which precisely two survived the war, an astonishingly high loss rate. There were also three classes of Type C attack submarines. The C1 class (3,561 tons) consisted of five boats completed in 1938-39 and this was followed by the virtually identical C2 class (three boats) and the slightly modified C3/C4 class (three boats). One C2 and one C3 surrendered in August 1945, all nine others being lost during the war.

During the war more aircraft-carrying submarines were built, which did not fit into the A/B/C series. First was the AM class (4,762 tons), which started on the design board as headquarters (A) type boats, but were then modified. They had a large hangar offset slightly to starboard, with the bridge above it and to port. The

AM carried two floatplanes and had a surface range of 21,000nm (38,900km). Large as they were, the two AM boats were overtaken in size by the STo boats (6,560 tons), which carried three floatplanes (and the parts of a fourth), had a very heavy armament and a range of no less than 37,500nm (69,450km). The STo class also had extensive staff facilities and were essentially an amalgamation of Types A and C.

Another field in which the IJN was innovative was the refuelling of flying-boats. Before the war trials were carried out with normal boats carrying extra supplies of aviation fuel, but later a special type of submarine, the SH was designed, which could carry 365 tons of aviation fuel, together with bombs, aerial torpedoes, ammunition and other stores. One (*I-351*) was completed in early 1945, being sunk six months later.

In the other development stream — the RO, or medium boats — the L4 Type (1,322 tons) of the early 1920s followed the L3, being essentially a further refinement of the Vickers' design. The Schneider-Laubeuf design, which had progressed through the K3 and K4 classes was developed into the K5 class (940 tons), of which two were produced in the mid-1930s. This series culminated in the K6 (1,447 tons), which joined the fleet in 1943-44, a well-designed and much more manoeuvrable design than most Japanese submarines. Another, somewhat smaller design, the KS (782 tons) was also produced in the early 1940s, intended for coastal defence missions. Total production amounted to two K5, eighteen K6 and eighteen KS, and of these just one K6 was still afloat at the surrender, all 37 other boats having been sunk by Allied ASW forces (35) or mines (2).

World War II

On 7 December 1941, the day of the attack on Pearl Harbor, 62 submarines were operational. Fifteen were the smaller, limited range RO class boats, the remainder I class, large, long-ranged and well-armed.

Below: *The IJN made widescale use of midget submarines throughout the war.*

The entire strength of the 6th Submarine Fleet (30 I class boats) took part in the Pearl Harbor operation, eleven of them carrying one floatplane each. Another five carried one Type A midget submarine each, which they launched some 10 miles (16km) off the entrance to Pearl Harbor in the early hours of 7 December. Despite the courage of the two-man crews, the result was a fiasco. Quickly detected, the midgets were harried and attacked by US aircraft and ships, all of them eventually being lost. The remaining fleet submarines operated against other US shipping, sinking some merchantmen and firing torpedoes at the carrier USS *Enterprise* (CV-6), albeit without success. Others headed for the US West Coast, where they shelled shore targets and attacked some shipping. After the Pearl Harbor operation *I-70*, a KD-6A boat, was discovered on the surface by aircraft from the *Enterprise* and sunk, becoming the first Japanese submarine casualty of the war.

The submarine force's operational areas expanded to match Japanese conquests and by mid-1942 they were operating all over the Pacific, and also in the South China Sea and the Indian Ocean. In January *I-6* torpedoed and damaged USS *Saratoga*, but, fortunately for the USA, the carrier was able to limp back into Pearl Harbor. One particularly serious event was the loss of *I-124* (a KRS type minelayer), which was sunk off Darwin, Australia. The hulk lay just 40ft (12m) below the surface and US Navy divers were able to enter and recover her codebooks, which was to prove a major disaster for the IJN in the longer term.

In March 1942 the submarine strategy was officially changed to attacks on merchant ships, although, somewhat ironically, the next success was against a British battleship lying at the anchorage in Diego Suarez, which was damaged by a midget launched from an I class submarine (a tanker was also sunk). One of the submarines in this group, *I-30* (B1 class) then sailed round the Cape of Good Hope, reaching the German U-boat base at Lorient on 5 August 1942. She loaded with technical material for Japan and returned to the Far East, where she hit a mine off Singapore and sank.

During the Battle of Midway IJN submarines generally failed to achieve very much except for the sinking by *I-168* (KD6A class) of the carrier USS *Midway*, which had already been damaged by IJN carrier aircraft, and an accompanying destroyer. This success could not, however, alter the course of the battle, following which the US Navy went from strength to strength and the IJN slipped inexorably towards defeat.

During the landings on Guadalcanal in August 1942 a mass of US shipping was menaced by no less than fifteen IJN submarines. Several unsuccessful attacks were carried out, but the carrier USS *Saratoga* was damaged on 31 August and one week later *I-19* with one six torpedo salvo sank the carrier USS *Wasp* and severely damaged the battleship *North Carolina* and the destroyer *O'Brien*. A

month later in the same area *I-176* damaged the cruiser USS *Chester*, followed a few weeks later by the destruction of another cruiser, USS *Juneau*. In all, this period represents the apogee of the IJN submarine force.

At about this time the ever-growing Allied use of radar in both ships and aircraft began to make running on the surface, necessary both to recharge batteries and for rapid transits, increasingly hazardous. Also, IJN tactics were being shown up as inflexible and inadequate, especially so when USS *England* (DE-365), with the aid of two other escort vessels, rolled up a sentry line of IJN submarines, sinking six in twelve days in the most devastating ASW operation ever. By the end of 1944 simple arithmetic was telling against the

submarine force: 54 submarines lost and a meagre 38 new submarines taken into commission in that year alone.

The final act in the war was the appearance of the *kaiten* suicide submarines. Most were launched from submarines, the first such operation taking place in November 1944. The IJN persuaded themselves that the results were far better than was the case and the *kaiten* force was expanded in order to undertake further missions. Whereas the first two *kaiten* attacks had been against ships in anchorages the third mission was against ships at sea on the supply route to Okinawa, but was equally unsuccessful.

Below: *The IJN commissioned very large submarines during World War II: here are* I-47, I-36, *and* I-402.

Similar patterns were repeated throughout the year until the ninth and final mission in July when six submarines carrying 33 *kaiten* sailed. Three of the submarines had to return to port due to mechanical problems with the *kaiten* but the remaining three, through a mixture of *kaiten* and their own torpedoes, were responsible for sinking one heavy cruiser (USS *Indianapolis*) (sunk by torpedoes from *I-58*) and a destroyer-escort, and damaged a transport.

The three STos and two AMs undertook their only major mission in August 1945. One AM was sunk en route to the operational area, but the others were preparing to launch an aerial attack when the surrender was announced and all four surrendered to the US Navy at sea.

Like Germany, the IJN's thoughts had turned to developing the potential of high-speed submarines. *Number 71* appeared in 1938, a small submarine with a design speed of 25kt submerged, considerably earlier than the better-known German *Elektroboote*. However, the two operational high-speed designs which followed, the ST and STS, like their German counterparts (Types XXI and XXIII) did not enter service before the war's end. Both Axis partners missed a golden opportunity, since all four designs were far in advance of anything possessed by their enemies.

The unexpected problem of resupplying isolated island garrisons in waters dominated by US ships and aircraft gave rise to an urgent need for transportation of men and material by submarine. At first, a variety of combat submarines were employed for such tasks, room for stores usually being created by removing some torpedoes, although deck guns were often also removed to enable landing craft to be carried. This misuse, together with the high loss rate, exacerbated the already critical shortage of such boats and in 1942 specialised transport submarines were ordered. Two classes of large submarine were ordered (D1 and D2 classes) and one class of small boats (SS class). Only the original D1 class saw significant service, eight out of the twelve becoming war losses.

One extraordinary episode was the construction by the Japanese Army of its own transport submarines. On discovering these plans the IJN offered help in design and construction, but this was declined. It appears that 26 boats of the Yu1 and Yu1001 classes were built, of which six survived the war, the others presumably being war losses.

A related problem was the desperate shortage of fuel in Japan, which became

Japanese Submarines of World War II

KAIGUN DAI (KD), LARGE ATTACK SUBMARINES

Class	Lead Boat	Displacement (tons)	In Service	Built (no)	War Losses	Remarks
KD1	No 44 (I-51)	2,430	1921	1	—	Stricken 1941
KD2	No 51 (I-52)	2,500	1922	1	—	Stricken 1942
KD3A/3B	No 64 (I-53)	2,300	1927-30	9	1	Used for training from 1942. 1 lost in pre-war accident
KD4	I-61	2,300	1927-29	3	1	1 lost in pre-war accident
KD5	I-65	2,330	1932	3	2	1 lost in pre-war accident
KD6A/6B	I-68	2,440	1934-38	8	8	
KD7	I-76	2,602	1942-43	10	9	1 lost in training accident 1943

C TYPE, LARGE ATTACK SUBMARINES

Class	Lead Boat	Displacement (tons)	In Service	Built (no)	War Losses	Remarks
C1	I-16	3,561	1940-41	5	5	
C2	I-46	3,564	1944	3	2	
C3/C4	I-52	3,644	1943-44	3	2	

JUNSEN (J), LARGE SCOUTING SUBMARINES

Class	Lead Boat	Displacement (tons)	In Service	Built (no)	War Losses	Remarks
J1	I-1	2,791	1926-29	4	4	
J1M	I-5	2,921	1932	1	1	
J2	I-6	3,061	1935	1	1	
J3	I-7	3,583	1937-38	2	2	

B TYPE, LARGE SCOUTING SUBMARINES

Class	Lead Boat	Displacement (tons)	In Service	Built (no)	War Losses	Remarks
B1	I-15	3,654	1940-43	20	18	1 lost on sea trials 1944
B2	I-40	3,700	1943-44	6	6	
B3/B4	I-54	3,688	1944	3	2	

A TYPE, LARGE COMMAND SUBMARINES

Class	Lead Boat	Displacement (tons)	In Service	Built (no)	War Losses	Remarks
A1	I-9	4,149	1941-42	3	3	
A2	I-12	4,172	1944	1	1	

Japanese Submarine Accessions and Losses in World War II

Year	1941	1942	1943	1944	1945	Totals
Start Strength	62	59	62	72	57	
New Boats						
Japanese Built	—	20	36	38	14	108
Ex-German	—	—	1	1	4	6
Ex-Italian	—	—	—	—	2	2
Losses	3	17	27	54	28	129
End Strength	59	62	72	57	49	

Japanese Submarine Losses 1941-1945						
CAUSE	1941	1942	1943	1944	1945	Totals
Land-based aircraft		2	1	1	1	5
Carrier-based aircraft	1		1	2	5	9
Land-based aircraft and surface ships			1	2		3
Carrier-based aircraft and surface ships			1	2	3	6
Surface ships		9	16	38	10	73
Submarines		4	2	7	7	20
Mines		1	2		1	4
Operational losses	2		2	4	1	9
Totals	3	17	27	54	28	129

progressively more isolated from its sources of supply as the war progressed. Again the submarine force was tasked with finding an answer and a number of submarines were pressed into service as tankers.

There is no doubt that the IJN submarine force did not perform as well in the war as had been expected. The areas to be covered were vast, stretching from the east coast of Africa to the west coast of the Americas. Further, it found itself pulled into roles which were neither anticipated nor wanted, such as transporting fuel to Japan, and carrying men and supplies from Japan to the outlying island garrisons. The submarine force also became involved in the *kamikaze* saga, which, in the event, proved to be a singularly fruitless undertaking and far less productive than normal attacks using the submarines' own torpedoes.

The production efforts of the Japanese shipbuilding industry do not seem to have been harnessed effectively. Too many classes were ordered and an apparent fascination with size and special roles resulted in yards, even at the height of the war, being constrained to produce monsters like the AM and STo classes, and special-role types such as seaplane support boats. Then, when the yards could have been really productive in constructing the revolutionary high-speed submarines, they became involved in the *kaiten* programme, with the result that the boats which might have had a real effect never reached operational status.

Tactically, too, the IJN submarines could have done better. They certainly sank a number of warships, including two aircraft carriers, two cruisers and ten destroyers, and damaged many more. They also sank 184 merchant ships (907,000grt). However, they showed a great degree of inflexibility, and captains often let targets pass because they were precluded from engaging by their very precise orders. Strict rules against breaking radio silence were also counter-productive and the extraordinary success of USS *England* was due, at least in part, to the refusal of the IJN submarines to broadcast news of what was happening to them before they sank.

The IJN practice of admirals accompanying groups of submarines to command their operations on the spot seems also to have been less than successful. Whilst this may have been due to some extent to the large distances involved, this system proved far less effective than that exercised by their ally Admiral Dönitz in far-off Europe.

However, this is not to deny that the officers and men of the submarine service fought a dangerous and courageous war. It was also fought to generally the same rules as those used by the submariners of other nations, although there were a number of bad incidents, which were punished by the Allies after the war. One hundred and twenty-nine Japanese submarines were lost in World War II, of which 120 were due to enemy action.

Post-War
On the Japanese surrender all surviving submarines were brought together and inspected by the victorious Allies. A few boats were taken to the USA for further examination, but by mid-1946 all the surrendered boats had been scuttled in either Japanese or American waters.

The Japanese Maritime Self-Defense Force was raised in the early 1950s and its first submarine was an unmodified Gato class boat, USS *Mingo* (SS-261), on loan from the US Navy. Named *Kurushio* (S-501) she helped train crews for the new submarine force from 1955 to 1966. However, the first post-war Japanese submarine was commissioned in 1959, *Oyashio*, followed by the four-boat Hayashio class in the early 1960s. Since then there have been a number of classes of increasingly sophisticated, diesel-electric powered attack submarines, culminating in today's Yuushio class. The JMSDF maintains a force of about 15-18 submarines, with a new class appearing about every ten years.

Japanese Submarines of World War II

AIRCRAFT-CARRYING SUBMARINES

Class	Lead Boat	Displacement (tons)	In Service	Built (no)	War Losses	Remarks
AM	I-13	4,762	1944-45	2	1	
STo	I-400	6,560	1944-45	3	—	

KRS, MINELAYING SUBMARINES

Class	Lead Boat	Displacement (tons)	In Service	Built (no)	War Losses	Remarks
KRS	No 48 (I-21)	1,768	1927-28	4	3	

SH, SEAPLANE SUPPORT

Class	Lead Boat	Displacement (tons)	In Service	Built (no)	War Losses	Remarks
SH	I-351	4,290	1945	1	1	

ST, HIGH-SPEED ATTACK

Class	Lead Boat	Displacement (tons)	In Service	Built (no)	War Losses	Remarks
ST	I-201	1,450	1945	3	—	No operational missions

FOREIGN SUBMARINES (I SERIES)

Class	Lead Boat	Displacement (tons)	In Service	Built (no)	War Losses	Remarks
Type IX-D₂	I-501	1,804	1945	2	—	Ex-German
Marcello	I-503	1,220	1945	1	—	Ex-Italian
Marconi	I-504	1,489	1945	1	—	Ex-Italian
Type XB	I-505	2,177	1945	1	—	Ex-German
Type IX-D₁	I-506	1,799	1945	1	—	Ex-German

RO SERIES, MEDIUM SUBMARINES

Class	Lead Boat	Displacement (tons)	In Service	Built (no)	War Losses	Remarks
L3	No 46 (RO-57)	1,195	1922-23	3	—	Used for training from 1941
L4	No 59 (RO-60)	1,322	1922-27	9	5	Used for training from 1942
K5	RO-33	940	1935-37	2	2	
KS	RO-100	782	1942-44	18	18	
K6	RO-35	1,477	1943-44	18	17	

FOREIGN SUBMARINES (RO SERIES)

Class	Lead Boat	Displacement (tons)	In Service	Built (no)	War Losses	Remarks
Type IXC	RO-500	1,232	1943-44	2	1	Ex-German. RO-501 was lost during delivery voyage

STS, SMALL HIGH-SPEED ATTACK SUBMARINES

Class	Lead Boat	Displacement (tons)	In Service	Built (no)	War Losses	Remarks
STS	HA-201	493	1945	10	—	No operational missions

D TYPE TRANSPORT SUBMARINES

Class	Lead Boat	Displacement (tons)	In Service	Built (no)	War Losses	Remarks
D1	I-361	2,215	1943	12	8	} Gun armament, no torpedo tubes
D2	I-373	2,240	1945	1	1	
SS	HA-101	493	1944	10	0	

K Class

(Patrol submarines)

Displacement:
K1 735 tons surfaced; 1,030 tons submerged
K2/K3 755 tons surfaced; 1,050 tons submerged
K4 770 tons surfaced; 1,080 tons submerged

Performance:
Max speed K1 18kt surfaced; 9kt submerged
K2/K3/K4 17kt surfaced; 9kt submerged
Range K1 4,000nm/10kt surfaced; 85nm/4kt submerged
K2/K3/K4 6,000nm/10kt surfaced; 85nm/4kt submerged

Maximum Operational Diving Depth:
Not known

Dimensions:
K1 227ft 0in (69.2m) x 20ft 9in (6.3m) x 11ft 3in (3.4m)
K2/K3 230ft 0in (70.1m) x 20ft 0in (6.1m) x 12ft 1in (3.7m)
K4 243ft 6in (74.2m) x 20ft 9in (6.3m) x 11ft 3in (3.4m)

Machinery:
Two Sulzer diesel engines, 2,600bhp; two electric motors, 1,200shp; two shafts

Complement:
K1 44
K2/K3/K4 45

Construction:

K1 (2 boats)	Kure Navy Yard. Two boats. *Nos 19 (RO-11), 20 (RO-12)*. Launched 1917.
K2 (3 boats)	Kure Navy Yard. Three boats. *Nos 22 (RO-14), 23 (RO-13), 24 (RO-15)*. Launched 1920-21.
K3 (10 boats)	Kure Navy Yard. Four boats. *Nos 34 (RO-16), 35 (RO-17), 36 (RO-18), 37 (RO-19)*. Launched 1921-22. Yokosuka Navy Yard. Four boats. *Nos 38 (RO-20), 39 (RO-21), 40 (RO-22), 41 (RO-23)*. Launched 1920-21. Sasebo Navy Yard. Two boats. *Nos 42 (RO-24), 43 (RO-25)*. Launched 1919-20.
K4 (3 boats)	Sasebo Navy Yard. Two boats. *Nos 45 (RO-26), 62 (RO-27)*. Launched 1921-22. Yokosuka Navy Yard. One boat. *No 58 (RO-28)*. Launched 1922.

Design: The early boats constructed for the Imperial Japanese Navy (IJN) were small, coastal types, which, while useful for gaining experience, were of limited tactical use. Clearly, to be effective, the Japanese submarine force needed longer range and the IJN placed an order for two French Schneider-Laubeuf designs, to be constructed at the Creusot yard, in 1911. These had a range of 2,050nm (4,000km), armed with four 18in (457mm) torpedoes in Drzewiecki drop-collars, a Russian invention popular with French submarine designers at that time. One of these boats was delivered in 1916 (S1 class), the other having been taken over by the French Navy and commissioned as *Armide*, although a second, slightly modified boat (S2 class) was built at the Kure Navy Yard, being completed in 1920.

Pacific waters were much deeper and more dangerous than those for which contemporary European boats were designed (principally, the Mediterranean, Baltic and North Seas) and the IJN did not consider that the European designs fully met their needs for ocean-going submarines. In particular, they required greater hull strength and much more precise control.

Accordingly, in 1916 they modified the French design to their requirements to produce the first Japanese class of submarine, the K1 class. The result was a somewhat larger boat and a strengthened hull, with many more internal sub-divisions than in European designs, together with more substantial frames and outer skin. Submerged displacement inevitably increased from 665 tons for the S1 to 1,030 tons.

The K1s proved successful in service and the design was modified slightly to produce the K2 class. The main differences were in the shape of the bow and stern. Yet further minor changes were incorporated into the K3 class, which, comprising nine boats, was the largest single class of submarine yet built for the IJN. Finally, the three boats of the K4 class were slightly longer, mainly in order to accommodate the 21in (533mm) torpedo tubes.

Armament: The S1 class had been armed with four 18in (457mm) torpedoes, all in Drzewiecki drop-collars, while the S2 had four bow-mounted tubes and only two torpedoes in drop-collars. The K1 class retained the latter arrangement, carrying ten torpedoes altogether, as well as mounting one 3in (76mm) deck gun.

The K2 and K3 classes classes had the same armament as the K1 class. The K4, however, was the first Japanese class to be fitted with 21in (533mm) tubes, four being mounted in the bows, the drop-collars being deleted.

Above: *No 69 of the KT class was similar to the K4 class, but with better range.*

Below: *K1 class No 19 was armed with four bow 18in (457mm) torpedo tubes, with two drop-collars on the upper casing. K2 and K3 classes were similarly armed but the K4 and KT classes were fitted with four 21in (533mm) torpedo tubes and no drop collars. Also shown is a 3in (76mm) deck gun.*

Service History: The two K1 boats joined the fleet in 1919 and during fleet exercises that year managed to ram each other. The damage was extensive, but due to their great strength they survived and limped back to port for repairs. In common with all other Japanese submarines then in service, they were renumbered on 11 November 1924, *No 19* becoming *RO-11* and *No 20 RO-12*. Both were stricken in 1931.

The first two boats of the K2 class were commissioned in 1919, the third in 1920. All were renumbered in 1924 using the new system. All were stricken in 1931, although *RO-14* was used as a training hulk for many years, surviving until 1948, when she was broken up.

The K3 boats were completed between 1921 and 1923. *No 43* was involved in a collision with the cruiser *Tatsuta* on 19 March 1924, but was recovered and refitted, although her subsequent service was as a trials boat. All were stricken in 1932 except for *RO-17* and *RO-18*, which survived until 1936. *RO-20* and *RO-21* were disposed of in a uniquely Japanese manner, being sold to serve as submerged breeding grounds for fish!

The K4 class were commissioned in 1923-24, being renumbered later that year. All were stricken in 1940.

Thus, none of this large class of eighteen boats saw war service, being just too late for World War I and having disappeared by the time of the attack on Pearl Harbor. However, they gave many years of useful service and provided valuable experience to many of the officers and men who were to serve in the IJN submarine force in World War II.

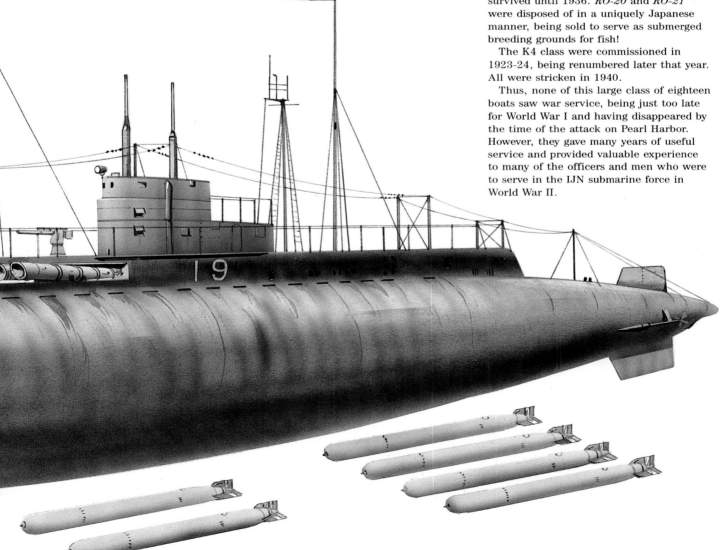

No 71 Class

(Experimental high-speed submarine)

Displacement:
213 tons surfaced; 240 tons submerged
Performance:
Max speed 13.20kt surfaced; 21.34kt submerged
Range 3,830nm/12kt surfaced; 231nm/7kt submerged

Maximum Operational Diving Depth:
265ft (80m)
Dimensions:
140ft 5in (42.8m) x 10ft 10in (3.3m) x 10ft 2in (3.1m)
Machinery:
One diesel engine, 300bhp; one electric motor, 1,800shp; one shaft
Complement:
11
Construction:
Kure Navy Yard, No 71. One boat. Launched August 1938.

Design: For many years submarines were very slow underwater and had a limited endurance. One reason was the generally low electrical storage capacity of the batteries, but more important was the extraordinary external clutter of guns, protuberances (such as cleats and antennas), safety rails and a general lack of streamlining, all of which caused a great deal of hydrodynamic drag.

One early endeavour to overcome this was the British R class of 1918, which represents the first attempt to design a specialised anti-submarine submarine. For this a very high underwater speed was needed and the R class was, in fact, the first ever to have an underwater speed higher than that on the surface. They were single-hull boats with a submerged displacement of 503 tons and had an underwater speed of 15kt. With very clean lines, they achieved the speed required of them, but were very difficult to control at high submerged speeds and were not a great success in service. All were stricken in the early 1920s, except for one which survived until the early 1930s.

The Japanese had produced a series of boats throughout the 1920s and 1930s which, apart from large size and long range, did little to extend the boundaries of submarine technology. Then, in 1938,

they launched *No 71*, a small but very fast submarine, which was intended (at least in theory) to be the prototype of a class of short-range, coastal defence submarines. With exceptionally clean lines, *No 71* had the classic high-speed features of an uncluttered hull, a streamlined sail, a single propeller, no forward hydroplanes and cruciform after control surfaces.

She was designed to achieve 25kt underwater, but never exceeded 21.25kt, although this was by far the highest speed recorded by any submarine up to that date. That she failed to achieve her design speed is not surprising since the phenomenon of instability at high speeds was neither recognised nor understood until the 1950s when the first nuclear-propelled boats were carrying out their trials. The solution, tested and proved in USS *Albacore*, was in a shorter, beamier hull, but the pre-war Japanese designers were not to know that.

No 71 never achieved her surface design speed of 18kt, either, but for different reasons. The original design called for a Daimler-Benz diesel of 1,200bhp, but this could not be obtained. Instead a Japanese diesel of very much lower power had to be used, with a consequent degradation in performance.

These shortcomings aside, *No 71* was a

remarkable achievement, pre-dating the much better known German high-speed submarines by 3-4 years.

Armament: Despite her small size *No 71* was given an armament of three 17.7in (450mm) torpedo tubes. These were mounted in the bow and there were no reloads, since such a short-range local defence boat was reckoned to be able to return to port to re-arm.

Service History: *No 71* carried out a series of intensive tests over the period 1938 to 1940 and was then scrapped. However, her great value came in the lessons learned, which were incorporated into two operational classes: the ST and STS type high-speed submarines.

The ST (or I-201) class (ST = *sen taka* = high speed submarine) displaced 1,450 tons and were armed with four 21in (533mm) torpedo tubes and two deck-mounted 25mm machine-guns. They had a long, very clean, all-welded hull, with twin diesel engines (2,750hp) and twin electric motors (5,000shp). They had a surface speed of 15.75kt and a design submerged speed of no less than 19kt (although only 17kt was achieved in practice), twice as fast as any submarine in service at that time, except for the German Type XXI. They were designed for rapid, mass-production, but, in the event, only three were completed out of a projected 100 units.

Apart from the streamlining of the hull, the high underwater speed was achieved by greater battery power. The German Type XXI used more batteries, but the Japanese took a different course, obtaining increased electrical energy storage in a limited volume by using a new type of high-

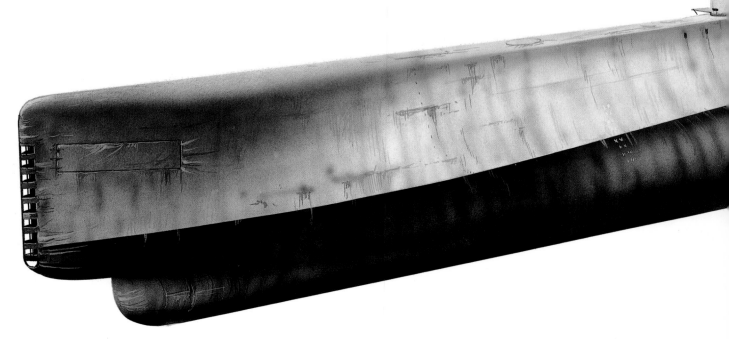

capacity, short-life batteries.

The other direct descendant of *No 71* was the STS type, a much smaller submarine than the ST, displacing 493 tons. With a single shaft they had a 400hp diesel (11.8kt) and a 1,250shp electric motor, giving a submerged speed of 14kt. Two 21in (533mm) torpedo tubes were fitted, but there was no gun.

It had been discovered that hulls were stable without forward hydroplanes and

the designers sought to do away with such devices. The submariners themselves, however, insisted upon them for low-speed control and to avoid broaching during the period immediately following the launch of a torpedo. On the STS the forward hydroplanes were fitted not on the bow, but on the hull admiships.

Like the ST, the STS class was designed with large scale mass production in mind, but only ten were completed before the war's end and no operational patrols were undertaken.

Above: *Much has been written about the German high-speed submarines developed during World War II. Much less has been written about the Japanese No 71, launched in 1938, which had an equally revolutionary, streamlined hull form. She attained an underwater speed of 21.25kt, the fastest in the world at that time by a very wide margin.*

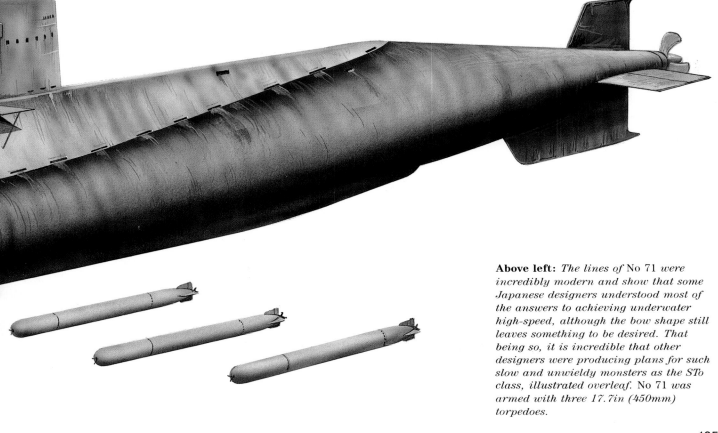

Above left: *The lines of* No 71 *were incredibly modern and show that some Japanese designers understood most of the answers to achieving underwater high-speed, although the bow shape still leaves something to be desired. That being so, it is incredible that other designers were producing plans for such slow and unwieldy monsters as the STo class, illustrated overleaf.* No 71 *was armed with three 17.7in (450mm) torpedoes.*

STo **Class**

(Aircraft-carrying submarines)

Displacement:
5,233 tons surfaced; 6,560 tons submerged
Performance:
Max speed 18.75kt surfaced; 6.5kt submerged
Range 37,500nm/14kt surfaced; 60nm/3kt
submerged
Maximum Operational Diving Depth:
330ft (100m)
Dimensions:
400ft 3in (122.0m) x 39ft 4in (12.0m) x 23ft 0in
(7.02m)
Machinery:
Four diesel engines, 7,700bhp; two electric
motors, 2,400hp; two shafts
Complement:
144
Construction:
Kure Naval Yard, *I-400*. One boat. Completed
1944.
Sasebo Navy Yard. *I-401, I-402*. Two boats.
Completed 1945.

Above: *At the end of the war the giant submarines* I-400, I-401 *and* I-14 *lie alongside a US Navy tender in Tokyo Bay, their crews supervised by their captors.*

Design: During the inter-war years many navies tried to produce an effective aircraft-carrying submarine, in which the natural 'stealth' capability of the submarine would be complemented by the long-range reconnaissance capability of aircraft. For all navies the concept was essentially the same: a small, dismantlable seaplane/floatplane was carried in a deck-mounted, watertight cylindrical hangar. To launch the aircraft the submarine had to surface, open the hangar door, and assemble the aircraft, which was then either floated off the deck of the submarine, lifted onto the water by crane, or catapulted off.

The US Navy carried out experiments using the submarine *S-1* (SS-105) in 1923 with a Martin MS-1 floatplane, but did not pursue the idea further. The British M-2 was converted in 1928 to take a small seaplane, but was lost with all hands in 1932. The French produced the *Surcouf*

(q.v.) in 1935, which carried a Besson MB411 floatplane, but although the submarine served for a number of years, the aircraft was removed when war broke out in 1939 and was not used in action.

Only the IJN produced a workable series of aircraft-carrying submarines, the first being the J1M class scout submarine *I-5*, which carried a Watanabe E9W1 biplane with twin floats. There were two hangars, with the fuselage and floats in one, the wings in the other. There was no catapult. The J2 and J3 classes followed a similar arrangement, but a stern-facing catapult was installed on the afterdeck. The A1, A2 and B1 classes represented a great improvement with the hangar forward of the conning-tower and a forward-facing

catapult, which enabled the aircraft to take additional advantage of the wind over the deck. Next came the AM class which could carry two floatplanes.

The STo (STo = *sen-toku* = special submarine) were designed to carry aircraft which would bomb American cities, but this mission was changed, at the suggestion of Admiral Yamamoto, the IJN commander-in-chief, to attacks on the locks of the Panama Canal. To this day the STo class remain the largest diesel-electric submarines ever constructed and were only overtaken in size by the US Navy's SSBN *Ethan Allen* (SSBN-608) when she was launched in 1960.

The original design, begun in 1942, would have accommodated two floatplanes, but this was later enlarged to take three aircraft, plus the parts for a fourth. The aircraft were housed in a long hangar offset slightly to starboard, with the bridge above and offset to port. The aircraft could be warmed up in the hangar and were then pulled out, one at a time, onto an 85ft (25.9m) catapult track, where their floats, which were stowed separately, were fitted. All three aircraft could be launched within 45 minutes of surfacing.

The STo's hull was of a complex nature and must have been difficult to construct. Aft it was circular in cross-section, but this changed into a horizontal figure-of-eight configuration from the engine-room to the forward end of the officers quarters, where it again changed first to circular and then to a vertical figure-of-eight right forward, which gave two torpedo rooms, one above the other. The main object of this complex arrangement was to use as broad a beam as possible to obtain stability, especially during the aircraft launch.

Aircraft: The first operational aircraft for IJN submarines was the Watanabe E9W1 (nicknamed by the Allies, 'Slim'), a slow, but reasonably effective biplane with twin floats. The second, and most widely used aircraft was the Yokosuka E14Y1 (Glen) monoplane, again with twin floats. The final aircraft in this series was the Aichi M6A1 *Seiran*, which was specifically

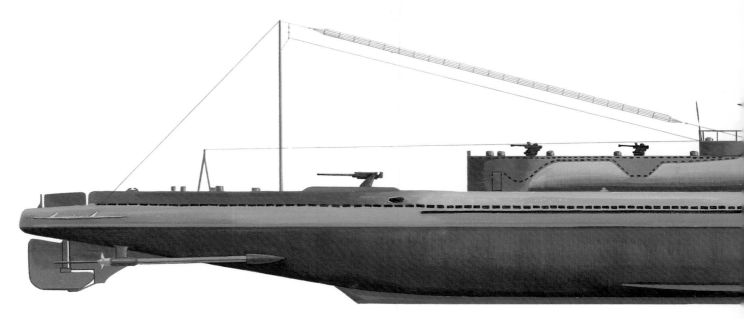

developed for operations from the STo submarines. A single-engined, low-winged monoplane it had two large floats and a crew of two. Weapon load comprised either two 550lb (250kg) bombs or a single 1,760lb (798kg) bomb, or one torpedo. Fixed, forward-firing machine-guns had been planned but were not installed and the only defensive armament was a single 13mm machine-gun operated by the observer. Maximum speed was a very respectable 300mph (483km/hr).

Armament: The STos were armed with eight 21in (533mm) torpedo tubes, located in two torpedo rooms: twenty torpedoes were carried. Surface armament comprised one 5.5in/50 (140mm) gun on the after deck and ten 25mm AA guns, with two triple mountings and one single mount on the after superstructure, and one triple mount before the conning tower.

Service History: Originally some 19 STo units were planned, but this was

Above: *A US Navy crew brings* I-14 *alongside* I-401. *Note the huge hangar and the bridge offset to port.*

progressively cut back and only five were actually laid down. Of these, one was cancelled on the ways and another was sunk by US aircraft when 90 per cent completed. Three were completed: *I-400* and *I-401* as aircraft carriers, and *I-402*, which was modified during construction and completed as a tanker to transport urgently needed oil from the East Indies to Japan.

In May 1945 *I-400* and *I-401* were combined with two AM class aircraft carriers, *I-13* and *I-14*, to form the 1st Submarine Division for an attack on the Panama Canal, the four submarines carrying a total of ten aircraft. There were repeated delays due to shortages of fuel for both submarines and aircraft, late delivery of the completed aircraft and damage to

Below: *The STo class submarine I-402, with an Aichi M6A1 Seiran positioned on the catapult ready for launch. The ultimate realisation of the aircraft-*

I-401 when she activated a magnetic mine. However training started against models of the canal locks, but the target was then changed to Ulithi, a major US Navy anchorage south of Guam.

The new plan called for the two AM class submarines to use their E14Y1 aircraft for reconnaissance over the anchorage, following which the six M6A1 aircraft from the larger submarines would carry out suicide attacks. *I-13* was sunk en route to Truk by aircraft from USS *Anzio*, but the others arrived there safely and planned the raid for 17 August. This was frustrated, however, by the broadcast of Emperor Hirohito's order for immediate surrender on 15 August. *I-400* surrendered at sea on 27 August 1945 and *I-401* followed her into captivity two days later. Their tanker sister, *I-402*, never carried out any resupply voyages; she surrendered to the US Navy and was scuttled on 1 April 1946.

carrying submarine, the STo class were too large, too unwieldy and took up too many resources late in the war, when there were higher priorities elsewhere.

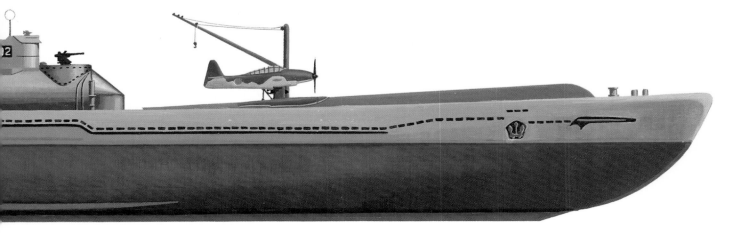

KD Class

(Ocean-going patrol submarines)

Displacement:
KD1 1,500 tons surfaced; 2,430 tons submerged
KD2 1,500 tons surfaced; 2,500 tons submerged
KD3 1,800 tons surfaced; 2,300 tons submerged
KD4 1,720 tons surfaced; 2,300 tons submerged
KD5 1,705 tons surfaced; 2,330 tons submerged
KD6A 1,785 tons surfaced; 2,420 tons submerged
KD6B 1,810 tons surfaced; 2,564 tons submerged
KD7 1,833 tons surfaced; 2,602 tons submerged

Performance:
Max speed
KD1 20kt surfaced; 10kt submerged
KD2 22kt surfaced; 10kt submerged
KD3 20kt surfaced; 8kt submerged
KD4/KD5 20kt surfaced; 8.5kt submerged
KD6/KD7 23kt surfaced; 8.25kt submerged
Range
KD1 20,000nm/10kt surfaced; 100nm/4kt submerged
KD2/5 10,000nm/10kt surfaced; 60nm/3kt submerged
KD3 10,000nm/10kt surfaced; 90nm/3kt submerged
KD4 10,800nm/10kt surfaced; 60nm/3kt submerged
KD6A 14,000nm/10kt surfaced; 65nm/3kt submerged
KD6B 10,000nm/16kt surfaced; 65nm/3kt submerged
KD7 8,000nm/16kt surfaced; 50nm/5kt submerged

Maximum Operational Diving Depth:
KD1/3/4 200ft (60m)
KD2 175ft (53m)
KD5 230ft (70m)
KD6A 245ft (75m)
KD6B 278ft (85m)
KD7 265ft (80m)

Dimensions:
KD1 300ft 0in (91.4m) x 29ft 0in (8.8m) x 15ft 0in (4.57m)
KD2 330ft 9in (100.8m) x 25ft 0in (7.6m) x 16ft 9in (5.1m)

Above: *The IJN built a series of KD submarines, starting with the KD1 class in 1924 and culminating in the KD7 class of 1942-44, to which I-176, seen here, belonged. Of the ten KD7s built, not one survived the war. Nine of these losses were due to enemy action and one to an accidental flooding.*

KD3A 330ft 0in (100.0m) x 26ft 3in (8.0m) x 15ft 9in (4.82m)
KD3B 331ft 4in (101.0m) x 26ft 0in (8.0m) x 16ft 0in (4.9m)
KD4 320ft 6in (97.7m) x 25ft 6in (7.8m) x 15ft 9in (4.8m)
KD5 320ft 6in (97.7m) x 26ft 9in (8.2m) x 15ft 6in (4.7m)
KD6A 343ft 6in (104.7m) x 26ft 11in (8.2m) x 15ft 0in (4.57m)
KD6B 344ft 6in (105.0m) x 26ft 11in (8.2m) x 15ft 0in (4.57m)
KD7 346ft 0in (105.5m) x 27ft 0in (8.25m) x 15ft 1in (4.6m)

Machinery:
KD1 Four diesel engines, 5,200bhp; two electric motors, 2,000shp; four shafts (see notes)
KD2 Two diesel engines, 6,800bhp; two electric motors, 2,000shp; two shafts
KD3 Two diesel engines, 6,800bhp; two electric motors, 1,800shp; two shafts
KD4/5 Two diesel engines, 6,000bhp; two electric motors, 1,800shp; two shafts
KD6 Two diesel engines, 9,000bhp; two electric motors, 1,800shp; two shafts
KD7 Two diesel engines, 8,000bhp; two electric motors, 1,800shp; two shafts

Complement:
KD1/2/3/4 60
KD5 75
KD6 70
KD7 86

Construction:

KD1 (1 boat)	Kure Navy Yard. *I-51*. One boat. Completed 1924.
KD2 (1 boat)	Kure Navy Yard. *I-52*. One boat. Completed 1925.
KD3A (4 boats)	Kure Navy Yard. *I-53, I-55*. Two boats. Completed 1927-28. Sasebo Navy Yard. *I-54*. One boat. Completed 1927. Yokosuka Navy Yard. *I-58*. One boat. Completed 1928.
KD3B (5 boats)	Kure Navy Yard. *I-56, I-57*. Two boats. Completed 1929. Sasebo Navy Yard. *I-60, I-63*. Two boats. Completed 1928-29. Yokosuka Navy Yard. *I-59*. One boat. Completed 1930.
KD4 (3 boats)	Mitsubishi, Kobe. *I-61, I-62*. Two boats. Completed 1929-30. Kure Navy Yard. *I-64*. One boat. Completed 1930.
KD5 (3 boats)	Kure Navy Yard. *I-65*. One boat. Completed 1932. Sasebo Navy Yard. *I-66*. One boat. Completed 1932. Mitsubishi, Kobe. *I-67*. One boat. Completed 1932.
KD6A (6 boats)	Kure Navy Yard. *I-68*. One boat. Completed 1934. Mitsubishi, Kobe. *I-69, I-72*. Two boats. Completed 1934-36. Sasebo Navy Yard. *I-70*. One boat. Completed 1934. Kawasaki, Kobe. *I-71, I-73*. Two boats. Completed 1934-35.
KD6B (2 boats)	Sasebo Navy Yard. *I-74*. One boat. Completed 1938. Mitsubishi, Kobe. *I-75*. One boat. Completed 1938.
KD7 (10 boats)	Kure Navy Yard. *I-76, I-81*. Two boats. Completed 1942-43. Kawasaki, Kobe. *I-77, I-79, I-83*. Three boats. Completed 1942-43. Mitsubishi, Kobe. *I-78*. One boat. Completed 1942. Yokosuka Navy Yard. *I-80, I-82, I-84, I-85*. Four boats. Completed 1944.

Below: *I-70, a KD6A submarine, was a rather more successful attempt at a 'fleet submarine' than was achieved by other navies, having a high surface speed and long range. Their underwater performance, however, was much less satisfactory and many were lost in the course of the war.*

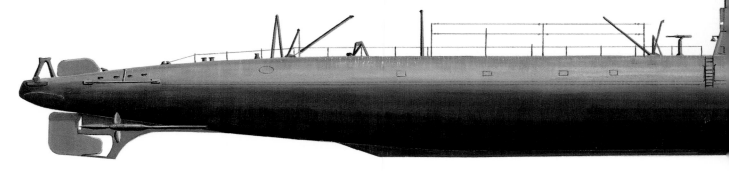

Design: Like a number of other navies, the IJN was interested in the early 1920s in the concept of a 'fleet' submarine which could act in concert with the main surface battlefleet. Combined with this was the problem that any Japanese fleet actions would take place (it was hoped) at great distances from the homeland, requiring trans-Pacific ranges. Thus, like the United States, the IJN needed submarines which were fast, with long range and heavy armament, together with sufficient reloads. They also needed reasonable habitability, although Japanese requirements in this respect were less than those of the Americans.

The programme to produce such boats started in the early 1920s and benefitted from the allocation to the IJN of a number of ex-German submarines. Several series of submarines were produced, but typical of these inter-war developments was the KD (*kaigun dai* = large) series. This consisted of nine sub-types and a total of 35 boats constructed over eighteen years, each type representing a small but significant advance on its predecessor.

First in the series was the single submarine KD1 class, *No 44*, later *I-51*, by far the largest submarine built in Japan up to that time. British assistance was given in the design and she was armed with eight 21in (533mm) torpedo tubes and two deck guns. Her most spectacular capability, however, was a surface range of no less than 20,000nm (37,040km) at 10kt, almost certainly greater than that of any other operational submarine at that time.

Next in the series was the KD2 type, of which six were originally planned, but the Washington Naval Treaty of 1922 intervened, as a result of which only one (*I-52*, later *I-152*) was, in fact, completed. Her design incorporated lessons learnt from examination of the German *U-139*, one of the surrendered boats allocated to Japan. Slightly larger than the KD1 she displaced 2,500 tons, but had just half the surface range (10,000nm, 18,500km).

The nine KD3A/KD3B were launched between 1925 and 1929; these were virtually identical with the KD2, except that one gun was deleted. The next three boats, KD4, launched 1927-29, were very similar again, except for an 8 per cent increase in surface range and a reduction in the number of torpedo tubes. The three KD5 boats, launched in 1931 had a

marginally greater displacement than the KD4, but the armament was changed again.

Next came the KD6A/6B class of eight boats, which had the exceptionally high surface speed of 23kt, although maximum submerged speed was still 8.25kt. The two KD6B boats had strengthened hulls, giving them a slightly greater diving depth than the KD6A; surface range was also slightly less.

Armament: There were constant minor changes in the armament of these various types. This reflects changing tactical ideas, differing perceptions of the threat, feedback from operational boats and, as in all navies, changing views of senior officers!

The KD1 class, first in the series, had a particularly heavy armament of eight 21in (533mm) torpedo tubes, all in the bow (sixteen reloads), together with one 4in (102mm) and one 3in (76mm) deck guns. It was very unusual at this time for patrol submarines to be built without stern tubes and in the KD2 class, while the total number of tubes remained the same, two were moved to the stern and reloads reduced to eight, while the main gun was upgraded to a 4.7in (120mm). In the KD3 the complete torpedo battery was once again moved to the bow, with eight reloads, and, while the 4.7in (120mm) gun was retained, the 3in (76mm) was removed.

KD4 reverted to the six bow, two stern torpedo tube layout of the KD2, with reloads reduced to six, but had only one 4.7in (120mm) gun as in the KD3. KD5, KD6 and KD7 classes all had six bow torpedo tubes with eight reloads (six in KD7). KD5 and KD6A both had one 3.9in (100mm) gun and one 13mm AAMG, while KD6B had a 4.7in (120mm) gun in place of the 3.9in (100mm). KD7 also had the 4.7in (120mm) main gun, but AA defence was provided by twin 25mm cannon.

Service History: The two oldest submarines did not see war service, both having converted to the training role, *I-51* in 1930 and *I-52* in 1940. They were stricken in 1941 and 1942 respectively.

I-63 sank after a collision in 1939 and, although recovered, was immediately scrapped. Of the remaining boats in the KD3 class one, *I-60*, was sunk by a British submarine in 1942 and the others were relegated to training duties in mid-1942. Four were converted to *kaiten* carriers in 1945, their deck guns being removed to accommodate the suicide submarines. None was lost on suicide operations and, together with the unconverted training boats, they survived the war, to be scrapped or scuttled in 1946.

One of the three KD4 boats was sunk in a collison in 1941 and the second was sunk by a US submarine in 1942. The third became a training boat in 1944, but was converted to a *kaiten* carrier in 1945; however, she survived the war to be scuttled in 1946.

Of the three KD5 boats, one was lost in an exercise two years before the war, one was sunk by a British submarine in 1944, and the third, having been converted to a *kaiten* carrier, was sunk by US naval aircraft whilst on a mission with the suicide boats in 1945.

There were eight KD6s, every one of which was lost in the war. Three boats, *I-171*, *I-174* and *I-175* (formerly *I-71*, *I-74* and *I-75*, respectively), were converted to transports in 1942, which involved removing the deck gun and most of the spare torpedoes. This enabled them to carry stores internally, and vehicles and a *Daihatsu* landing craft on the upper casing. The US Navy sank six, four being sunk by surface ships, one by a submarine and one by aircraft. Of the two others, one was accidentally flooded during an air attack on Truk and the last was lost at sea, causes unknown, in 1944.

Not one of the KD7s survived the war, either, the US Navy sinking no less than nine: surface ASW ships sank seven; naval aircraft, one; and submarines, one. The final loss was due to accidental flooding in 1943.

These boats sank 38 enemy merchantmen (146,948grt) during the war and damaged a further 11 (57,382grt). They also damaged a number of small warships. In essence, they were good on the surface, having high speed, long range and a good weapons fit. However, their submerged performance was barely adequate and this possibly accounts for their large proportion of war losses.

Yuushio Class

(Diesel-electric attack submarines) (SSK)

Displacement:
2,250 tons surfaced; not known submerged
Performance:
Max speed 12kt surfaced; 20kt submerged
Range not known
Maximum Operational Diving Depth:
984ft (300m)
Dimensions:
250ft 0in (76.2m) x 32ft 6in (9.9m) x 24ft 7in
(7.5m)
Machinery:
Two Mitsubishi/M.A.N. V8/V24-30 AMTL
Kawasaki diesel generator sets, 1,700bhp; one
Fuji electric motor, 7,220shp; one shaft
Complement:
80
Construction:
Mitsubishi, Kobe. *Yuushio* (SS-573), *Nadashio*
(SS-577), *Akishio* (SS-579), *Yukishio* (SS-581).
4 boats. Launched 1979-89.
Kawasaki, Kobe. *Mochishio* (SS-574), *Setoshio*
(SS-575), *Okishio* (SS-576), *Hamashio* (SS-578),
Takeshio (SS-580), *Sachishio* (SS-582). 6 boats.
Launched 1980-88.

Above: *A Yuushio class submarine of the Japanese Maritime Self-Defense Force (JMSDF) at high speed on the surface. This is one of the most capable diesel-electric classes ever built by any navy. Performance compares favourably with most SSNs except, obviously, with regard to underwater endurance.*

Left: *The submarine* Mochishio *(SS-574), the second of her class to be completed. The lines of this class are exceptionally clean, giving an outstanding underwater performance.*

Design: The IJN had a large submarine fleet in World War II, but all were disposed of after the surrender. In the early 1950s the Japanese Maritime Self-Defense Force (JMSDF) received a surplus US Navy submarine for training, but as the economy gained strength Japan decided to restore a national shipbuilding capability.

The first post-war submarine was the *Oyashio* (1,420 tons) which was commissioned in 1959 and was followed by the improved four-boat Hayashio class in 1961-62. Yet further improvement came with the Ooshio class (1,650 tons), which were among the last submarines to be built with stern torpedo tubes.

The next class, Uzushio, was, like a number of other Western designs, based upon the US Navy's *Barbel*, with an *Albacore*-type teardrop hull for faster and quieter underwater performance and better controllability and manouevrability, particularly at high speed. Of 2,340 tons displacement (submerged) the hull was built of a very high quality steel to give a diving-depth of 656ft (200m). Seven boats were built between 1969 and 1977, and the first two were stricken in 1987 and 1988 after only 16 years' service.

The latest class to enter service is the Yuushio class, with all ten boats in service by December 1990. This is basically an all-round improvement on the Uzushio class, capable of slightly higher speeds. Like the previous class, the Yuushio class has its torpedo room admidships. The tubes are angled out at 10°, with their mouths just abaft the large bow sonar array, a feature they share with US Navy SSNs.

The Uzushio class was built of NS-63 high-tensile steel, but the Yuushios are built of even stronger NS-90, permitting an increase in diving-depth from 656ft (200m) to 984ft (300m).

Armament: There are six 21in (533mm) torpedo tubes and up to 15 torpedoes or missiles can be carried. Weapons include Mark 48 wire-guided torpedoes and Mark 37C ASW torpedoes, while boats from *Nadashio* (SS-577) onwards are fitted to launch Sub-Harpoon, as well.

Service History: *Yuushio (SS-573)* entered service in 1980 and the remaining nine boats followed at yearly intervals thereafter. These very sophisticated attack submarines are equivalent to SSNs in most features except for underwater endurance. This is pushing the JMSDF towards seeking a solution to the long-standing problem of discovering an effective and efficient air-independent propulsion system, which will free the non-nuclear submarine from the necessity of coming up to 'breathe' at regular intervals.

The next class of submarines for the JMSDF will be an improved version of the Yuushio class, slightly longer and with surface displacement increased from 2,250 tons to 2,400 tons. The first of class (SSN-584) is due to enter service in 1991.

Left: Yuushio *(SS-573), her lines making an interesting comparison with those of USS* Albacore *(AGSS-569) (see pages 38-39), from which she is descended by way of the Uzushio class. The six torpedo tubes are placed well back from the bows and can launch US Mark 37C short torpedoes (1) and Japanese GRX-2 torpedoes (2). The fifth of class onwards can also launch Sub-Harpoon (3) and the earlier boats are being modified to launch this missile as well.*

FRANCE

The first submersible to be built in France was *Nautilus*, constructed at Rouen in the early years of the 19th Century to a design by the American Robert Fulton. Although she worked after a fashion and certainly was able to submerge and surface again, she was propelled under water by a manually turned screw, which made her slow and very limited in range. Despite its revolutionary enthusiasms, the French Navy showed little interest in this vessel and Fulton went elsewhere in a vain attempt to market his ideas.

The first working French submersible was the *Plongeur*, which was designed by Admiral Siméon Bourgois and launched in 1863. The propulsion problem was solved by using a compressed-air engine, which proved to be very safe, but gave a poor performance, with a range of 5.7nm (10.5km) at 3.8kt submerged and a maximum speed of 4kt. Her only armament was a spar torpedo and after a series of trials she was stricken in 1872, fitted with a steam-engine and used as a harbour tender until 1935.

Goubet produced two submarines in the 1880s, which were reasonably successful, the second one even attracting an order from Brazil, although she was never delivered. Next to appear (in 1888) was *Gymnote*, a tiny, 31 ton submarine with all-electric power. She made over 2,000 successful dives and her major innovation was the use of hydroplanes for submerged control, three being fitted on each side. The next design, the *Gustave Zédé*, was also powered by electric motors and introduced a tall conning-tower and a rudimentary periscope. She was armed with one 17.7in (450mm) torpedo tube and three torpedoes, and carried out some 2,500 dives before being stricken in 1909. Both these types needed to return to port to recharge their batteries, which was a serious tactical limitation.

The real breakthrough came with *Narval*, which was the winner in a competition sponsored by the Minister of Marine. This very successful design, which is described in more detail in the following pages, established Maxime Laubeuf as one

Above: *The Goubet submarine consisted of a single bronze casting 16ft 5in (5m) long, 5ft 9in (1.75m) deep and 3ft 3in (1m) wide. The two-man crew sat back-to-back beneath a large dome with seven ports. Power was by batteries.*

of France's foremost submarine designers. *Narval* was launched in 1899.

Between 1900 and the end of World War I France built 116 submarines in 30 identifiable classes, although some were simply improved versions of an earlier class. At the time of the outbreak of war in 1914 the navy possessed 79 submarines of which 39 were actually in service, the remainder being in reserve. Some of the early classes were powered by petrol engines, but most were powered by diesels, the first of these being the submarine *Z*, launched in 1904. However, a number of classes were powered by steam engines, and although this meant that they were slow to submerge, the French appear to have had less trouble with such a propulsion system than the Royal Navy. However, the Dupuy de Lome class of 1915 was the last to be powered by steam, and all subsequent French submarines were diesel-powered until the appearance of nuclear-propulsion in the 1960s.

Below: *Pluviose, constructed in 1908, was a Laubeuf design. Eight torpedoes were carried, two of which were mounted in the cradles seen on the stern.*

All French submarines of this period were armed with 17.7in (450mm) torpedoes, of which some were launched from internal bow tubes. However, from a very early stage the French were keen on the torpedo 'drop-collars' invented by the Russian submarine designer Drzewiecki and sometimes also used simple external cradles to carry and launch torpdoes.

During World War I French submarines operated in the Mediterranean, the Adriatic, the Dardanelles, the Atlantic, the North Sea and the Channel. They were fairly successful, but were limited by their short range and an absence of large numbers of targets to engage. Construction during the war was on a small scale and at the end of the war the navy found itself with a submarine fleet of limited tactical value and with a high proportion of elderly boats. In the share-out of German submarines 44 were allocated to France, of which ten were actually commissioned, the remainder being scrapped.

The Inter-War Years

One of the notable incidents of the Washington Naval Conference of 1921-22 was the British proposal to ban submarine warfare completely, a suggestion which was strenuously resisted by France. Even so, France's financial position did not permit the major building programmes the navy would have liked. In 1922 six Requin class (1,441 tons) submarines were ordered, and thereafter, the modern

submarine fleet was gradually expanded.

The major building effort for many years was put into two series: the 600/630 tonne medium type and the 1,500 tonne large, ocean-going type (the metric tonne is specified here, as this was how the types were officially designated). In each case the navy issued standard specifications and then left individual yards to produce their own designs. First came the 600 tonne type in the mid-1920s, of which there were three designs, from Simonot-Loire (Sirène class), Normand-Fenaux (Ariane class), and Schneider-Laubeuf (Circé class), with four of each being built. An improved series of specifications was issued a few years later, leading to the slightly larger 630 tonne type: Schneider-Laubeuf (Argonaute class, five built), Normand-Fenaux (Diane class, nine built) and Loire-Dubigeon (Orion class, two built). The Admiralty then decided to achieve better standardisation and produced its own design for a yet further improved 630 tonne type, which became the Minerve class, of which six were completed between 1934 and 1938. The final version of this series was the Aurore class (1,170 tons submerged displacement), again to an Admiralty design, eight were ordered of which only the name-boat of the class was completed.

The second major group was the ocean-going 1500 tonne type, the first series of nineteen boats in the Redoutable class being constructed in the late 1920. They were good seaboats, with long-range and good surface speed. However, they suffered from two problems which affected most French submarines of this period: a slow diving time and complex torpedo

Above: Rubis, *launched in 1907 and seen here in 1911, was a single-hull Maugas design. A head-count suggests that just two crew members are in control below!*

arrangements. A second series of six boats with more powerful diesel engines was built in the early 1930s followed by another six of the third series in the mid-1930s, which had even more powerful engines. A fourth and greatly improved series was planned for the early 1940s, but was halted by the outbreak of war.

As with other navies, the French built some minelayers, of which the best was the Saphir class, completed between 1928 and 1935. Of the six completed the most famous was *Rubis*, which was the most successful minelayer of World War II. The French also built *Surcouf*, a giant (4,304 tons) cruiser submarine armed with two 8in guns, two 37mm AA guns, eight 21.7in (550mm) and four 15.7in (400mm) torpedo tubes, and carrying a reconnaissance seaplane. Designed to a flawed tactical concept, she remained a 'one-off' and was sunk in 1942, rammed by a merchant ship in the Caribbean.

Not one World War I submarine survived beyond 1935 and the oldest submarine in service on the outbreak of war was *Requin*, which had been launched in 1924. There were 75 submarines in service: 33 of the 600/630 tonne types, 29 of the 1500 tonne type, six of the Requin class, six of the Saphir class and *Surcouf*.

Below: Narval *was one of the first boats constructed after World War I, and incorporated the results of detailed examination of surrendered U-boats.*

All these submarines developed in the inter-war years had a very characteristically French torpedo armament. Virtually all other navies used the 21in (533mm) torpedo tube, and the normal arrangement was to mount the majority in the bow and a small number in the stern. Most of these tubes were housed internally, which meant that they could be reloaded. A few submarines also had fixed, external tubes, usually in the stern, which could not, of course, be reloaded while submerged. The French Navy, however, used rotating mounts, housing two, three or four topedo tubes, in many submarines. These mounts were situated either near the centre of the boat, or on the stern. The 1500 tonne-type submarines for example, were armed with nine 21.7in (550mm) and two 15.7in (400mm) tubes. Of the nine 21.7in (550mm) tubes, four were in the bows, three were in a rotating mount immediately abaft the conning-tower and two shared a rotating mount with the two 15.7in (400mm) tubes on the stern.

These mounts were mechanically complicated and had an additional disadvantage in that they set up asymmetric forces when rotated underwater prior to firing, making steering difficult. Further, they could not be reloaded while submerged. The gyroscopic motors in French torpedoes were unreliable when set for an angular course and so a 'spread' was obtained by using these rotating mounts. The reason for using the smaller 15.7in (400mm) calibre torpedoes was that they were adequate against smaller and less well-protected targets, such as merchant ships.

World War II

The French Navy's roles at the start of World War II were to protect France's trade routes, to defend the colonial territories of the French Empire, and to co-operate with the British in the North Sea, Channel, Atlantic and Mediterranean. However, the land defence against Germany collapsed and the instrument of capitulation was signed on 21 June 1940. Submarines under construction were destroyed on the ways, but the operational boats suffered a variety of fates. Some were already in British ports or sailed to such ports to escape capture; others came under Vichy control; some were scuttled. The seven French submarines in British ports were seized by the Royal Navy, but were later turned over to the Free French Navy, the most famous of these being *Surcouf* and the minelayer, *Rubis*.

Those submarines which came under Vichy control carried out numerous operational tasks, one of the major achievements being to damage the British battleship HMS *Resolution* (31,000 tons) during the Dakar action in September 1940. Sixteen submarines were lost during operations under the Vichy flag and three were scuttled in North African ports rather than be captured by the Allies. There were 21 French submarines moored in Toulon on 27 November 1942 when the Germans took over the naval base. Sixteen were scuttled or sabotaged by their crews and four escaped, of which one reached Spain and was interned, while the other three reached North African ports. In a concurrent action, nine submarines at Bizerta, all of which had been taken out of commission, were captured by German and Italian forces and were disposed of by them.

At the beginning of 1944 the submarine force of the Free French Navy numbered some 22 boats and that number was more or less maintained until the end of the war. Two were lost, but the Royal Navy bolstered the numbers by transferring one

Above: *When the Germans occupied Toulon on 27 November 1942 four submarines escaped, of which three reached North Africa. Here the crew of* Casablanca *recover from their voyage.*

captured Italian submarine and three newly-built British boats: one U and two V class. The end of the war found the French Navy with twenty submarines in service, over fifty having been lost, for various reasons, since 1939.

French Submarine Losses 1939-1945								
CAUSE	1939	1940	1941	1942	1943	1944	1945	Totals
Land-based aircraft				8				8
Surface ships		3		4	1			8
Submarines		2	1					3
Mines		2						2
Operational losses				1				1
Scuttled to avoid capture		4		21				25
Captured				9				9
Stricken					2			2
Sunk by friendly forces						1		1
Totals	0	11	1	43	3	1	0	59

Below: Aréthuse *was one of a class of four specialised ASW submarines completed 1958-60. They were intended specifically to operate in the choke-point between the toe of Italy and Tunisia.*

Post-War Developments

These twenty submarines were of outdated design and worn out after six years of war, but they had to serve on for at least a few years, while the fleet was recreated. The first 'new' boats to be commissioned into the post-war fleet were five boats of the pre-war Aurore class, which had not been completed due to the outbreak of war in 1939. They were finished and commissioned in the late 1940s and subsequently underwent further modifications, including some streamlining. All were scrapped in the 1960s.

In the division of German equipment the French received one Type XXI (*U-2518*) and one Type XXIII (*U-2326*). Although the latter was lost in the same year, the Type XXI was commissioned as *Roland Morillot* and served for some years. She was also used as the basis for the first new French design, the Narval class, which was ordered under the 1949-54 Programmes, the first-of-class, *Narval*, being laid down in 1951. Large and capable boats, well-streamlined and fitted with a schnorkel, they had a submerged displacement of 1,910 tons. Six were built, being modernised between 1966 and 1970; only one (*Dauphin*) remained in service in 1991, being used as an experimental vessel.

The navy still did not have sufficient hulls, however, and in 1951/52 four British S class submarines were transferred on

loan for use as targets in anti-submarine warfare training, as part of a NATO programme. One was lost in an accident and the remaining three were returned between 1958 and 1961.

After the Narval class came the Aréthuse class, much smaller (669 tons submerged displacement). They were handy and efficient submarines, and four were built.

An improvement on the Aréthuse class, the nine Daphné class submarines were launched between 1959 and 1967. With a submerged displacement of 1,038 tons they were initially popular and attracted a number of export orders, but a series of losses marred their repuation for some years. They were followed by the Agosta class (1,450 tons), which appears likely to be the final diesel-electric class built for the French Navy. Displacing 1,750 tons, French yards have built four of these submarines for the French Navy and two for the Pakistan Navy, while Bazan, Cartagena has built four for the Spanish Navy.

Design work had started on a French nuclear submarine in the 1950s and a hull was laid down in 1958. However, the project was cancelled in 1959 and work on the hull suspended. President de Gaulle decided in the late 1950s that France needed an independent nuclear deterrent and although land- and air-based systems were developed in parallel, the major resources and expenditure have been devoted to the sea-based element. Unlike any other navy, political pressure forced the French Navy to develop their first nuclear-propelled submarine for use as a ballistic-missile launcher, rather than as an attack submarine. This was a very tall order, requiring the simultaneous development and integration of a number of very advanced technologies — nuclear propulsion, missiles and warheads, missile guidance, missile launch from a submerged submarine and very precise navigation and position-fixing. In the event, and to the very great credit of French industry, it all worked.

One requirement of this very complex programme was to test the missiles at sea. To achieve this the unfinished hull of the still-born 1950s nuclear submarine was completed as the missile trials boat *Gymnote*, but with diesel-electric rather than nuclear propulsion.

The first SSBN, *Le Redoutable*, was laid down in 1964, launched in 1967, and became operational in 1971, a truly remarkable French national effort. This has been followed by four more similar SSBNs and a modified design, the single boat L'Inflexible class. The first submarine of the new 'SNLE-NG' class was laid down in 1989 and will enter service in 1994, being followed by two more before the turn of the century.

Having successfully got the SSBN force into service, the French Navy subsequently turned to the development of a nuclear-propelled attack submarine, which led to the Rubis class and its improved version, the Amethyste class. These are the smallest operational SSNs yet constructed by any navy.

Above: Le Redoutable, *the first French SSBN, was launched in March 1967 and became operational in December 1971, armed with sixteen M20 missiles.*

Below: L'Inflexible, *the sixth French SSBN, a development of the Le Redoutable class, is armed with sixteen M4 SLBMs.*

Narval Class

(Harbour defence submarine)

Displacement:
117 tons surfaced; 202 tons submerged
Performance:
Max speed 9.9kt surfaced; 5.3kt submerged
Range 345nm/8.8kt surfaced; 58nm/2.8kt
submerged
Maximum Operational Diving Depth:
50ft (15m)
Dimensions:
111ft 7in (34.0m) x 12ft 6in (3.8m) x 6ft 1in
(1.8m)
Machinery:
TE steam engine, 220ihp; one electric motor,
80shp; one shaft
Complement:
13
Construction:
Arsenal de Cherbourg. *Narval* (Q4). One boat.
Completed 1899

Design: In the early days of submarine
development the names of the designers
were internationally known; men of such
celebrity were, for example, Holland and
Lake in the USA, Pullino and Laurenti in
Italy, and Drzewiecki and Bubnov in
Russia. Among this elite group was the
French designer, Maxime Laubeuf
(1864-1939), whose name is associated
with a series of successful submarines.

In 1896 the new French Minister of
Marine sponsored an international
competition for a submarine with a
maximum displacement of 200 tons, a
surface range of 100nm (185km) and a
submerged range of 10nm (18.5km).
Twenty-nine designs were submitted from
various countries. Laubeuf won with a

design that introduced a number of very
significant innovations. Perhaps the most
important and farsighted development was
the idea of a double hull in which the
pressure body was surrounded by a lighter
streamlined casing, with the ballast tanks
and some accessories fitted in the gap
between the two. In this, *Narval* was the
precursor of virtually every subsequent
submarine design.

Laubeuf's other great advance was the
use of a practicable mixed propulsion
system, consisting of a surface propulsion
system (steam) and a submerged, air-
independent system (batteries), in which
the steam engine also charged the
batteries whilst propelling the submarine
on the surface. There had been battery-
powered submarines before, but all had
had to return to port for the cells to be
recharged, a shortcoming which Laubeuf
removed at a stroke. There had even been
a previous design for a mixed steam/
battery plant, produced by an American
named Alstitt in the 1860s, but his device
was unsuccessful and it was Laubeuf who
first made it a practical proposition.

Laubeuf selected an oil-fired steam
system for surface propulsion, since not
only did it utilise technology that was well
understood, but it was also very much
safer than the only realistic alternative of
that time, the petrol engine. There were,
however, certain unavoidable drawbacks to
steam propulsion, which neither Laubeuf
nor any other designer ever overcame.

Steam propulsion systems created very
high temperatures within the submarine,
which were both very unpleasant to work
in and also caused excessive condensation,
which had a harmful effect on other
equipment. Secondly, a funnel was
essential as an exhaust uptake, with a
valve needed to block off this opening
prior to submerging. This made the

submarine very vulnerable, since the
funnel was not only short but was also
inevitably placed on the very low
superstructure; thus, a high wave could
easily enter the uptake before the valve
could be closed, leading to swamping.
Thirdly, diving in a steam-powered
submarine was of necessity a slow
procedure since the furnaces had to be
damped down and at least some of the

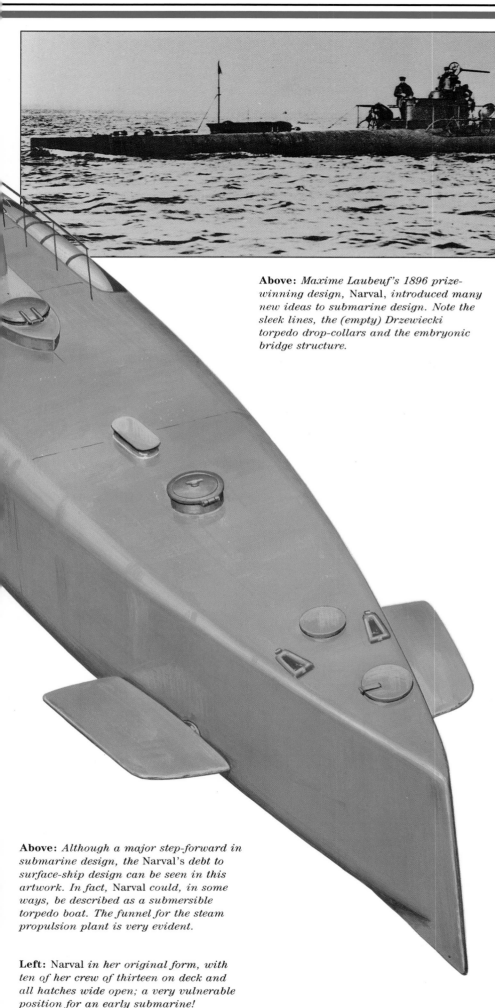

Above: *Maxime Laubeuf's 1896 prize-winning design,* Narval, *introduced many new ideas to submarine design. Note the sleek lines, the (empty) Drzewiecki torpedo drop-collars and the embryonic bridge structure.*

Above: *Although a major step-forward in submarine design, the* Narval's *debt to surface-ship design can be seen in this artwork. In fact,* Narval *could, in some ways, be described as a submersible torpedo boat. The funnel for the steam propulsion plant is very evident.*

Left: Narval *in her original form, with ten of her crew of thirteen on deck and all hatches wide open; a very vulnerable position for an early submarine!*

heat dissipated before the boat could dive. It took up to twenty minutes in *Narval* at first, although this period was later reduced to twelve minutes. This may not have mattered too much in peace, but was obviously a very major hazard in war!

There were other innovations in the *Narval*, too. These included a fairly substantial tower in the centre of the deck (an embryonic conning-tower) and one of the first submarine periscopes, which gave the commander a means of seeing what was happening on the surface, without exposing the complete hull.

Armament: *Narval* was fitted with four torpedo drop-collars, of the type developed by the Russian submarine designer/engineer Drzewiecki. These were mounted high on *Narval's* upper casing and took the then standard French 17.7in (450mm) torpedoes. Like all such installations the drop-collars were very prone to damage, as well as being inherently inaccurate, but they continued to be used on French submarines for many years.

Service History: *Narval* was launched on 21 October 1899, but was not ready to run trials until the end of the following year. Once started, however, the trials were very successful. She was commissioned into the French Navy and served with great success until 1909, when she was stricken and scrapped.

So promising was the design that a successor class was ordered on 20 May 1899; ie, six months before *Narval* was launched. The Sirène class, another Laubeuf design, was shorter by 12ft 4in (3.76m) but with a 2ft 1in (0.61m) greater draught. These boats had a slightly greater displacement (213 tons), a greatly increased surface range of 600nm (1,110km) at 8kt, and could dive in six minutes. However, they were otherwise identical with the earlier boat. Launched in 1901 the four boats of the Sirène class served throughout World War I in Cherbourg as part of a local defence flotilla. They were all scrapped in 1919.

It is worth noting that Laubeuf designed a number of classes of submarine powered by steam engines, twenty-five in all. Steam propulsion had many disadvantages, as described above, but these notwithstanding, not one of these boats sank due to faults in, or stemming from, her propulsion system.

Surcouf Class

(Ocean-going cruiser submarine)

Displacement:
3,252 tons surfaced; 4,304 tons submerged
Performance:
Max speed 18.5kt surfaced; 10kt submerged
Range 10,000nm/10kt surfaced; 70nm/4.5kt submerged
Maximum Operational Diving Depth:
262ft (80m)
Dimensions:
360ft 11in (110.0m) x 29ft 6in (9.0m) x 23ft 9in (7.25m)
Machinery:
Two Sulzer diesel engines, 7,600bhp; two electric motors; 3,400shp; two shafts
Complement:
118
Construction:
Arsenal de Cherbourg. *Surcouf.* One boat. Completed 1935

Below: *Designed specifically for operation from the* Surcouf, *the Besson MB 411 had a range of 215nm (400km), which could be increased to 400nm (740km) with the use of auxiliary tanks. The only example was destroyed on the ground in England in 1941 and was thus not on* Surcouf's *final trip to the USA.*

Design: The pressures of World War I gave rise to great improvements in design and performance of submarines. It became possible for submarines to do more than just lie in wait for targets and then attack them with either small guns or torpedoes, both of which had short ranges. Obviously, a larger gun would enable the submarine to attack surface targets at much greater ranges.

The British developed the K class, a so-called 'fleet' submarine. Eighteen were built between 1916 and 1918; they had a submerged displacement of 2,600 tons and were armed with two 4in (102mm) guns. The next step was the M class which had a 12in (305mm) gun in a large turret forward of the conning tower. Three were built, of which *M-1* was lost with all hands in 1925, *M-2* was converted into a seaplane carrier (and sank when the hangar door was inadvertently left open during a dive) and *M-3* was converted into a minelayer.

Surcouf, designed under the 1926 Naval programme, was, in her time, the largest submarine in the world, her vast dimensions being necessary to carry all the items considered necessary for her role of worldwide commerce-raiding. Her twin 8in (203mm) guns were the largest permitted on a submarine under the 1922 Washington Naval Treaty and were mounted in a turret forward of the conning-tower, controlled by a director and

a range-finder. Abaft the conning-tower was an aircraft hangar, with the AA guns mounted on its roof. In line with its role, a 16ft (4.9m) motor cutter was carried to take the boarding party to its prizes and a compartment was provided within the *Surcouf* for 40 prisoners.

Surcouf was the last of the submarine designs that sought to use guns as an alternative to torpedoes for major actions against surface ships. *Surcouf* spent most of her career in search of a proper role. Although the basic operational concept was not totally unsound, it was the technology that was deficient. Today's cruise-missile armed submarines are the realisation of that idea.

Armament: The main armament was two 8in (203mm)/50 guns, for which 600 rounds were carried. With a maximum range of some 26,250yd (24,000m) these enabled *Surcouf*, at least in theory, to deal with armed merchant cruisers and other lightly armed convoy escorts from considerably outside their guns' maximum range. The first rounds could be fired some two and a half minutes after surfacing. A large stereoscopic range-finder was mounted on the superstructure just forward of the bridge; it had a 13ft 1in (4m) base. However, the visual horizon of the director was little more than 12,300yd (11,265m), which established the effective range of the guns.

Secondary gun armament comprised two

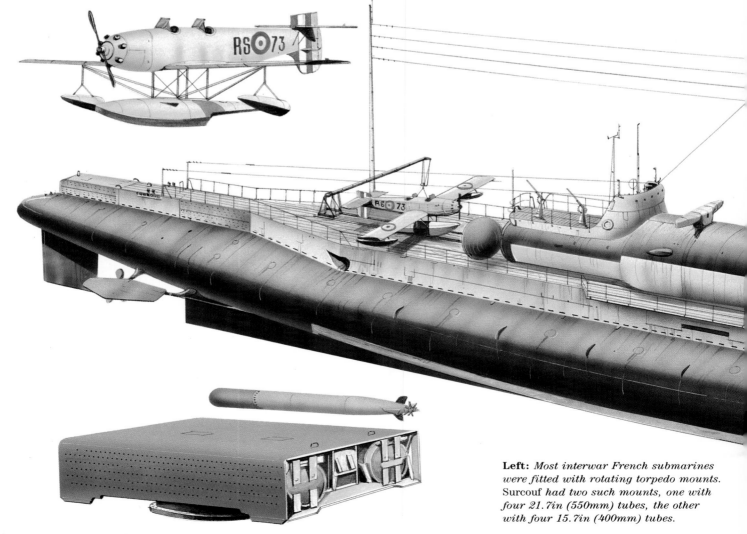

Left: *Most interwar French submarines were fitted with rotating torpedo mounts.* Surcouf *had two such mounts, one with four 21.7in (550mm) tubes, the other with four 15.7in (400mm) tubes.*

37mm (1,000 rounds) and two twin Hotchkiss 13.2mm AAMG (16,000 rounds). This alone was considerably more than the *total* armament of many submarines.

Twelve torpedo tubes were fitted: eight 21.7in (550mm) (four in the bows and four externally aft; fourteen torpedoes carried). Four 15.75in (400mm) tubes were in a separate traversing mount, for which eight torpedoes were carried. These smaller, faster torpedoes were intended for use against merchant ships.

Aircraft: The Besson MB 411 floatplane was developed specifically for this role. With a span of 32ft 4in (9.85m), length of 22ft 11in (7m) and a height of 7ft 10in (2.40m) the aircraft was very small. Powered by a 120hp Salmson air-cooled radial engine, it could be dismantled in 10 minutes and placed in a container 13ft 1in (4m) square and 22ft 11in (9m) long. The aircraft was not a success and had been removed by the outbreak of war in 1939. Its hangar was thereafter used as a storeroom.

Service History: Having taken some seven years to build, *Surcouf* was commissioned in 1935, and made several lengthy cruises before the outbreak of World War II. In 1939/40 she served as a convoy escort on several occasions, but left Brest on 18 June 1940 to avoid capture by the Germans.

She lay at Plymouth, England for some weeks before being taken over by force by the Royal Navy on 3 July, an action during which three Britons and one Frenchman were killed, and two men wounded. Thereafter *Surcouf* served with a French crew, but under British operational

Above: Surcouf *in peacetime, the diminutive figures of her crew showing just how large she was. Note the two masts for high-frequency radio antennas.*

Below: Surcouf *in Holy Loch, Scotland early during World War II. Designed for anti-shipping missions, she proved difficult to employ effectively.*

control. There was much discussion as to the best use to which this odd submarine might be put. She was used as convoy escort and for anti-surface raider patrols in the Caribbean and was also used (under French command) in the operation to bring the islands of St Pierre-et-Miquelon under Free French control in December 1941.

It was then decided to send her to the Pacific where she would be employed in the defence of the Free French Pacific Islands. She was transitting across the Caribbean when, on 18 February 1942 she was rammed and sunk with all hands. Ironically, having been built to sink merchantmen, it was a US merchant ship, the *Thomson Lykes*, which sank the *Surcouf*.

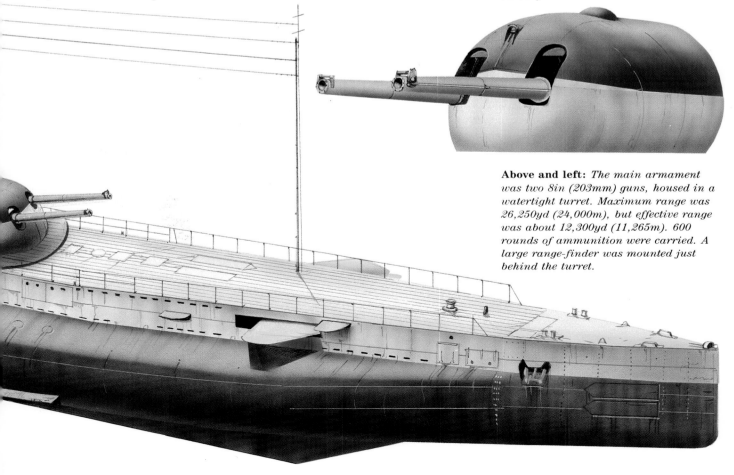

Above and left: *The main armament was two 8in (203mm) guns, housed in a watertight turret. Maximum range was 26,250yd (24,000m), but effective range was about 12,300yd (11,265m). 600 rounds of ammunition were carried. A large range-finder was mounted just behind the turret.*

Saphir Class

(Ocean-going minelaying submarines)

Displacement:
761 tons surfaced; 925 tons submerged
Performance:
Max speed 12kt surfaced; 9kt submerged
Range 4,000nm/12kt surfaced; 80nm/4kt
submerged
Maximum Operational Diving Depth:
262ft (80m)
Dimensions:
216ft 2in (65.9m) x 23ft 7in (7.2m) x 14ft 1in
(4.3m)
Machinery:
Two Normand-Vickers diesel engines, 1,300bhp;
two electric motors, 1,000shp; two shafts
Complement:
42
Construction:
Arsenal de Toulon. *Saphir, Turquoise, Nautilus,
Rubis, Diamant, Perle.* Six boats. Completed
1928 to 1935

Right: *The famous Free French submarine,* Rubis, *lying alongside in the Scottish port of Dundee in 1940. The broad ballast tanks housed the sixteen vertical mine-tubes of the Normand-Fenaux system, eight on each side, with two mines per tube.*

Above: *Free French sailors man the twin 13.2mm AAMG mount on a Saphir class submarine, probably* Rubis. *Aircraft became submarines' greatest menace and no submarine would have travelled in this manner in daylight later in the war.*

Below: *A fine shot of* Rubis. *Her mines accounted for a minelayer, seven patrol boats and fourteen merchant ships, and she sank another merchantman with a torpedo, making her the most successful Free French submarine of World War II.*

Above: Rubis, *showing her typical inter-war hull shape. Note the numerous protuberances, whose drag limited underwater speed and endurance.*

Design: Numerous navies pursued the idea of specialised minelayers in the inter-war years. The Saphir class were developed from the *Pierre Chailley*, the first French minelayer, which had been launched in 1921, and which tested and proved the very successful Normand-Fenaux minelaying system.

Laubeuf-type submarines with a double-hull, there was nothing particularly remarkable about their design, and their surface speed was surprisingly slow. Nevertheless, they were among the most successful of the French inter-war designs.

Armament: There were five torpedo tubes. Two 21.7in (550mm) were in the bow, with four torpedoes. There was also a rotating mount in the upper casing abaft the conning-tower, with one 21.7in (550mm) tube and two 15.7in (400mm) tubes, for which there were no reloads.

There was one 3in (76mm)/35 gun mounted on the forward casing and two 13.2mm AAMG.

Primary weapons were the mines, for which the excellent and reliable Normand-Fenaux system was used. This consisted of sixteen vertical tubes mounted in the ballast tanks, eight on each side and with two mines per tube.

Service History: Joining the French fleet in the early 1930s, the Saphir class served on routine peacetime tasks until the outbreak of war in 1939. Between then and the armistice in June 1940 four boats, *Saphir, Turquoise, Diamant* and *Nautilus* served in the Mediterranean, carrying out

a number of mining operations, mainly against ports on the Italian West coast. The other two, *Perle* and *Rubis* operated in the North Sea. In June 1940 *Rubis* found herself in a British port and promptly joined the Free French Navy.

Diamant was scuttled in Toulon harbour in November 1942; she was then raised but was later bombed. The remaining three Mediterranean boats were captured in Bizerta on 8 December 1942. Two were impressed into the Italian Navy: *Saphir* becoming the Italian FR-112 and being taken to Naples for use as a battery-charging hulk, while *Turquoise* became FR-116 and was scuttled in Bizerta harbour in May 1943. *Nautilus* was sunk at Bizerta in January 1943. *Perle* was sunk in error by an RAF aircraft, while operating in the Atlantic on 8 July 1944.

In contrast to this not very distinguished record, the sixth of the class, *Rubis*, became not only the most successful French submarine of the war, but also the most successful specialist minelayer in any navy, carrying out 22 minelaying patrols, during which she laid 683 mines, a total exceeded only by the British *Rorqual*, which laid 1,284. *Rubis*' mines sank fourteen merchantmen (21,000grt), a minelayer and seven patrol boats, and damaged several more. On top of this *Rubis* also sank one merchant ship (4,300grt) with a torpedo. She was stricken in 1949 and sank in the Mediterranean while *en route* to the breaker's yard.

Daphné Class

(Patrol submarines)

Displacement:
869 tons surfaced; 1,043 tons submerged
Performance:
Max speed 13.5kt surfaced; 16kt submerged
Range 4,300nm/7.5kt surfaced; not known submerged
Maximum Operational Diving Depth:
984ft (300m)
Dimensions:
189ft 6in (57.75m) x 22ft 2in (6.76m) x 17ft 3in (5.25m)
Machinery:
Two SEMT-Pielstick/Jeumont-Schneider 450kW diesel generator sets, 4,000bhp; two electric motors, 2,000shp; two shafts
Complement:
6 officers, 39 ratings
Construction:

Dubigeon, Nantes (7 boats)	French Navy: *Daphné, Diane, Eurydice, Minerve.* Four boats. Completed 1959 to 1960
	South African Navy: *Maria van Riebeeck, Emily Hobhouse, Johanna van der Merwe.* Three boats. Completed 1970 to 1971
Dubigeon, Normandy (4 boats)	Portuguese Navy: *Albacora, Barracuda, Delfim, Cachalote.* Four boats. Completed 1967 to 1969
Cherbourg Naval Dockyard (5 boats)	French Navy: *Doris, Flore, Galatée, Junon, Venus.* Five boats. Completed 1960 to 1966.
Brest Arsenal (3 boats)	French Navy: *Psyché, Sirène.* Two boats. Completed 1969 to 1970 Pakistan Navy: *Hangor.* One boat. Completed 1970
CN Ciotat, Le Trait (2 boats)	Pakistan Navy: *Shushuk, Mangro.* Two boats. Completed 1970
Bazan, Cartagena (4 boats)	Spanish Navy: *Delfin, Tonina, Marsopa, Narval.* Four boats. Completed 1973 to 1975

Design: Following World War II the French Navy had some fourteen different types of submarine in service, ranging in size from ocean-going types to midgets. One of these was an ex-German Type XXI, *U-2518*, taken over in 1945 and renamed *Roland Morillot* (S-613). An improved version of this design was produced in France as the Narval class; six were built in the early 1950s and rebuilt in the 1960s. Displacing 1,910 tons submerged and armed with six bow-mounted torpedo tubes all have now been stricken except for *Dauphin* (S-633), which serves as an experimental boat. In the late 1980s she was being used to test the design of the bow for the new Amethyste class SSNs.

The next to appear was the Aréthuse class, small hunter-killers, of which four were built between 1955 and 1958. They were armed with four torpedo tubes, firing ASW homing torpedoes; all have now been stricken.

Following the success of the Aréthuse class the French Navy produced an enlarged version, displacing 1,043 tons submerged, designated the Daphné class. Careful attention was paid to silence of operation; the exterior shape of the hull was tank-tested in great detail and all mooring equipment was made retractable. Microphones were fitted around the hull

Above: Daphné *(S-641), nameship of a successful class, twenty-five of which were built between 1959 and 1975. The long, narrow hull, the neat fin and the careful streamlining all attest to her* descent from the German Type XXI, one *of which served in the French Navy as the* Roland Morillot. *Displacing 1,043 tons submerged, these boats have an operational diving depth of 984ft (300m).*

which enabled those inside to monitor ambient noise-levels and to regulate speed or manoeuvre accordingly.

Armament: The Daphné class are fitted with twelve 21.7in (550mm) torpedo tubes, eight of which are in the bows. The other four are aft, two in the stern and two angled aft, all outside the pressure hull and without reloads. The Pakistani boats are all capable of firing Sub-Harpoon.

Service History: The Daphné class was an immediate success and eleven entered service with the French Navy between 1964 and 1970. A further ten were sold overseas (South Africa, 3; Pakistan, 3;

Portugal, 4) and four were constructed in Spain with French technical help. In 1968, however, misfortune struck; *Minerve* (S-647) disappeared in the Mediterranean without trace, followed in 1970 by *Eurydice* (S-644). These two mysterious losses were nearly followed in 1971 by *Flore* (S-645) when the schnorkel sprang a leak, but the alert captain took immediate remedial action and managed to save his boat. *Sirène* (S-651) flooded and sank in 1972, but was salvaged and returned to service. Modifications to the others cured the problems and there were no further losses, but nor were there any further orders.

The Pakistani Navy has four submarines of this class, of which three were bought from France and the other, *Ghazi* was bought from Portugal (*Cachalote*). *Hangor* (S-131) sank the Indian Navy frigate *Khukri* during the 1971 conflict.

The South African Navy's three boats were modernised in 1985-86 in South Africa. This navy is very keen to buy more submarines but has been prevented from doing so by the United Nations' arms embargo.

The Spanish and French Daphnés have all been modernised and all have a large sonar dome on the bow, with the sole exception of the original *Daphné* (S-641).

Above: *In 1968 and 1970 two Daphné class submarines were lost with all hands in the Mediterranean, possibly due to problems with the schnorkel. None has been lost since. This is* Daphné.

Above: *As is so often the case with French submarines, the Daphné class has an unusual armament. There are eight bow torpedo tubes in two vertical rows of four, but with no reloads. There are also four external tubes aft, again without reloads. The 21.7in (550mm) diameter tubes launch the older models of torpedo, such as the E14 (1) and the L3 (2).*

Rubis Class

(Nuclear-powered attack submarines)
(SSN)

Displacement:
2,385 tons surfaced; 2,670 tons submerged
Performance:
Max speed 25kt submerged
Maximum Operational Diving Depth:
980ft (300m)
Dimensions:
236ft 7in (72.1m) x 24ft 11in (7.6m) x 21ft 0in (6.4m)
Machinery:
One CAS-48 pressurized-water reactor, 48MWatt; two turbo-alternator sets, 9,500shp; one emergency electric motor; one shaft
Complement:
8 officers, 57 ratings
Construction:
Rubis, DCAN, Cherbourg. *Rubis, Saphir, Casabianca, Emeraude.* Four boats. Completed 1979 to 1986.
Amethyste, DCAN, Cherbourg. *Amethyste, Perle, Turquoise, Diamant.* Four boats. Completed 1991 to 1997(?)

Design: Other major navies developed their nuclear submarine fleets by first producing SSNs and then graduating later to SSBNs, since, in general terms, missile technology lagged behind that developed for nuclear-propulsion systems. The French Navy, however, entered the nuclear scene somewhat later and, under strong pressure from President de Gaulle, designed and constructed SSBNs first, since that was the political and strategic priority. Not surprisingly, such a massive programme, which, for political reasons, had to be seen to be entirely French in character, took up all the available resources for many years.

It was not until the 1974 programme that the French Navy was able to turn its attention to SSNs and their first design, the 2,670 ton Rubis class, are the smallest operational SSNs in any navy. The hull design was based fairly closely on that of the Agosta class of conventional submarines, although the nuclear submarines are externally distinguishable on the surface by the larger sail and the horizontal diving planes mounted about two-thirds of the way up it.

To be able to construct such a small nuclear-powered submarine suggests that the French Navy has achieved a significant development in nuclear reactor design, compared with the rather large devices in the Le Redoutable class SSBNs. Indeed, it was thought for some years that this had been achieved by the use of liquid-metal cooling in the reactor, but it has since been confirmed that the reactor is a pressurized-water design.

Armament: The armament, sonar and fire-control systems are based on those of the Agosta class. As with those boats, the four torpedo tubes are the internationally standardized 21in (533mm), indicating a final abandonment of the French 21.7in (550mm) torpedo. Torpedoes carried are all of French design, either F17 or L5 Mod 4.

Saphir (S-602) was the first to be fitted for SM39 Exocet, an adaptation of the very successful MM38 surface-launched, anti-ship missile. Like the US Navy's Sub-Harpoon, SM39 is tube-launched from a submerged submarine. *Rubis* (S-601) has since been modified to take SM39.

A total of fourteen torpedoes or missiles can be carried.

Service History: The first of class, *Rubis* (S-601) (originally named *Provence*), was laid down in December 1976 and launched on 7 July 1979. She joined the fleet on 28 February 1983 after extensive trials and has since been joined by the three remaining members of the class in 1984, 1987 and 1988, respectively.

There are two squadrons of these submarines, one based at Toulon, the other at Lorient. Unlike other navies, the French Navy has two crews for each of these SSNs, each of eight officers and 57 ratings; this ensures maximum utilization of the hull. The average patrol is estimated to last 45 days, with a maximum of 60 days.

The first of the next class of four boats was laid down in 1988 and will be commissioned in 1991. Designated Amethyste, this is both the name of the first of class and also the acronym for *Amelioration Tactique Hydrodynamique Silence Transmission Ecoute* (= reduced radiation emission). These boats will be marginally larger than the Rubis class with a length of 241ft 6in (73.6m), although submerged displacement will decrease marginally to 2,640 tons. The Rubis class boats are being brought up to the same standards in their first major refits over the years 1988 to 1995.

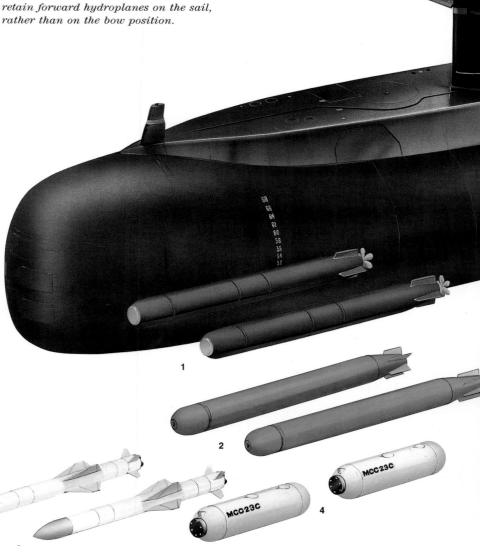

Below: Rubis, *showing the unique design of this first French SSN. The hull of the new Amethyste batch has a more rounded bow and does not have an upper casing coming to a point above the bows. The French Navy is now one of the few to retain forward hydroplanes on the sail, rather than on the bow position.*

Above: *Armament is wire-guided F17 torpedoes (1), L5 acoustic homing torpedoes (2), and SM39 Exocet missiles (3). Two mines (4) can also be carried.*

Right: Amethyste *is launched on 14 May 1988. A little larger and even quieter than the Rubis class, these are the smallest SSNs in service with any navy.*

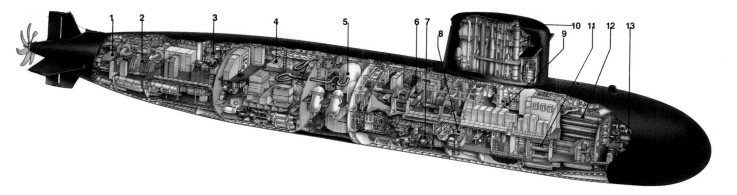

Above: Amethyste *shows how very crowded is the interior of a modern submarine:* **1** *Emergency motor.* **2** *Main motor.* **3** *Machinery control room.* **4** *Turbo-alternators.* **5** *Steam generator.* **6** *Officers' quarters.* **7** *Auxiliary machinery.* **8** *Galley.* **9** *Command centre.* **10** *Periscope.* **11** *Crew's quarters.* **12** *Torpedoes.* **13** *Torpedo tubes.*

ITALY

The first Italian submarine, *Delfino*, was constructed between 1892 and 1895 to a design by Engineer Lieutenant Giacinto Pullino and was accepted into the Italian Navy in 1896. With a submerged displacement of 108 tons she had a long, cylindrical hull with a single horizontal propeller. However, like several other contemporary designs, she also had two vertical propellers to assist in submerging and surfacing. Originally, she had only battery propulsion, but a petrol engine was added in 1902. She was later rebuilt and was operational throughout World War I, a remarkable achievement for the navy's first, experimental submarine.

The second class to be built, the Glauco class, was the first to be designed by Engineer-Lieutenant Cesare Laurenti, and from then on numerous classes were produced by Italian yards. Up to about 1918 Italian designs enjoyed an excellent international reputation and several foreign navies ordered Italian boats, either in small classes or just as a 'one-off' for comparison with others on the market. Even Germany, Great Britain and the United States placed orders, although, due to the outbreak of war, Germany never received her boat, while both Britain and the US were not at all happy with theirs.

At the outset of World War I there were twenty-one Italian submarines in service, of which many were quite elderly. Production was stepped-up, but, despite a thriving domestic industry, the Italian Navy still felt it necessary to purchase more submarines from abroad. The only purely foreign design was the Electric Boat Company's very successful H class, of which eight were delivered in 1916-17. The British sold three S class which had been built in Scotland to a Laurenti design

Above: Serpente, *an Argonauta class 600 ton type, was launched in 1932 and scuttled on 12 August 1943.*

and four W class, which had been built in England to a French design, both types being highly unpopular in British service. In addition, some forty submarines were built in Italian yards during the war.

During World War I Italian submarines operated primarily against Austria-Hungary in the Aegean. Twelve submarines were lost.

In the inter-war years Italy built up a very large submarine fleet, intended to counter the French and to protect her colonial possessions in North and East Africa. They were thus designed to operate either in the Mediterranean or in the Red Sea/Indian Ocean. In the mid-1920s numerous small classes were built to test the various basic designs. Larger numbers of boats were ordered in the early 1930s and a speed-up in the production rate was ordered in the late 1930s when war appeared imminent.

On the outbreak of World War II Italy

Below: *Acciaio class* Nichelio *surrenders in September 1943. She was ceded to the Soviet Navy in 1949.*

possessed one of the largest submarine fleets in the world; there was a total of 115 boats in commission, of which 84 were operational, and a further 30 were completed between then and the end of the Italian war. On that day, 8 September 1943, 53 submarines were in service, of which 34 were surrendered to the Allies and the balance were either scuttled, sabotaged or captured by the Germans.

The Italian Navy's submarine service had perhaps the most exciting and certainly the most far-ranging campaign of any element of the country's armed forces. They served throughout the Mediterranean, in the North and South Atlantic, in the Indian Ocean and the Red Sea, and travelled as far east as Singapore and Japan. In the course of these travels they sank numerous Allied merchant ships and a significant number of warships, including four light cruisers.

The larger, longer-ranged patrol boats were sent, at the suggestion of the Italian authorities, to the French port of Bordeaux to operate under German command in the Battle of the Atlantic. Two boats were also sent to the Baltic port of Gdansk (Gdynia) so that Italian crews could train alongside the German training flotillas. The Bordeaux base became

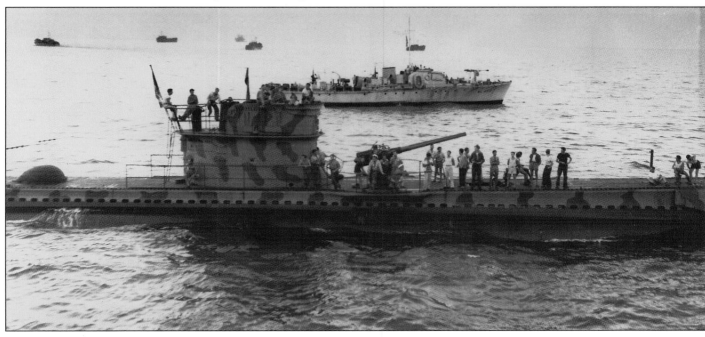

operational on 23 August 1940 and three submarines left on their first Atlantic patrols on 10 October. The maximum number operating out of Bordeaux was 27 (June 1941), dropping to 11 in December 1942 and to six at the time of the surrender in September 1943. However, despite some sinkings it was not a successful enterprise, with the Italians finding the Atlantic conditions quite unlike anything for which they had trained. Their submarines proved too slow and unmanoeuvrable for this type of warfare.

Many Italian submarines were used as transports. In the Mediterranean they carried supplies to the beleaguered Axis forces in North Africa, whilst other, longer ranged types were used to bring supplies back from the Far East. These were standard service submarines, but in early 1943 seven of the boats at Bordeaux were taken in hand by the Germans for a proper conversion to the transport role. In return nine new Type VIICs were ceded to the Italian Navy (who designated them the S class), but the crews were still training in them at the time of the surrender and the boats were subsequently commissioned into the *Kriegsmarine*.

Italy also designed a class of specialised transport submarines. The R class boats (2,606 tons) had four holds and a surface range of 12,000nm (22,225km) at 9kt, but although two were launched none ever undertook an operational mission.

The Italians built a small number of minelayers, but these were not particularly successful, mainly because the mines were dangerous to lay.

After Italy's surrender she became a co-belligerent and a number of her boats were used as targets for anti-submarine warfare training, during which another two boats were lost in accidents.

After the war Italy was ordered to cease all new construction and to give up her existing submarines, with two submarines being transferred to each of the victorious powers as reparations. In the event, only those destined for the USSR were

transferred, all remaining submarines being scrapped between 1945 and 1949, except for two, which were retained for training, and a third which had been damaged in an air attack in 1945 and which had to be completely rebuilt between 1955 and 1961.

When Italy joined NATO and the Navy again needed submarines, nine boats came from the USA, seven of them being former World War II fleet submarines. The first two, Guppy IBs, were transferred in 1954-55, followed by a fleet schnorkel in 1960 and two more, specially modified for the Italian Navy (essentially fleet schnorkels, but with a streamlined fin) in 1966. Then there were two Guppy III's,

transferred in 1977. The remaining ex-US Navy submarines were two post-war Tang class, which were sold in 1973-74. All of these were scrapped in the 1970s and 1980s.

Italian submarine-building restarted in 1965, four of the small, 593 tons submerged displacement Enrico Toti class being completed in the late 1960s. They were joined by four of the somewhat larger (1,637 tons) Nazario Sauro class in the early 1980s and four of the Improved Sauro class in the late 1980s/early 1990s. Italy now intends to keep her submarine force at a strength of about ten to twelve boats, with a new class of four boats appearing at ten year intervals.

Above: Enrico Dandolo *(S-513), a* Toti *class submarine launched in 1967, is designed for Mediterranean operations.*

Below: Salvatore Pelosi *(S-522), name-boat of a class of four modified Nazario Sauro class submarines.*

Medusa Class

(Coastal submarines)

Displacement:
250 tons surfaced; 305 tons submerged
Performance:
Max speed 12.5kt surfaced; 8.2kt submerged
Range 1,200nm/8kt surfaced; 54nm/6kt submerged
Maximum Operational Diving Depth:
131ft (40m)
Dimensions:
148ft 2in (45.15m) x 13ft 9in (4.20m) x 9ft 10in (3.00m)
Machinery:
All except *Velella*. Two Fiat diesel engines, 650hbp; two Savigliano electric motors, 300shp; two shafts
Velella Two M.A.N. diesel engines, 650bhp; two Siemens electric motors, 300shp; two shafts
Complement:
2 officers, 19 ratings
Construction:
Fiat-San Giorgio, La Spezia, *Medusa*, *Velella*, *Argo*, *Jalea*. Four boats. Completed 1912 to 1913.
Cantieri Navali Riuniti, Muggiano. *Salpa*, *Jantina*. Two boats. Completed 1912 to 1913.
Cantieri Orlando, Livorno. *Fisalia*, *Zoea*. Two boats. Completed 1912 to 1913.

Above: Velella *of the Medusa class. These boats were the first in the Italian navy to be fitted with diesel engines, which substantially increased their safety.*

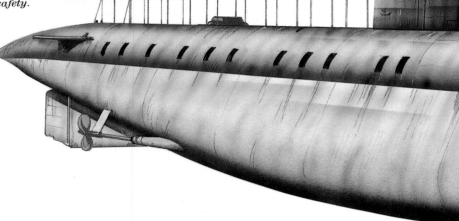

Design: The Medusa class proved to be a very successful design. The first Italian submarines to be fitted with diesel engines, no less than 41 of this and a slightly improved design were built between 1912 and 1918 for six navies.

Engineer-Lieutenant Cesare Laurenti, who designed the Medusa class, had also been responsible for the second class of Italian submarines, the Glauco class, five of which were completed between 1905 and 1909. As with many other contemporary boats they were powered by petrol engines. This was a potentially hazardous power source, but they served until 1918 (*Glauco* until 1916) without a calamity. On the other hand, a development, *Foca*, was almost destroyed soon after she was commissioned. *Foca* had three shafts, each driven by a Fiat petrol engine, with a total power output of 800bhp. Commissioned on 15 February 1909 she suffered a disaster only two months later (26 April) in Naples harbour, when an accumulation of battery gases was ignited by a spark, which in turn set fire to the fuel tanks. She was sunk to extinguish the fire and subsequently raised, refitted and returned to service.

As a result of this experience (and of several other disasters) with petrol engines the Royal Italian Navy decided to switch to diesel engines and the Medusa class was the first to be fitted with this new type of engine. There were protracted trials until the diesels were properly adjusted, but thereafter they proved to be useful and popular boats.

All boats of the class, except one, were fitted with Fiat diesels and Savigliano electric motors. The second to be completed, *Velella*, was however given M.A.N. diesels and Siemens electric motors for purposes of comparison. Fortunately the German motors were not selected for subsequent boats as this source would have dried up in 1915 when Italy joined the Allies against the Central Powers.

This design featured a long, low hull with only a very small conning-tower, which led the Royal Navy to claim that they were not sufficiently 'seaworthy' for use in the North Sea. They had the typical Laurenti partial double-hull and a wide flat, 'duck's tail' stern. There was a high degree of internal subdivisioning, with no less than ten watertight bulkheads. Their hulls were not cylindrical in order to give extra volume, another Laurenti trade-mark, and the Japanese, in particular, regarded this as a grave weakness. They mounted both bow and stern hydroplanes, and proved to be exceptionally manoeuvrable underwater.

Armament: Sole armament were two 17.7in (450mm) torpedo tubes, with two reloads. No guns were fitted, even during the war, although the Japanese fitted a 3in (76mm) gun to theirs in the early 1920s.

Service History: After a somewhat lengthy settling-down period due to the novel diesel engines, the boats of the Medusa class entered service with the Royal Italian Navy in 1912-13. The class was initially deployed in two squadrons of four boats each, but for most of World War I *Velella* was based at Brindisi and the remainder at Venice. The Medusa class was, in fact, the largest single class of submarines in the Royal Italian Navy until the arrival in service of the closely-related F1 class in late 1916, which eventually numbered 21 boats.

Two of the class were sunk in the war (*Medusa* and *Jalea*, both in 1915). The remainder were scrapped in 1918.

An improved version of the Medusa class was ordered by a number of foreign navies. Three navies each ordered three boats — Brazil (F1 class), Portugal (Foca class) and Spain (A class) — which were all built in Italy. Great Britain also ordered three, but these were constructed in a Scottish yard (S class). Japan ordered two, which were built by Kawasaki at Kobe (F1 class). Finally, the Royal Italian Navy took delivery of 21 of these boats, in whose service they were designated the F class.

Above: Medusa *heads out to sea, with the hatches open to aid ventilation below.*

Below: *Sole armament for most boats in the class was two 17.7in (450mm) torpedo tubes in the bow, with two reloads. Only the Japanese boats had guns.*

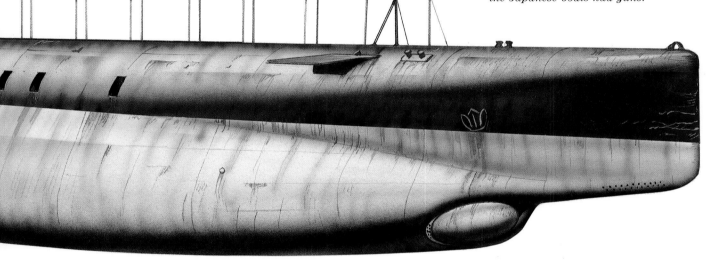

Below: Fisalia, *seen here in 1913, running at speed. The British built three similar boats, but disliked the low freeboard and considered them to be very poor sea-boats and unsuitable for North Sea conditions.*

Brin Class

(Ocean-going patrol submarines)

Displacement:
1,016 tons surfaced; 1,266 tons submerged
Performance:
Max speed 17.3kt surfaced; 8kt submerged
Range 9,000nm/7.8kt surfaced; 90nm/4kt
submerged
Maximum Operational Diving Depth:
328ft (100m)
Dimensions:
237ft 10in (72.5m) x 21ft 11in (6.7m) x 14ft 11in
(4.55m)
Machinery:
Two Tosi diesel engines, 1,500bhp; two Ansaldo
electric motors, 550shp; two shafts
Complement:
7 officers, 47 ratings
Construction:
Tosi, Taranto. Brin, Galvani, Guglielmotti,
Archimede, Torricelli. Five boats. Completed
1938 to 1939.

Design: The Royal Italian Navy built no less than 26 classes of submarine between the end of World War I and the Armistice in 1943; typical of these was the Brin class of five boats constructed in the late 1930s. They were long-range submarines, intended primarily for operations in the Red Sea and the Indian Ocean in the defence of Italy's East African empire.

They were designed and built by Tosi at Taranto, and were based on the earlier Archimede class (1,259 tons), of which Tosi had built four between 1931 and 1935. The Brin class had partial double-hulls, but of a more streamlined shape, giving them higher speed for the same power plant. In general, they proved to be a satisfactory design.

Armament: The Brin class were fitted with eight 21in (533mm) torpedo tubes, four in the bow and four in the stern. There were a total of twelve reloads.

As built, the 3.9in (100mm)/43 gun was mounted in a very unusual position at bridge level at the *after* end of the large sail, a feature confined to this and the

contemporary Italian Foca class. Quite what tactical benefit was expected from this is not clear and, in any event, early in the war this mounting was removed from both Brin and Foca classes and replaced by a 4.72in (120mm)/47 mounted on the foredeck. For anti-aircraft defence four 13.7mm machine-guns were carried on single mounts.

Service History: The first three of the class, *Brin*, *Galvani* and *Guglielmotti* were launched in 1938. The final pair, however, were built in secret to replace two submarines which had been covertly transferred to the Spanish Nationalist navy and, to aid the subterfuge, were even given the names of those two boats: *Archimede* and *Torricelli*.

In June 1940 all the boats of the class were based in the Red Sea, apart from *Brin* which had returned to Italy. Two of these were sunk by British warships very early in the war: *Torricelli* on 23 June 1940 and *Galvani* just one day later, but in a quite separate engagement. The former was, in fact, scuttled by her own crew after a very heavy surface engagement in the Red Sea with three British destroyers and a sloop, in the course of which one British destroyer was sunk.

In May 1941 all remaining Italian boats east of Suez, including *Archimede* and *Guglielmotti* sailed back to Bordeaux, France by way of the Cape of Good Hope, being replenished by the German armed merchant cruiser *Atlantis* en route. This was no mean achievement at that stage of the war. Once at Bordeaux the *Archimede* and *Guglielmotti* were joined by *Brin* and the three boats were responsible for sinking or damaging seven Allied merchant ships (53,200grt).

Guglielmotti was torpedoed by the

Above: *Italy transferred two Archimede class submarines to Spain during the Civil War and built two new Brin class* *submarines to replace them, giving them the same names. Here the Brin class* Torricelli *is launched on 26 March 1939.*

Above: Brin *in Cagliari harbour in 1942, with a mass of cables bringing power aboard from the shore supply. The Italians were unusual in camouflaging the upper decks of their submarines.*

British submarine *Unbeaten* in the Mediterranean (17 March 1942) and *Archimede* was sunk by depth-charges dropped by a US Catalina flying-boat off the Brazilian coast on 14 April 1943.

Only *Brin* survived the war, being surrendered to the Allies in 1943. She was sent to Colombo, Ceylon (present-day Sri Lanka) and used as an ASW target until the end of the war, when she returned to Italy. She was stricken in 1948.

Above: *Originally the Brin class were armed with a 3.9in (100mm) gun on the aft end of the bridge structure, but this was deleted and replaced by a 4.72in (120mm) gun on the foredeck, as shown here on* Brin *in 1942.*

Left: *The Brin class was typical of Italian inter-war submarines, large boats with a long range and good armament. The relatively good hull shape, the folding hydroplanes and the long-range radio antennas are all clear in this drawing. The device on the bows is a net-cutter, invented by the Germans in World War I, which was supposed to saw a way through anti-submarine nets.*

Sauro/Pelosi/ Improved Pelosi Class

(Diesel-electric attack submarines)

Displacement:
Sauro 1,450 tons surfaced; 1,637 tons submerged
Pelosi 1,476 tons surfaced; 1,662 tons submerged
Improved Pelosi 1,580 tons surfaced; 1,760 tons submerged

Performance:
Max speed 11kt surfaced; 19kt submerged
Range Sauro 11,000nm/11kt surfaced; 250nm/4kt submerged
Pelosi 11,000nm/11kt surfaced; 250nm/4kt submerged

Maximum Operational Diving Depth:
984ft (300m)

Dimensions:
Sauro 209ft 6in (63.85m) x 22ft 5in (6.83m) x 18ft 8in (5.70m)
Pelosi 211ft 2in (64.35m) x 22ft 5in (6.83m) x 18ft 7in (5.66m)
Improved Pelosi 217ft 10in (66.40m) x 22ft 5in (6.83m) x 18ft 7in (5.66m)

Machinery:
Three GMT A210 16NM diesel generators; one twin Marelli electric motor; 4,270shp; one shaft

Complement:
Sauro 6 officers, 43 ratings
Pelosi/Improved Pelosi 7 officers, 43 ratings

Construction:

Sauro	CRDA, Monfalcone. *Nazario Sauro* (S-518), *Carlo Fecia di Cossato* (S-519). Two boats. Completed 1976 to 1977.
	Italcantieri, Monfalcone. *Leonardo da Vinci* (S-520), *Guglielmo Marconi* (S-521). Two boats. Completed 1979 to 1980.
Pelosi	Fincantieri, Monfalcone. *Salvatore Pelosi* (S-522), *Giuliano Prini* (S-523). Two boats. Completed 1988 to 1989.
Improved Pelosi	Fincantieri, Monfalcone. Two boats. Completed 1993(?)

Design: Italy did not begin to build submarines again in the post-war period until 1965, when the first of the Enrico Toti class was laid down. Four of these small 593 tons submerged displacement boats were built and three were still in service in 1991, *Attilio Bagnolini* (S-505) having been stricken in 1990.

The second post-war class was the Nazario Sauro class, which are much larger (displacing 1,637 tons) and more heavily armed than the Toti class. Two were ordered in 1967, but building was postponed a year later due to budgetary problems, being reinstated in the 1972 programme and completed in 1976 and 1977. Two more were ordered in 1976 and completed in 1981-82. The Sauro class is of conventioinal design, with the forward hydroplanes mounted on the sail.

The first two of the Salvatore Pelosi class (also known as the 'Improved Sauro class') are 1ft 8in (0.5m) longer, a plug having been inserted amidships to accommodate an additional watertight bulkhead. Improved sensors are also fitted. The second two are 6ft 7in (2.0m) longer still.

Below: *The submarine* Nazario Sauro *(S-518). Completed in 1976 she was the first in a successful series, now eight strong, for the Italian Navy. Note the sonar domes on the upper casing.*

Above: Salvatore Pelosi *(S-522) is slightly longer than the original Sauro class to accommodate new equipment and an additional watertight bulkhead. Two of this type have been built.*

Armament: All three types are equipped with six 21in (533mm) torpedo tubes. The Nazario Sauro class carry twelve Whitehead Type A-184 torpedoes. The Salvatore Pelosi class is fitted to launch Sub-Harpoon, although no actual missiles have yet been procured; a mix of up to twelve torpedoes or Sub-Harpoon can be carried.

Service History: The Nazario Sauro class submarines entered service between 1980 and 1982, and will all be given a mid-life refit between 1990 and 1995. This will involve replacement of the batteries, replacement of some machinery and improvements to the living accommodation for the crew. It is also anticipated that reliability will be increased, as well.

The Salvatore Pelosi class replaced the

US-supplied Tang class fleet submarines, which had been acquired in the early 1970s, thereby fulfilling the navy's plan to have a fleet of twelve Italian-designed submarines.

For the future, the Italian Navy is planning to build at least two of a yet further improved and larger version of the Sauro class, to be designated the Type S90. This will have a submerged displacement of 2,490 tons and, at least according to present plans, will have conventional diesel-electric propulsion rather than air-independent system. The Type S90 will replace the ageing Toti class, giving the Italian Navy a balanced fleet of relatively large and very modern attack submarines, which will carry them into the 21st Century.

Above: *The six 21in tubes launch either A-184 heavyweight torpedoes (to be replaced by the A-290 high-speed torpedo) or SM-600 mines.*

CHINA

The Chinese Navy did not emerge from the era of sailing-junks until the 1860s, when a few steam-driven ships began to appear, at first constructed abroad, but later built within the country. By 1894 the navy was reasonably modern, although not very large. It found itself deeply embroiled in the war which broke out with Japan over the control of Korea. There were two principal naval engagements in which the main Chinese fleet, commanded by Admiral Ting Ju-Ch'ang, lost on both occasions: the Battle of the Yalu (17 September 1894) and the Battle of Weihaiwei (2-12 February 1895). Nevertheless, both the Chinese officers and sailors acquitted themselves very well and fought hard against a more experienced and better equipped enemy.

In the early years of the 20th Century a number of ambitious naval plans were prepared and a few modern ships were built, but the chaotic situation within the country, particularly following the overthrow of the Manchu dynasty in 1911-1912, caused repeated cancellations. The Chinese played little part in World War I apart from declaring war on the Central Powers in 1917 and seizing some German warships in Chinese ports.

The first attempt by the Chinese Navy to

Above: *The USSR supplied 15 submarines to China in the early 1950s, one of which was this Series XIIbis.*

acquire submarines was made in 1915 when a team was sent to the USA for training on the Electric Boat Company's H class submarines, which had already been ordered by the United Kingdom, Italy and Russia. Unfortunately, lack of money prevented an order being placed. Two years later a second attempt was made when the last six of the boats ordered by Imperial Russia became available following the October Revolution. Once more China sought to make a purchase, but, again, failed to find the funds and the boats went to the US Navy, instead.

In the 1920s the warlords flourished and fought one another on land, while the navy declined to a very run-down state. When Chiang Kai-shek and the Kuomintang gained power in 1929 more plans to improve the navy were made, but again they failed to reach fruition. Some surface ships and two Type IIB submarines were

ordered from Germany in the mid-1930s, but yet again the Chinese Navy was thwarted. The reason this time was the outbreak of World War II in Europe, which caused the German *Kriegsmarine* to requisition the boats, commissioning them as *U-120* and *U-121*.

The Communists under Mao Tse-Tung gained power in 1949 and they quickly set about reorganising the country, which was in a chaotic state after so many years of civil warfare. Interestingly, they gave a high priority to the creation of a powerful navy with three aims: to pursue the aim of finally annihilating the Nationalists who had sought refuge on the island of Taiwan, to control the seas bordering China's eastern and southern coasts, and to establish China's position as a Great Power. At first the navy was helped by the fellow-Communist power in the Soviet Union and it was from that source, and after so many years of trying, that the Chinese Navy finally received its first submarine in 1953, a Soviet Series XV. In all, eleven elderly submarines were

Han Class

(Nuclear-powered attack submarines) (SSN)

Displacement:
4,500 tons submerged
Performance:
Max speed 25kt surfaced; 30kt submerged
Maximum Operational Diving Depth:
Not known
Dimensions:
295ft 4in (90.0m) x 26ft 3in (8.0m) x 27ft 11in (8.52m) (Estimated)
Machinery:
One pressurized-water nuclear-reactor, turbo-electric drive; one shaft
Complement:
75
Construction:
Huludao Shipyard, Liao Ning province, PRC.
Five boats (401-405). Completed 1974 to 1992?

Design: The first Han class SSN appears to have been completed at about the same time as the first of the Ming class diesel-electric submarines, although its building had been delayed by problems with the nuclear-propulsion plant. The Han class has a highly streamlined Albacore-type hull, which bears little resemblance to the Ming class and can thus be assumed to be a totally new design. There is a large fin

placed well forward, with the forward hydroplanes sited high on it. Aft there is a single propeller and conventional cruciform control surfaces.
Armament: The Han class is armed with six (possibly eight) 21in (533mm) torpedo tubes. It has also been reported that at least one of the class may be fitted with launchers abaft the fin for the C-801 sea-skimming missile. However, as these

missiles can only be launched from the surface, such an installation seems to place a very expensive and tactically valuable submarine unnecessarily at hazard.
Service History: The first-of-class was apparently launched in 1972 and entered service in about 1975. She was followed by the second in 1980, the third in 1984 and the fourth in 1988. All serve in the North Sea Fleet. It has been reported that

supplied by the USSR in 1954 and 1955.

The Chinese wanted, however, to establish their own submarine-construction capability and in 1956 they were supplied with the parts for five Soviet Whiskey class submarines, which were assembled at a new yard at Jiangnan. Thereafter, the submarines were built completely in China, some 15 being constructed in the 1960s. Next the parts for three Romeo class were supplied by the USSR and this type proved very popular with the Chinese Navy as no less than 87 were then built, plus eight more for export (four to Egypt and four to North Korea). As far as is known, the final assistance given to China by the USSR was the supply of plans for the Golf class, diesel-electric, ballistic-missile submarine (SSB), of which one was built at Luda in 1964.

The first indigenous Chinese diesel-electric design was the Ming class (Type ES5C/D), three of which were built in the 1970s. They have an Albacore-type hull. They do not seem to have been particularly successful, and one suffered a serious fire and was subsequently scrapped. The problems appear to have been rectified as production of a modified design (Type ES5E) restarted in 1987 at the rather slow rate of one hull per year. These are relatively large boats with a displacement of 2,113 tons submerged, but retain a twin-shaft arrangement, which enables them to have two stern torpedo tubes (in addition to six in the bows). It is, however, also somewhat unusual in modern submarines as it creates considerable underwater noise.

Below: *The Chinese ES5G, a development of the Soviet-designed Romeo class, fires its C-801 missiles from the surface, a hazardous tactical undertaking.*

The same hull appears to have been used for the Modified Romeo class cruise-missile submarine, designated by China as the Type ES5G. This submarine has six missile bins in neat housings either side of the fin, but launching is only possible when surfaced, a serious tactical drawback in today's conditions. The missile is the C-801 *Ying-ji*, a sea-skimming, Mach 0.9 cruise-missile, with a 22nm (40lm) range and a distinct visual resemblance to the French Exocet.

Development of nuclear-powered attack submarines started in the mid-1960s and the first Han class SSN was laid down in 1971 and completed in 1974. Since then three have been completed, with another three on order. The nuclear programme has also led to the Xia class SSBN, which, although it has taken a long-time in development, nevertheless represents a major national achievement.

Left: *The Chinese Navy took an extraordinary leap forward with its Han class SSNs, the first of which was launched in 1972. There have been major delays in getting the class into service and only four had joined the fleet by 1991. However, it is clear that the Chinese are now catching up rapidly with Western technology. Armament comprises six 21in (533mm) torpedoes.*

reliability is poor.

As with the Xia class the fact that the Han class has taken a long time to develop and may be suffering from some problems in service should not be taken as an indication that production or development will cease. China needs a powerful fleet to underpin its conception of itself as a world power and all major navies have nuclear-powered submarines.

Xia Class

(Nuclear-powered ballistic missile submarines) (SSBN)

Displacement:
7,000 tons submerged
Performance:
Max speed 20kt submerged
Maximum Operational Diving Depth:
Not known
Dimensions:
394ft 0in (120.0m) x 33ft 0in (10.0m) x 26ft 3in (8.0m) (Estimated)
Machinery:
One pressurized-water nuclear reactor, turbo-electric drive; one shaft
Complement:
84?
Construction:
Huludao Shipyard, Liao Ning province, PRC. Three boats. One completed 1987.

Design: 'Xia' is a Western designation for the first class of Chinese SSBNs, which represent a remarkable national achievement and illustrate the intention of the People's Republic to take its rightful place among the superpowers. Prior to the spectacular rift between the two countries the USSR provided the PRC with the plans for its Golf-II class, diesel-electric powered, ballistic missile submarine. The plans were modified slightly by the Chinese to meet the needs of the PRC and then one submarine was constructed, being launched in 1964. Whereas the original Golf class had three tubes for the Soviet SS-N-5 missile, the Chinese boat was fitted with two tubes for the CSS-N-3, as the latter missile had a greater diameter. The first known launch of CSS-N-3 from this submarine was on 12 October 1982.

Meanwhile the Chinese nuclear warhead, nuclear propulsion, missile and submarine development programmes were

Left: A CSS-N-3 Ju Lang SLBM streaks skywards after a successful launch. Twelve of these missiles are carried by the Xia class SSBN. The single-stage missile has a range of about 2,000nm.

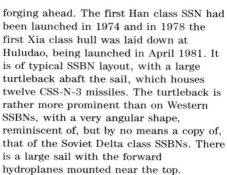

forging ahead. The first Han class SSN had been launched in 1974 and in 1978 the first Xia class hull was laid down at Huludao, being launched in April 1981. It is of typical SSBN layout, with a large turtleback abaft the sail, which houses twelve CSS-N-3 missiles. The turtleback is rather more prominent than on Western SSBNs, with a very angular shape, reminiscent of, but by no means a copy of, that of the Soviet Delta class SSBNs. There is a large sail with the forward hydroplanes mounted near the top.

Development of the Xia class represents a very remarkable national achievement and if the PRC received foreign help in the design or construction of this submarine, this remains a well-kept secret.

Armament: Like all combat submarines the Xia class is armed with six 21in (533mm) torpedo tubes, all in the bows. The main armament, however, is the CSS-N-3 ballistic missile, twelve of which are housed abaft the sail. The CSS-N-3 is a two-stage, solid-fuel missile, capable of delivering a single 2MT warhead over a range of 1,460nm (2,700km). The first trial launch of the first version of this missile (the CSS-NX-3) took place from a specially-constructed submerged pontoon in the Yellow Sea in April 1982, following which a second missile was launched from

Below left: *The Chinese Xia class SSBN and its CSS-N-3 SLBMs, which are launched while the submarine is submerged. The Xia is also armed with six standard 21in (533mm) torpedo tubes for self-defence. The production of this strategic submarine and weapons system is a great technical achievement by the navy of the People's Republic of China.*

Right: *A fine shot of Xia at sea showing the prominent 'turtleback' below which lie twelve CSS-N-3 missiles. The lines of the bow show well through the exceptionally clear water.*

the Chinese Golf class SSB in October 1982. This led to a launch of the definitive CSS-N-3 from the Xia class SSBN on 28 September 1985, although this was apparently less than successful and it was only in July 1988 that an acceptable launch was achieved. These problems should not, however, be overrated as both the US and Soviet navies have suffered some spectacular and expensive problems during their missile development programmes.

Service History: The first Xia class SSBN (406) became operational in 1988. It is to be assumed that it has, like other SSBNs, two crews and that it carries out patrols of about 60 days' duration. But, it will have to spend some time in port between each patrol and will also have to undergo periodic short refits. It will thus be available for only about 40 per cent of the time (perhaps, even less) and thus the PRC's submarine deterrent cannot be credible until a minimum of two more SSBNs have been completed. However, having shown the determination and capability to get this far, it is highly unlikely that the PRC will fail to construct a sufficient number of SSBNs to fulfil this mission.

ARGENTINA

rgentina, Brazil and Chile, the 'ABC' countries, have long competed with each other in Latin America, and nowhere more so than in naval matters. At the turn of the 19th Century a naval race between Argentina and Chile developed which concluded in 1904 with the Argentine Navy possessing no fewer than five battleships and eight cruisers, a force out of all proportion to her real needs.

Unfortunately, Brazil then started to build up her navy and Argentina felt that she had to respond with yet more acquisitions. These included three more dreadnoughts, although only two were, in fact, delivered.

Surprisingly, despite the size of her surface fleet, Argentina was the last of these three countries to purchase submarines. An Argentine naval mission visited virtually all European yards in the late 1920s and eventually ordered three boats from Italy. Forming the first Santa Fe class, these 920-ton displacement (submerged) submarines were armed with eight 21in (533mm) torpedo tubes (4 bow, 4 stern) and served in the Argentine fleet from 1932 to 1959.

In 1960 Argentina purchased two Balao class submarines from the USA, which

were named *Santa Fe* (S-11) and *Santiago del Estero* (S-12). These were unmodified boats, although they were later fitted with a more streamlined sail. They were replaced by two Guppy converted boats in 1971, which, confusingly were given the same names: *Santa Fe* (S-21), a Guppy IIA and *Santiago del Este* (S-22), a Guppy IA. In 1974 two German Type 209s were delivered, named *Salta* (S-31) and *San Luis* (S-32). These boats were assembled in Argentina from sections supplied by Howaldtswerke in Kiel.

When the Falklands War broke out in 1982 the Argentine Navy possessed these four submarines, although *Salta* was undergoing a refit and never managed to get to sea. *Santa Fe* was sent to South Georgia, where she called in at Grytviken, departing just after dawn on 25 April 1982. Just as she was about to submerge she was discovered by a helicopter from the approaching Royal Navy task-force, which dropped two depth-charges, damaging the submarine sufficiently to make it impossible for her to dive. She therefore returned to Grytviken, harried all the way by helicopters which fired at her with a torpedo, seven AS.12 missiles and fire from machine-guns, rifles and even a sub-machine gun. These inflicted

sufficient damage to render her unseaworthy, making her the first submarine to be defeated by helicopters. Unfortunately for *Santa Fe*, a modern submarine has no air defence weapons of any sort; had she still had the two 40mm cannon carried in her earlier existence as USS *Catfish* (SS-339) the result might well have been quite different.

San Luis operated near the Falkland Islands and her mere presence had a disproportionate effect on the main British task-force, which had to devote a tremendous ASW effort to keep her away from the two aircraft carriers, which were absolutely crucial to the success of the mission. *San Luis* is reported to have fired six torpedoes, none of which hit a target. At least one report suggests that the torpedoes were launched below the manufacturer's recommended maximum depth, which, if correct, could account for her lack of success.

Since the war the Argentine Navy has disposed of the surviving Guppy *Santiago del Este* and has taken delivery of two TR-1700 submarines, with at least one more under construction in Buenos Aires. The two Type 209s remain in service. However, the navy, like the rest of the country, is suffering from desperate financial problems and there have been reports that some of the four submarines have been offered for sale abroad. However, of all the South American navies equipped with submarines over the past ninety years, the Argentine Navy remains the only one to have used them in action.

Left: Santa Cruz *was the first of the TR-1700s to be completed by Thyssen Nordseewerke for the Argentine Navy. Note the very low mounting of the forward hydroplanes on the fin.*

Right: *The fine and uncluttered lines of the TR-1700 design are clear in this drawing. The TR-1700 has six 21in (533mm) torpedo tubes. As delivered they were equipped to launch SST-4 torpedoes (bottom), an export development of the German* Seeal *wire-guided heavyweight torpedo, and the US Mark 37C short anti-submarine torpedo (top).*

TR-1700 Class

(Patrol submarines)

Displacement:
2,150 tons surfaced; 2,364 tons submerged
Performance:
Max speed 15kt surfaced; 25kt submerged
Range 12,000nm/8kt surfaced; 110nm/15kt submerged
Maximum Operational Diving Depth:
984ft (300m)
Dimensions:
216ft 6in (66.0m) x 23ft 11in (7.30m) x 21ft 4in (6.50m)
Machinery:
Four MTU 16V652 MB80 1,100kw generator sets, one Siemens 6,600kw electric motor; 8,970hp; one shaft
Complement:
30
Construction:
Thyssen Nordseewerke, Emden. *Santa Cruz* (S-41), *San Juan* (S-42). Two boats. Completed 1984 to 1985.
Manuel Domecq Garcia, Buenos Aires. *Santa Fe* (S-43), *Santiago del Estero* (S-44), plus (S-45). Three boats. Completed 1991 onwards (see Notes).

Design: The Argentine Navy took delivery of two Type 209 submarines, *Salta* (S-31) and *San Luis* (S-32) in 1974 and, like many other users, found these German submarines excellent value for money. Further, in a country eager to establish its own shipbuilding industry, the navy was impressed by the fact that the submarines were shipped out in sections for final construction in Argentina. When, therefore, in the late 1970s they looked to expand their submarine fleet they turned again to Germany, although on this occasion to Thyssen Nordseewerke rather than Howaldtswerke. The initial order was for the TR-1400, but this was changed in February 1982, a month before the invasion of the Falkland Islands, to the larger TR-1700.

The TR-1700 is a large submarine, with a submerged displacement of 2,364 tons, making it only marginally smaller than the British Upholder class. It has a particularly well streamlined shape and high power, enabling it to achieve the very high underwater speed of 25kt, making it the fastest operational diesel-electric submarine in any navy. Only the US Navy's experimental diesel-electric submarine *Albacore* (AGSS-569) has been capable of a higher speed. Such a speed incurs a high drain on the batteries and could not be sustained for long; it is, nevertheless, a major achievement.

Above: *Santa Cruz in German waters prior to her delivery to Argentina in 1984.*

The TR-1700 is a single-hull design, with a 158ft (48m) pressure-hull, which is of uniform diameter throughout, except for a short tapered section aft. Internally, it is divided into three sections by two transverse bulkheads. The adoption of extensive automation means that a crew of just 30 men is needed.
Armament: There are six 21in (533mm) bow torpedo tubes for which 22 German-made SST-4 wire-guided torpedoes are carried. US Mark 37C ASW short torpedoes may also be carried. An autoload mechanism enables the tubes to be reloaded in 50 seconds.
Service History: The first-of-class, *Santa Cruz* (S-41), was launched in 1982 and commissioned in October 1984. This was to have been the only one of the six ordered to be built in Germany, but a second boat, *San Juan* (S-42) was also built by Thyssen Nordseewerke. It reached Argentina in 1985. Of the three that were to have been built in Argentina one should be completed in 1991, but, because of financial problems, the future of the other two is in doubt. Indeed, the German government is known to have granted permission for all of the class to be sold abroad, if the Argentine Navy wishes to do so, but this has not happened, so far.

AUSTRALIA

Despite its geographical remoteness from Europe, Australia took a very early interest in naval defence, primarily in the context of a Commonwealth system, based on the then dominance of the world's oceans by the Royal Navy. This interest led to the adoption of a submarine component in 1913, with two of the British E class being ordered as the AE class. Designated *AE-1* and *AE-2* they were crewed by RN personnel and were delivered to Australia in 1914, by far the longest voyage then undertaken by submarines. On the declaration of war by Australia in 1914 they deployed to the Bismarck Archipelago to seek the German destroyer *Geier*, where on 14 September *AE-1* disappeared without trace, the first Allied submarine to be lost in the war. The other boat, *AE-2* was later sent to the Dardanelles where she was

scuttled by her own crew after being seriously damaged by gunfire from a Turkish MTB in April 1915, while operating in the Sea of Marmora.

In early 1924 the British Labour government shelved plans to develop the Singapore Naval Base, as a result of which Australia instituted a fleet expansion programme, which included two ocean-going submarines. *Oberon*, then building at HM Dockyard, Chatham for the RN, suited the RAN's needs and two generally similar boats were ordered from Vickers, Barrow as the Oxley class (1,872 tons). The most noticeable difference from

Below: *Four of the six Oxley class submarines of the Royal Australian Navy:* Oxley *(nearest the camera),* Otway, Onslow *and* Otama. *All were built in Scotland between 1964 and 1969.*

Oberon was that they had an improved hull shape, including an unusual ram-shaped bow, which gave them marginally better underwater performance.

Despite a subsequent Conservative decision to proceed with the Singapore base, the RAN stuck to its order and the two boats, *Oxley* and *Otway*, were delivered in 1928. However, a budget crisis in 1930 led to the two submarines being put into reserve in 1930, following which they were presented as a free gift to the RN in 1931. *Oxley* became the first Allied submarine to be lost in World War II, being sunk by another British submarine in a tragic accident on 10 September 1939.

No further submarines operated with the RAN until the purchase of six submarines from Britain in the 1960s. As in the 1930s, the British design was designated the Oberon class and the RAN version the Oxley class! These six boats have undergone a major modernization in the 1980s and will continue to serve beyond the year 2000. They will, however, be joined and progressively replaced by the new Collins class, an Australian-built version of a Swedish Kockums' design.

Collins Class

(Diesel-electric attack submarines)

Displacement:
2,450 tons surfaced; 2,700 tons submerged
Performance:
Max speed 10+kt surfaced; 20+kt submerged
Range 11,500nm surfaced; 9,000nm/10kt
schnorkel; 490nm/4kt submerged
Maximum Operational Diving Depth:
Not known

Dimensions:
246ft 1in (75.0m) x 25ft 7in (7.8m) x 22ft 4in
(6.8m)
Machinery:
Four Garden Island-Hedemora V-8 VB210
diesel generator sets, 6,900bhp; one electric
motor, 5,000shp; one shaft
Complement:
41 (plus 5 trainees)
Construction:
Australian Submarine Corporation, Port
Adelaide. *Collins, Waller, Dechaineux, Sheean,
Rankin,* plus three. Eight boats. Completed
1995 to 2005(?)

Design: In the early 1980s it was
announced that the RAN was looking for a
successor to its Oxley class submarines.
These were identical with the Royal Navy's
Oberon class and, like all of Australia's
previous submarines, had been designed
and built in Great Britain. The
competition for a successor was, however,
international, with British, German,
French, Italian and Swedish firms
competing for one of the most important
submarine contracts ever.

Although the success of Kockums designs
serving with the Royal Swedish Navy was
well-known, no Swedish submarine had
ever been exported before. In any case, it
was considered that a company which had
concentrated on designs optimised for
service in the special conditions of the
Baltic would be unlikely to produce a
design suitable for service in the very
different waters of the Pacific and Indian
Oceans. Nevertheless, after a lengthy and
very detailed examination and testing of
the competing designs (and somewhat to
the surprise of the naval community), the
winner was the Swedish Type 471, a
Kockums' design based closely on the
Royal Swedish Navy's Västergötland, albeit
somewhat larger.

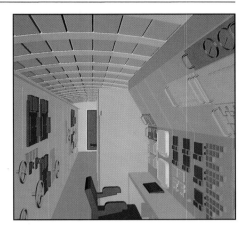

Above: *A CAD (computer-aided design)
image of the propulsion control room for
the Australian Collins class submarines.
Following their success with the RAN
order, Kockums have also won an order
for two submarines for the Royal
Malaysian Navy.*

The Type 471, to be known as the
Collins class in the RAN, is a typical
Kockums' design, with a long cylindrical
hull, minimal upper-casing, a mid-set sail
with the forward hydroplanes placed half-
way up it, X-configured after control
surfaces and a seven-bladed, skew-back
propeller. It is designed to meet the very
demanding RAN requirement of 3,500nm
at 10kt submerged plus 47 days at 4kt on
station.

The hull is constructed of a Swedish
Micro-alloy steel, which is claimed to give
the strength of HY-100, but with much
improved fabrication and welding. The hull
is coated in an anechoic cladding.
Propulsion in the first six boats is by
diesel-electric drive, with batteries being
used for underwater propulsion. However,
the RAN has become closely associated
with Kockums in the development of the
Stirling air-independent propulsion system
and it is possible that the seventh and
eighth of the Collins class will be longer in
order to accommodate such a system.

Armament: The Collins class is fitted
with six 21in (533mm) torpedo tubes
arranged in port and starboard banks of
three each. They are designed to launch
either Mark 48 torpedoes or Sub-Harpoon
missiles, a total of twenty-three such
weapons being carried. It is also possible
that an Australian designed and
constructed 'strap-on' minelaying system
may be ordered for use on these
submarines.

Service History: The first-of-class will
enter service in early 1995 with the
remaining boats following at approximately
yearly intervals thereafter. The area to be
patrolled is vast and with Australia's
increasing concentration on political and
economic affairs around the Indian Ocean
rim it seems likely that they will spend
most of their operational lives in that part
of the world.

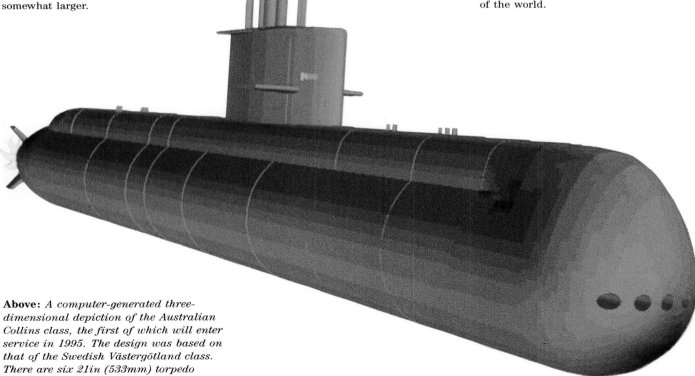

Above: *A computer-generated three-
dimensional depiction of the Australian
Collins class, the first of which will enter
service in 1995. The design was based on
that of the Swedish Västergötland class.
There are six 21in (533mm) torpedo
tubes, for which a total of twenty-three
torpedoes will be carried.*

AUSTRIA-HUNGARY

The Austro-Hungarian Empire, ruled by the Hapsburg dynasty, covered a vast area of central Europe, included a bewildering number of nationalities, and possessed just 340 miles (547km) of coastline along the Adriatic. Covering such a huge land mass, it was not surprising that the Army was by far the predominant service, a situation that was reinforced by the Hungarian objection to any signficant expenditure on the navy, which would, of course be of no benefit to them. Nevertheless, the Empire had a navy, which had, in fact, defeated a superior Italian squadron at the famous Battle of Lissa (20 July 1866).

Like their German neighbours to the north, the Imperial Austro-Hungarian Navy did not venture into submarines until it was clear that other major navies, such as the British, American and French, were fully committed to this new weapon. It was decided to order three competing designs, two of each being built and commissioned in 1908-09, following which the best design would be built in larger numbers.

Two boats (U-1 class) were built at Pola to the design of the American Simon Lake, which, like many of his submarines, proved to be unsatisfactory, although they did eventually serve as training boats for some years.

Germaniaweft, Kiel, built two boats (U-3 class), which were towed to Pola via the Bay of Biscay; they proved more satisfactory than the Lake design and both served in the war. Finally, the Whitehead yard at Fiume built three boats to a Holland design (U-5 class), of which two were delivered in sections from the USA and the third was built as an improved version by Whiteheads.

The Navy then specified its requirements for a 500-ton boat with an underwater speed of 12kt, a very interesting demand, as it was one of the first to recognise the need for a high underwater speed. Five boats were ordered from Germaniawerft (U-7 class) in February 1913, but when war broke out it was considered that they would be unable to make the voyage from Kiel to the Adriatic and they were sold to Germany.

With an urgent need for submarines, five of the newly developed German UB-1 type coastal submarines were ordered in April 1915 (U-10 class) and sent across Europe by rail in sections, while another four coastal submarines were built to plans prepared by Whitehead for the Royal Danish Navy (U-20 class). Eight boats were built to the German UB-II design (U-27 class) and another two of the same design were handed over by the Germans in 1917 (U-43 class). Finally, there was U-14, whose extraordinary story is described on the facing page.

The result of these muddled plans was that just 27 submarines saw service with the Imperial Austro-Hungarian Navy, all of which served in the Mediterranean, seven of them becoming war losses. Despite this, they were remarkably successful, sinking two cruisers, five destroyers, two submarines and damaging one battleship, two cruisers and a destroyer. They also sank or captured 108 merchantmen

Above: *Sailors of the Austro-Hungarian Navy transfer a torpedo below prior to setting out on a World War I patrol.*

(196,102 grt) and damaged a further 11 (41,000 grt). (It should be added that many of the 'merchantmen' were very small coastal sailing vessels).

The Austro-Hungarian Empire collapsed as the war ended and with it the Imperial Navy. Its fleet was disbanded and the ships and submarines allocated to the victorious allies, but, with only a very few exceptions, all were scrapped in the early 1920s.

Below: *U-12 of the U-5 class was a Holland-designed boat, built under licence by the Whitehead yard at Fiume.*

U-14 Class

(Coastal patrol submarine)

Displacement:
397 tons surfaced; 551 tons submerged
Performance:
Max speed 12.6kt surfaced; 9kt submerged
Range 6,500nm/10kt surfaced; 84nm/5kt submerged
Maximum Operational Diving Depth:
Not known
Dimensions:
171ft 3in (52.2m) x 17ft 1in (5.2m) x 10ft 6in (3.2m)
Machinery:
Two diesel engines, 840bhp; two electric motors, 660shp; two shafts
Complement:
28
Construction:
Arsenal de Toulon, France. *Curie*. Completed 1912 (see Notes).

Design: This submarine had a most curious history. She was built in France in 1912 as the *Curie*, one of the sixteen-strong Brumaire class. A double-hulled Laubeuf design, the Brumaire class was essentially a diesel-engined version of the steam-powered Pluviôse class. They were powered by M.A.N 480bhp diesel engines produced under licence in France, which gave them a surface speed of 13kt and a surface range of 1,700nm (3,150km) at 10kt.

Following her sinking by the Austro-Hungarian Navy (described below) she was salved, refitted and returned to service. However, after a year she was returned to the yards where she was given a number of substantial improvements, which considerably enhanced her performance and combat capability. Her engines were replaced by more powerful units giving the performance shown in the specifications above; she was also given a proper

Above: *U-14's captain for most of her career in the Austro-Hungarian Navy was* Oberleutnant *von Trapp, later the hero of the story 'The Sound of Music'.*

conning-tower instead of the French lookout platform and her armament was changed.

Armament: The original French weapons fit of the Brumaire class was a decidedly peculiar mix. There was one fixed torpedo tube in the bows, itself relatively unusual as it was far more common to have two. It was the devices on the upper casing, however, which were the more puzzling, consisting of four Drzewiecki drop-collars and two external cradles on top of the tanks and angled outwards. At this remove it is not possible to guess why there was such a mixture; even six drop-collars would have seemed less strange. A total of eight 17.7in (450mm) torpedoes were carried; ie, one per drop-collar/cradle, and one in the bow tube plus one reload. No gun was fitted.

When the *Curie* was being refitted by the Austro-Hungarians as *U-14* in 1915, the bow tube was replaced by a new 21in (533mm) tube and the external cradle and drop-collars were retained but altered to launch 21in (533mm) torpedoes. A 3.5in (88mm) gun was fitted on a wet-mounting on the foredeck and a 47mm cannon was mounted at the after end of the new

Below: *The Austro-Hungarian* U-14 *was originally a French submarine: the* Curie *of the Brumaire class.*

bridge. In 1918 two of the drop-collars were removed and replaced by two, fixed, aft-firing torpedo launchers.

Service History: As *Curie* this submarine served in the French Navy's Mediterranean Fleet and on 20 December 1914 she managed to enter the main Austro-Hungarian naval base at Pola, but ran into the anti-submarine net. She was forced to the surface and came under gunfire, as a result of which she sank. She was raised in February 1915, refitted and commissioned as *U-14* of the Imperial Austro-Hungarian Navy. She underwent further refits from February to November 1916 and again in 1918.

Her captain from 1916 onwards was the Austrian aristocrat, *Oberleutnant* Georg Ritter von Trapp, who had previously commanded *U-5*. In these two submarines he became the highest-scoring submarine ace of his navy. His sinkings included the French armoured cruiser *Leon Gambetta* (11,959 tons) which he sank with heavy loss of life on 27 April 1915, the Italian submarine *Nereide* (320 tons) on 5 August 1915 and twelve merchantmen (45,668grt). Von Trapp achieved considerable fame for these achievements in his own country, but he later achieved even greater renown as the father of the 'von Trapp family singers' in the musical 'The Sound of Music'.

U-14 was reclaimed by France at the end of World War I and was recommissioned in the French Navy. She served on for another nine years, before being stricken in 1928.

BRAZIL

Brazil is by far the largest and most populous country in Latin America and is potentially a world power. She has the largest population in the southern hemisphere — 150,189,000 — and her 324,200-strong armed forces are the second largest in the Americas. Despite this, somehow her aspirations never seem to be realised.

Brazil declared its independence from Portugal in 1822, but fighting with the colonial power continued into the following year. However, the Brazilian naval squadron, which was under the command of the British Admiral Cochrane, harried a Portuguese convoy of troop transports escorted by thirteen warships and then, having surmised its destination of Maranhao, sailed ahead, captured the port and despatched its garrison back to Portugal. Thus, when the convoy arrived

there was nowhere for them to land and they were forced to sail off ignominiously to Portugal. The Brazilian Navy thus started its existence with a major victory and a substantial contribution to its country's independence.

In 1865 Brazil became involved in the War of the Triple Alliance (with Argentina and Uruguay) against the Paraguayan dictator Lopez. It was primarily a land campaign, although the navy was able to play a part in riverine operations. The war ended in 1870 with the death of Lopez, whose megalomania had reduced his country's population from 1,400,000 to 221,000.

In the late 19th Century the Brazilian Navy sought to purchase a submarine from France. Designed by the inventor Goubet, the sale fell through.

By the turn of the century Brazil was a very prosperous country, controlling the world's supply of coffee and rubber and with even greater wealth in prospect. This encouraged the navy to seek to become not just a continental power, but a global power. To further this aim Brazil ordered two dreadnoughts in 1906 and a third, and

even larger, dreadnought in 1910. Unfortunately, the economy collapsed, leading to a mutiny on board the battleship *Minas Gerais* and the third battleship, *Rio de Janeiro*, was sold to Turkey, whilst still on the stocks.

Part of the 1904 Programme for a balanced fleet was the purchase of three Laurenti-Fiat submarines and a submarine depot ship from Italy. Of 305 tons displacement, the F1 class were armed with two 18in (457mm) torpedo tubes and served from 1913 to 1933. Brazil joined the Allies on 6 October 1918 and deployed a squadron to the coast of West Africa, while her two surviving dreadnoughts were sent to the USA for refit prior to joining the Grand Fleet in Scapa Flow. However, the war ended before this could be completed. The small submarine squadron played no part in the war.

A new submarine, *Humaita* (1,884 tons) was purchased from Italy in 1927 and for five years (1933-38) this was the only submarine in the fleet until the arrival of the three boats of the Tupi class (853 tons), which were purchased from Italy in 1938. Brazil joined the Allies relatively early in World War II (22 August 1942) and took part in operations in the Atlantic, Pacific and Mediterranean campaigns. The four submarines operated in home waters and did not encounter any enemy shipping.

After the war the Brazilian Navy did not receive any modern submarines until 1958, when two US Navy Gato class fleet submarines were transferred. They were given some minor modifications prior to transfer and lasted seven years before being banned from diving due to deterioration of the hull. Another two fleet submarines of the Balao class were transferred in 1963. In 1972-73 all four of these elderly and outdated boats were replaced by seven Guppy type boats: five Guppy IIs and two Guppy IIIs.

These Guppys were supplemented by three new British-built Oberon class submarines between 1973 and 1977, giving Brazil a fleet of no less than ten large, modern, well-equipped boats, by far the strongest in South America. Of these, one Guppy II, one Guppy III and the three Oberons remain in service in 1991.

In the 1970s the Brazilian Navy initiated another fleet expansion programme, which once again included submarines. The country was also particularly keen to establish its own submarine building capability and, not unnaturally, its attention turned to the German firm of HDW, who have an excellent reputation for good submarine design coupled with a willingness for technology transfer. So, in August 1982 Brazil ordered three Type 1400 submarines (1,900 tons), of which one was built by HDW at Kiel and the other two are still building at the Arsenal de Marinha yard in Rio de Janiero.

Brazil has announced the intention to build a 2,200 ton submarine of Brazilian design (NAC-1 class) after completion of the two Type 1400s. There have also been several reports that this class will be followed by an SSN design.

Above: *F-3, one of three Fiat-Laurenti submarines bought from Italy in 1913 as part of a major naval expansion.*

Below: *The three submarines of the Tupi class, 853 tons submerged displacement, which were bought from Italy in 1938.*

Humaita (Oberon) Class

(Diesel-electric patrol submarines)

Displacement:
2,030 tons surfaced; 2,400 tons submerged
Performance:
Max speed 17.5kt surfaced; 15kt submerged
Range 11,000nm/11kt schnorkel; not known
submerged
Maximum Operational Diving Depth:
656ft (200m)
Dimensions:
294ft 11in (89.9m) x 26ft 6in (8.07m) x 18ft 0in
(5.48m)
Machinery:
Two Admiralty Standard Range 16 VVS-ASR1
diesel engines, 3,680bhp; two electric motors,
6,000shp; two shafts
Complement:
5 officers; 57 ratings
Construction:
Vickers-Armstrong, Barrow-in-Furness. *Humaita*
(S-20), *Tonelero* (S-21), *Riachuelo* (S-22). Three
boats. Completed 1973-77.

Design: After World War II the Royal
Navy, like the US Navy, found itself with a
large number of wartime submarines in
fairly good condition, but which were
obsolescent due to the advances made by
German designers. As a result, the initial
British post-war policy was to update A
and T class submarines in a programme
similar to that of the US Guppy.

With the failure of the hydrogen-
peroxide propulsion programme, and
despite the prospect of nuclear submarines
in the near future, the Royal Navy then
decided to produce a new class of diesel-
electric submarines, which were the
equivalent of the American Tang class.
This first post-war design fell into two

Above: Humaita, *2,400 tons submerged
displacement, one of three Oberon class
submarines bought from Great Britain in
the 1970s.*

groups: first was the Porpoise group of
eight boats completed 1958-61 and second
the Oberon group of 13 boats completed
1960-67. The Oberon design was a virtual
repeat of the Porpoise, but with improved
electronic and detection equipment, and
the ability to fire homing torpedoes.

All eight boats of the Porpoise class were
constructed for the Royal Navy. However,
the Oberon class was widely exported:
Australia receiving six, Brazil three,
Canada three and Chile two. The first
Brazilian order for two Oberon class was
announced in 1969, followed by an order
for a third boat in 1972. *Tonelero*, second
of class, suffered a major fire at a late
stage during her construction, which
resulted in her being towed from Barrow to

Below: Tonelero *(S-21) was the victim of
a major fire during her construction in
Britain, which resulted in a lengthy
delay in completion and delivery.*

Chatham Naval Dockyard for repair work
and then being towed back to Barrow for
completion. Thus, having been laid down
in November 1971 she was not
commissioned until December 1977, which
must be something of a record.

Armament: The Brazilian submarines are
fitted with six 21in (533mm) tubes in the
bow, for which a total of eighteen UK
Mark 24 or US Mark 37 torpedoes are
carried. The submarines were built with
two 21in (533mm) stern tubes for short
Mark 23 torpedoes, but these are no longer
used.

Service History: *Humaita* was
commissioned in 1973, followed by
Riachuelo in March 1977 and finally by
Tonelero, after her fire, in December of
that year. The boats have all had several
refits but are now approaching the end of
their useful lives, although all have
recently received new fire control systems.

Brazil's current submarine fleet consists
of one Tupi class, a new Type 1400
constructed in Germany, two elderly
Guppys and these three Oberon class.
However, it will become stronger as the
building programme develops.

CHILE

Chile, a former Spanish colony which obtained its independence in the early 19th Century has a long naval tradition. It was conquered by Spain between 1540 and 1561, but there were repeated insurrections over the years, culminating in the war of independence between 1817 and 1819. This war included some spectacular naval successes by a squadron under the command of the British Admiral Cochrane, which left an enduring anglophile legacy.

Worsening relations with Peru and Bolivia led to the War of the Pacific (1879-84) in which the Chilean Navy was particularly successful, sinking the Peruvian monitor *Huascar* and carrying out several amphibious landings. Chile obtained what it wanted from the war, but its effect was to create simmering problems with Peru and Bolivia, leading to further armed clashes in the period 1921-29. Eventually, the USA arbitrated and settled the dispute.

Since then Chile has not been directly involved in any international wars. However, there has been tension over the Beagle Channel with Argentina, while Chile appears to have been a not totally disinterested observer in the 1982 Falklands War.

Throughout all this, the Chilean Navy has maintained a small, but notably efficient fleet, whose main purpose has been to keep a wary eye on its neighbours Peru to the north and Argentina to the east. Like other South American navies, the Chilean Navy for many years operated one battleship, together with a force of cruisers and destroyers, supported by a small number of submarines.

The first submarine was locally constructed in 1864, but does not appear to have been successful. Then, in 1911 two submarines were ordered from the USA. They were completed in 1914, but following the trials the Chilean Navy refused to accept them, as they did not meet the specifications. (They were then

Above: Thomson, *one of two US Navy Balao class submarines transferred to Chile in the 1960s. They did not receive Guppy conversions but were given streamlined fins, as shown here, during refits.*

put up for sale and bought by the Premier of British Columbia for local defence in August 1914, following which they served in the RCN as the CC class).

In 1914 there were a number of Chilean warships under construction in British yards which were taken over and commissioned into the Royal Navy. This outstanding debt was met in part in 1917, by offering the Chilean Navy five H class submarines, which had been constructed for the Royal Navy in the USA, but had been impounded by the then neutral US Government in 1915. They were released on the entry of the USA into the war, but were no longer required by the British. They were accepted by Chile who ordered one more new construction boat to make a squadron of six. These boats served in the Chilean Navy from July 1917; three were stricken in 1945, one in 1949 and the remaining two in 1953. One, *Rucumilla*, sank in an accident in 1927 with loss of

Below: Quidora *(ex-H-4), one of five H class submarines built for the Royal Navy in 1915, but then ceded to Chile in 1917. A sixth, new boat was also built.*

her complete crew but was raised and returned to service.

Next came the three O'Brien class described opposite, and there was then a gap in submarine purchases until two surplus US Navy Balao class were purchased in 1961-62; one served until 1972, the other until 1982. These were standard fleet submarines and did not have any Guppy conversion or schnorkel, although streamlined fins were fitted at their first refit.

Two British Oberon class submarines were acquired, which arrived in 1976, well over a year late, due to building delays; both are still in service. Then in 1984, Chile purchased two submarines from Germany, IKL Type 1300, which are essentially the standard design except for a raised sail required on account of the rough seas encountered in the South Pacific.

Thus, the Chilean Navy has maintained a small but efficient force since 1917. They have purchased new boats sparingly, but except for the two US Balao class, which were elderly, the boats have been well up with the latest technology at the time of commissioning. They have then remained in service for many years, although the Chilean Navy's reputation for the highest standards of maintenance has ensured that they were always fully operational.

Capitan O'Brien Class

(Patrol submarines)

Displacement:
1,412 tons surfaced; 2,020 tons submerged
Performance:
Max speed 15kt surfaced; 9kt submerged
Range 7,000nm/10kt surfaced; not known submerged
Maximum Operational Diving Depth:
300ft (91m)
Dimensions:
260ft 0in (79.25m) x 28ft 0in (8.53m) x 13ft 6in (4.5m)
Machinery:
Two Vickers diesel engines, 2,750bhp; two electric motors, 1,300shp; two shafts
Complement:
54
Construction:
Vickers-Armstrong, Barrow. *Capitan O'Brien, Almirante Simpson, Capitan Thomson.* Three boats. Completed 1928-29.

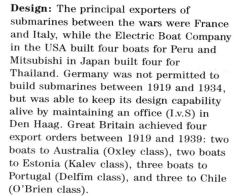

Right: *The unusual ram bow, used only in O'Brien, Oxley and Odin classes.*

Above: Captain Thomson *showing the typically British 4.7in (120mm) gun installation at bridge level.*

Design: The principal exporters of submarines between the wars were France and Italy, while the Electric Boat Company in the USA built four boats for Peru and Mitsubishi in Japan built four for Thailand. Germany was not permitted to build submarines between 1919 and 1934, but was able to keep its design capability alive by maintaining an office (I.v.S) in Den Haag. Great Britain achieved four export orders between 1919 and 1939: two boats to Australia (Oxley class), two boats to Estonia (Kalev class), three boats to Portugal (Delfim class), and three to Chile (O'Brien class).

The Chilean Navy had long had close

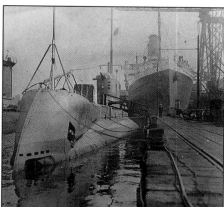

ties with the Royal Navy and most Chilean surface warships were built in British yards. When, therefore in the mid-1920s the Chilean Navy needed to buy three modern submarines it was natural that they should turn to Vickers of Barrow, England. The design selected was based on the Royal Navy's Odin class, which was being completed as the Chilean boats were laid down.

Externally the O'Brien class, like the British Odin class, was characterised by a most distinctive rearwards sloping ('ram') bow. They also had a very large bridge structure, which incorporated the gun mounting.

The three boats were constructed at the Vickers yard in Barrow-in-Furness, the first being launched in 1928 and the other two in early 1929.

Armament: Main armament was a battery of eight 21in (533mm) torpedo tubes, six in the bow, two in the stern.

One 4.7in (120mm) gun was installed, mounted in a special mount just forward of, and at the same level as the bridge. This was very similar to the arrangement in the British O class, but was slightly higher in the Chilean boats. This had been developed originally in the earlier L class and was intended to enable the gun crew to get into action more quickly on surfacing, since they did not have to emerge from the conning-tower onto the foredeck.

Service History: At the time of commissioning these were the most modern and capable submarines in the southern half of Latin America. Peru possessed four somewhat smaller US R class submarines (755 tons) bought in 1926, while the Argentine Navy did not have any submarines at all until they took delivery of the three Santa Fe class boats (920 tons) from Italy in 1931-32. The three Chilean boats were, thus, far larger and more effective than either of the classes operated by their neighbours.

The three submarines of this class served for many years, operating in the difficult waters off the Chilean coast. In common with most warships in the Chilean Navy they had very long service lives, *Almirante Simpson* and *Capitan O'Brien* being stricken in 1957 and *Capitan Thomson* in 1958.

Below: *A splendid picture of the Chilean* Almirante Simpson *running trials off the Scottish coast in 1929.*

DENMARK

Right: *Three submarines of the Havmanden class which were all scuttled in 1943. In the centre is* Havhesten.

Below: Neptun *of the B class, the first class to be built in Denmark in 1915-16.*

Denmark, like Turkey, has the dubious honour of controlling one of the world's major naval choke-points. The Baltic Sea's exit to the North Sea is through the Kattegat, a narrow channel running through a maze of islands, which no ship or submarine could transit in the face of determined opposition from the shore. A second strategic consideration for Denmark has been the presence of a powerful neighbour to the south.

In the early years of this century the Danish defence budget was very tight, and between 1900 and 1910 only one coastal battleship and one torpedo boat joined the surface fleet, at a time when other European navies were expanding rapidly. It is thus not surprising that the Royal Danish Navy was one of the last European navies to establish a submarine service, ordering her first boat in 1908 from Italy. This boat, the *Dykkeren* (132 tons), was followed by a class of six, designed by the Whitehead yard at Fiume, of which three

were built at Fiume and three in the Royal Dockyard at Copenhagen, one of them paid for by public subscription. Delivered between 1911 and 1914, the Havmanden or A class (204 tons) were small, handy boats, but with an exceptionally light armament of two 18in (457mm) torpedo tubes and one 8mm machine-gun, fitted in 1917. They were quickly followed by the five-boat Aegir or B class (235 tons), which were slightly larger, and with an additional stern torpedo tube and a 57mm cannon. Finally in this first series came the three boats of the Rota or C class (369 tons); these were larger still and with four torpedo tubes, which, strangely, were mounted three in the bows and one in the stern (except for *Rota*, which had five tubes).

The Daphne class (381 tons) joined the navy in 1926, followed by the Havmanden class (402 tons) in 1937 to 1940. These

Below: Dryaden, *a Daphné class boat.*

small submarines were all built at the Royal Dockyard in Copenhagen and all were scuttled on 29 August 1943, the hulks being raised and sold for scrap in 1950.

The first post-war submarines were the four boats of the Delfinen class (643 tons), which were constructed in Copenhagen between 1954 and 1963, and stricken in the 1980s. These were followed by two German Type 205 boats, the Narvhalen class, designed by IKL but constructed in Copenhagen. These were modelled on the Type 207 built for the Royal Norwegian Navy and entered service in 1970. After very considerable hesitation it was decided not to construct a new class of submarine to replace the ageing Delfinen class and, instead, three surplus Type 207 Kobben class submarines were bought from Norway and completely modernised. Thus, Denmark's submarine fleet will comprise just five boats, all constructed in the 1960s, for some years to come.

Dykkeren Class

(Petrol-engined patrol submarine)

Displacement:
105 tons surfaced; 132 tons submerged
Performance:
Max speed 12kt surfaced; 7.5kt submerged
Range 100nm/8kt surfaced; 40nm/5kt submerged
Maximum Operational Diving Depth:
148ft (45m)
Dimensions:
113ft 10in (34.7m) x 10ft 10in (3.3m) x 7ft 3in (2.2m)
Machinery:
Two Fiat petrol engines, 600bhp; two electric motors, 210shp; two shafts
Complement:
9
Construction:
Fiat-San Giorgio, La Spezia. *Dykkeren*. One boat. Completed 1909.

Design: In the early 1900s the Royal Danish Navy decided to add the first submarines to its small fleet and, like many other countries, she turned to Italy as a potential source. The Italian submarine designers at this time enjoyed a considerable international reputation and many smaller navies ordered their first class of submarines from them, while a number of major navies ordered a small number for comparison with their own designs. As a result, the Italians sold a remarkable number of boats!

The leading Italian submarine designer at the time was Engineer Lieutenant-Commander Cesare Laurenti, whose vessels were normally constructed by the Fiat yard at La Spezia. His designs had certain common characteristics. They had a double hull for about three-quarters of their length and a high reserve of buoyancy, making them somewhat skittish in a seaway. They took a long time to dive, but in those pre-radar days that was not too much of a disadvantage. They had a remarkable number of internal watertight bulkheads, as many as ten in some.

Despite this pedigree, they proved to be remarkably unpopular in some navies. The Royal Navy, for example, disliked their three S class so much that when Italy joined the Allies on 25 May 1915 they

Below: Dykkeren, *the first Danish submarine, which was built in Italy in 1909 to a Fiat-Laurenti design.*

were handed over to the Royal Italian Navy with almost indecent haste.

The Danish *Dykkeren* was based on the Italian Glauco and Foca classes. In common with them, the petrol engines were unreliable and the fuel dangerous.
Armament: *Dykkeren* was armed with two 18in (457mm) torpedo tubes.
Service History: She was commissioned into the Royal Danish Navy in June 1909, but suffered many mechanical problems which led to her spending a lot of time in the Royal Dockyard in Copenhagen. *Dykkeren* was sunk on 9 October 1916 in a collision with a Norwegian merchant-ship. She was raised in 1917 but was not returned to service.

The next class of submarine destined for the Royal Danish Navy was ordered in 1910, but not from Italy. Instead they turned to a competing company: the Whitehead Yard at Fiume in Austria-Hungary.

ESTONIA

The small country of Estonia, a province of the Russian Empire, was brought under Soviet rule in the Revolution, but quickly proclaimed its independence on 24 February 1918. It was occupied the very next day by German troops. The Germans remained until the end of World War I, withdrawing on 11 November 1918. The forces of the Soviet Union then advanced, taking Narva in a few days, and eventually they occupied just over half of the country. British assistance in the Intervention War in early 1919 stemmed the Soviet advance and this, combined with a very active Estonian land campaign, led to the liberation of the country in May 1919. Captured Russian ships were immediately impressed into the newly-created Estonian Navy and sent into action, mostly against land targets.

By the time the peace treaty was signed at Dorpat on 2 February 1920, the main elements of the Estonian Navy were two destroyers, two gunboats and two minelayers. The two destroyers, *Wambola* and *Lennuk*, were former Soviet warships which had been captured at sea by a British squadron on 27 December 1918 and presented to the Estonians. The remaining ships were captured in harbour and were either former Soviet or German warships.

In 1933 the two destroyers were sold to Peru as part of a plan to modernise and expand the navy. The main element of this plan was the purchase from Great Britain of two minelaying submarines, which were the largest and most modern warships in the small Estonian fleet on their arrival in 1937. The Latvian Navy had followed a similar path, buying two submarines from France in 1927. It is clear that both countries felt that the most cost-effective way for such small navies to exercise naval power was through submarines, rather than through surface warships.

In the event, the two Kalev class submarines were unable to fight for the defence of Estonia as their country was overwhelmed in a series of diplomatic moves by their giant neighbour, the USSR. A Non-Aggression Pact was signed between the two countries in 1932 and a Treaty of Mutual Assistance was signed in 1939 following the German conquest of Poland. This allowed a small Soviet garrison to be stationed on Estonian soil. In June 1940 the Estonians were accused of acts of provocation against these troops and a new and more friendly (to the USSR) government was set up. A few weeks later the country was declared a Soviet Socialist Republic and on 6 August it was integrated into the USSR, with the Estonian Navy becoming part of the Soviet Navy.

That was not the end of the story, however, as in 1989 the Estonians again made a bid for liberty. Although an act of secession from the Soviet Union was not to be achieved on that occasion, there can be no doubt that Estonians remain determined to be free, and when they achieve that aim they will doubtless reform their small, but very efficient naval force.

Kalev Class

(Minelaying submarines)

Displacement:
620 tons surfaced; 850 tons submerged
Performance:
Max speed 13.5kt surfaced; 8.5kt submerged
Range not known
Maximum Operational Diving Depth:
Not known
Dimensions:
190ft 3in (58.0m) x 23ft 11in (7.30m) x 10ft 10in (3.30m)
Machinery:
Two Vickers diesel engines, 1,200bhp; two electric motors, 790shp; two shafts
Complement:
38
Construction:
Vickers-Armstrong, Barrow-in-Furness, England. *Kalev, Lembit,* Two boats. Completed 1936-37.

Above: Kalev *coming alongside a British submarine. The two Estonian boats were built by Vickers-Armstrong in England, their design being based on that of the British P class, but they were slightly smaller and with added mine chutes.*

Below: *The Estonian submarine Kalev. She was armed with only four torpedo tubes, all in the bow (there were no stern tubes), mines mounted in vertical tubes, and two light AA cannon.*

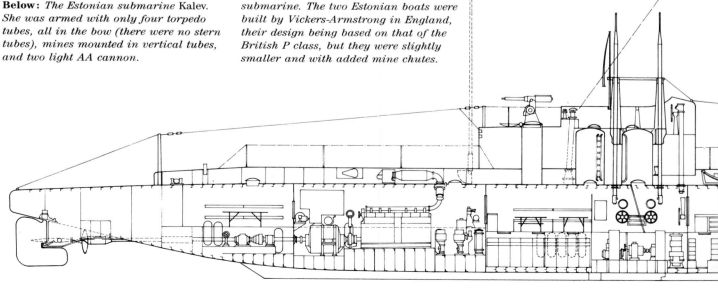

Above: Lembit *undergoing builder's trials.* Lembit *was taken over by the Soviet Navy in 1940 and survived the war. She is preserved as a memorial.*

Below: Kalev. *Faced with a limited defence budget and a wish to expand a very small navy, the Estonians decided to build these two submarine minelayers.*

Design: When the Estonian Navy found itself in a position to expand in the early 1930s top priority was given to the purchase of two submarines. The decision was possibly influenced by the acquisition of two submarines by the Latvian Navy, Latvia being a country whose geographical position and historical background was very similar to that of Estonia. The decision to fit them as minelayers is an interesting one and was possibly the result of studying the very successful use of mines in the Baltic in World War I.

The order was placed with the British firm of Vickers-Armstrong, who based their design on that of the Royal Navy's P class, although the Estonian boats were slightly smaller, displacing 850 tons as opposed to the P's 2,040 tons. As with the British World War I E and L class minelayers, the mine chutes were sited vertically in the saddletanks, five on each side abreast the conning-tower.

Armament: The armament of these boats was somewhat unusual. There were four 21in (533mm) torpedo tubes, all in the bow, with none in the stern, although this was the prevailing fashion. Further, there was no large calibre deck gun, such armament being confined to two AA cannon, one of 40mm the other 20mm. Twenty mines were carried, two in each of the ten vertical tubes.

Service History: The pride of the Estonian Navy, these two submarines were commissioned in 1937. When Estonia was occupied by the Soviets in 1940 the two submarines were incorporated into the Soviet Navy, but they retained their original names.

Kalev was sunk off Hangö (the southernmost tip of Finland) while serving as a transport submarine. *Lembit* appears to have been used in her intended role as a minelayer, and survived the war. She was redesignated first to *U-1* in 1945 and then to *S-85* in 1949. She was used for experimental purposes from 1956 to the early 1970s. She was stricken in 1979 and moved to Tallinn where she was preserved as a memorial, and is believed still to be there.

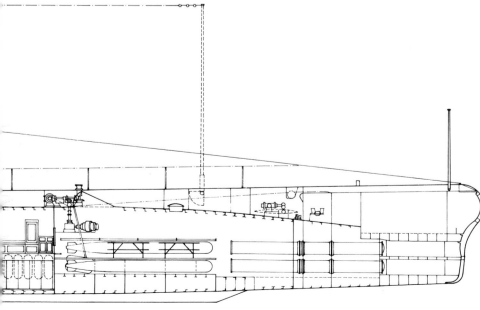

GREECE

reece was a vassal state of the Turkish Ottoman Empire for many centuries, but fought a long war of independence from 1821 to 1829, in which naval forces played a prominent part. Volunteer adventurers flocked to support the Greeks, including the British Admiral Cochrane, who arrived in 1825 and was given command of the Greek Navy. However, the Turks retained effective control of the country until the British, French and Russians sent a joint fleet, which defeated the Turkish-Egyptian fleet at the Battle of Navarino (20 October 1827).

From that day onwards the Greek Navy's primary mission was to face the Turkish Navy and it was with this role in mind that it bought the Nordenfelt- and Garrett-designed submarine *Nordenfelt I* (60 tons) in 1885, an action which caused the Turks to buy *Nordenfelt II*. The Greek submarine never became operational and was scrapped in 1901.

Tension throughout the Balkans rose at the start of this century and the Greek Navy again invested in submarines. This time the boats were much better, being two Schneider submarines ordered from France in 1909 and delivered in 1911 and 1912. Named *Delfin* and *Xifias*, these 460 tons Laubeuf-designed boats arrived in time to take part in the first Balkan War (1912 to 1913). It was during this conflict that Lieutenant-Commander Paparrigopoulos carried out the first-ever submerged attack on a surface warship at sea when, on 9 December 1912, he attacked the Turkish light cruiser *Medjidieh* (3,250 tons), which emerged

Above: Pipinos *(ex-HMS* Veldt*) was one of six British submarines transferred to the Greek Navy between 1943 and 1946.*

Below: Papanikolis, *formerly USS Hardhead (SS-365), was a Guppy IIA conversion transferred to Greece in 1972.*

from the Dardanelles accompanied by five destroyer escorts. The Greek submarine closed to within 550yd (500m) and fired a single torpedo. The missile failed to function properly and veered off course, a fate that has dogged submarine captains of many nations since then!

Two more Laubeuf submarines were ordered from France in 1912, while it was also planned to order five U-boats from Germany, but both orders were cancelled by the suppliers on the outbreak of war. The next submarines actually to reach the Greek Navy were six French boats of the Katsonis and Proteus classes, which were delivered between 1926 and 1928. Four were sunk during World War II: one by the Italians and three by the Germans.

After the Greek surrender in 1941 the

Below: *The Greek submarines* Proteus *(nearest the camera) and* Nereus. *These were similar to the Katsonis class, but had the torpedo tubes mounted internally.*

surviving Greek warships operated under Royal Navy command in the Mediterranean. They proved very active allies and the Royal Navy lent them six submarines and presented them with a seventh. Four V class submarines were lent between 1943 and 1946, being returned in 1957/58, while two U classes were lent in 1945 and returned in 1952. The seventh submarine was the former Italian *Perla*, which had been captured at sea off Beirut in 1942 by the British, who presented it to the Greeks, by whom it was commissioned as *Matrozos*.

In the early 1950s the Greek Navy, keeping, as always, a watchful eye on Turkey, observed their build-up of ex-US fleet submarines, which had started in 1948. They sought to counter-balance this and the US Navy supplied three fleet schnorkel conversions, one each in 1957, 1958 and 1965, which were subsequently replaced by two Guppy conversions, one Guppy IIA, *Papanikolis*, in 1972 and a Guppy III, *Katsonis*, in 1973.

In the 1960s the Greek Navy found itself with a few rather elderly ex-US submarines and decided that it was time to expand, placing orders for a number of the then relatively untried German Type 209 submarines from Howaldtswerke at Kiel. These were, in fact, the first of many foreign orders for this type, and eight entered service between 1971 and 1980. Four are being upgraded in the early 1990s, a process which will include fitting them to launch the Sub-Harpoon missile.

The Greek Navy's submarine force consisted in 1991 of ten boats. There are the eight Type 209s, plus the elderly ex-US Guppy III, which is used for sea training, and the Guppy IIA which is used for pier-side training.

Katsonis/ Proteus Class

(Patrol submarines)

Displacement:
Katsonis 595 tons surfaced; 778 tons submerged
Proteus 750 tons surfaced; 960 tons submerged

Performance:
Max speed Katsonis/Proteus 14kt surfaced; 9.5kt submerged
Range Katsonis/Proteus 3,500nm/10kt surfaced; 100nm/5kt submerged

Maximum Operational Diving Depth:
Katsonis 262ft (80m)
Proteus 278ft (85m)

Dimensions:
Katsonis 204ft 9in (62.40m) x 17ft 5in (5.30m) x 11ft 2in (3.40m)
Proteus 225ft 1in (68.60m) x 18ft 10in (5.73m) x 13ft 9in (4.18m)

Machinery:
Katsonis Two Schneider-Carels diesel engines, 1,300bhp; two electric motors, 1,000shp; two shafts
Proteus Two Sulzer diesel engines, 1,420bhp; two electric motors, 1,200shp; two shafts

Complement:
Katsonis 39
Proteus 41

Construction:
Katsonis   F.C. de la Gironde, France. *Katsonis, Papanikolis.* Two boats. Completed 1926
Proteus   Ateliers et Chantiers de la Loire. *Proteus, Nereus, Triton.* Three boats. Completed 1927 to 1928
Chantiers Navale Français (CNF), Blainville. *Glavkos.* One boat. Completed 1928

Below: Katsonis. *Note the externally-mounted bow and stern torpedo tubes, and the bridge-mounted gun, which were characteristic of this class.*

Design: After World War I the first French medium displacement submarines to be built were a series of ten boats under the designation 600 tonne-type, followed by sixteen of the improved 630 tonne-type. Within each of these groups a standard specification was issued and companies were then able to produce their own design, as a result of which there were slight differences within each 'type'. Thus, there were three designs of the 600 tonne-type: Design A, Simonot-Loire (three built); Design B, Normand-Fenaux (three built); and Design C, Schneider-Laubeuf (four built). Similarly, there were three versions of the 630 tonne-type: Design D, Schneider-Laubeuf (five built); Design E, Loire-Dubigeon (two built); and Design F, Normand-Fenaux (nine built).

The 600 tonne-type was not totally satisfactory, all three designs proving to have poor habitability and to suffer from a degree of lateral instability when submerged. Their armament was also less than ideal (see below). These faults were overcome in the improved and slightly enlarged 630 tonne-type.

When Greece was seeking new submarines in the early 1920s they turned to the supplier of their earlier boats, France, and ordered, first, two of the 600 tonne-type Design C (Schneider-Laubeuf) and later four of the 630 tonne-type Design E (Loire-Simonot). The first two had modified armament, but the later boats were identical to their French counterparts, apart from the armament.

Armament: The French 600 tonne-type was armed with seven torpedo tubes: three in the bow (one internal and two in the casing), two externally aft and two in a revolving mount abaft the conning-tower. This was a rather complicated arrangement for a submarine of this size and also meant that only the single internal bow tube could be reloaded at sea. Thirteen torpedoes were carried.

The Katsonis class had a simplified arrangement, with six 21.7in (550mm) torpedo tubes, four in the bow and two in the stern, but with two of the bow tubes mounted internally. The remaining two

bow tubes and both stern tubes were in the upper casing. Main gun armament was one 4.0in (102mm)/40 mounted at the forward edge of the conning-tower on a rotating platform, which was designed to ease control and to enable the gun to be brought into action rapidly on surfacing. A light AA gun was mounted during the war.

The French 630 tonne-type was fitted with six 21.7in (550mm) and two 15.75in (450mm) torpedo tubes. Of the larger tubes, three were in the bow, all internal, two in the stern on a rotating mount and one in the stern in a fixed, external mount. The two smaller tubes were also aft, in a rotating mount.

In the Proteus class this was again considerably simplified with eight 21.7in (550mm) torpedo tubes (six bow, two stern), all mounted internally. The 4.0in (102mm) gun was mounted on the casing at the forward edge of the conning-tower rather than at bridge level. A 40mm cannon was also mounted for AA defence.

Service History: The two boats of the Katsonis class (*Katsonis* and *Papanikolis*) entered service in 1926 and the other four boats of the Proteus class in 1927 (*Proteus* and *Nereus*) and 1928 (*Glavkos* and *Triton*). When Italy attacked Greece on 28 October 1940 all six were in service. *Proteus* was rammed and sunk by *Antares*, an Italian submarine-chaser, on 19 December 1940. The Axis forces invaded Greece in April 1941 and when defeat became inevitable the surviving units of the fleet, including the five remaining submarines, escaped to British-held ports in the Mediterranean.

The five Greek boats spent the rest of the war under the operational control of the Royal Navy, operating out of Alexandria and Malta. They achieved some successes against German and Italian targets, but a further three were lost before the conflict ended. Two were rammed and sunk by German submarine-chasers: *Katsonis* on 14 September 1943 and *Triton* on 16 November 1942. *Glavkos* was sunk by bombing on 4 April 1942.

Thus, only *Papanikolis* and *Nereus* survived the war to be stricken in 1945.

INDIA

The Royal Indian Navy was raised by the British as an adjunct to the Royal Navy for Imperial defence tasks. By the end of World War II it had grown to encompass some 400 ships and approximately 26,000 men, but this establishment was rapidly run down to a mere 11,000 men, four sloops, two frigates and one corvette by the time of Independence in 1947. From that low-point it has expanded steadily until today it is one of the world's major navies and is growing faster than any other maritime force.

In 1991 the Indian Navy possessed a front-line strength of two aircraft-carriers, five destroyers, nineteen frigates, numerous smaller vessels and auxiliaries,

and sixteen submarines. This force is designed for two principal missions. First is the ever-present threat of war with Pakistan, whose navy possesses two Agosta class (1,725 tons) and four Daphné class (1,043 tons), all designed and built in France. Second is a scarcely-concealed wish to be the predominant naval power in the Indian Ocean.

The Indian submarine fleet was established with the delivery of Soviet-supplied Foxtrot class boats, the first of which arrived in 1968. All of new construction, the class built up steadily, peaking at eight in 1975. This was a very sensible buy for a first submarine class, as the Foxtrot has a good reputation as a simple, rugged and reliable boat, and was quite sufficient for the Indian Navy's needs at that stage in its development. After a gap of some years the Indian Navy negotiated with the German firm of HDW for the purchase of Type 209 submarines, of which two would be built in Germany and the remainder in Bombay, thus

establishing an Indian submarine-construction capability.

However, when difficulty was experienced with the Type 209 programme, it was decided to order a number of Soviet Kilo class (3,000 tons), diesel-electric submarines as well. The first of these, *Sindhugosh* (S-55), was delivered in 1986 and orders now stand at ten, seven of which had been delivered by the beginning of 1991. However, it is believed that the Indian Navy may then seek a licence to construct further Kilo class boats in India.

The Type 209 and Kilo programmes have already given the Indian Navy the largest and most modern submarine fleet in the Indian Ocean. However, events have not stopped there, as on 8 January 1988 a Soviet Charlie class SSGN arrived in Bombay, crewed by a predominantly Indian crew, on long loan to the Indian Navy. This is the first nuclear-powered submarine to be lent to any developing navy and indicates not only a high level of sophistication in Indian Navy training and

Shishumar Class

(Patrol submarines)

Displacement:
1,660 tons surfaced; 1,860 tons submerged
Performance:
Max speed 11kt surfaced; 22.5kt submerged
Range 13,00nm/10kt surfaced; 524nm/4kt submerged
Maximum Operational Diving Depth:
853ft (260m)
Dimensions:
211ft 3in (64.40m) x 21ft 4in (6.50m) x 20ft 4in (6.20m)
Machinery:
Four MTU 12V493 TV60 (AZ 80) diesel engines, 2,400bhp; two Siemens electric motors, 5,000shp; one shaft
Complement:
8 officers, 28 ratings
Construction:
Howaldtswerke, Kiel. *Shishumar* (S44), *Shankush* (S45). Two boats. Completed 1986 Mazagon Dockyard, Bombay. *Shalki* (S46), plus one (S47). Two boats. Completed 1991 to 1993(?)

Above: Shankush *(S45), second Type SSK-1500 for the Indian Navy.*

Below: Shishumar *(S44) on trials in the Skaggerak bearing the German ensign.*

technological expertise, but also a major extension of its maritime ambitions. It has been officially stated that this submarine, named *Chakra* in Indian service, has no SS-N-8 anti-ship missiles or nuclear-tipped torpedoes, which suggests that it is regarded only as a training boat. Unconfirmed reports suggest that *Chakra* has suffered from a number of propulsion problems and that it has been exchanged for a second, similar boat, possibly named *Chitra*.

The Indian Navy clearly plans to dominate the Indian Ocean and it is also becoming obvious that submarines will be a major element of the fleet. Further, their acquisition of the *Chakra*, the establishment of a submarine-construction capability in Bombay and the already known missile and nuclear-warhead capability, suggest that the long-term plans almost certainly include a force of SSBNs armed with SLBMs. Such a strategic force would be supported by domestically-designed and built SSNs and SSKs.

Above: Shankush, *one of two Type 1500s built in Germany. Two others are being* built in India, but progress has been slow and Kilos ordered to fill the gap.

Design: The Type 1500 is one of the German IKL Type 209 series of submarine designs and was ordered by India in December 1981. It is the second-largest version of that very successful design (only the Brazilian Type 1400 has a greater displacement). It differs from the others in that it is the first to incorporate the Gabler escape sphere. This device is an autonomous rescue system which, in the event of an accident, is used to accommodate the complete crew. It is situated just forward of the sail and once ready for the escape it is released from the submarine and rises to the surface, where it floats to await the arrival of rescuers. The sphere contains all necessary life-support systems, including oxygen for eight hours, radios and distress beacons.

The original order was for four submarines, of which two were to be built by HDW at Kiel and two assembled from HDW-supplied parts at the Mazagon Yard in Bombay. The order was later increased to six, the two further boats also to be built by Mazagon. The two HDW boats were delivered as planned in 1986, but there have been repeated delays in the construction work at Mazagon and the order for the fifth and sixth boats has been allowed to lapse.

Armament: These submarines are armed with eight 21in (533mm) torpedo tubes, all in the bow. Fourteen AEG-designed SUT wire-guided torpedoes are carried. In addition, HDW strap-on minelaying pods have been purchased, which enable the submarines to carry 24 mines in addition to a complete outfit of torpedoes, should the tactical situation demand it.

Service History: The two German-built submarines were delivered on schedule in 1986 and now serve in the ever-growing Indian Navy. However, the two Indian-built boats (the first submarines to be built in India), have been seriously delayed and will not join the fleet until 1992/93 at the earliest.

The construction of the two boats at Mazagon has clearly caused major problems. However, modern submarines are highly complex devices — and these HDW boats are more sophisticated than most — and their construction demands

Below: *The HDW rescue sphere on the surface after a live test.*

very high skills in a number of areas, not least in fabricating the critically important pressure-hull. Thus, it is not surprising that Mazagon should have experienced difficulties with their first submarines.

Above: Shishumar *surfaces after the test; in real life the hulk would lie below.*

NETHERLANDS

espite her fine naval traditions, both in fighting and in building excellent warships, there appear to have been no 19th Century Dutch inventors designing submarines and endeavouring to interest the Naval Staff in their projects. The lead was eventually taken by the De Schelde shipyard, who decided to construct the first Dutch submarine as a private venture using plans purchased from J.P. Holland's Electric Boat Company in the USA. The boat, named *Luctor et Energo* was laid down in June 1904 and launched one year later. Although completed in June 1906, it was not until December of that year that a somewhat reluctant navy purchased the boat, designating her *Onderzeeboot 1*.

For some years thereafter the Royal Netherlands Navy (RNethN) looked to foreign firms for submarine designs, although all the boats were built in Dutch yards. Several classes were built to designs produced by the Hay-Whitehead company, based at Fiume in Austria-Hungary, while other early classes were built to designs of the Scottish Hay-Denny Company.

The Dutch had two quite separate naval areas to defend. The first was the homeland, a small country with a relatively short North Sea coastline, and as the nation had declared herself neutral, the main mission was defence of that neutrality. The second area, however, was the huge, sprawling imperial territory (the third largest European empire) in the Dutch East Indies (present-day Indonesia). To meet these two missions the Dutch for many years produced two types of submarine. The first type, intended for homeland defence, were small and with a short range: they were designated *'Onderzeeboot'* ('O') and given Arabic numbers (eg, *0-9, 0-12*, etc). The second type were larger, longer-ranged boats, designated *'Kolonial'* ('K') and given Roman numbers (eg, *K-XI, K-XIV*, etc).

This distinction lasted from 1913 to 1936, when it was realised that it would be cheaper and more effective to have just one type of submarine. Consequently, the K-IV class was the last of the purpose-built *Kolonial* boats and from the *0-16* onwards only the 'O' designations were used.

The Netherlands had succeeded in remaining neutral throughout World War I and this, coupled with economic problems in the 1920s and early 1930s, resulted in the fleet being somewhat neglected. Despite this, some eighteen submarines were built in Dutch yards between 1918 and 1933, when a limited rearmament plan started. The boats built prior to the outbreak of World War II (0-19 and 0-21 classes) were really excellent in quality and fully up to international standards of armament, performance and habitability. They also introduced to service a rudimentary form of air-tube which enabled the diesels to be run safely while the boat remained submerged. When the Germans captured examples of Dutch submarines in 1940 they saw the potential of this device and developed it into the 'schnorkel', which is now a standard fitting on every diesel-electric submarine.

Dutch submarines served with the Allies during World War II in both European and Pacific theatres, the RNethN receiving four brand-new British submarines between 1942 and 1944. The Dutch boats achieved numerous successes, including sinking *U-95* in the Mediterranean and *U-168* in the Java Sea, while a Japanese aircraft carrier and a cruiser were seriously damaged. Ten submarines were lost in action, eight of them in the Far East.

After the war there were four remaining 0-21 class boats, plus three British boats provided during the war. In the late 1940s plans were made to construct a new class of diesel-electric submarines and an intense debate developed over whether future Dutch boats should be nuclear-powered. It was finally decided that The Netherlands could not afford such expensive systems and construction of the Dolfijn class restarted, but they reached service much later than had been planned. This class utilised an unique form of treble hull to obtain the maximum possible operating depth from the steel then available.

In the late 1960s work started on the two-boat Zwaardvis class, which used both the newer steels then available and the basic design of the US Navy's Barbel class to produce one of the most efficient submarines of the 1970s. Two of an improved version of this class have been sold to the Republic of China (Taiwan) as the Sea Dragon class, and more would have followed but for objections from Beijing.

The Zwaardvis class was followed in the late 1980s by the six-boat Walrus (or Zeeleeuw) class, another exceptional type. One of the largest diesel-electric boats, they are also the largest submarines ever to be fitted with X-form after hydroplanes.

Since the 1950s Dutch submarines have been firmly integrated into NATO plans, and these modern and highly capable boats would all operate in the North Atlantic Ocean and the Norwegian Sea in a conflict.

Left: *An impressive picture of the Dutch submarine* Walrus, *showing her stream-lined hull and sail to full advantage.*

O-19 Class

(Overseas minelaying submarines)

Displacement:
998 tons surfaced; 1,536 tons submerged
Performance:
Max speed 19.25kt surfaced; 9kt submerged
Range not known
Maximum Operational Diving Depth:
320ft (100m)
Dimensions:
265ft 9in (81.0m) x 24ft 7in (7.5m) x 13ft 1in
(4.0m)
Machinery:
Two Sulzer diesels, 5,200bhp; two electric
motors, 1,000shp; two shafts
Complement:
55
Construction:
Wilton-Fijenoord, Schiedam. *O-19, O-20.* Two
boats. Completed 1938 to 1939.

Design: The Dutch for a long time
developed two types of submarine: 'O'
class for home service and 'K' class for
service in the Dutch East Indies. The first
of these, *K-I*, was completed in 1913 and
displaced 386 tons compared with the
contemporary O-2 class which was
considerably smaller, displacing only 150
tons. The colonial boats had to cope with
much hotter temperatures and longer
cruises, and hence needed greater internal
space.

No less than nine colonial submarines of
four distinct classes were laid down during
World War I, even though The Netherlands
remained neutral, but they all took a long
time to complete, joining the fleet between
1921 and 1923. The K-II and K-V classes
(of one and three boats, respectively)
were, like *K-I*, of the Hay-Denny type, but
the K-III and K-VII were of the Holland
pattern.

The first truly post-war design was the
K-XI class (815 tons) completed by
Fijenoord in 1925. They were followed in
the early 1930s by the K-XIV class, which
were an enlarged version of the O-12 class
then building for use in home waters. The
K-XIV (1,008 tons) were by far the largest
submarines built by The Netherlands up to
that time, and had a heavy armament of
eight 21in (533mm) torpedo tubes, four in
the bows, two in the stern and two in a
rotating mount in the upper casing.

The next class of colonial submarines
were to have been designated the K-XIX
class, but it was decided to drop the
different K and O prefixes that previously
distinguished between the two types of
submarine and so they became the O-19
class, instead. This design was based upon
that of two minelaying submarines, *Orzel*
and *Sep*, which had been designed and
built for the Polish Navy by the Rotterdam
Dry Dock Co only two years previously.
The engines were some 60 per cent more

Right: *O-19 underway in a Scottish loch
after escaping from Holland and before
her departure to the Dutch East Indies.*

Above: *O-20 was severely damaged by a
Japanese destroyer in the Dutch East
Indies and had to be scuttled.*

powerful than those in the O-16 class,
their output of 5,200bhp giving a very
high surface speed of just over 19kt.

All contemporary submarines spent a
large part of their patrols running on the
surface, but in the case of the colonial
submarines this meant that they became
very hot and airless, and thus very
uncomfortable for the crew. To try to
overcome this a Dutch naval officer
conceived the idea of an air-breathing
tube, which would enable the diesels to be
run with the boat submerged at periscope
depth. The tube, which was first fitted to
the O-19 class boats, incorporated an air
intake and an engine exhaust, with an
automatic cut-off valve to prevent
accidental flooding. It was this that led to
the more sophisticated German 'schnorkel'
later in the war.

Armament: This class was armed with
eight 21in (533mm) torpedo tubes. Four

tubes were in the bows, two in the stern
and two in a remotely-controlled, trainable
mount in the upper casing. Fourteen
torpedoes were carried.

Gun armament comprised one 3.4in
(88mm)/45 gun forward of the conning-
tower and two 40mm Bofors in single,
disappearing mounts, one at either end of
the bridge structure. A 12.7mm AAMG was
also carried.

They were also equipped to carry mines,
using the French Normand-Fenaux system.
Forty mines were carried in 20 vertical
tubes, 10 on each side of the hull in the
ballast tanks, each tube containing two
mines.

Service History: Both these submarines
were completed in time to escape the
German attack and reached the Far East
safely. In 1941 O-20 was severely damaged
by depth charges from the Japanese
destroyer *Uranami* and had to be scuttled.
Her sister, *O-19*, operated in Far Eastern
waters throughout the war until she was
wrecked in the South China Sea in
mid-1945 and had to be abandoned.

Dolfijn Class

(Diesel-electric patrol submarines)

Displacement:
Dolfijn group 1,494 tons surfaced; 1,826 tons submerged
Potvis group 1,509 tons surfaced; 1,831 tons submerged

Performance:
Max speed 14.5kt surfaced; 17kt submerged
Range not known

Maximum Operational Diving Depth:
985ft (300m)

Dimensions:
Dolfijn group 260ft 10in (79.5m) x 25ft 7in (7.8m) x 15ft 9in (4.8m)
Potvis group 256ft 11in (78.3m) x 25ft 7in (7.8m) x 16ft 5in (5m)

Machinery:
Dolfijn group Two M.A.N. diesels, 2,800bhp; two electric motors, 4,200shp; two shafts
Potvis group Two Pielstick PA 4 diesels, 3,100bhp; two electric motors 4,400shp; two shafts

Complement:
67

Construction:
Rotterdamsche Droogdok Maatschappij, Rotterdam. Dolfijn group: *Dolfijn* (S-803), *Zeehond* (S-809). Two boats. Completed 1961. Wilton-Fijenoord, Schiedam. Potvis group: *Potvis* (S-804), *Tonijn* (S-805). Two boats. Completed 1965 to 1966.

Design: The first post-war boats to be built in The Netherlands, they were subjected to lengthy delays during construction, due to discussions on whether, or not, they should be nuclear-powered. Thus, although approved in 1949, the first two (*Dolfijn* and *Zeehond*) were not completed until 1961 and the second pair (*Potvis* and *Tonijn*) until 1965-66.

This very interesting design was the work of M.F. Gunning, who had been the chief naval constructor to the RNethN for some years. He argued that the three separate, but interconnected pressure hulls in a 'treble-bubble' arrangement had a number of significant advantages.

The uppermost (and largest) contained the control centre, the torpedo tubes (four at each end), storage spaces, and the crew accommodation. Below were two parallel hulls, slightly shorter and of smaller diameter, containing machinery, the drive-train, batteries and stores. The advantage of this layout was that it gave great strength and compactness, and made the best possible use of the steel then available. However, this was somewhat offset by the cramped conditions in the two lower hulls, and mechanical maintenance at sea was particularly difficult.

This, coupled with the high cost of construction and the development of much stronger steels, meant that the design was not repeated. Nevertheless, these Dutch boats had an exceptional diving depth for their day and were very quiet; and were very highly regarded by other NATO navies.

Gunning's ideas of multiple pressure-hulls, which he developed in the 1940s, seem to have reappeared in the Soviet Typhoon class of the 1970s. These huge submarines also have two parallel pressure-hulls containing the machinery, with a third hull above housing the command and control facilities. Gunning, of course, would not have thought of making facilities for the SLBM launchers, but that apart there is some similarity in the basic concept.

Armament: These submarines are armed with eight 21in (533mm) torpedo tubes, four in the bow and four in the stern.

Service History: *Dolfijn* and *Zeehond* were authorised in 1949, but were not laid down until 1954, eventually joining the fleet in 1961. The second pair, *Potvis* and *Tonijn* were not authorised until 1962, and completed in 1965-66, with minor differences from the earlier two.

Dolfijn was placed in reserve in 1983 and sold for scrap in 1985. She should have been joined by the others as they were replaced by the Walrus class, but a fire during the construction of the name-ship of that class led to a considerable delay. As a result *Zeehond*'s service life was extended for an indefinite period, while, after initially announcing an intention to scrap the other two, the RNethN decided to refit and modernise them in 1988-90. The plans were then changed again and *Zeehond* was purchased by Rotterdamsche Droogdok Maatschappij (RDM) for use in trials of a new air-independent propulsion system, which began in 1990.

Below: *These plans show the unique construction of the Dolfijn class, with the main pressure hull placed on top of two smaller pressure hulls. The latter contained the diesel engines, electric motors and batteries, together with storage facilities. It was an ingenious idea, but the lower hulls were cramped.*

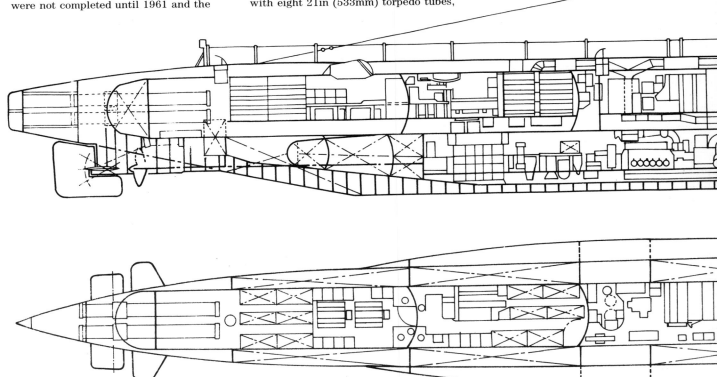

Above: Dolfijn *(S-803) running on the surface with both forward and after torpedo derricks in place.*

Right: Potvis *(S-804) (see here) and* Tonijn *were the second pair of Dolfijn class vessels to be built, being completed in 1965-66.*

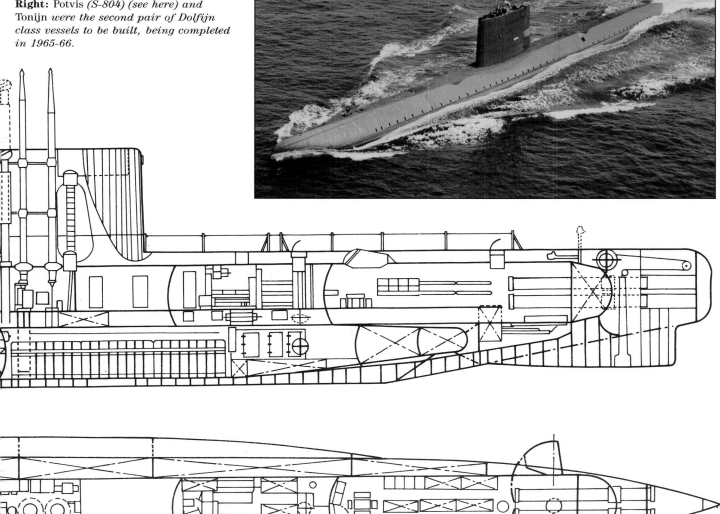

NORWAY

Above: *The first Norwegian submarine was initially named* Kobben, *but was later redesignated* A-1. *She was very similar to the German* U-1.

Norway is a country in which few people live far from the sea. It has 13,000 miles (20,920km) of coastline indented with many deep-water fiords and no less than 150,000 islands. For many years Norway was under the control of Denmark, until in 1814 it was ceded to Sweden. In 1815 it achieved a degree of autonomy, being given the status of a independent kingdom with its own parliament, although still under the rule of the King of Sweden. After considerable nationalist agitation this union was ended in 1905, when Norway achieved full independence, and Prince Carl of Denmark ascended the throne as Haakon VII.

A very small navy had been established in the 19th Century, but even after full autonomy was achieved it was not expanded greatly, as no specific threat was perceived. In 1914 the fleet consisted of a small number of coastal battleships and monitors, two cruisers, four destroyers, eleven gunboats and around forty torpedo boats. However, many of these were very elderly and of limited value.

When submarines started to enter service with the major navies, the Royal Norwegian Navy (RNorN) was quick to see their potential for protecting its country's long coastline and in 1908 they ordered their first submarine, *Kobben* (later redesignated *A-1*) from Germaniawerft at Kiel in Germany. This small (259 tons submerged displacement) submarine was

Below: *A Norwegian B class submarine (possibly* B-3*) being recovered after scuttling in 1940. The six boats of this class were built in the USA to a Holland design and launched between 1922-29.*

similar to the *U-1*, which had recently been completed for the Imperial Germany Navy. This was followed by an order for the A-2 class (353 tons), three being ordered in 1911 and a further one in 1912. As with most RNorN warships these all had exceptionally long lives, *A-1* being sold for scrap in 1933, the remainder being still in service on the outbreak of World War II.

Norway remained neutral throughout World War I, and then in the 1920s reduced her already small defence expenditure yet further. However, during the war an order had been placed for the first (and still the only) submarines to be built in Norway. These were constructed at the Horten Navy Yard, to a design by the American Electric Boat Company. Designated the B class, they displaced 545 tons, and were armed with four bow 17.9in (457mm) torpedo tubes and one 76mm deck gun. Inevitably construction took a long time and although ordered in 1915 the first boat was not launched until 1922, followed by two in 1923, one in 1924 and the final two in 1929.

The German invasion in 1940 took the Norwegians by surprise and, despite a heroic resistance, they were not equipped for a war against the modern armed forces of Nazi Germany. Of the nine submarines in service *A-2*, *A-3*, *A-4* and *B-3* were scuttled, while *B-2* and *B-4* were abandoned after attempts had been made to scuttle them. They were taken over by the Germans but never used by them. *B-5* and *B-6*, however, were captured by the Germans and put into service for a short period as *UC-1* and *UC-2*. The only Norwegian submarine to escape to Britain was *B-1*, which served for several years as an Asdic training target, but was paid off in 1944.

A large number of RNorN officers and sailors reached Britain determined to continue the war and this force was allocated three Royal Navy submarines, one in 1941 (*Uredd, ex-P-41*), one in 1943 (*Ula, ex-Varne*) and one in 1944 (*Utsira, ex-Variance*). One of these, *Uredd*, was sunk in the North Sea in 1943, but the others survived the war. They were joined in 1946 by three more British V class submarines, which became *Utstein, Utvaer* and *Uthaug* in Norwegian service. These five remaining ex-British boats served until the mid-1960s when they were sold for scrapping.

The seas around Norway were especially important during the Cold War as the country lay alongside the only route by which the Soviet Northern Fleet, and in particular its submarines, could reach the Atlantic. Thus, the East:West confrontation was particularly fraught in this area and Soviet submarines frequently

Above: Utstein *was given to the Norwegian navy in 1946. As HMS* Venturer *she was the first submarine ever to sink another submarine (*U-864*) while both combatants remained submerged.*

penetrated Norwegian territorial waters, sometimes even entering the fiords in clear breach of international law. It was apparent that, had war broken out, Soviet forces would have carried out immediate land, sea, air and amphibious attacks on Norway to remove any threat to their passage to the Atlantic. Thus the RNorN had an urgent need for a strong naval force and especially for submarines.

In the 1950s as the Cold War developed

Below: Kobben *(S-318), a Type 207 submarine, built in Emden and commissioned in 1964, carried the same name as the first Norwegian submarine, pictured at the top of page opposite.*

the RNorN sought modern submarines and they eventually selected the German IKL Type 205 (five of which were in service with the West German Navy), but modified to meet Norwegian requirements, particularly increased diving depth. Designated Type 207, fourteen were purchased, paid for jointly by Norway and US mutual assistance funds, all being built by Rheinstahl-Nordseewerke (later Thyssen Nordseewerke) at Emden between 1964 and 1967. This was a very successful programme and nine are being modernised between 1988 and 1992, six for continued service with the RNorN and three for sale to Denmark.

The latest submarine in the RNorN is the Type P 6071, six of which are being built by Thyssen Nordseewerke as the Ula class. When they are complete the RNorN will have a very modern and efficient submarine fleet of twelve boats, capable of serving well into the next century.

A-2 Class

(Coastal patrol submarines)

Displacement:
268 tons surfaced; 353 tons submerged
Performance:
Max speed 14.5kt surfaced; 9kt submerged
Range 900nm/10kt surfaced; 76nm/3.3kt
submerged
Maximum Operational Diving Depth:
164ft (50m)
Dimensions:
152ft 7in (46.5m) x 15ft 9in (4.8m) x 8ft 10in
(2.7m)
Machinery:
Two Germania 6-cylinder, 4-stroke, non-reversing
diesel engines, 700-750bhp; two electric
motors, 380shp; two shafts
Complement:
17
Construction:
Germaniawerft, Kiel. *A-2, A-3, A-4, A-5 (U-A).*
Four boats. Completed 1913 to 1914.

Design: Imperial Germany began to export
submarines from a very early stage, its
customers being Imperial Russia, Austria-
Hungary and Norway. The first Norwegian
boat, *Kobben* was similar to *U-1* in
German service, but with a greater diving
depth, an improved design of conning-
tower, hydroplanes operated from the
control room and a stern torpedo-tube
above the waterline in addition to the two
bow tubes. It also, however, had the
Körting paraffin engine, with its smelly
fuel and telltale white smoke-plume. In
general, however, the Norwegians were
happy with its performance, and in
November 1910 they asked a number of
shipyards to tender for a new class.

Germaniawerft submitted a design based
on that of a submarine they were building
for the Italian Navy, the *Atropo*, and in
May 1911 Norway placed an order for
three submarines to be designated *A-2* to
A-4. However, in the following year they
ordered one more boat, to be designated
A-5.

Above: A-2 *was the first of four boats
built for Norway by Germaniawerft at
Kiel in 1913-14. The first three were
delivered in 1913, but A-5* was
requisitioned by the Imperial German
Navy and served as U-A *in the war.*

This design was the first to have the
after hydroplanes placed abaft the
propellers, and it was fitted with a radio
and a gyroscopic compass. An unusual
device was a transverse propeller in a
tunnel in the bows, which was used when
the boat was stationary to make small
alterations of direction when aiming
torpedoes. As in the *Atropo*, two
periscopes were fitted, one being used in
the conning-tower, the second in the
control-room below.

The Germania diesel engines, a great
improvement in many respects over the

Below: A-2 *and her two sisters served
from 1913 right through to 1940, when
A-2 was stricken and broken up, while
A-3 and A-4 were scuttled to avoid
capture by the invading Germans, at
which time the boats were totally out-of-
date and of very limited value, anyway.*

previous paraffin types, were non-reversing
and thus variable-pitch propellers were
fitted. The Italian *Atropo* had the same
engines which proved troublesome during
trials, but the problems had been rectified
by the time the Norwegian boats were
constructed.
Armament: The original design offered by
Germaniawerft had four torpedo tubes, two
in the bows and two in the stern. However,
as constructed the class had only three
tubes, two in the bows and one mounted
externally in the stern. All were the then
standard 17.7in (450mm), with five
torpedoes carried.

The boat requisitioned by Germany,
U-A (ex-*A-5*) was fitted with a single
50mm (2in)/KL40 in 1917, but the
Norwegian boats were never given a deck
gun.
Service History: The three submarines of
the original order were handed over to the
RNorN in early 1914 at Kiel and they then
proceeded under their own power to the
Norwegian submarine base at Horten. The
fourth boat, which was to have been *A-5*
and which had been ordered later, was
still building at the time of the outbreak of
World War I and was requisitioned, being
commissioned into the Imperial German
Navy as *U-A*. After two years on
operations she was transferred to a
training role and after the war was sent to
the United Kingdom, where she was
scrapped.

The three other boats (*A-2* to *A-4*) served
throughout World War I and the inter-war
years with the Royal Norwegian Navy.
Incredibly, all three were still in service
when Germany invaded Norway in early
1940, the oldest submarines in any navy in
the world at that time. Together with the
six B class boats they endeavoured to put
up some resistance to the invaders, but all
were either broken up or scuttled in
harbour, except for *B-1* which escaped to
Britain. The Germans raised two of the
scuttled B class submarines, together with
A-3. It is suggested in some accounts that
they considered recommissioning her as
UC-3, but this seems improbable on
account of her antiquity.

Ula Class

(Diesel-electric patrol submarines) (SSK)

Displacement:
1,040 tons surfaced; 1,150 tons submerged
Performance:
Max speed 11kt surfaced; 23kt submerged
Range 5,000nm/8kt schnorkel
Maximum Operational Diving Depth:
820ft (250m)
Dimensions:
193ft 7in (59.00m) x 17ft 9in (5.40m) x 14ft 9in
(4.50m)
Machinery:
Two MTU 16V652 MB diesel engines, 2,520bhp;
two three-phase NEBB generator sets, electric
drive, 6,000shp, one shaft
Complement:
3 officers; 15-17 ratings
Construction:
Thyssen Nordseewerke, Emden. *Ula* (S-300),
Utsira (S-301), *Utstein* (S-302). *Utvaer* (S-303),
Uthaug (S-304), *Uredd* (S-305). Six boats.
Completed 1990 to 1992.

Design: The RNorN had a particularly successful relationship with the German design firm of IKL and the shipbuilding firm of Thyssen Nordseewerke during the Type 207 Kobben programme. As a result, when they started to look for a new submarine to replace half the Type 207s they turned to the same concerns. The result of this collaboration is the Type P 6071 or Ula class, which is considerably larger than the Type 207 and much more capable. With a submerged displacement of 1,150 tons the Type P 6071 has a typical IKL hull-form, but with X-configured after control surfaces, the first to be fitted in a German-designed submarine.

The design originated in the design office of IKL as the Type 210. But, when the building contract was given to Thyssen Nordseewerke, the latter completed the detailed construction design work, and the type designation was changed to the Norwegian project number P 6071.

The Type P 6071 programme illustrates

Above: Sklinna *(S-305) and* Utvaer *(S-303), two of the fourteen Type 207s built in Germany for the Royal Norwegian Navy between 1964 and 1967.*

how modern submarines are composed of items from a multiplicity of international sources. The first pressure-hull was constructed in Germany, but the remaining five are being made by Kvaerner Brug in Oslo and then shipped to Kiel. The sensors also come form a variety of sources. The radar is British (Kelvin-Hughes Type 1007), as is the EW suite (Racal Sea Lion), while the sonar is German (Krupp Atlas DBQS-21F) and the conformal arrays French (Thomson-CSF). The periscopes are Italian (Riva-Calzoni Trident non-pressure-hull-penetrating masts) and the navigation system American (Rockwell-Collins NAVSTAR GPS). The torpedoes (AEG Seeal) and tubes are German, but the fire-

Below: *The Type P 6071 submarine* Ula *(S-300) is the lead-ship in a class of six being built for the Royal Norwegian Navy by Thyssen Nordseewerke at Emden in Germany. They are very sophisticated boats with an excellent performance.*

control system is Norwegian (Norsk Forsvarsteknologie MSI-90U). System integration of equipment from such a variety of sources is obviously a challenge and the logistic support must be complicated, but, on the other hand, such an approach enables the best equipment in its field to be obtained.

Armament: The Ula class submarines are armed with eight 21in (533mm) torpedo tubes, all in the bow. Standard torpedo is the German Seehecht DM2A3, of which fourteen are carried. These dual-purpose, wire-guided torpedoes have a range of up to 15nm (28km) at 23kt or 7nm (13km) at 35kt.

Service History: The first Type P 6071 (*Ula*) was launched in July 1988 and ran a long series of trials starting in April 1989, not being commissioned until April 1990. During these trials she was hit by a rogue practice torpedo, which she had launched herself, incurring minor damage, by no means the first boat to suffer such a fate.

The remaining five submarines are joining the Norwegian fleet between 1990 and 1992, when they will provide a very effective force for the protection of Norway's long coastline.

PERU

The first Peruvian submarine was built by a local pioneer in 1879. Little is known about the builder, Federico Blume, or his boat, but it was considered worth destroying to prevent its capture by the Chilean Navy during the War of the Pacific (1879-1883). That war had a devastating effect on the Peruvian Navy and there seems to have been little desire to rebuild the fleet for some years. In 1906 two modern cruisers were acquired from Great Britain, but the arrival of a French naval mission in 1908 played a key role in ensuring that when it was decided to order two submarines, the model selected was a Laubeuf design. These two boats, the first modern submarines in a South American Navy, were named *Ferre*

and *Palacios*; they were built by Schneider-Creusot, displaced 400 tons and were delivered in 1913. Due to the war in Europe spares were difficult to procure and they were discarded in 1919, a remarkably short ship's life by Peruvian Navy standards.

The French mission having left, they were replaced in the early 1920s by a US naval mission. Consequently when it was decided to order a new class of submarine the choice fell on an American design. Six boats of the R class were ordered in 1924 from the Electric Boat Company, but only four were actually delivered: two in 1926 and two in 1928.

Peru was not involved in World War II and did not order any further submarines until 1953, when six Dos de Mayo class were ordered, again from the Electric Boat

Company. As before, only four were actually purchased, these arriving between 1954 and 1957.

In 1969 the Peruvian Navy decided to order some much larger submarines, purchasing two ex-US Navy Guppy IAs in July 1974. A third boat, (USS *Tench* (SS-417)), was partly cannibalized to prepare the other two for transfer to Peru and her hulk was later towed out to Peru for further cannibalization, as necessary. The two active boats, named *La Pedrera* (SS-49) and *Pacocha* (SS-48) in the Peruvian Navy remain in service.

In the early 1970s the Peruvian Navy became one of the first in South America to order submarines from Germany, with six Type 209s being delivered between 1973 and 1983. There are thus twelve boats in service in 1991: six Type 209, four Dos de Mayo class and two Guppy IAs, a considerably larger force than can be assembled by most other South American navies, particularly Peru's neighbour and rival, Chile.

Below: Peru is one of many nations to operate the very successful German Type 209 design. This is Islay, *one of six delivered between 1975 and 1983.*

R Class

(Patrol submarines)

Displacement:
576 tons surfaced; 755 tons submerged
Performance:
Max speed 14.5kt surfaced; 9kt submerged
Range 3,700nm/10kt surfaced
Maximum Operational Diving Depth:
200ft (60m)
Dimensions:
186ft 3in (56.77m) x 17ft 6in (5.33m) x 15ft 0in (4.57m)
Machinery:
Two NELSECO diesel engines, 1,200bhp; two electric motors, 934shp; two shafts
Complement:
30
Construction:
Electric Boat Company, Groton. *R-1, R-2, R-3, R-4*. Four boats. Completed 1926 to 1928.

Design: The first two of these four submarines were commissioned into the Peruvian Navy in 1926 and stricken in 1960, an operational life of 34 years! They

were ordered in 1924, being completed in 1926 (*R-1* and *R-2*) and 1928 (*R-3* and *R-4*). Their design was virtually identical with that of the Electric Boat Company's version of the US Navy's R class, of which 20 had been built by the company between 1917 and 1919 (a further 7 were built by Lake to a slightly different design).
Armament: These submarines were fitted

Below: R-1, one of four R class submarines delivered to the Peruvian Navy by the Electric Boat Company in 1926-28. They were refitted in 1935-36 and 1955-56, and stricken in 1960. They were delivered under their own power, making the voyage from Connecticut to Callao without problems. Armament comprised four 21in (533mm) bow torpedo tubes and one 3in deck gun.

with four 21in (533mm) torpedo tubes, all in the bow, with a total of eight torpedoes carried. One 3in (76mm)/50 gun was mounted on the foredeck.
Service History: These boats entered service in 1926 (*R-1* and *R-2*) and 1928 (*R-3* and *R-4*). Another two were projected, but in the event were not ordered. During the 1933 dispute with Colombia two of the R class submarines were despatched with the cruiser *Almirante Grau* to control the mouth of the River Amazon. They served for many years, being refitted in 1935-36 and 1955-56. In 1957, somewhat late in their careers, they received names: *R-1*, *Islay*; *R-2*, *Casma*; *R-3*, *Pacocha* and *R-4*, *Arica*. They were scrapped in 1960, by which stage they must have been thoroughly worn out.

Dos de Mayo Class

(Patrol submarines)

Displacement:
825 tons surfaced; 1,400 tons submerged
Performance:
Max speed 16kt surfaced; 10kt submerged
Range 5,000nm/10kt surfaced (schnorkel)
Maximum Operational Diving Depth:
288ft (90m)
Dimensions:
243ft 1in (74.1m) x 22ft 0in (6.7m) x 13ft 10in (4.3m)
Machinery:
Two General Motors 12-278A diesel engines, 2,400bhp; two electric motors; two shafts
Complement:
40
Construction:
General Dynamics (Electric Boat) Groton. *Dos de Mayo* (SS-41), *Abtao* (SS-42), *Angamos* (SS-43), *Iquique* (SS-44). Four boats. Completed 1954 to 1957.

Design: These four submarines' main claim to fame is that two of them have retained a deck gun armament into the 1990s, some thirty years longer than any other navy. A second claim is that they are directly descended from one of the most unpopular submarine designs in the US Navy. Thirdly, they are the last new-construction submarines to have been built in the United States for a foreign customer.

In the 1930s the US Navy's submarine force was developing a very satisfactory line of 'fleet submarines', which started with the P class of 1933 (1,960 tons), and evolved through the S class (2,198 tons) and the T class (2,370 tons) to the outstanding and very successful Gato class (2,424 tons), the first of which joined the fleet in 1941. However, the surface admirals were not very happy with this, considering that too much money was being devoted to submarines and, further, that the submarines themselves were growing too big, complicated and expensive. In vain the submariners argued that they needed size to cope with the long ranges required in a Pacific war, both to house the fuel and to give the crew reasonable living conditions for the many weeks they would be at sea.

The submariners were outvoted and were compelled to include in their 1938 programme two smaller boats in order to determine whether they would be of value; one suggestion was that they could be used for short-range defensive tasks off the Panama Canal or the Philippines. This gave rise to the M class of two boats: *Mackerel* (SS-204) and *Marlin* (SS-205). With a submerged displacement of 1,190 tons, they were armed with six 21in (533mm) torpedo tubes (four bow, two stern), one 3in (76mm) gun and two 0.5in or 20mm AAMGs, a heavy weapons fit for their size. They were unpopular in service and operated for a while in the Atlantic before being relegated to training tasks. They were scrapped shortly after the end of the war.

In the late 1940s the Peruvian Navy approached the USA seeking new submarines that were somewhat smaller than the numerous 'war-surplus' fleet submarines boats then becoming available. The order was originally for six boats, but this was later reduced to four. The Electric Boat Company took the plans of the Mackerel class and modernised them, streamlining the hull and sail, and adding up-to-date sensors. However, the Peruvian Navy insisted on a gun armament and a 5in (127mm)/25 was duly fitted.

Armament: Primary armament is six 21in (533mm) torpedo tubes, four in the bow, two in the stern, firing US Mark 37 homing torpedoes. The curious feature of this class, however, is not only that they were built in the 1950s with a gun armament, but that two boats, *Dos de Mayo* and *Abtao*, actually retain it, in 1991 the very last submarines in the world to do so. The gun is a 'wet' 5in (127mm)/25 mounted abaft the sail. Quite why such an antiquated concept should be retained is not clear, as it is difficult to envisage a tactical situation in which such a weapon could be of value.

Service History: When commissioned these submarines were named *Lobo* (SS-41), *Tiburon* (SS-42), *Atun* (SS-43) and *Merlin* (SS-44), but these names were changed later to those listed in the specifications above.

They appear to have given satisfactory service in the Peruvian Navy, as they have been regularly modernised over the past thirty-five years of service. Two underwent a major refit at the Electric Boat Company in 1965, the other pair in 1968, when, among other changes, their original stepped sails were replaced by unstepped models, based on those installed in US Navy Guppy IIIs. New batteries were installed in 1981 and a new sonar with a large bow dome has also been installed.

Below: Dos de Mayo, *one of four boats built in the USA in the 1950s combined an advanced hull design with an outmoded 5in (127mm)/25 deck gun, still retained by two of the class.*

POLAND

The independent republic of Poland came into existence on 11 November 1918; the navy was officially created on 28 November, with the shadow of impending war with the newly-created USSR hanging over the country. Poland defeated the Soviet Bolsheviks in the short war (1920-21) and at the peace talks demanded some naval vessels, including five submarines, in addition to territories she had seized. In the end, while she received the territories she claimed, she did not take possession of any of the ships.

Poland then started buying a number of small ships and in 1926 she was in a position to order two modern destroyers and three submarines from France. These, the first class of submarines in the young but very ambitious navy, were the Wilk class (1,250 tons), enlarged versions of the French Saphir class minelayers. They proved to be somewhat noisy and unreliable, and were delivered very late.

The Orzel class was ordered in 1935 and as a result of the dissatisfaction with the Wilk class they were built in the Netherlands. They proved to be excellent boats and an order for a further improved and modified pair was placed, surprisingly, in France. However, they had not been completed when the Germans invaded.

All five Polish submarines patrolled the Baltic during the very short hostilities with Germany and were then forced to head for neutral ports as they could not return to Poland. Rys and Zbik (both Wilk class), together with Sep (Orzel class) put into Stavnas in Sweden where they were interned for the duration, being returned to Poland in 1945.

Meanwhile, Wilk and Orzel both reached England where they served under the operational control of the Royal Navy. Orzel was lost in 1940, but Wilk served as a training boat until 1942 and was then put into reserve. She was returned to Poland in 1951 for scrapping.

The crew of the decommissioned Wilk

Above: Zbik, *a Wilk class minelayer, launched in 1931, was built to a design based on that of the French Saphir class.*

Below: Sokol *was a British U class boat which achieved considerable success, as so clearly testified by her Jolly Roger.*

demanded an active role in the war and were allocated the ex-US Navy S class submarine S-25, which was commissioned into the Free Polish Navy as the *Jastrzab*. She was sent on a convoy screening operation only to be sunk in error by a Norwegian destroyer and a British minesweeper on 2 May 1942.

Two British U class submarines were also transferred to the Poles, *Urchin* becoming

Below: Bielik, *a Soviet Whiskey class boat, was one of three transferred to Poland. All have now been stricken.*

Sokol and P-52 becoming *Dzik*. They served valiantly in the Mediterranean, and were eventually returned to Britain, being handed back to the Royal Navy in 1946.

In the 1950s Poland found herself a member of the Warsaw Pact and was supplied with three Whiskey class submarines. These served for many years and were due to be replaced by four Kilo class submarines. However, following delivery of the first of the order financial difficulties led to a delay and two Foxtrot class submarines are being lent to the Polish Navy to tide them over.

Orzel Class

(Ocean-going patrol submarines)

Displacement:
1,100 tons surfaced; 1,650 tons submerged
Performance:
Max speed 20kt surfaced; 9kt submerged
Range 7,000nm/10kt surfaced; 100nm/5kt
submerged
Maximum Operational Diving Depth:
260ft (79.25m)
Dimensions:
275ft 7in (84.00m) x 22ft 0in (6.70m) x 13ft 8in
(4.17m)
Machinery:
Two Sulzer diesel engines, 4,740bhp; two
Brown-Boveri electric motors. 1,100shp; two
shafts
Complement:
60
Construction:
De Schelde Navy Yard, Vlissingen, Netherlands.
Orzel. One boat. Completed 1939.
Rotterdam Dock Yard, Netherlands. *Sep.* One
boat. Completed 1939.

Design: The two submarines of the Orzel
class were designed and constructed in the
Netherlands. They were ordered as a result
of worsening relations with Germany and
the first, *Orzel*, was paid for by public
subscription. The second, *Sep*, was paid
for out of normal Naval Directorate funds.

The Dutch had built some very good
submarines in the inter-war years and it
was thus not surprising that the Poles
should turn to them to build this new
class. The design was similar to that of the
Dutch Navy's 0-19 class, which was
building at the same time. They were of
double-hull design and the pressure-hull
was divided into five compartments.
Armament: These two boats were very
heavily armed for the time, possessing
twelve 21.7in (550mm) torpedo tubes.
Four of these were in the bows, four in the
stern and two in a French-type rotating
mount in the upper casing before the
conning-tower. A total of twenty torpedoes
was carried.

Gun armament was also rather heavy. It
comprised one 105mm/41, two single
40mm/60 Bofors and one twin 13.2mm
heavy machine-gun mount.

For mines the boats were fitted with
'Normand-Fenaux' vertical tubes, similar
to those installed on the French-built Wilk
class. There were ten tubes on each side
installed in the ballast tanks, each taking
two mines.
Service History: Both boats were
launched in 1938 and commissioned in

*Below: The Orzel class was armed with
no less than twelve torpedo tubes.*

Above: Orzel, *paid for by public
subscription, had a fine war record.*

1939, although *Sep* cut short her builder's
trials to reach Poland in April as invasion
appeared imminent. When war did break
out both were on patrol, but, due to the
lightning overthrow of their country and
German air superiority, neither was able to
return home. *Sep* made for the port of
Stavnas in Sweden where she was interned
on 17 September 1939, eventually being
returned to Poland on 25 October 1945.

Orzel experienced mechanical problems
during her first war patrol and on 15
September 1939 she put into the Estonian

port of Tallinn for repairs, in accordance
with International Law. Contrary to that
law she was interned on her day of arrival
and some essential equipment was removed
in an attempt to prevent her escape. On 18
September, however, she escaped, carried
out a Baltic patrol and then set sail for
England. Having avoided minefields and
the German Navy, she arrived at Rosyth in
Scotland on 14 October 1939. It was a
courageous and daring voyage which was
viewed with great admiration at the time.

She sailed under the operational control
of the Royal Navy until 8 June 1940 when
she disappeared 'cause unknown' while on
patrol in the North Sea.

Above: Orzel *escaped German capture to
reach Britain on 14 October 1939.*

Below: *A fine view of* Orzel *as she
prepares to receive formal visitors.*

Kilo Class

(Ocean-going patrol submarines) (SSK)

Displacement:
2,300 tons surfaced; 2,900 tons submerged
Performance:
Max speed 16kt surfaced; 20kt submerged
Range Not known
Maximum Operational Diving Depth:
Not known
Dimensions:
239ft 6in (73.0m) x 32ft 6in (9.9m) x 21ft 4in (6.5m)
Machinery:
Two diesel-generators; 6,800bhp; one motor, one shaft
Complement:
12 officers; 41 ratings
Construction:
Admiralty Yard, Sudomekh, USSR. *Orzel*. One boat (plus three on order). Completed 1986.

Design: In the 1970s the Soviet Navy built eighteen Tango class diesel-electric submarines, of which, unlike the previous Foxtrot and Whiskey classes, not one was exported. There was some thought at the time that the Soviet Navy, might, like the US Navy, decide to build only nuclear submarines in future, but in 1980 a totally new design appeared — the Kilo class.

Apart from serving in the Soviet Navy a number of Kilo class submarines have been exported. Known export orders include Algeria (2), India (8), Romania (1) and Poland (4). Other orders may be placed by Cuba and Libya. The Polish order has been slowed down due to financial problems, with the second boat now due to be delivered in 1993-94.

The Kilo appears to represent a major change in Soviet diesel-electric submarine design. Whereas the Tango class had a long, narrow hull reminiscent of the German Type XXI the Kilo class has a shorter, fatter hull, similar to, but by no means identical with, the US 'Albacore' hull. Like the Tango, the Kilo's hull is coated with anechoic tiles to reduce her sonar signature.

Armament: The Kilo class is armed with six bow 21in (533mm) torpedo tubes. Twelve torpedoes or twenty-four mines are carried. Some reports suggest that there is a launch position at the rear of the sail for a hand-held SA-7 'Grail' SAM launcher. Should this be correct, it seems tactically

Above: *The Soviet-designed Kilo class has proved to be very successful and is now in service with at least four navies, with production continuing at a steady rate at two yards, one at Komsomolsk-na-Amur and the other at Gorky.*

3

unsound as any hostile airborne target would be likely to be armed with air-to-surface missiles which would have greater range than the SA-7. In such a situation the submarine's captain would be better advised to dive.

Service History: The first Kilo class in Polish service is named *Orzel*, after her illustrious World War II predecessor. She was delivered on 21 June 1986 and serves with the Polish Navy in the Baltic Sea.

Right: *A Soviet navy Kilo class submarine — the Polish Navy's boats are identical. The forward hydroplanes are fully retractable to reduce damage whilst on the surface during Arctic operations.*

Below: *The lines of the Kilo class are quite unlike those of any previous Soviet-designed diesel-electric submarine, having a much greater beam: length ratio. The hull is completely covered in anechoic tiles to reduce the sonar signature.*

Left: *Kilo class submarines are armed with six torpedo tubes and are estimated to carry 12 torpedoes/missiles. These may include anti-ship torpedoes (1), ASW homing torpedoes (2) and mines (3), two of which can be carried instead of one torpedo. SS-N-15 missiles may also be carried.*

SPAIN

The Spanish Navy has a long and very distinguished history. For several centuries she was one of the mightiest naval forces in the world, a power that was necessary to maintain a global empire. This empire gradually broke up and a period of stagnation in the latter part of the 19th Century led to neglect of the fleet. Thus, when war broke out with the United States in 1898 the Spanish Navy suffered defeats (and heavy losses) in both the Philippines and Cuba.

The first submarine to be constructed in Spain was designed by two engineers, Narcisco Monturiol and Cosmo Garcia, and was launched at Barcelona in 1859. Named *El Ictineo*, it was tested by the designers in 1860 and 1861 before undergoing a series of official trials. The boat was powered by steam, and armed with a cannon and a steam-operated auger for boring holes in enemy ships' hulls. Despite what seem to have been successful tests, including no less than sixty dives, a projected larger boat was not built.

After a gap of some years an even more successful submarine was designed and built in 1887-8 by Lieutenant Isaac Peral, but even this failed to receive the encouragement from the naval authorities that it deserved. This was a fate that befell many submarine pioneers in other countries during those pioneering days.

Spain remained neutral during World

Above: *Lt Isaac Peral (1851-1895).*

War I, but was a close observer of the German U-boat campaign, as she not only lost a number of merchantmen but on several occasions was forced to allow U-boats to use her ports for repairs under the neutrality rules. The Spanish authorities terminated such arrangements in mid-1917 and thereafter any belligerent submarine entering a Spanish port was interned.

The Spanish Navy's first operational submarine — a Holland-type boat — was purchased from the USA in 1916 and named the *Isaac Peral*. At the same time six boats of the B class were laid down in the Spanish Cartagena Dockyard. These were improved versions of the *Isaac Peral*; construction took a long time, the first not being finished until 1921 and the last in

1923. These were followed by a third Holland design, the C class (1,290 tons), completed between 1927 and 1930 at Cartagena.

Like many other navies of the period, the Spanish Navy purchased three Italian Fiat-Laurenti submarines in 1917; ie, interspersed in the line of Holland designs. The Fiat-Laurenti type were designated the A class in Spanish service and served until the mid-1930s.

The Civil War broke out in July 1936 and lasted until March 1939. Most naval ships and port facilities fell under the control of the Republicans, although the majority of naval officers sided with the Nationalist cause. The Republicans thus initially had all the submarines: six B class and six C class. However, the Nationalists received active submarine support from the German and Italian navies. In addition, the Italians transferred two submarines to the Nationalist Navy in 1937, which served until 1959. The Italians also lent four submarines complete with crews to the Nationalist Navy for a short period.

Republican submarines were very active during the Civil War. Merchant ships were attacked, and a determined but unsuccessful attack on the German cruiser, *Leipzig*, resulted in Germany and Italy ceasing to take part in the International Patrol. The Nationalist navy and its allies did not suffer any submarine losses, but, of the twelve Republican submarines, five were war losses. Two were sunk by aircraft and one was scuttled after being severely damaged by bombs; another was sunk by an Italian submarine and one disappeared — 'causes unknown' — in the Bay of

Peral Class

(Experimental submarine)

Displacement:
87 tons surfaced
Performance:
Max speed 10kt surfaced
Range not known
Maximum Operational Diving Depth:
not known
Dimensions:
70ft 0in (21.3m) x 8ft 6in (2.6m) x n.k.
Machinery:
Two electric motors, 60hp; two shafts
Complement:
6
Construction:
Carraca, Cadiz, *Peral*. One boat. Completed 1888.

Design: One of the outstanding submarines of the late 19th Century was that designed by Lt Isaac Peral y Caballero of the Spanish Navy. It was laid down in 1887 and commissioned into the Spanish Navy in 1890. Peral's submarine was powered by batteries, which enabled her to travel a reasonable distance but she had to return to port for a recharge. Diving and

Above: *Peral's submarine of 1888 is still displayed as a monument in Cartagena.*

surfacing were achieved using a combination of ballast tanks and vertical propellers. There were two such propellers, one forward and the other aft, just forward of the rudder.
Armament: *Peral* was armed with one torpedo tube in the bow. Three Schwartzkopf torpedoes were carried.
Service History: Launched in 1888, the *Peral* appears to have been successful during trials, but was not followed up by the authorities. Lieutenant Peral died in

Right: *The Spanish Delfin class is a licence-built version of the French Daphné class, constructed between 1973 and 1977 at the Bazan yard, Cartagena.*

Biscay. In addition, three were scuttled at the end of the war and although later raised, were not returned to service.

An exhausted Spain was again neutral in World War II and only one B class and two C class submarines remained in service. They were supplemented by two D class, whose construction had started in 1933-34 but had been abandoned during the Civil War. These were completed in 1944, followed by a third similar boat laid down in 1945 and completed in 1952. These D class boats were the largest yet built in Spain, with a displacement of 1,480 tons and armed with six 21in (533mm) torpedo tubes and one 4.7in (120mm) and four 37mm guns.

The next addition to the submarine force did not occur until 1959, when one US Balao class submarine was converted to 'fleet schnorkel' standard and transferred, followed by four more US boats, all Guppy IIAs, between 1971 and 1974. However, there were no new boats available from the United States, which had by now adopted an 'all-nuclear' policy, and so the Spaniards turned to France, building four Daphne class submarines as the Delfin (S-60) class, between 1973 and 1975. These were followed in the 1980s by four more submarines of the Galerna (S-70) class, Spanish-built versions of the French Agosta class. These eight submarines are all in service in 1991, with a plan to replace the Delfin (S-60) class with a new S-80 class in the late 1990s.

1895 and his historic submarine was eventually discarded in 1909. Fortunately she was not scrapped and her hull remains on display as a national monument in Cartagena, Spain.

The next Spanish submarine was not ordered until 1915, when the Spanish Navy placed a contract with an American shipyard for a Holland-type boat of 750 tons displacement, armed with four 18in (457mm) torpedo tubes and one 3in (76mm) gun on a disappearing mount. With some justice she was named *Isaac Peral*.

Right: Peral *photographed during her brief service career, 1888 to 1909.*

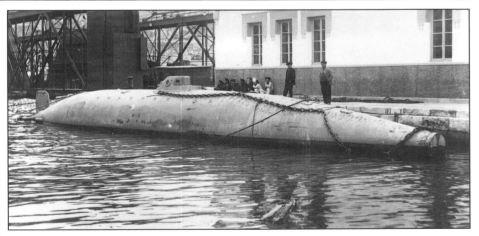

Below: *Apart from the very blunt cap to the bow torpedo tube, the shape of the Peral was exceptionally clean and very advanced for her day.*

Galerna (S-70) Class

(Diesel-electric attack submarines)

Displacement:
1,490 tons surfaced; 1,740 tons submerged
Performance:
Max speed 12kt surfaced; 20.5kt for five minutes, 17.5kt for 60 minutes submerged
Range 8,500nm/9kt (schnorkel), 178nm/3.5kt (creep motor)
Maximum Operational Diving Depth:
984ft (300m)
Dimensions:
221ft 9in (67.6m) x 22ft 3in (6.8m) x 17ft 8in (5.4m)
Machinery:
Two SEMT-Pielstick 320-16 PA4-185 diesel-generator sets, 2,540bhp; one Jeumont-Schneider 3,500kw propulsion motor, plus one 23hp 'creep' motor; one shaft
Complement:
7 officers; 43 ratings
Construction:
Bazan, Cartagena. *Galerna* (S-71), *Siroco* (S-72), *Mistral* (S-73), *Tramontana* (S-74). Four boats. Completed 1983 to 1986. (Spanish order)
DCN, Cherbourg. *Agosta* (S-620), *Béveziers* (S-621), *La Praya* (S-622), *Ouessant* (S-623). Four boats. Completed 1977 to 1978. (French order)
Dubigeon, Nantes. *Hashmat* (S-135), *Hurmat* (S-136). Two boats. Completed 1979 to 1980. (Pakistan order).

Design: The Galerna is a Spanish-built version of the French-designed Agosta class which was somewhat larger than the previous Daphné class. It was designed for distant water operations, to enable the French Navy to play its part in the protection of France's substantial remaining overseas interests.

Great attention has been paid to silent operating. The design incorporates a double-hull, with the space between the two being used for fuel, ballast and acoustic equipment. All equipment which protrudes through the deck, such as sonar housings, is retractable to ensure a smooth

Above: *A submarine of the Galerna class, four of which were built for the Spanish Navy by Bazan in the 1980s.*

waterflow at speed, and machinery is mounted on rafts. One unusual feature is the fitting of a small 23hp electric motor for very quiet, low-speed cruising while on patrol, a device first used on the German Type XXI.

If the French Navy maintains its announced intention to concentrate in future on nuclear-powered submarines the Agosta will prove to be the last of a very distinguished and consistently interesting

Right: *The French, Spanish and Pakistan versions of the French Agosta class SSK are all fitted with four bow tubes and carry 20 torpedoes, normally the French L5 Mod 3 (1) or F17 Mod 2 (2). The French boats can launch the Exocet missile (3), and the Pakistani boats the Sub-Harpoon. TSM 3510 mines (4) can be carried.*

Left: *The Spanish Navy's Galerna at sea off the Spanish coast. The current Spanish submarine fleet comprises four Galernas and four Delfins.*

Above: *The Spanish submarine* Galerna *leaves Portsmouth, England, on 5 September 1989, after a formal visit.*

equipment is of Spanish origin. The Pakistan Navy also has two Agosta class, which were originally ordered by the South African Navy, but the order was cancelled by the French to comply with the United Nations arms embargo.

Armament: Only four torpedo tubes are fitted, but with 20 reloads and special devices for rapid reloading. The torpedo tubes are of 21in (533mm) calibre, the first time that the French have used this international standard, rather than their earlier 21.7in (550mm). Normal weapon load is a combination of French-designed and manufactured L5 Mod 3 or F 17 torpedoes, or SM-39 Exocet anti-ship missiles. The Spanish boats can carry 19 mines in lieu of 9 torpedoes. The Pakistan submarines have been modified to fire Sub-Harpoon.

Service History: The first of the Galerna class joined the Spanish fleet in 1983 and has since been joined by three more, completing the order. One, *Siroco* (S-72) collided with a destroyer in October 1985, but has been repaired. It had been planned to build another new class of submarine to replace the Delfin class, as part of the Spanish Navy's impressive modernisation programme, but this has been postponed and both the Delfin and Galerna classes are being modernised.

The four Agosta class submarines in the French Navy have also been refitted, but are scheduled to reach the end of their service lives in 2002 (three boats) and 2003 (the remaining boat).

The two boats of the Pakistan order were completed in France and delivered to the Pakistan Navy in 1977-78; as built, they were identical with those delivered to the French Navy, but have since been modified to take the US Sub-Harpoon anti-ship missile. Egypt is also understood to have made enquiries about purchasing Agostas in the late 1970s, but no order was ever announced, four Chinese-built Romeos being purchased instead.

line of French diesel-electric submarines.

The Spanish Navy's first French-designed submarines were the four boats of the Daphné class, designated in Spain the Delfin (S-60) class, which were built by Bazan at Cartagena between 1968 and 1974. These have proved very successful and were refitted between 1983 and 1988 to enable them to serve through until the late 1990s, at least.

The Spanish Navy was, thus, content to continue the good relationship by ordering four of the more advanced Agosta class, also to be built by Bazan. Just under 70 per cent of the submarines' structure and

SWEDEN

The Royal Swedish Navy (RSwN) and the Swedish submarine industry have evolved along a remarkably similar path to that of the country's air force and military aircraft industry. In both fields a very small indigenous requirement has nevertheless proved just sufficient to support a highly proficient and technologically advanced industry. Further, just as over the past thirty years the military aircraft industry has been in the hands of one firm — Saab Scania — so, too, has Kockums A/B of Malmö dominated the submarine industry.

Such a situation stems from Sweden's policy of neutrality and her desire not to be beholden to another nation for any major item of defence equipment. That she has been successful when two hot wars and a lengthy Cold War have taken place on her front doorstep speaks highly both for the capability of her politicians and the efficiency of her Armed Forces. That her neutrality needs to be actively defended was never more clearly demonstrated than in 1982 when a Soviet Whiskey class ran aground well inside Sweden's territorial waters.

The first sign of an interest in submarines can be recognised in a wooden model of a submersible constructed in 1770 by D.P. Thunberg, which now lies in the National Maritime Museum in Stockholm, although no actual craft appears to have resulted. Two submarines were constructed in 1869 and 1870 by A.B. Sandahl and S.V. Zethelius, but with little apparent success and it was the famous arms manufacturer, T. Nordenfelt, who constructed the first successful Swedish submarine in 1883. Like many submarine pioneers he failed to interest his own navy in the project, but he sold one to Greece, following which Turkey ordered two similar boats, which were built in Great Britain. The design was not satisfactory and the two relatively unsophisticated navies soon lost interest in them.

Once submarines began to appear a viable proposition, however, the RSwN appreciated that they could be particularly useful in defending the neutrality of their long Baltic coastline with its many scattered islands. So they sent a naval engineering officer to the USA to examine the work of Holland and Lake. This led to the construction of *Hajen* in 1904, a small submarine of 107 tons displacement. It was a fairly effective submarine, although its paraffin engine was unreliable and, like the similarly powered German submarines, left a long cloud of white smoke.

Since then the Swedish navy's submarine arm has been constantly operational, with a small but highly proficient fleet. Only two submarines have been imported from abroad. *Hvalen*, was purchased from Italy in 1909 in order to

Above: Hvalen *was built in Italy and travelled 4,000nm to Sweden.*

examine a leading European design, and a midget submarine, *Spiggen* (37 tons), was bought from Britain as a target demonstrator in 1959. All the remaining vessels have been constructed in Swedish yards, although foreign expertise has been bought-in at various stages. Thus, during and immediately after World War I the experience of Weser AG of Bremen, Germany was influential in the construction of several classes. Similarly, French expertise in minelaying systems was utilised in the construction of several classes of minelayers in the 1920s and 1930s. Like all navies the RSwN absorbed

Above: *The Hajen class submarine* Sälen *(see here in 1920) was built by Kockums at Malmö to a German design.*

Below: *The nine strong U-1 class was built between 1940 and 1944, and stricken between 1960 and 1976.*

the lessons of the German Type XXI to produce new streamlined hulls in the late 1940s. Unlike the victors Sweden was not able to share in the captured submarines, but fortunately *U-3503* had sunk near Göteborg in the final days of the war and the RSwN was able to raise it and examine it in great detail.

Finally, US technology resulting from the tests of the experimental submarine *Albacore* appears to have been used to develop the new hull shape of the Sjöormen class in the late 1960s. It would be quite wrong, however, to assume that the Swedes have merely copied overseas ideas, and, particularly since the 1960s, they have produced some very exciting and challenging designs. There is clear evidence that Swedish designers have moved on from the *Albacore* design and their submarine hulls have a very individual shape. Their excellence was demonstrated when Kockums won the strongly contested international competition for the new Australian submarine, now being constructed as the Type 471 (Collins class).

Swedish submarines are designed to operate primarily in the Baltic waters of the Swedish archipelago in defence of their country's neutrality; they are thus essentially defensive in nature. For example, in the days when virtually all foreign submarines carried deck guns in order to sink merchant ships without expending precious torpedoes, only one class of Swedish submarine ever mounted anything heavier than anti-aircraft weapons (these were the three boats of the 1926 Draken class, which mounted a 105mm gun).

Torpedo armament has usually been at least adequate. Up to the 1925 Valen class the RSwN used 17.7in (457mm) torpedoes,

always in the bow, and it was the 1926 Draken class which introduced both 21in (533mm) tubes and stern mounting. The 1936 Sjölejonet class then introduced the trainable mount in the upper casing, but this feature only appeared in one more class and was then dropped. The Sjöormen (1967) class was the first to deploy a mixed bow armament of four 21in (533mm) and two 15.7in (400mm) tubes; such mixed batteries have been installed in all following classes, the present

Above: *A submarine of the Swedish Hajen class, which was built between 1954 and 1958.*

Västergötland having no less than six 21in (533mm) and three 15.7in (400mm) tubes.

Since the 1960s the RSwN has paid particular attention to automation in order to reduce the requirement for highly trained and expensive crew. For example, the World War II British A class submarine had a crew of 61, whereas today's

Västergötland, with a similar internal volume, has a crew of just 20.

Sweden has lost three submarines, all in World War II, although none was the result of deliberate hostile action. One, *Ulven*, was sunk when she struck a German mine, while the two others, *Illern* and *Sjöborren*, collided with surface vessels. Today a small submersible, *URF* (50 tons), is maintained as a rescue vessel, but, so far as is known, it has never been used other than in practice.

Hajen Class

(Patrol submarine)

Displacement:
107 tons surfaced; 127 tons submerged
Performance:
Max speed 9.5kt surfaced; 7kt submerged
Range not known
Maximum Operational Diving Depth:
50ft (15m)
Dimensions:
70ft 10in (21.6m) x 11ft 10in (3.6m) x 9ft 10in (3.0m)
Machinery:
One Avance paraffin-oil engine, 200bhp; one Luth & Rosén electric motor, 70hp; one shaft
Complement:
11
Construction:
Stockholm Naval Shipyard. *Hajen*. One boat. Completed 1904.

Design: The first submarine for the Royal Swedish Navy (RSwN) was designed by Commander (Engineer) Carl Richson, who was sent in 1900 to the USA to study submarine developments. He returned to Sweden and produced a design which was then built under conditions of the strictest secrecy. The boat was laid down in the Stockholm Navy Yard in 1902 and launched on 16 July 1904. Named *Hajen*, she seems to have been remarkably

Below: Hajen, *the first submarine to be designed and built in Sweden, was launched in 1904 and is now in a museum.*

successful, especially considering that she was the first operational boat in the RSwN. She remained in service for 18 years and even proved to be worth a rebuild in 1916, at a time when submarine design had improved out of all recognition.
Armament: *Hajen* was armed with one 18in (457mm) torpedo tube, for which three torpedoes were carried.
Service History: *Hajen* entered service in 1904. In 1909, when Sweden's second submarine, *Hvalen*, entered service, she was designated a 'second-class submarine' and at the same time was given the designation *Undervattensbåten* 1 (Submarine No1). She underwent a major reconstruction in 1916, in which her length was increased by 5ft 11in (1.8m) so that the unreliable paraffin engine could be replaced by a 4-cylinder diesel (135hp). She was withdrawn from service in 1922 and became an exhibition item at the Marinmuseum, Karlskrona, where she remains to this day.

Sjölejonet Class

(Patrol submarines)

Displacement:
580 tons surfaced; 760 tons submerged
Performance:
Max speed 16kt surfaced; 9kt submerged
Range not known
Maximum Operational Diving Depth:
Not known
Dimensions:
210ft 8in (64.2m) x 21ft 0in (6.4m) x 11ft 2in
(3.4m)
Machinery:
Two M.A.N diesels, 2,100bhp; two electric
motors, 1,000shp; two shafts
Complement:
35
Construction:
Kockums, Malmö. *Sjölejonet, Sjöbjörnen,
Sjöhunden, Svärdfisken, Tumlaren, Dykaren,
Sjöhästen, Sjöormen, Sjöborren.* Nine boats.
Completed 1936 to 1941.

Above: Sjöborren *leaves harbour on 18
December 1941, shortly after completion.*

Below: *Sjölejonet class submarine*
Sjöhästen *at sea in the Baltic in 1941.*

Below: Sjölejonet, *nameship of a class of
nine submarines completed between 1936
and 1941. Torpedo armament was
curious, with three bow tubes, one stern
tube and two in a French-style traversing
mount. There were also two 40mm Bofors
AA guns on complicated disappearing
mounts.*

Design: At the end of World War I the RSwN found itself with fifteen submarines in service; in fact, all the submarines that had ever been built in Sweden, since they had not suffered a single loss. The two oldest were stricken in the early 1920s, but the remainder served on, most being scrapped in the early 1930s. During the war the Swedes had obtained a licence to use Weser AG plans, which they utilised to develop the second Hajen class; three boats of 600 tons displacement launched in 1917-18. A further three boats of a generally similar design were launched in 1921; the Bävern class (650 tons).

Having observed the success of the small German minelayers, the RSwN built one such boat of their own in 1925, *Valen* (730 tons), a second class of three in 1934-35, the Delfinen class (720 tons), and a third class in 1942, the Neptun class (730 tons).

Above: Sjölejonet *at sea during World War II. Sweden's defence forces played an active role in protecting their country's neutrality and three submarines were sunk, albeit none as a result of direct hostile action.*

All used the French Normand-Fenaux system, in which 20 mines were stored in vertical tubes in the outer ballast tanks.

The second post-war class of patrol submarines was the Draken class, launched between 1926 and 1930. The largest Swedish-built submarines to date, with a submerged displacement of 850 tons, they were armed with four 21in (533mm) torpedo tubes and a 105mm/41 gun, the only Swedish submarines ever to carry such a large-calibre weapon.

In the mid-1930s the RSwN, clearly sensing the coming conflict, altered its previous practice of building classes of three boats at about five year intervals by ordering no less than nine of the Sjölejonet class. Still showing traces of the German influence dating back to the contacts with Weser AG in 1916-17, these relatively small (760 tons displacement) submarines were designed for operations in the Swedish archipelago.

Armament: The Sjölejonet class was very conventional except for its armament. The disposition of the six 21in (533mm) torpedo tubes was unusual, with three in the bow, one in the stern and two in a traversing, remotely-controlled mount in the upper casing. These were the first Swedish submarines to have such a mounting, which had long been popular with French designers.

The two 40mm guns were on disappearing mountings. This, too, is surprising, since disappearing mounts were both complicated and heavy, and had gone out of fashion some years previously with other navies. In addition, they had seldom been used for such small weapons.

Service History: Commissioned between 1938 and 1942, these boats served for over twenty years. *Sjöborren* collided with a service vessel and sank on 4 September 1942, one of two Swedish submarines to suffer such a fate during the war. She was subsequently raised, repaired and returned to service.

All were comprehensively refitted in the 1950s. The sail was streamlined, the guns removed and the twin external torpedo tubes suppressed. They were stricken between 1959 and 1964.

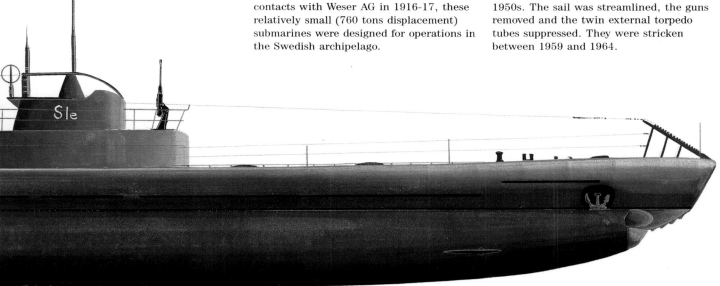

Västergötland (Type A-17) Class

(Diesel-electric patrol submarines)

Displacement:
1,070 tons surfaced; 1,140 tons submerged
Performance:
Max speed 11kt surfaced; 20kt submerged
Range not known
Maximum Operational Diving Depth:
984ft (300m) (plus)
Dimensions:
159ft 1in (48.50m) x 19ft 11in (6.06m) x 20ft 0in (6.10m)
Machinery:
Two Hedemora V12A/15-Ub diesels, 2,160bhp; two Jeumont-Schneider 760kw electric generators, one ASEA electric motor, 1,800shp; one shaft
Complement:
20
Construction:
Kockums AB, Malmö. Västergötland, Hälsingland, Södermanland, Östergötland. Four boats. Completed 1987 to 1990.

Design: The oldest submarines in service with the RSwN in 1991 are a few remaining members of the Draken class (Type A-11), which joined the fleet in 1961-62. The largest boats yet built for the RSwN at the time of their commissioning, they have a displacement of 1,110 tons, and their design incorporates the lessons learned from the salvaged German Type XXI, U-3503. They are being phased out as the new Type A-17 class boats enter service.

Above: Swedish submarine Västergötland *is launched on 17 September 1986.*

Next came five submarines of the Sjöormen class (Type A-12), commissioned 1967 to 1969, with a displacement of 1,400 tons. These are of a radically different design: they do not have the long, thin hull of the Draken class, but instead have a shorter, beamier hull, with a large sail positioned well forward. The forward hydroplanes are positioned low on the sail.

This design also introduced X-configured after control surfaces, which have a number of advantages over the conventional +-design.

The three-boat Näcken class (Type A-14) (1,125 tons) continued the development of a short, stubby 'Swedish' hull, with the sail positioned virtually amidships. This class also has the forward hydroplanes on the sail and X-configured after control surfaces. Diving depth is no less than 984ft (300m).

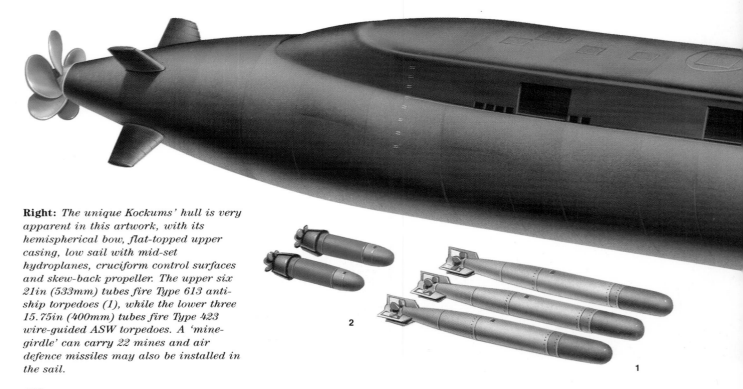

Right: *The unique Kockums' hull is very apparent in this artwork, with its hemispherical bow, flat-topped upper casing, low sail with mid-set hydroplanes, cruciform control surfaces and skew-back propeller. The upper six 21in (533mm) tubes fire Type 613 anti-ship torpedoes (1), while the lower three 15.75in (400mm) tubes fire Type 423 wire-guided ASW torpedoes. A 'mine-girdle' can carry 22 mines and air defence missiles may also be installed in the sail.*

Näcken herself has been lengthened by 19ft 8in (6m) in order to house a United-Stirling A-275 air-independent propulsion system. This has proved a great success and *Näcken* is now fully operational using this system, which enables her to operate without even recourse to her schnorkel for periods of up to 21 days.

Continuing the success of the Näcken class, the RSwN has built the four-strong Västergötland (Type A-17) class, launched between 1986 and 1989. Like all Swedish submarines since the Draken class these are assembled at the Kockums Yard in Malmö, who also build the centre section, while the bow and stern sections are fabricated by Karlskrona.

Armament: There are no less than nine torpedo tubes, all in the bow, one of the heaviest batteries ever installed in any submarine, let alone one as small as this. The torpedo tubes are arranged with six

21in (533mm) tubes uppermost, for which twelve Type 613 hydrogen-peroxide powered anti-ship torpedoes are carried. Below these are three shorter 15.75in (400mm) tubes; these launch the Type 423 15.75in (400mm) wire-guided anti-submarine torpedo, of which six are carried. There are separate reload magazine compartments.

Consideration is being given to fitting these boats with four vertical launch tubes in the sail for RBS-17 anti-ship missiles. This missile is a version of the Saab RBS-15 surface-skimmer, powered by a solid fuel booster rocket and a turbojet sustainer. It has terminal-homing guidance.

Below: Västergötland *at sea, with the officers' figures giving an idea of the small size of these exceptionally powerful and successful submarines.*

This class, like other modern Swedish submarines, can be fitted with the specially developed 'mine-girdle'.

Service History: The four boats of the Västergötland-class entered service between 1987 and 1990.

In a very important commercial triumph Kockums won the fiercely-fought international competition for the next generation of Australian submarines. The winning design, a development of the Västergötland, is described under the entry for the Type 471. This is Sweden's first-ever export order for submarines.

Now under development is the next Swedish submarine, the Type A-19 (UB-90 Project) which is scheduled to start replacing the Sjöormen class from 1995 onwards. The hull will be developed from that of the Västergötland-class, but it is virtually certain that Stirling-cycle external combustion engines will be used.

TAIWAN

The ancient land of China has had a turbulent history in the 20th Century. One of the major figures in that drama was General Chiang Kai-shek, who first gained prominence as the commandant of the Whampoa Military Academy in 1924. A member of the Kuomintang movement, Chiang was commanding an army in 1926 and in 1928 he established a Nationalist government in Nanking. He soon had full charge of the movement and found himself fighting first the Communists and then the invading Japanese. Gaining Allied support during World War II he battled against the Japanese but kept a wary eye on Mao Tse-Tung and the Communists.

After the eventual submission of Japan, the fight with the Communists turned into a major civil war, in which the tide swung inexorably in favour of the Communists, who gradually pushed the Nationalists further and further south. Finally, in December 1949 Chiang Kai-shek, his government and his troops withdrew to the island of Formosa (Taiwan) where they formed the Nationalist Republic of China. They also managed to retain control of three small, offshore islands: Quemoy, Tachen and Matsu.

These small islands were the scene of sporadic activity in the 1950s and 1960s, with Communists' artillery bombardments being countered by Nationalist resistance, with strong United States' support. There were also several invasion scares, but, in the event, Communist forces never actually attempted to cross the narrow waters to the islands. All this naturally led to the building-up of large defence forces on Taiwan, which, supported by the island's burgeoning economy, have obtained some very sophisticated weapons systems. Unfortunately for the Taiwanese the support given by the United States diminished rapidly after the latter's *rapprochement* with the Communist government of the People's Republic of China and Taiwan found itself increasingly isolated.

The mission of the Taiwanese Navy is to defend Taiwan and the offshore islands against invasion or attack by sea and, at least in theory, to maintain a capability to invade mainland China, although such an operation is increasingly improbable. To achieve this, the bulk of the Taiwanese Navy has long consisted of a large number of somewhat elderly ex-US Navy destroyers and frigates, most of which have undergone several refits and refurbishments.

The first submarines were two ex-US Navy Guppy IIs, which were transferred in 1973, ostensibly as targets for ASW training for the surface fleet. When delivered, no torpedoes were included in the order and the torpedo tubes had actually been welded shut by the United States' authorities. This was quite insufficient to thwart the resourceful Taiwanese, who soon had the tubes working again and managed to find torpedoes somewhere on the world markets, as a result of which the two submarines became operational, albeit with a limited capability.

Having trained the nucleus of a submarine force, the Taiwanese next sought modern boats and managed to place an order in The Netherlands for two modified Zwaardvis class boats. The Dutch withstood strong political pressure from the PRC, and delivered two of the Hai Lung class, but Chinese pressure has prevented any repeat orders.

The Taiwanese have since sought to place an order with IKL for the Type 2000. This was the design submitted by the German submarine builders IKL for the Australian submarine competition, but which lost to the Swedish Kockums Type 471. The plan is to build one in Germany for delivery in the mid-1990s; with a number of further boats being built in Taiwan. There is still some doubt as to whether the German government will issue permission for the order to go ahead and doubtless the Beijing government is bringing strong pressure to bear in an attempt to prevent such a deal from being completed. It has also been reported that Taiwan has expressed interest in buying at least one of Argentina's current fleet of submarines, but no firm plans have been announced.

Hai Lung Class

(Attack submarines)

Displacement:
2,376 tons surfaced; 2,660 tons submerged
Performance:
Max speed 11kt surfaced; 20kt submerged
Range 10,900nm/9kt surfaced
Maximum Operational Diving Depth:
984ft (300m)
Dimensions:
219ft 7in (66.92m) x 27ft 7in (8.40m) x 21ft 11in (6.70m)
Machinery:
Three Bronswerk/Stork-Werkspoor 12 ORUB 215 diesel engines, 4,050bhp; one electric motor, 5,100shp; one shaft
Complement:
8 officers, 59 ratings; (maximum complement 79 men)
Construction:
Wilton-Fijenoord, Schiedam. *Hai Lung, Hai Hu.* Two boats. Completed 1987 to 1988

Right: *The two Hai Lung class SSKs were constructed by the Dutch firm of Wilton-Fijenoord and delivered in 1987-88.*

Design: The Hai Lung class is a modified version of the RNethN very successful Zwaardvis class and the first post-war Dutch submarine export order. The first Dutch post-war submarine design was the three-boat, triple-hull Dolfijn/Potvis class, the last of which was launched in June 1965. Meanwhile, design work had already started on the next class, which was based on the Barbel class, the last diesel-electric submarines to be built for the US Navy.

Like the Barbel class the Dutch boats have a teardrop hull, but the design was modified to allow Dutch equipment to be used. Special attention has been paid to silent running and all noise-producing machines are mounted on a spring-mounted false-deck. Two boats were built for the RNethN, being launched in 1970 and 1971, following which the new Walrus/Zeeleeuw class was designed, with four submarines launched between 1985 and 1991.

The Taiwanese class was ordered in 1980, named after the lead-ship *Hai Lung* (*Sea Dragon*). These are of the same

Above: Hai Hu, *second of the class, undergoing maker's trials in The Netherlands prior to acceptance by the Taiwanese. The Beijing government prevented an order for further boats.*

dimensions as the Dutch boats and with the same armament, but have a slightly more powerful power-train and different sensors. They are highly automated and have a target data system capable of tracking eight targets simultaneously.

Armament: Six 21in (533mm) torpedo tubes are fitted, all in the bow. The remarkable load of twenty-eight torpedoes is carried, a large number for this size of submarine, of which two types are available to the Taiwanese Navy. First is the German-designed SUT, a wire-guided, anti-submarine torpedo, of which 200 were ordered in 1988 from Indonesia, where they are manufactured under licence. Second is the US Mark 37, a homing torpedo, primarily for use against surface targets.

Under development in Taiwan is the

Hsiung Feng II missile, which is equivalent in performance and role to the US Harpoon, versions for land, air and surface-ship launch have been developed and tested, while the submarine-launch version is currently under development. It is powered by a small turbojet and has a rocket booster motor.

Service History: The programme was dogged with difficulties. First, the Beijing government protested over the original order for two boats and the Dutch had to withstand the political pressure brought to bear on them. Then the shipyard suffered from considerable financial difficulties, which caused delays in construction. However, the Dutch government resisted the pressures and the shipyard survived, and delivery eventually took place in October 1987 (*Hai Lung = Sea Dragon*) and April 1988 (*Hai Hu = Sea Tiger*), both boats being delivered as deck cargo on heavy-lift ships. However, further pressure from Beijing prevented the Dutch government from authorising acceptance of an order for two more.

Below: *This internal view of the Hai Lung class shows how, typical of a modern submarine, the propulsion system takes up virtually half of the volume of the vessel. Forward of the engine room is the twin-level control and accommodation area, with the sonar and torpedo spaces discreetly screened, except for the sonar, whose circular array can be seen low in the bows.*

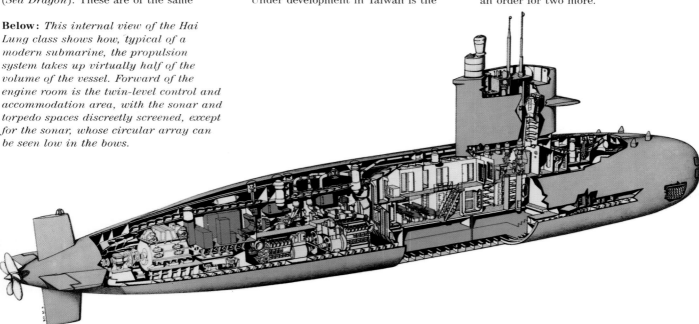

TURKEY

Turkey lies at the junction of Europe and Asia, with shores on the Mediterranean, the Black Sea and the Aegean. She shares borders with the USSR and Iraq to the East, while to the West lies her old adversary, Greece, with whom there exists a very uneasy relationship, despite a common membership of NATO. Added to all this is control of one of the most important naval choke points in the world: the Dardanelles.

Loss of the Turkish Straits to a hostile power would not only be a disaster to Turkey, but would also make a very significant change to the balance of power in the region. Thus, naval power is very important to Turkey and she maintains a large navy, the primary element of which is one of the strongest and most up-to-date submarine forces in the Mediterranean.

This elite force has a long history. Two Nordenfelt boats were obtained in 1887, but proved to be failures and never entered service. Then a French submarine was captured during World War I, but never commissioned. The submarine service's first two successful submarines were the *Birindci Inönü* and *Ikinci Inönü* (literally, *Number One* and *Number Two*), which were built by Fijenoord in the Netherlands in 1927 to a German design. These were followed in 1931 by two Italian-designed boats (*Dumlupynar* and *Sakarya*) and then another German-designed boat a year later (*Gur*) but built this time in Spain. Then came three more German boats (the Ay class 1938/39), two being built in Germany, the third in Turkey.

Due to the outbreak of war, the next five boats ordered ran into problems, the Germans taking over the nearly-completed minelayer *Batiray*, while the British requisitioned the four boats of the Oruc Reis class. The German submarine never reached the Turkish Navy, being scuttled in 1945, but three of the four British boats eventually arrived, the fourth having been lost in action.

Above: Ikinci Inönü, *formerly the 'Fleet Schnorkel' USS* Blueback (SS-326). *She was one of twenty-one ex-World War II fleet submarines transferred 1948-1971.*

After the war the US Navy modified most of their vast stock of fleet submarines to incorporate schnorkels, increased battery power and streamlining, together with new sonars and radars. No less than 21 of these US submarines were transferred to Turkey over a period of 25 years, the largest number to any single navy, the first four arriving in 1948.

The pre-war boats were scrapped during the 1950s and in 1960 the Turkish Navy was equipped with ten relatively modern and quite large (2,000 tons submerged) ex-US Navy submarines. (One boat, lost in an accident in 1953, had been replaced from US stocks). However, by this time even these submarines had limited performance and outdated sensors, and these shortcomings were addressed by obtaining more advanced conversions, designated Greater Underwater Propulsive Power (Guppy), of which ten were transferred

Below: Murat Reis *was built by Vickers in Great Britain and launched in 1940. She was then seized by the Royal Navy and commissioned as HMS P-612, but was delivered to Turkey in 1942.*

between 1970 and 1973. The final submarines supplied by the US Navy were two Tang class, the penultimate class of diesel-electric submarines built by the United States, which were leased in the early 1980s and sold outright in 1987.

Meanwhile, when the Turkish Navy started to look for new submarines in the late 1960s there were no United States' designs on the market. Instead they turned to a previous source, Germany, twelve of the new Class 209/Type 1200 (1,185 tons submerged displacement) being ordered. The first three were built in Germany by Howaldtswerke, but all subsequent boats have been constructed by the Turks themselves at the Gölcük Naval Shipyard. Six of the Type 1200 are now in service, but the remainder were cancelled, to be replaced on the ways at Gölcük by six of the larger Type 1400 (1,586 tons submerged displacement).

The Turkish submarine force now comprises six modern Class 209/Type 1200, with another class under construction, The Class 209/Type 1200 boats are equipped with modern torpedoes and sensors, while the new Type 1400s will be even more effective, being armed with Sub-Harpoon SSMs. The two Tang class will serve on for some years, but the seven very elderly Guppy conversions will doubtless be stricken in the near future.

Nordenfelt II Class

(Steam-driven submarines)

Displacement:
100 tons surfaced; 160 tons submerged
Performance:
Max speed 8kt surfaced; 4-5kt submerged
Range not known surfaced; 14nm/4kt
submerged
Maximum Operational Diving Depth:
50ft (15.2m)
Dimensions:
100ft 0in (30.5m) x 12ft 2in (3.7m) diameter
Machinery:
One Lamm steam compound engine, 250ihp;
one steam accumulator for underwater
propulsion
Complement:
7
Construction:
Des Vignes Co, Chertsey, England. *Abdul Hamid, Abdul Medjid*. Two boats. Completed 1886 to 1887.

Design: Among the submarine pioneers in the latter part of the 19th Century were the Swedish armaments manufacturer Nordenfelt and an eccentric Church of England pastor, the Reverend George Garrett. These two designed and built a boat in Sweden in 1885, which was bought by Greece in 1886. Known as *Nordenfelt I*, she was of cylindrical shape and displaced 60 tons on the surface.

Turkey, Greece's former suzerain and current enemy, was alarmed by this purchase and also by reports that another potential enemy, Czarist Russia, was

Above: *The sinister shape and two determined gunners look menacing, but* Nordenfelt II *was a dismal failure.*

constructing 50 miniature submarines. (These latter reports were, in fact, true, but the Drzewiecki midgets were intended only for close defence of ports and fortresses. Powered by a man-driven treadle and quite incapable of moving in the open sea they were not a significant threat to the Turks).

Nevertheless, the Turks went ahead and ordered two enlarged and improved Nordenfelt boats from England. Like the Greek boats they were powered on the surface by a steam engine, with some of the steam being fed into a special

Below: *The complicated steam engine of* Nordenfelt II *was not a success.*

accumulator tank. There it passed through a heat-exchanger where it heated the water in the accumulator tank before being fed by a pump back to the boiler. On submerging, the super-heated water in the accumulator was fed into the main boiler, where it became steam and drove the pistons.

This was an ingenious idea and worked after a fashion, but it had a number of inherent disadvantages. One of these was that steam had to be raised in harbour a full three days prior to putting to sea, in order to heat the accumulator sufficiently.

Another unsatisfactory design feature was that the boat had positive buoyancy and was fitted with two vertical propellers. To submerge, some water was allowed into the main tank until the boat was just under the surface, at which point the propellers were engaged and they literally drove the boat down under the water. Of course, these propellers had to remain turning to maintain depth until it was necessary to surface when they were stopped and positive buoyancy carried the boat upwards. Thus, while other submarines of the time found it more difficult to surface than submerge, Nordenfelt's design had the opposite characteristic!

Armament: Main armament was two 14in (356mm) torpedo tubes mounted externally in the bow. There were also two (25mm) Nordenfelt machine-guns mounted on the upper deck.

Service History: These two boats were constructed at a yard on the River Thames and then dismantled and sent in sections to Constantinople for reassembly. Their trials were disastrous, the boats totally failing to perform satisfactorily. So bad were they that, despite the well-justified reputation for bravery of Turkish sailors and soldiers, it was not possible to assemble a crew to operate the craft. Eventually Garrett, who had become a commander in the Imperial Ottoman Navy to supervise the trials, was forced to leave the country somewhat precipitately. The two hulls were then laid up and allowed to rust quietly away.

Ay Class

(Ocean-going patrol submarines)

Displacement:
934 tons surfaced; 1,210 tons submerged
Performance:
Max speed 20kt surfaced; 9kt submerged
Range 8,100nm/12kt surfaced; 65nm/4kt submerged
Maximum Operational Diving Depth:
330ft (100m)

Dimensions:
262ft 6in (80.0m) x 21ft 0in (6.4m) x 14ft 0in (4.26m)
Machinery:
Two Burmeister & Wain diesel engines, 3,500bhp; two electric motors, 1,000shp; two shafts
Complement:
44
Construction:
Germaniawerft, Kiel. *Atilay, Saldiray*. Two boats. Completed 1938.
Gölcük Yard, Istanbul. *Yildiray*. One boat. Completed 1939.

Design: Following successful experience with the German-designed Birindci Inönü and Gur classes (which had been built in The Netherlands and Spain respectively) the Turkish Navy again turned to Germany for a new class of ocean-going submarines in the late 1930s. However, by this time Germany had thrown off the shackles of the Versailles Treaty and was once again not only designing but also building its own submarines.

The new Ay class was based closely upon the Type IXA U-boat design, but with certain modifications to meet Turkish requirements. Design work on the Type IXA had started in 1935, with the intention of producing a boat capable of a lengthy stay in the Western Mediterranean (operating from a base in Germany) whilst carrying a load of fuel, torpedoes, ammunition and supplies sufficient to undertake worthwhile operations there. The first of the Type IXA were ordered in 1936, with a displacement of 1,153 tons and range of 8,100nm at 12kt on the surface and 65nm at 4kt submerged.

The Turkish order was placed in 1937 and two of the boats were built by Germaniawerft at Kiel. However, the third was built at the Turkish naval yard at Gölcük near Istanbul, the first submarine to be constructed there.

Armament: The Ay class was armed with six 21in (533mm) torpedo tubes, four in the bow and two in the stern. Gun armament comprised one 3.94in (100mm) gun and a 20mm AAMG. The 100mm gun was mounted on a level with the conning-tower and fitted with a wrap-around shield. This was similar to *Gur* and *Batiray*, but quite unlike other boats designed by Germany.

Service History: The three boats joined the Turkish fleet respectively in 1939 (*Atilay, Saldiray*) and 1940 (*Yildiray*). They were to have been joined by a slightly larger, minelaying submarine from Germaniawerft, *Batiray*, but this was requisitioned by the German *Kriegsmarine* and commissioned as *U-A*. It was scuttled in 1945.

Four other submarines on order from Great Britain were also requisitioned in 1940, two were delivered in 1942 and the third in 1945, the fourth having being lost while serving in the Royal Navy.

All this left the three boats of the Ay class as Turkey's most modern submarines during most of the war. *Atilay* was lost during an exercise in July 1942, but the other two served on until being stricken in 1957.

Above: *The Turkish* Saldiray *is launched at Germaniawerft, Kiel, on 23 July 1938, bearing the Nazi swastika on her bow.*

Below: Saldiray's *design was based on the German Type IXA, but with some differences such as the gun mounting.*

Guppy III Class

(Modified fleet submarines)

Displacement:
1,970 tons surfaced; 2,870 tons submerged
Performance:
Max speed 17kt surfaced; 14kt submerged
Range 10-12,000nm/10kt surfaced; 95nm/5kt submerged
Maximum Operational Diving Depth:
400ft (122m)
Dimensions:
326ft 6in (99.52m) x 27ft 0in (8.23m) x 17ft 0in (5.18m)
Machinery:
Four General Motors 16-278A diesel engines, 6,500bhp; two electric motors, 5,200shp; two shafts
Complement:
8 officers; 78 ratings
Construction:
USS Cobbler (SS-344), USS Corporal (SS-346). Balao class. Built by Electric Boat Company, Groton; completed 1945. Converted to Guppy II 1948-49 and to Guppy III 1962. Transferred to Turkey 21 November 1973 as Canakkale (S-341) and Ikinci Inönü (S-333).

Above: Ikinci Inonu (S-331) was an unmodified Balao class boat.

Below: USS Sabalo (SS-302) received only the Fleet Schnorkel limited conversion.

Design: In the late 1940s the Soviet naval threat appeared to US analysts to be increasing rapidly. In particular, the submarine threat was ominous, as Stalin was known to have initiated a large-scale submarine construction programme. The US Navy found itself with a large fleet of relatively new Gato, Balao and Tench class fleet submarines, but these had been rendered obsolescent by the German Type XXI and other Elektroboot designs. However, the excellent fleet boats had plenty of potential and they became the basis of a series of a number of very successful conversions, one such programme being called 'Guppy' (Greater Underwater Propulsive Power).

The Guppy Is had a streamlined sail and hull, and more powerful batteries, two being converted in 1947. These were followed by 24 Guppy IIs which had the same modifications as the Guppy Is but with an added schnorkel tube. A later programme saw ten boats being given a less drastic modernisation, particularly internally, and these were designated Guppy IA. Four of an austere version of the Guppy IA were completed for the Italian and Norwegian navies as Guppy IBs in 1953-54. Another version of the Guppy IA was developed for the US Navy which was virtually identical with the IA except that one diesel engine was removed in order to create more room internally; 16 of these Guppy IIAs were converted in 1952-54.

An even less expensive and more austere conversion was known as the Fleet Schnorkel, which simply had a streamlined sail, a schnorkel tube and a number of other, very minor, alterations. Little was done to remove the clutter on the upper deck and some even retained their 5in (127mm) guns. Nineteen were converted between 1947 and 1952.

Finally, nine of the Guppy IIs were given a more radical update, which included the lengthening of the hull by 15ft (4.57m), a higher and more streamlined sail, and a completely updated and refurbished interior. The latest sensors were fitted, including the PUFFS passive ranging sonar with its instantly recognisable triple domes on the casing. Nine of these Guppy IIIs were converted between 1959 and 1962, but they only saw some ten years service before being displaced by the ever-increasing number of SSNs.

Armament: Ten 21in (533mm) torpedo tubes, six in the bow, four in the stern. 24 to 28 torpedoes carried.

Service History: During the post-war period many foreign navies sought replacements for elderly submarines. So, as the US Navy finished with boats they were either lent or sold to such friendly navies, Turkey receiving more vessels than any other.

The first four boats were unmodified Balao class fleet submarines, which were transferred in May 1948 and subsequently uprated to Fleet Schnorkel standard in 1953. A further seven already-modified Fleet Schnorkels were transferred between 1950 and 1960, one of which was sunk in an accident in 1953.

Later the Turkish fleet was strengthened considerably by the transfer of eight Guppy IIAs in 1970-72, followed by two Guppy IIIs in 1973. Finally, two Tang class submarines were transferred, members of the first class of diesel-electric submarines to be built for the US Navy after the war.

Of all these US transfers only five Guppy IIAs, two Guppy IIIs and two Tangs remained in service in 1991.

Left: Ikinci Inonu (S-346), a Guppy IIA and former USS Threadfin (SS-410).

PICTURE CREDITS

The publishers would like to thank the many museums, manufacturers and private collectors who generously supplied photographs reproduced in this book. Special thanks are due to Aldo Fraccaroli who kindly provided numerous important historical photographs from his own extensive collection. The photographs published in this book are here credited by page number.

Marius Bar, Toulon: 21 top; 112 bottom; 113 bottom
Bazan, Cartagena: 172 bottom
John Batchelor: 16 bottom; 87 top (MoD photograph); 92
Bildstelle der Marine, Wilhelmshaven: 81 lower
Chilean Embassy, London: 147 top and middle
CPMIEC, Beijing: 135
DCN, France: 20 middle; 115 bottom; 125 top; 125 bottom
Ch. L. Dert, Vlissingen: 167 top (via Aldo Fraccaroli)
Deutsches Museum, Munich: 70 lower
E.C.P. Armées: 115 top; 122
Fincantieri SpA: 127 both; 133
FFV Ordnance: 14 bottom; 15 top
Aldo Fraccaroli Collection: 11 middle; 18 top; 39 (US Navy photograph); 50; 98 top; 98 lower (Shizuo Fukui photograph); 99 (Shizuo Fukui photograph); 108 (Shizuo Fukui photograph); 128; 129 bottom; 131 both; 142 both; 143 bottom; 144 top (G. Gotuzzo photograph); 144 bottom; 146 both; 149 top; 150; 151 lower; 152 top (Anthony and Joseph Pavia photograph); 152 middle and bottom; 153; 160 bottom; 161 both; 162 top; 166 top (Ossi Janson photograph); 166 middle (M. Wojennej photograph); 166 bottom; 167 top (CH. L. Dert photograph); 167

bottom; 171 top (M. Ramirez Gabarrús photograph); 174 top and middle (Ossi Janson photographs); 174 bottom (Otto Ohm photograph); 176 both (Otto Ohm photographs); 177; 182 bottom (Anthony and Joseph Pavia photograph); 184 bottom; 185 bottom
Shizuo Fukui: 98 lower (via Aldo Fraccaroli); 99 (via Aldo Fraccaroli); 105; 108 (via Aldo Fraccaroli)
M. Ramirez Gabarrús Collection: 171 top (via Aldo Fraccaroli)
General Dynamics: 20 bottom; 29 bottom; 42; 44 top; 45
G. Gotuzzo: 144 top (via Aldo Fraccaroli)
Howaldtswerke-Deutsche Werft (Foto HDW): 69 bottom; 80; 81 top; 82; 83 all; 154 both; 155 all; 164 top
Imperial War Museum, London: 11 bottom; 16 top; 22 top; 68 (via Mars); 84 bottom; 85 top; 89; 91 top; 106; 115 lower
Italian Naval Historical Branch: 126 top; 132
Ossi Janson: 166 top (via Aldo Fraccaroli); 174 top and middle (via Aldo Fraccaroli)
Kockums Marine AB; 19 bottom left and right; 25 bottom; 141 both; 178; 179
Leningrad Central Naval Museum: 47 top and middle; 52, 54; 57
Mike Lennon: 173
Marinemuseet, Norway: 162 bottom
Marinha do Brasil: 145 top
Marinstaben, Stockholm: 175
Military Archive and Research Services (Mars): 26 top (US Navy photograph); 26 bottom; 32 (US Navy photograph); 68 (IWM photograph); 78 top (Public Records Office photograph); 84 top; 100 (US Navy photograph)
Musée de la Marine, Paris: 116; 117
National Archives, Washington D.C.: 22 bottom; 126 bottom
Netherlands Ministry of Defence, Royal Netherlands Navy Archives: 18 bottom; 157 both;

159 both
Otto Ohm: 174 bottom (via Aldo Fraccaroli); 176 both (via Aldo Fraccaroli)
Anthony and Joseph Pavia: 152 top (via Aldo Fraccaroli); 182 bottom (via Aldo Fraccaroli)
Peruvian Naval Archives: 164 bottom; 165
Public Records Office, London: 78 top (via Mars)
RDM Technology: Endpapers; 24 bottom; 156
H. Roger-Viollet, Paris: 112 top; 113 top
Royal Danish Embassy, London: 149 bottom
Royal Navy Submarine Museum, Gosport: Half-title; 11 top; 14 top; 30 top; 31 bottom; 33 both; 34; 35; 46; 65; 73; 77; 78 bottom; 90; 91 lower; 110 top; 120 both; 121; 129 top; 130; 140; 143 bottom; 145 bottom; 147 both (Vickers photograph); 160 both; 170 top; 170 lower; 183 both; 184 top
Spanish Naval Archives: 171 lower; 172 top
Strachan & Henshaw: 15 middle and bottom
Thyssen Nordseewerke, Emden: 138; 139; 161 bottom; 163 bottom
UK Ministry of Defence, Navy: 30 bottom; 87 top (via John Batchelor); 96
US Navy: 13 top; 17 top and bottom; 23 bottom; 25 top; 26 top (via Mars); 27 both; 28; 29 top; 31 top; 32 (via Mars); 36; 37; 38; 39 (via Aldo Fraccaroli); 41 both; 43; 44 bottom; 48; 49; 58; 59; 60; 61; 62; 63; 69 top; 100 (via Mars); 103; 107; 114 top; 134; 168; 169; 182 top; 185 top and middle
VSEL, Barrow-in-Furness: 8-9; 13 bottom; 19 top; 85 lower; 87 lower; 94 both; 95; 97; 147 bottom (via RN Submarine Museum); 151 top
Wilton-Fijenoord B.V.: 180; 181 both
Marynarki Wojennej Collection: 166 middle (via Aldo Fraccaroli)
Wright & Logan, Portsmouth: 114 bottom; 123
WZ-Bilddienst: 12; 23 top; 24 top; 47 bottom; 66; 67 both; 70 top; 71; 72 both; 74; 75 both; 115 top; 163 top
Xinhua News Agency: 136; 137